# UMBRIA

*'...the Umbrians have long memories and know deep in their hearts that the ancient Romans learned all their simple and honest virtues from their ancestors.'*

Dana Facaros & Michael Pauls

# About the Guide

The **full-colour introduction** gives the authors' overview of the region, together with suggested **itineraries** and a regional **'where to go' map** and **feature** to help you plan your trip.

Illuminating and entertaining **cultural chapters** on local history, art, architecture, food, wine and culture give you a rich flavour of the region.

**Planning Your Trip** starts with the basics of when to go, getting there and getting around, coupled with other useful information, including a section for disabled travellers. The **Practical A–Z** deals with all the **essential information** and **contact details** that you may need while you are away.

The **regional chapters** are arranged in a loose touring order, with plenty of public transport and driving information. The author's top **'Don't Miss'** ★ **sights** are highlighted at the start of each chapter.

A **language and pronunciation guide** and a comprehensive **index** can be found at the end of the book.

Although everything we list in this guide is **personally recommended**, our authors inevitably have their own favourite places to eat and stay. Whenever you see this **Author's Choice** ★ icon beside a listing, you will know that it is a little bit out of the ordinary.

## Hotel Price Guide (*see also* p.67)

| | | |
|---|---|---|
| Luxury | €€€€€ | over €230 |
| Very expensive | €€€€ | €150–230 |
| Expensive | €€€ | €100–149 |
| Moderate | €€ | €60–99 |
| Inexpensive | € | under €60 |

## Restaurant Price Guide (*see also* p.73)

| | | |
|---|---|---|
| Very expensive | €€€€ | over €45 |
| Expensive | €€€ | €30–45 |
| Moderate | €€ | €20–29 |
| Inexpensive | € | under €20 |

# About the Authors

Dana Facaros and Michael Pauls, now based in southwest France, spent three years in a tiny Umbrian village, where they suffered massive overdoses of food, art and wine, and enjoyed every minute of it. They have written over 40 guides for Cadogan.

**4th edition published 2009**

# 01 INTRODUCING UMBRIA

*Above, from top: Stone barn; Umbrian foods on display*

It's debatable whether this book should contain the warning label 'Beware: Umbria can get seriously under your skin'. It happens almost imperceptibly, and you'll probably only realize that you've been bagged when you leave and cross over the border into Lazio, the Marches or even Tuscany: somehow, after Umbria, they seem less solid and reliable, more busy and badgered. The reason for this subtle increase in atmospheric pressure, on the authority of a spiky-haired Turinese motorcyclist who roared into our village one day, is because 'Umbria has the best karma in Italy'.

That this little region, the 'green heart of Italy', is bewitchingly beautiful has something to do with it. Umbria may not have a coastline, or mountains as spectacular as the Alps or Dolomites, but the gentler charms of its wooded hills, lush valleys and placid lakes – the landscapes of Perugino – are the visual equivalent of the centre of your favourite chocolate. And it comes spiked with art; the regional tourist board claims that Umbria has the densest quantity of works in Italy. Perugia, Assisi, Orvieto, Gubbio, Spoleto, Città di Castello, Todi and a hundred smaller towns are crammed with ancient, medieval and Renaissance treasures (don't come here for Baroque or anything later; in much of Umbria, time stopped around 1530). Even the towns themselves are works of art, pink and white dream cities piled on silvery hills of olives and vineyards. There's art in the kitchen, too; no one in this nation of fussy eaters is as traditional as an Umbrian. You may never get any *nuova cucina*, but the food, even in cheap *trattorie*, is the most consistently delicious and reliable in Italy. For gastronomic enlightenment, Umbrian style, try the fresh truffles, homemade pasta, wild asparagus or a bottle of blood-red Sagrantino di Montefalco.

*Above: Monti Sibillini*
*National Park*

*Opposite: Orvieto*

In spite of these sensual delights, Umbria's most important contributions to civilization have been spiritual and otherworldly. As the nun on the bus put it, 'Umbria speaks in silences.' It is Italy's cradle of saints and mystics, including Benedict, the founder of western monasticism, and Francis, the most gentle of spiritual revolutionaries. It is his lingering influence that makes Umbria a centre that holds in the Italian whirlwinds of fashion, fame and political kerfuffles. Isolated from outside influences, the only region neither to touch the sea nor to border another country, Umbria in its miniature time-warp may be conservative in its ways (but not in its politics – its nickname is 'Red Umbria'), but it's also an immensely hospitable and wise place to be.

# Where to Go

Umbria boasts both peaceful landscapes and delightful towns. **Perugia**, the atmospheric capital, is one of the country's greatest art cities. This is your best bet if you are intending to try to visit all of Umbria from a single base: it's central and has the most public transport. Perugia's citizens also enjoy their own 'riviera' at nearby **Lake Trasimeno**. Within view of Perugia is lovely pink and cream **Assisi**, home of St Francis and a very fine art collection. No visit to Umbria would be complete without seeing this wonderful and world-renowned landmark.

**Northern Umbria** boasts some of Italy's most sparsely populated countryside, full of tobacco farms and olive groves, but frescoes and hill towns hold your attention, as does a splendid natural park. The magnificent, sun-drenched **Valle Umbra** has some of the world's most attractive countryside as well as many of Umbria's most beautiful hill towns.

The **Tiber Valley**, the corner of Umbria that is closest to Rome, has its own distinctive character, much of it concentrated in historically rich Orvieto with its majestic cathedral. Rounding off Umbria is the **Valnerina**, much of which remains an Italian secret, protected as a natural park.

*Below: Signorelli frescoes, Orvieto*

# Chapter Divisions

10 km
5 miles

N

TUSCANY

THE

MARCHES

Citta di Castello

Morra

Montone          Gubbio

Umbertide    **08**
**NORTHERN UMBRIA**

Lago
Trasimeno    **07**          Perugia
**PERUGIA,**
**LAKE TRASIMENO & ASSISI**          Assisi

Spello

Bevagna  **09** Foligno
**THE VALLE UMBRA**

Trevi

U M B R I A

Parco

Nazionale

dei Monti

Sibillini

Norcia

Todi

Spoleto

**10**

Orvieto  **THE TIBER VALLEY**          **11**   Cascia
**THE VALNERINA**

Amelia

Terni

Narni

Viterbo

L A Z I O

*Above: Todi*

# Umbria's Top Ten

1 Perugia, Umbria's capital and one of Italy's greatest art cities, pp.81–104

2 Assisi, the beautiful rose-tinted town of St Francis, pp.116–29

3 Spoleto, the gorgeous setting for the Two Worlds Festival, pp.176–88

4 Orvieto, famous for its wine, Etruscans, and a Cathedral, housing frescoes of the Last Judgement by Luca Signorelli that inspired Michelangelo's Sistine Chapel, pp.199–214

5 The luminous mirror of Lake Trasimeno, set in the emerald hills, pp.106–13

6 The Monti Sibillini and the vast, wildflower-filled meadow of Piano Grande, pp.252–3

7 Atmospheric, utterly medieval Gubbio and the traditional *Corsa dei Ceri* on 15 May, in honour of patron saint Ubaldo, one of the maddest races in all Italy, pp.145–54

8 The lush Cascata delle Marmore, Italy's most beautiful waterfall, created by the ancient Romans, p.238

9 The hill town of Todi, set in sumptuous rolling hills, pp.190–6

10 The views from Montefalco, the 'balcony of Umbria', pp.169–71

*From top: Gubbio;
Duomo, Orvieto*

*Above: The 'ruins' of La Scarzuola near Montegiove*

# Umbrian Curiosities

It's not all lovely landscapes, hill towns, frescoes and homemade pasta – Umbria is also a land of quirks and oddities. Among the most notable are:

1 The naturally mummified bodies in Ferentillo, including a pair of Chinese honeymooners, pp.240–1

2 The Pozzo di San Patrizio in Orvieto – a well seven storeys deep, dug by the Renaissance architect Antonio da Sangallo, so big it has two sets of spiral steps wide enough for donkeys, p.211

3 Garden follies: the 20th-century La Scarzuola near Montegiove, with its 'ruins' and stage sets, pp.215–16, and the late Renaissance Monster Park of Bomarzo, pp.222–3

4 Perugia's 'underground city'– medieval streets and palaces, buried under the Renaissance-era Rocca Paolina, pp.93–4

*Above: Teatro della Concordia, Montecastello di Vibio*

5 The tiny version of La Scala – the Teatro della Concordia in Montecastello di Vibio, p.196

6 Paintings in the Terni art museum by local shoemaker Orneore Metelli, Umbria's Douanier Rousseau, p.236

7 The Botte dei Canonici – a wine barrel as big as a house, under Gubbio cathedral, p.149

8 The world's only Chocolate School, in the suburb of San Sisto, near Perugia, p.101

9 The Virgin Mary's wedding ring, kept in Perugia's cathedral, p.90

10 Umbrian bread has no salt owing to a boycott that began in 1538 in protest against a papal salt tax, p.87

# Medieval Art and Architecture

Umbria was a feisty place in the Middle Ages, when its miniature city-states flourished and fought with the best of them, before being assumed into the Papal States and nodding off into a deep slumber that lasted for centuries – but which, like Sleeping Beauty, preserved them remarkably intact. Some of the very best examples of the region's artistry are:

1 The beautifully frescoed upper and lower Basilicas of San Francesco, Assisi, pp.119–25

2 Orvieto Cathedral – a jewel box with reliefs by Lorenzo Maitani, pp.203–7

3 Perugia's magnificent Palazzo dei Priori and Fontana Maggiore, pp.88–9

4 Spoleto's ornate Lombard Romanesque church of San Pietro, in Monteluco, pp.184–5, and Gattapone's astonishing bridge and aqueduct, the Ponte delle Torri, p.180

5 The early medieval abbey of San Pietro in Valle, near Ferentillo, pp.241–2

6 The lively medieval façades of Foligno's Duomo, p.164

7 Gubbio's Palazzo dei Consoli – one of the most extraordinary civic buildings in Italy, p.148

8 Bevagna's little churches in Piazza Silvestri, pp.167–8

9 Todi's monumental Piazza del Popolo, a superb medieval set-piece, pp.192–3

10 The exotic Romanesque Collegiata di Santa Maria Assunta, Lugnano in Teverina, pp.221–2

*Below: Upper Basilica of San Francesco, Assisi*

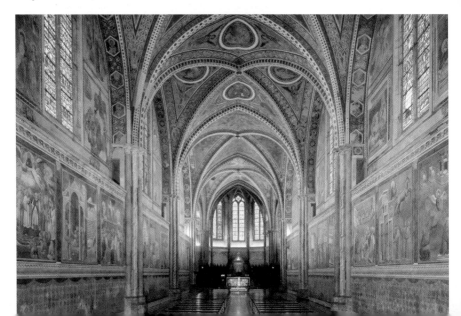

*Above: Ponte delle Torri, Spoleto*

*Right: Palazzo dei Priori and Fontana Maggiore, Perugia*

*Above, from top: Classic Umbrian landscape; Lake Trasimeno*

# Dream Landscapes

More rugged than Tuscany, the landscapes of Umbria resemble the frescoes that fill its churches and palaces; even if you live there for years, they still have the power to take your breath away. An extraordinary number of major saints came from the region, beginning with Benedict, Francis, Clare, Valentine and Rita, and no one is quite sure whether a quality innate to the countryside inspired their spiritual vocation or whether their holy presence somehow imbued the land with its mystical beauty.

1 The Fonti del Clitunno, near Trevi: springs famous since Roman times, next to a Dark Age temple, pp.174–5

2 The Valnerina, where medieval hill towns hang high over the rugged valley, p.225

*Above: Dawn view, Assisi*

3 Lake Trasimeno and its velvet green hills, the inspiration for Perugino, pp.106–13

4 The sunny Valle Umbra, between Assisi and Spoleto, p.157

5 The Piano Grande, a former glacial lake, set under the Monti Sibillini above Norcia, pp.252–3

6 Monte Subasio, above Assisi, filled with memories of St Francis, p.130

7 East of Gubbio, the meadows and beech forests of the Parco Naturale del Monte Cucco, pp.152–3

8 The peaceful Upper Tiber Valley, one of the least populated areas in Italy, p.189

9 The rolling Martani hill country, around Bevagna and Montefalco, p.167

10 The mountain lake of Piediluco above Arrone, pp.239–40

*Above, from top:
Perugina Chocolate
House; Porta Marzia,
Perugia*

*Below: Ceramics,
Orvieto*

# Itinerary: A Week
# In and Around Perugia

Umbria's capital, founded by the Etruscans, is highly evocative, and often as uncanny as it is picturesque. Home to a major university for foreigners, as well as for Italians, it has one of the youngest and liveliest populations in Umbria. It makes chocolates (the famous *bacci*, or kisses), hosts a well-known jazz festival, and has more than its share of surprises.

**Day 1**  Spend the morning with the masterpieces in the **Galleria Nazionale dell'Umbria** in the Palazzo dei Priori. After lunch, visit the **Cathedral of San Lorenzo**, the **Fontana Maggiore** and the **Palazzo dei Priori** itself to see its two beautifully decorated rooms, the Collegio del Cambio and Collegia della Mercanzia, and the Sala dei Notari.

**Day 2**  Discover Etruscan and Roman finds in Perugia's **Archaeology Museum**, and the nearby church of **San Domenico**, the **Orto Medievale** and the ornate church of **San Pietro**. In the afternoon, ride the escalator down into the 'underground city' of the buried **Rocca Paolina**, then visit the surviving bastions and Etruscan gate, the **Porta Marzia**.

**Day 3**  Explore Perugia's oldest streets, the **Etruscan Well** and the Etruscan-Roman **Arco di Augusto**, then take a stroll over a medieval aqueduct into the Borgo Sant'Angelo; see the **Roman mosaic** in the Institute of Chemistry, the **church of Sant'Agostino**, the ancient **Tempio di San Michele Arcangelo** and the **Porta Sant'Angelo** as well as the important churches of **San Francesco al Prato** and **San Bernardino**.

**Day 4**  Hire a car for a lazy day around **Lake Trasimeno**; visit Perugino's home town **Città della Pieve**, and check out **Corciano**'s cashmere outlets on the way back to Perugia.

**Day 5**  Soak up more big-time culture in **Assisi** – the **Basilica of San Francesco**, the **Temple of Minerva**, the **Cathedral**, the **Basilica di Santa Chiara**, and the surrounding Franciscan sites and landscapes around **Monte Subasio**.

**Day 6**  Take the Perugino chocolate tour in **San Sisto** and visit the Etruscan **Ipogeo dei Volumni**, before having lunch in **Torgiano**. Visit the **wine museum**, and then head over to **Deruta** to be tempted by the lovely ceramics and majolica.

**Day 7**  Drive up to **Gubbio** to visit the **Duomo**, the **Museo Civico** and **Palazzo Ducale**; take the *funivia* up **Monte Ingino**.

# CONTENTS

# Reference

# History and Art

02

# History

Umbrian history is not a nice thread with events hanging on it like beads, but rather a ball of yarn that a naughty kitten has pounced on. Most of the time, of course, the naughty kitten was Rome. Being just upriver from the Big Noise on the Tiber has proved a mixed blessing.

## Early Days

Umbria has always been green, but long ago it was very wet, too, drowned under the prehistoric 'Lago Tiberino' that submerged all but the highest hills, which were covered with lush vegetation and giant sequoias. Some of these, fossilized in the mud, were uncovered by chance in a quarry near Todi in the 1980s, and now form the petrified forest of Dunarobba. As sediment filled in the shores and the water receded, the first people moved in, although no one is sure where they came from: a cave on Monte Peglia, northeast of Orvieto, was inhabited in the Lower Palaeolithic (c. 500,000 BC), by people of the Pebble Culture who managed to bag deer, porcupines and sabre-toothed tigers. Finds from the Middle Palaeolithic (Abeto, near Norcia, Mousterian site, from c. 70,000–35,000 BC) and Upper Palaeolithic (the Tane del Diavolo, near Parrano, c. 30,000 BC) show that the first residents of Umbria kept up with the Stone Age Joneses across Europe and beyond. They also kept up with the first artistic trends, and produced at least one tiny but buxom female fertility figure, the 'Venus of Trasimeno', discovered at Castiglione del Lago and now at the archaeology museum in Florence.

No one knows much about Mesolithic Umbria, but the wide variety of Neolithic artefacts from various cultures show that this central, landlocked region was already something of a cultural sponge at an important crossroads. These Late Stone Age inhabitants were shepherds, and eventually farmers, but it seems that they hadn't settled down for long when the new metal cultures were introduced from the coasts; bronze made better tools, but also better weapons, and in general people took to the hills for defence, and there they would stay for thousands of years, safe from invaders and from the malarial vapours that would plague the region until the end of the Second World War.

It was in the Bronze Age (1600–1000 BC) that the first Indo-Europeans appeared, who by the Iron Age can be defined as the **Umbrii** who occupied a good portion of central Italy. According to Pliny the Elder these sober, serious-minded folk were the most ancient of all inhabitants in Italy (the modern Umbrians agree) and they spoke an Italic language similar to Latin. They founded many of Umbria's towns, including Città di Castello, Todi, Spoleto, Terni, Assisi and Amelia; in Amelia they left an astonishing set of travertine cyclopean walls from the 5th century BC, similar to those built by the Latins and other central Italian peoples.

Beginning in the 9th century BC, the **Villanovan culture** prevailed on the western edge of the region. The Villanovans were peaceful farmers who lived in huts (they made their funerary urns in the same shape as their homes, so we know what they looked like) and were the first in the area to cremate their dead; they were also fairly arty potters and metalworkers, as can be seen in Perugia's archaeology museum. Near the end of the 8th century BC, they came into contact with the first

Greek colonists down by the Bay of Naples, who introduced more advanced metal and ceramic techniques, writing, and a taste for luxury goods.

When or how or why the Villanovans evolved into **Etruscans** is a mystery: according to Herodotus, writing in the 5th century BC, they came out of Lydia in Asia Minor in the 13th century BC, during a famine, and after sailing about for a while 'came to Umbria, where they settled, building the cities in which they all lived. Because they wanted to change their name they assumed the name of *Tirreni*, deriving it from the prince who led them there.' This is close to the Etruscans' own version of events, and goes some way towards explaining their non-Indo-European language (the only inscriptions similar to Etruscan have been found on the northeastern Greek island of Limnos) and also coincides with the tales of the 'Sea Peoples' who wandered over the Mediterranean during Mycenaean times and the Dark Age that followed (1500–1000 BC). In the oldest Egyptian records they are the *Tursha*, who once invaded the Nile Delta along with the Achaeans, the Shardana of Sardinia and the Sicans of Sicily.

By historical times in the western Mediterranean, however, the Greeks regarded them as pirates, the *Tyrennoi*, who gave their name to the Tyrrhenian Sea. Their maritime empire got in the way of the ambitions of their rival thalassocrats, the Greeks, to exploit the mines of Elba and the Tuscan coast. In the 7th century BC the Etruscans emerge as the most powerful people of Italy. According to inscriptions, their own name for themselves was *Rasena*. The Latins called them *Tuscii* (hence Tuscany). Their city states controlled that region, parts of Emilia-Romagna, northern Lazio, and parts of what is now western Umbria, including Orvieto (*Volsinii Veteres*), one of their most important cities and the guardian of the great federal religious sanctuary called the *Fanum Voltumnae*. By the 6th century they had pushed the native Umbrians east over the Tiber. A desire to control the fertile plain around Trasimeno led to the founding of Perugia by the Etruscans of Chiusi (*Camars*).

In spite of their violent rivalry, the Greeks and Etruscans traded like crazy. The luxury-loving Etruscans adored Greek vases, and imported them in great numbers from the 7th century on. Later they learned to imitate them. When the Greeks started building temples in the 8th century BC, so did the Etruscans, although theirs were of wood, with projecting rafters and beams in a style that seems a curious cross between the Classical Greek and something Japanese. They were very religious and superstitious, obsessed with divination and death; nearly all their surviving architectural works are tombs, and most of their surviving art was found there too. The Etruscans borrowed the Greek alphabet, but as far as we know they never produced an imaginative literature. They excelled in sculpture and portraiture, and intricate gold and metal work in the 'minor arts'; they learned fresco from the Greeks and decorated their tombs, usually with joyful and life-filled scenes.

The less sophisticated Umbrii never liked the *nouveaux riches* Etruscans much, but they learned to live with them. Towns on the frontier like *Tuder* (Todi) and Perugia were bilingual, and the Etruscans exerted a powerful cultural and economic influence. Nevertheless, the Umbrii retained their own ethnic identity especially in the more easterly towns of Assisi and Spello. The most important inscription ever found in the Umbrian language, the so-called **Eugubine tablets** (in

Gubbio, *see* p.148) date from the 3rd and 1st century BC. The earliest, significantly, are written in the Etruscan alphabet, later ones in the Latin script, a clear sign of the power shift of the times. Mostly devoted to religious practices, the tablets also ask that the gods protect the locals (the Ikuvini) from three groups of troublesome people, the *Narharkum nomen*, the *Japuzkem nomen* and the *Turskem nomen*, who are believed to be, respectively, the people from the Nera valley, the people from the coast of Croatia, and the Etruscans. The astonishing thing is that the tablets offer instructions on how to sacrifice any one of the above peoples (or anyone from nearby Gualdo Tadino) if the Ikuvini should happen to nab them. Umbria does seem to have been an exceptionally conservative hillbilly backwater – but then, the early Romans practised human sacrifice too.

In ancient Umbria it may have been very much every city state for itself, as in the case of Etruria. Another inscription, found in Spello and known as the **Constantine Rescript**, dates from the AD 330s and records the emperor's acquiescence to Spello's request to hold their own religious ceremonies and gladiatorial games rather than send the usual priest to the federal Etruscan sanctuary at *Fanum Voltumnae*. So if the Ikuvini in Gubbio were ready to sacrifice any Etruscan they met, the Umbrians in Spello worshipped side by side with the Etruscans, centuries after both people had been subjugated by the Romans.

## Roman Umbria

The Romans had one talent and one delight: making war. Almost everything else we associate with them they got from the Etruscans: their religious practices and art, togas, concrete, sewers, road building, rectilinear town planning, races and gladiators. But the Etruscans were hardly conquered overnight. Things began to go wrong for them in 550 BC when the Greeks of Cumae defeated their attempts to expand in Campania. Etruscan kings were booted out of Rome a few years later, and the next century saw the Romans take the upper hand in the slow battle to the death with Veii, the first of the many Etruscan cities they gobbled up. In 299 BC the Romans destroyed the strategic Umbrian town of *Nequinum* (Narni) and replaced it with a Roman colony. This drove the Umbrians to ally themselves with the Etruscans, the Gauls and the Samnites to fight the intruders. It was all too little, too late, and the Romans soundly defeated them in 295 BC at the Battle of Sentinum.

One reason why the Etruscans fell to their protégés may have been the fact that they were an elite, and that the plebeians and slaves weren't especially interested in fighting for their cause. *Volsinii Veteres* (Orvieto) was conquered in 280 BC, which led to social upheaval and strife between the old aristocratic leadership and the plebeians who took power. Eventually the aristocrats appealed to the Roman Senate for assistance; the Senate responded, but, as an added and probably unwanted bonus, razed the town and resettled everyone in the new foundation of *Volsinii Noves* (Bolsena, in Lazio). Etruscan Perugia took note, and never challenged the rising power. In 241 BC the Romans consolidated their power to the east by founding a colony at the ancient Umbrian town of *Spoletium* (Spoleto).

One of the first and most important acts of the Romans in Umbria was the construction in 222 BC, financed by the wealthy Roman politician Gaius Flaminius, of the **Via Flaminia** from Rome to Rimini, passing through the heart of the region;

this link between east and west and north and south grew more and more important as time went on, and to this day it remains a busy route. In 217 BC, during the Second Punic War, the same Gaius Flaminius would return to Umbria in an attempt to head off Hannibal at Lake Trasimeno, only to ignore the omens and his Etruscan diviners (*haruspices*) and walk into a terrible Carthaginian trap (*see* p.110). It was one of the greatest defeats ever suffered by Rome, but none of the Etruscan or Umbrian towns in the neighbourhood took advantage of the opportunity to revolt. Perugia in particular went out of its way to take in the Roman survivors from the battle. Spoleto and Spello likewise shut their gates to Hannibal.

Rome rewarded Umbria's loyalty with peace and prosperity; drainage schemes opened up new lands to the farmers. In 90 BC, under the *lex Julia*, all Umbrians were made Roman citizens. Many towns, especially along the two branches of the Via Flaminia (it splits at Narni into easterly and westerly routes), were built up by the Romans, and to this day they retain important remains of antiquity's master engineers. But it wasn't all roses: in 40 BC the Perugians and Norcians made the mistake of siding with Mark Antony, and were attacked by Octavian for their error; after Perugia went up in flames, however, the now-emperor Augustus took pains to restore Perugia as *Perusia Augusta* and it continued to prosper.

When Augustus divided Italy into administrative districts, he based his divisions on ethnic lines, and made Umbria the Sixth Region, which included the modern region east of the Tiber, but also much of the Marche, and parts of Lazio (but excluding Perugia and Orvieto, which were in Etruria, and Norcia, which was in Samnium). The Romans were fond of Umbria, where they built many villas. Virgil and Propertius (the poet of Assisi), Ovid and Pliny the Younger wrote lovingly of the idyllic springs of Clitumnus, where white oxen were purified for sacrifice by a temple to the river god.

Thanks to its proximity to Rome, Umbria carried on blithely over the next pair of centuries. By the end of the 3rd century AD it had started its conversion to Christianity, showing an early propensity for producing saints. Most of these were martyrs in the persecutions of the time – the most famous, outside Umbria at any rate, was St Valentine, a bishop of Terni. At the same time, echoes of troubles on the empire's frontier began to resound at home. When Diocletian split the empire into more manageable eastern and western sections, he reordered the boundaries, dividing Umbria between the new province of *Flaminia et Picenum* east of the Tiber, and *Tuscia et Umbria* west of the Tiber. Soon the name 'Umbria' was dropped, and forgotten until the 17th century, when it was revived by classical scholars.

Diocletian's splitting of the empire had, for Umbria, the slow but same inexorable effect of splitting the atom, especially once **Constantine**, emperor of the west, defeated his co-emperor of the east, and became the single emperor of the Roman Empire, only to move its capital east to Constantinople. No longer at the centre of the world, Rome and Umbria and the west went into a tailspin. And to add insult to injury, when it was decided that the west needed a capital after all, Ravenna was chosen (404). Four years later Alaric and the Visigoths marched down the Via Flaminia to besiege and later plunder Rome. The Vandals followed suit (455) and in 476 the Roman empire was given its *coup de grâce* when the last feeble emperor was packed off and replaced by the first Ostrogothic King of Italy, Odoacer.

Four years later, **St Benedict** was born in Norcia. In hindsight it seems that the man who would one day be proclaimed the Patron Saint of Europe was born just in time to establish his Rule for western monasticism, creating an efficient model of order, labour, spirituality, authority and learning in a world turned upside down. Another, rather original contribution to Umbria's mystical reputation was the hundreds of Syrian ascetics who arrived in 514, fleeing the persecutions of the Arian Byzantine emperor Anastasius to live in small communities and caves around the Valnerina.

## The Greeks and Goths, and especially the Lombards

In the early Middle Ages, Umbria's once cosy position near Rome on the Via Flaminia became its great misfortune. Although Italy revived a little under Odoacer's successor, King Theodoric, after he died the Byzantine emperor Justinian saw his chance to reclaim the west, and sent his general Belisarius to Italy to start the ruinous **Greek–Gothic wars** in 535. Caught between Rome and Ravenna, Umbria became a doormat for armies marching back and forth, armies that often destroyed the towns along the way. Perugia endured a seven-year siege by the Gothic king Totila, but the behaviour of the imperial side was little better: important towns such as Carsulae were abandoned for ever. The Byzantines finally prevailed in 552, when Narses decisively defeated Totila and the Ostrogoths near Gualdo Tadino.

The wars left Italy on its knees, making it easy prey for the next invaders, the **Lombards** (*Longobardi*, the 'people of the long axe'), a Germanic tribe that made its Gothic and Frankish cousins look like choirboys. The Lombards kept the rain off by coating themselves in bear grease, and they drank their wine out of their enemies' skulls. They easily captured most of northern Italy, made Pavia their capital, and set up various feudal states elsewhere, as in Tuscany, Campania and Umbria (571). The Umbrian Duchy of Spoleto proved to be the longest lasting of all these, enduring until 1250: it encompassed all of eastern Umbria from Gualdo Tadino to Terni as well as parts of Abruzzo, Lazio and the Marche. Fortunately for Spoleto, the Lombards soon mellowed, and gave up their Arian heresy to become pious Catholics; among their contributions to the cultural life of the area were the endowments of the powerful Benedictine abbeys of San Pietro in Valle in the Valnerina and Sant'Eutizio near Preci.

With the exception of Orvieto (which was in the Lombard duchy of Tuscany) the rest of Umbria remained Byzantine, a province of the Exarchate of Ravenna, with Perugia as its administrative seat. The delicate political balance between the Byzantines and Lombards ended in 751, when the Lombards conquered Ravenna and threatened Rome; the pope, in alarm, summoned in the **Franks** and Pepin the Short, who kicked the Lombards out and gave Ravenna to the popes. A similar appeal in 774 to Pepin's son **Charlemagne** was met with an equally enthusiastic response; Charlemagne married the daughter of the Lombard king Desiderius, and then forced him to abdicate. He crowned himself King of Italy, then repudiated his new wife.

It was around this time that one of the popes pulled an underhand stunt that would affect Umbria for centuries, by forging a document called the **Donation of**

Constantine, which was presented as a 4th-century testament from the emperor written before he went east, willing the popes perpetual control over Rome and Italy as a token for his conversion to Christianity (the document was often challenged by lawyers, and in the 1450s, humanist Lorenzo Valla categorically proved it a fake). When Pepin gave the Exarchate of Ravenna to the popes, they used the 'Donation' to justify their temporal control of the former Byzantine territories, as well as their ambition to control central Italy, as a buffer around Rome but also one rich with farms and taxes. In the hopes of gaining Frankish support for this policy, Pope Leo III confirmed Charlemagne's hold over much of Europe by crowning him Holy Roman Emperor in 800, reviving a title that would be a bugbear in Italy for 1,000 years, especially as later popes came to think of themselves as the true heirs of the Roman emperors. For the next six centuries the pope and the German emperor would be at one another's throats.

After Charlemagne's death, however, any kind of central control fell apart under the pressure of raiding **Saracens** from Sicily, who came right up the Valnerina in the 800s, and from the **Magyars**, who marched down the Via Flaminia in the 900s. The Duchy of Spoleto held on under the auspices of the emperors, although the dukes were now more Frankish than Lombard.

## Comuni, Guelphs and Ghibellines

*In the republics there is greater life, greater hatred, and more desire for vengeance.*

Machiavelli

When the curtain rises again, around the year 1000, the towns of Umbria, as in the rest of Italy, while nominally pledging their allegiance to either pope (eventually to be known as the **Guelph party**, *see* pp.38–9) or emperor (the **Ghibellines**), emerged as little city states that spent much of their energy clobbering one another. Yet as rough and tumble as it was, the 11th to mid-14th century was a golden age for Umbria, the period when its towns and landscapes formed their character, when it built its greatest monuments, and when **St Francis of Assisi** started the religious revival that would sweep across Italy and Europe in the 1200s. Even Francis as a young man fought in the wars, and was captured by Perugia and spent time in its prison.

As the threat of outside invasion lessened, people returned to the old Umbrian–Etruscan–Roman towns; the population began to grow, agriculture revived, and trade took off. Although the papacy gained a new militancy and prestige on a European scale, it was still too weak to assert itself at home. Umbria, like all the papal possessions, was plagued by problems of succession, schisms and challenges to its authority by various Church councils, heresies and secular rulers. In the vacuum of any central authority from Rome, local abbots and bishops organized councils of men from the established families to attend to each town's defence, its militia and communal improvements. These informal associations led, throughout northern Italy in the 11th century, to the formation of the secular *comune* (plural *comuni*). Similar to the city states of ancient Greece, the *comuni* were at first dominated by town-dwelling nobles, though each citizen was directly involved in current affairs. The piazza became the *agora* or *forum*, and the patron saint was a comune's tutelary divinity.

The first battles were over land, as each *comune* fought to increase its control of the surrounding land, the *contado*, at the expense of smaller towns, feudal lords and monasteries. The garden-like appearance of Umbrian landscapes in frescoes dates from the age of the *comuni* (also the bare brown hills you often see – massive deforestation took place, before problems of erosion led the comuni to initiate reforestation programmes). The majority of the population were farmers, and they lived in a city or village and worked in the surrounding fields. During the rare interludes of peace, good health and good crops, it was a small but perfectly manageable world. As agriculture remained the economic backbone in Umbria, the *comuni* were more self-sufficient but also more conservative and inward-looking than, say, in neighbouring Tuscany, and feelings of loyalty to the *comune*, or *campanilismo* (the attachment to one's own bell tower) as it is still known, were intense. While people certainly travelled, they rarely married or moved outside their *comune*.

Although each *comune's* Grand Council kept the peace at first, trouble began as more and more feudal lords moved into the towns, bringing into the streets the battles they once fought in the countryside, now with Guelph and Ghibelline labels attached; each family had its band of faithful clients and dependants ready to spring into action. The new men, the *popolo*, who owed their wealth to trade, opposed the nobles' endless quarrels and demanded a greater say in running the towns. Eventually the *comuni* came up with an ingenious solution to the rising factionalism: they would elect a **podestà** (formerly an appointive imperial office), a respected and impartial umpire, nearly always someone from another town. He would serve for an appointed period, usually from six months to a year, and with his entourage of judges and notaries would set up housekeeping in the Palazzo del Comune. Many men made a career of being *podestà*, travelling from town to town, bringing to all of Umbria's *comuni* the same institutions: the council, a *Capitano del popolo* (in charge of the citizen militia) and the council of *Anziani* or Priors, of leading guild members, who were especially powerful in Perugia. What they lacked was a police force, and most disputes were still settled with vendettas.

Occasionally players from the First Division burst in on Umbria's parochial cocoon and made a nuisance of themselves. Emperor Frederick Barbarossa came down and wrecked havoc in the 1150s. The powerful **Pope Innocent III** toured Umbria in an attempt to assert his temporal authority before the Perugians poisoned him (1216). A few decades later, Barbarossa's grandson, **Frederick II 'Stupor Mundi'**, promised to give the Church the Duchy of Spoleto, but then fell out with the pope; when the pope excommunicated him, Frederick responded by seizing much of Umbria, and took up residence in Foligno, where he held a grand parliament in the cathedral. The Ghibellines of Umbria were in their ascendancy, but after his death in 1250, the Guelphs clawed their way back.

By 1300, Umbria's *comuni* had reached their peak in wealth and population. Streets and squares were paved, fountains and sewers brought water to the hill towns and took it away again, wooden houses were replaced with stone ones, markets were established, cathedrals and Franciscan churches were built, and people began to dress in fine linens, wool tunics and furs, and light their houses with candles. Perugia, far and away the richest and most populous city in Umbria with *c.* 28,000 in 1300 (down from 40,000 in Etruscan times), had a university reputed for law. Yet at the same time the system was becoming untenable. The nobles and high churchmen and bourgeois had become so partisan that they couldn't agree on a candidate for *podestà*; on occasion they would even elect two.

## The Signoria

A combination of internal factionalism and external events tolled the death knell for the *comuni*. The papacy's leave of absence in Avignon (1305–76) at first limited meddling from that quarter, but in 1313 the announced arrival in Orvieto of German emperor Henry VII, who died in Siena before he even reached Umbria, sparked off a battle that involved Guelphs and Ghibellines from all over the region, ending in a horrific massacre at Orvieto (*see* p.202).

The real troubles began in 1347. The crops failed, leading to a famine, which was followed by something even worse: the Black Death. In 1348 the plague took with it some 100,000 Umbrians, striking the towns especially hard: Spoleto lost two-thirds of its population. The same area was subject to a devastating earthquake. Umbria was a mess, and in 1353 Pope Innocent VI in Avignon made the most determined attempt yet to take the papal dominions under his wing when he appointed the Spanish **Cardinal Gil Albornoz** to assert his authority. A nobleman who had fought the Moors in Spain, Albornoz came with an army to crush any who opposed him, notably Spoleto, which still thought of itself as an Imperial city, and Perugia, which was loath to give up its independence and was besieged by the famous White Company led by the English *condottiere* (mercenary captain) Sir John Hawkwood. Although Perugia never surrendered, it was weakened enough for Albornoz to subdue the towns of its territory. The Cardinal built mighty fortresses in Spoleto, Narni, Assisi and elsewhere to keep them in line; he also divided the Papal States into administrative provinces, and wrote the so-called **Egidian Constitutions**, a law code that would remain in place until 1816.

Once Albornoz was dead, the *comuni* tried to go back to their old ways, but things had changed, and in the social turmoil and confusion strong men took advantage of the situation to seize power. It happened first in Orvieto in 1334, when the first Monaldeschi seized power in the confusion after the massacre; in Perugia it came in 1416 when the *condottiere* **Braccio Fortebraccio** captured the city. The *condottieri* and their companies generally thrived in the confusion of the day, and Fortebraccio was one of the more successful, in spite of being excommunicated twice by Pope Martin V for horning in on his territory; he ruled all of Umbria and part of southern Tuscany until he died in battle in 1424.

After Fortebraccio, the popes and the *signori* gradually worked out an arrangement: the Church defended the lords' right to rule their turf, and the lords acknowledged the Church as their overlord; as an added sweetener, the pope exempted Umbria from the papal salt tax, although henceforth the region had to get its supply from the papal pans. Pope Alexander VI sent his son Cesare Borgia with an army through the region to remind the *signori* who was boss, and he briefly installed his teenage daughter Lucrezia as governor of Spoleto. In Perugia, however, the gangster noble families, the Baglioni and Oddi, made papal authority a distant rumour; the mayhem and violence and vendettas became legendary, and the

Baglioni ultimately outdid even the Medici in the body count in their day. In 1540, **Pope Paul III** finally got rid of the Baglioni by provocatively levying the hated salt tax on Perugia; refusing to negotiate, he sent his son with an army to crush them once and for all in the **Salt War**.

## The Papal States
*They seem to stay alive only because the earth refuses to swallow them.*

Goethe

Goethe saw Umbria in the 1780s, but the poverty, bad roads, backward agricultural practices and bigoted ignorance he and many other travellers found in that century did not happen to Umbria all at once. Nor did the curse of papal rule happen to all parts of the region at the same time and to the same degree. While Perugia was clobbered into submission, Città di Castello, for instance, managed to maintain much of its autonomy under the Vitelli family for a long time in respect for their long support of the popes, while Gubbio escaped by belonging to the Montefeltro Dukes of Urbino, at least until 1624.

Once all the potential rival *signori* had been crushed and replaced with papal supporters, the Egidian Constitutions of Cardinal Albornoz was dusted off and clerical administrators were installed. The bottom line is that the popes, whose political activities soon gave them much bigger fish to fry, simply lost interest in Umbria, except as a tax cow to be milked to fund their beautification projects in Rome and as the occasional escape hatch when events in the Urbs became too hot to handle – most notably, Clement VII's retreat to Orvieto in 1527, during the sack of Rome by Emperor Charles V. Taxes doubled, then doubled again. The wars inside and outside the towns of Umbria ceased, but **brigandage** increased by leaps and bounds, many of the culprits coming from the noble families on the outs with the pope. When the popes in the late 1500s took action, they executed on average a thousand bandits each year.

Except for a few churches, building ground to a halt, and investment in agriculture or trade dried up; apart from the shameless greed and nepotism most popes practised for their families, their policies were so shortsighted and incompetent that those with any money invested only in land, taking advantage of every drought and misfortune to buy up the small landowners. Farmers were forced into sharecropping or *mezzadria*, which, although on the surface it seemed fairer, was little better than feudal serfdom; although the farmer split the harvest fifty-fifty with the landowner, he bore all the other costs, from seed to transport, and in many cases could not marry without the landowner's consent, or even leave the countryside once the lease was over. The towns were still very much dependent on their immediate surrounding territory, or *contado*, for food, and the peasants who tried to escape were often compelled to return to the land. On the other hand, there were increasingly fewer mouths to feed as populations dwindled – by 1800 Perugia's had shrunk to 13,000, while Orvieto could barely muster 5,000 souls.

Anyone with talent or ambition took orders or simply left the region. Trade and contacts with the outside world dried up, and the Church's war on thought in the Counter-Reformation confirmed the Umbrians in their provincialism and *campanilismo*. The 17th and 18th centuries were not good ones for Italy, and in

Umbria they brought stagnation. At the same time the very first **Grand Tourists** began to trickle into Umbria, usually only because they were on the way to somewhere else (most travelled from Venice and Ravenna to Rome on the Via Flaminia); if they came from the well-run Grand Duchy of Tuscany they were invariably appalled at conditions just over the border in Umbria. In 1766 Tobias Smollett found that 'the inns are dismal and dirty beyond all description; the bedclothes filthy enough to turn the stomach of a muleteer; the victuals cooked in such a manner that even a Hottentot could not have beheld them without loathing'. Goethe, 20 years later, discovered that the Umbrians were 'all bitter rivals: they indulge in the oddest provincialism and local patriotism, and cannot stand one another'. The Irish writer Lady Morgan (Sydney Owenson) came in the 1820s and found desolation: 'Something like population was visible, in the swollen, squalid, hollow figures, who steal from straw sheds, or appear at work in the pestilential marshes; many of them were ghastly spectres, with nothing of humanity but its sensibility to suffering.'

This, of course, was after **Napoleon** burst into the somnolent province in 1798 and made it part of the 'Republic of Rome'; he divided it into two provinces, and sent in French administrators to undo centuries of papal misgovernment. While some cheered, pious peasants joined Catholic guerrilla bands who attacked the Jacobins and began a reign of terror in the countryside. The clergy returned when Napoleon signed his concordat with Pius VII, but then left again when Napoleon declared himself Emperor in 1808 and imprisoned the Pope. There was another flurry of activity, including an attempt to refound the University of Perugia, before Napoleon was overthrown in 1814. Umbria returned to the status quo, and two years later suffered one of its periodic famines and epidemics.

But even here, in this embalmed, browbeaten backwater, there was no going back. Reactionary popes such as Gregory XVI (1831–46) and Pius IX (1846–78) pushed some Umbrians to join in the general European revolutions, and to fight with Garibaldi and Mazzini to defend the short-lived Roman Republic in 1848–9. Pius had begun his papacy as a promising moderate reformer, but the revolution gave him an obsessive horror of anything connected with the modern world; typically, he refused to allow railways in Umbria for fear that the passengers might snog in the tunnels. When it became increasingly apparent that there was no use in waiting for Rome to reform, the Perugini rose in 1859 in support of the Risorgimento and the Piemontese king Vittorio Emanuele II. Pius sent in the Swiss Guards to quell the revolt, which they did with such brutality that all of Europe was shocked. But the Pope could hardly find anyone else to support his dying state. Two years later, Umbria along with the rest of the Papal States was joined to the new kingdom of Italy. The monasteries were dissolved, and the Perugini took the greatest pleasure imaginable in seizing the Rocca Paolina, the huge fortress that had become the ultimate symbol of papal oppression, and turning it into rubble.

## The Green Heart of Italy

Unfortunately, joining the new kingdom of Italy did not improve things for many Umbrians; for decades it made things worse. The majority were trying to scrape a living from the land, but the reactionary Piemontese kings were the last ones to rock the boat when it came to property and privilege. There were new taxes, and *mezzadria* would continue for another whole century, while even worse off were the *braccianti*, day labourers, who survived hand to mouth. Many were so overworked and so malnourished that they became easy prey to pellagra and other diseases. Over the next few decades, tens of thousands emigrated to survive, mostly to France and Germany. But, at the same time, major investments by the state ended Umbria's isolation, both physical and economic. Railways were finally built, and Terni, with its cheap hydroelectric power, was chosen to be the first centre of heavy industry in Italy: armaments, steel, jute and chemical factories were established here, and other centres, such as Narni, followed. Terni boomed to the position it holds today, as Umbria's second city.

Side by side with this modernization was a general awakening (by outsiders, mostly) to the region's special beauty that had begun with the early 18th-century Romantics. In 1870, the name Umbria was revived for the first time since Roman days as an administrative region, and only a few years later the poet Giosuè Carducci became the first to call it *Umbria Verde!* (Green Umbria) in one of his poems. As the Industrial Revolution chugged ahead, there was a revival of interest throughout Europe in St Francis, the nature-loving saint: parallels were drawn with his life and Christ's, and Umbria was proclaimed the Galilee of Italy.

But this green Umbria was also rapidly taking on a new colour: red. In 1919 the first post-war elections in Umbria gave the Partito Socialista Italiano an absolute majority, as the long oppressed farm and newly exploited industrial workers united. Reaction was not long in coming, in January 1920, when landowners formed the first Fascist group in Perugia, and immediately began to clash with the Socialists. A decade later the only Socialists were in Terni, though they had to remain clandestine as Mussolini went about busting up their union. For Terni was important to the Fascists, especially once Italy entered the war. The industry earned it unwanted attention from the Allied bombers; in the raids 2,000 were killed and medieval Terni was all but wiped off the map. Northern Umbria, where partisans harried the Germans, suffered severe reprisals.

After the war, 72 percent of Umbrians voted for a republic over a monarchy and on the whole it has done well by them. The ancient curse of malaria was eradicated with DDT. New opportunities in industry and immigration proved to be the death knell at last for *mezzadria*, especially after a freak frost in 1956 killed nearly all of the region's olive trees. Small industrial zones now surround most towns, some of them processing the foods Umbria is famous for, from Buitoni pasta to sausages, wine and Perugina chocolates and truffles. Perugia's university with its well-known school for foreigners has recaptured much of its old glory. Natural parks have been set up to preserve Umbria's remarkable natural beauty. And the region that was for hundreds of years a cultural desert has become a cultural dessert, serving up delights such as the Spoleto and Umbria Jazz Festivals to go with Umbria's innumerable art treasures and the spiritual lure of its saints. In the past two decades tourism has grown in leaps and bounds, and an average of two million visitors pass through every year.

Umbria has long suffered from earthquakes, and the one in September 1997 was a serious setback, especially as the region was preparing for the Jubilee Year

2000. Assisi managed to get the Basilica of San Francesco open on time for the celebrations, but almost every Umbrian town and village is still swathed in scaffolding as major restoration works continue to repair the damage (*see* pp.36–8).

The perils of climate change have not passed Umbria by and green initiatives are beginning to spring up. The Castello Monte Vibiano Vecchio olive oil farm, southwest of Perugia, is aiming to be Europe's first completely carbon-neutral farm, and the Lungarotti vineyards in Torgiano are running a pilot scheme for creating biomass energy from vine prunings and grape waste.

# Art in Umbria

Umbria is full of treasures from the Middle Ages and Renaissance, and many of them can still be found in the church or convent or palazzo they were designed for. Much of this remarkable heritage was contributed by non-Umbrians, especially by painters and sculptors from the neighbouring art powerhouses of Florence, Siena and Rome, who worked on the prestigious projects at the Basilica of San Francesco in Assisi and the Cathedral of Orvieto. Native Umbrian artists learned from the works they left behind.

When we read accounts by the Grand Tourists of the 18th century, it comes as a shock to realize that they sniffed at and disdained the frescoes we travel thousands of miles to see. Even Goethe 'turned away in distaste' from the trecento treasurehouse of the Basilica of San Francesco. After centuries of neglect, the first to take up the cause of Umbrian art, especially of Perugino and his school, were the German Nazarenes in the early 19th century. In the 1820s, the French painter Valéry made illustrations of the frescoes in Assisi, the Pinturicchios in Spello and the Peruginos in Città della Pieve and Panicale, and awakened a new interest in Umbrian art just as the Romantic poets were awakening a new interest in the landscapes. In the mid-19th century, the Pre-Raphaelites led a revival of interest in Perugino and the Umbrian school, the 'holy painters' who by some geo-psycho process of osmosis were influenced by the landscape and the mysticism of the region's saints to create a more spiritual art.

## The Pre-Peruginos

The first frescoes of note in Umbria are in the abbey of San Pietro in Valle, in the Valnerina, dated at around 1190 and among the most important in Italy for the time: not only because they have survived, but also because they show the first inklings of a whole new western or Latin sensibility in art as opposed to the Greek Byzantine styles that had dominated the early ages in Ravenna and Rome. The anonymous **Master of the St Francis Cycle**, who worked in the great basilica in Assisi, is believed to have been an Umbrian; he worked in the mid-1200s, with the Florentine **Cimabue** (*c.* 1240–1302), who took the art of San Pietro in Valle a giant step further along the western road. The frescoes of the Master of St Francis and Cimabue in the basilica were only the first of many by great artists who would inspire generations of Umbrian painters. The most important of these was **Giotto** (*c.* 1266–1337), Cimabue's student, whose contribution to the basilica was as powerful as its exact nature is controversial. He and/or his disciples led the way, in the great *Life of St Francis* cycle in the upper church, in exploring new ideas in composition and expressing psychological meaning and humanity in his subjects. Through his intuitive grasp of perspective, Giotto was able to go further than any previous artist in representing his subjects as actual figures in space. In a sense Giotto actually invented space; it was this, despite his often awkward draughtsmanship, that so astounded his contemporaries. The recognizable Assisi settings were the precursors of the Umbrian fondness for localizing settings that would become a trademark of Perugino.

Along with the revolutionary Florentines, the other major contribution to Umbria's heritage and to its own trecento style came from Siena. In the 13th and 14th centuries, Siena's artists, while less innovative, rivalled and often surpassed those of Florence. The pivotal figure was **Duccio di Buoninsegna** (d. 1319), the catalyst who founded the essentials of Sienese art by uniting the beauty of Byzantine line and colour with the sweet finesse of western Gothic art. Two of Duccio's greatest followers, **Pietro Lorenzetti** (d. 1348) and **Simone Martini** (d. 1344), worked in Assisi. The elegant and rarefied Martini was the great exponent of International Gothic – a flowery and ornate style – while Lorenzetti, known for his emotional expressiveness, left his most powerful works in Assisi. His talented brother-in-law and assistant, **Lippo Memmi** (d. 1347), contributed his masterpiece to Orvieto cathedral.

Their Umbrian followers were usually just as colourful if less sophisticated. In the next generation, the itinerant painters **Giovanni di Corraduccio** of Foligno and **Cola Petruccioli** introduced the International Gothic style around the region. Its greatest master, **Gentile da Fabriano** (c. 1360–1427), came from just over the border in the Marche, but left Perugia a fine altarpiece now in the Galleria Nazionale and a pretty fresco in Orvieto cathedral; his near contemporary, **Ottaviano Nelli** (c. 1375–1440), had a delicate sense of colour and harmony, and left most of his work in his home town of Gubbio. Another Umbrian painter active in this period was the Dominican **Bartolomeo di Tommaso** of Foligno, more workmanlike and less original but still worth a look – one of his best works is based on the Divine Comedy, in Terni's church of San Francesco. **Masolino da Panicale** (c. 1383–1447) was the greatest of the native Umbrian painters of the time; he worked alongside the revolutionary Masaccio in the famous Brancacci Chapel in Florence, but was otherwise known for his lyrical decorative work. In Umbria he left only one mediocre fresco, in San Fortunato in Todi.

Fresh influences came from Tuscany in the 15th century. The spiritual **Beato Angelico** (1400–55) worked in Orvieto and Perugia in the last decade of his life and left a major altarpiece now in Perugia's Galleria Nazionale, but most of all he left Umbria his student **Benozzo Gozzoli** (c. 1421–97), who learned much of his master's grace and sweetness if little of his spirituality. Gozzoli left a number of works in Umbria, but none of them equals to the worldly fairytale pageant he created for the Medici palace in Florence; his fresco cycle on the life of St Francis at Montefalco seems soft, sweet and sentimental, but would exert a slippery influence on many Umbrian artists. One was the prolific and polished **L'Alunno** (Nicolò di Liberatore,

c. 1430–1502) of Foligno; although his later works show more drama, they still rarely challenge the imagination.

Along with the spirituality of Angelico, another powerful inspiration for the region's artists was the work of **Piero della Francesca** (c. 1415–92), who is often considered an honorary Umbrian. Piero explored the limits of perspective and geometrical forms to create some of the most compelling, haunting images of the quattrocento, fusing geometry, light, colour and landscapes (many of his native Upper Tiber) to create a mystical total atmosphere. His subjects are often archetypes of immense psychological depth, not to be fully explained now or ever. His altarpiece in the Galleria Nazionale in Perugia is his only work in Umbria proper, but some of his masterpieces are just over the border in Borgo Sansepolcro and Monterchi.

Perugia in particular produced a group of fine painters in the generation before Perugino. There's the meticulous **Benedetto Bonfigli** (c. 1420–96), known for his painted banners in Perugia churches; his best works, the Cappella dei Priori frescoes, show the spatial influence of Piero. The elegant and colourful **Bartolomeo Caporali** (1420–1503) was closer to Gozzoli, and a great lover of natural detail; many of his paintings still decorate the churches in and around Perugia. A third Perugian, **Fiorenzo di Lorenzo** (c. 1440–1525), changed his style so often that attributions are often a problem; one of his best frescoes is now in the Pinacoteca of Deruta. Outside Perugia, two painters who worked mainly around their home towns were **Pierantonio Mezzastris** (c. 1430–1506) of Foligno and **Matteo da Gualdo** of Gualdo Tadino (c. 1430–1503), who created conventional, colourful, stylized works and had probably never heard of Florence.

## Perugino and the Umbrian School

When most art historians talk of an 'Umbrian School of art', they start with Pietro Vannucci, better known as **Perugino** (c. 1450–1523), of Città della Pieve near Lake Trasimeno. Like Leonardo da Vinci, Perugino was a student of Andrea Verrocchio, who instilled a love of nature and landscapes in both of his students. They would both make their landscapes a very integral part of their paintings – Leonardo preferring the dramatic scenery of the Italian lakes, Perugino opting for the more idyllic, soothing countryside around Trasimeno. Another tradition has it that Perugino studied under Piero della Francesca; true or not, he certainly absorbed Piero's lessons of space and clarity, and developed a distinctive idealized type of figure. He was one of the most famous painters of his time, with commissions from all over Italy; the pope summoned him to Rome with Botticelli and Ghirlandaio to paint the walls of the Sistine Chapel. Although he was adept at fresco and portraiture, most of his commissions were for devotional paintings, which his patrons couldn't get enough of. At his best he created works of genius, along with countless idyllic nativity scenes, each with its impeccably sweet Madonna and characteristic blue-green tinted landscape, filled with the stillness of Umbria. His art – classic, Virgilian, eulogic, serene, beautiful – turned its back on the individualist, restless, innovative spirits of Leonardo and Michelangelo. When not at his best, Perugino walks a fine tightrope over the Umbrian tendency to tumble into sweetness. Some of his later works are so awful they make you want to brush your teeth, although in most cases he wasn't completely at fault: in his cynical old age he let his workshop sign his name to anything.

Perugino is perhaps best known for his precocious pupil **Raphael** (1483–1520). Raphael's painter-humanist father, Giovanni di Santi, was a great admirer of Perugino, and during his son's earliest phase as an independent artist, working around Umbria and Tuscany, Perugino's influence is overwhelming even as Raphael quickly surpassed him. He left quite a few works in Umbria, but unfortunately his reputation as the greatest painter who ever lived saw most of them looted by Napoleon's troops, and none were ever returned: the superb *Betrothal of the Virgin*, painted for the Franciscans in Città di Castello, was carried off to the Brera in Milan; the *Madonna di Foligno* is now in the Vatican museum; the *Crucifixion* from San Domenico in Perugia is now in the National Gallery in London. The only Raphaels in Umbria today are Città di Castello's standard and some frescoes he painted as a teenager in the Collegio del Cambio and San Severo in Perugia.

Another student or rather colleague of Perugino was **Pinturicchio** (Bernardino di Betto, 1454–1513) of Perugia, who earned his name for his use of gold and rich colours. Pinturicchio was never an innovator, but as a virtuoso in colour, style and charming decorative effects few could beat him; he followed the Gozzoli of the Medici frescoes rather than the Gozzoli of Montefalco. He was another establishment artist, especially favoured by the popes, and, like Perugino, he was slandered most vilely by Vasari; in Umbria his best works are in Spello's Santa Maria Maggiore and in Perugia's Galleria Nazionale.

The most exceptional works in Umbria from this period, however, are the frescoes in Orvieto cathedral by **Luca Signorelli** (*c.* 1441–1523), a pupil of Piero della Francesca from Cortona, just north of Lake Trasimeno. Signorelli never painted anything else like these six great scenes of the end of the world; his imaginative, forceful compositions, combining geometrical rigour with a touch of unreality, owe something to Piero, while his vigorous, expressive male nudes were derived from a study of the Florentine Antonio Pollaiolo. Michelangelo took a good long look at them on his way to painting his own *Last Judgement* in the Sistine Chapel.

Other Umbrian artists of the 16th century followed the leaders: **Lo Spagna** (Giovanni di Pietro, *c.* 1450–1528) at his best incorporates the more delicate aspects of Perugino's sweetness with some of the compositional mastery of Raphael. Others who followed Perugino to a degree included **Tiberio d'Assisi** (*c.* 1470–1524), **Giannicola di Paolo** (*c.* 1460–1544) and **Pier Matteo d'Amelia** (d. 1508); the latter is best known for his work with Fra Lippi in Spoleto cathedral. Another, **Eusebio da San Giorgio** (*c.* 1470–1540), was a follower of Raphael, while **Dono Doni** of Assisi (d. 1575) and **Domenico di Paride Alfani** of Perugia (d. 1554) looked towards Michelangelo. Non-Umbrians such as the Pisan painter **Niccolò Pomarancio** and his son Antonio worked extensively in the region, and there's an excellent **Rosso Fiorentino** in Città di Castello, along with a couple of **Guercinos**. Afterwards Rome sucked in all the money and talent, leaving almost nothing of note in or from Umbria until the 20th century and **Alberto Burri** of Città di Castello (1915–95), whose visceral reaction to the horrors of the Second World War was to seek a more honest and moral art in the detritus of modern civilization.

# Topics

03

# After the Earthquakes: Art versus People

According to geologists, the earthquakes that jolted Umbria and the Marche twice on 26 September 1997, killing 11 and wounding many more, the aftershocks that continued throughout 1998, when over 10,000 minor and not so minor tremors were registered, and the subsequent earthquake and aftershocks which again rocked the region in 2005 and 2006 were merely part of a million-year-old trend as the Apennines yawn and stretch and adjust to fit their crust. The 100,000 people in Umbria and the Marche whose homes were rendered uninhabitable by the tremors obviously didn't find much comfort in their scientific long-range perspective, but in the immediate aftermath of the 1997 disaster things could have been worse. The government, both on a local and national level, responded quickly, so that by Christmas everyone was housed as close to their villages as possible, in rental accommodation, in prefab housing or, as a last resort, in shipping containers (fitted with doors, windows, room dividers, electricity and plumbing). People got on with their lives relatively quickly; nor was it long before the famous skylines of the hill towns were dominated by cranes and scaffolding, much of which is still in place. After all, there's a certain familiarity with earthquakes in the area; a serious one rocked the eastern Valnerina and parts of the Valle Umbra in 1979.

This one, however, grabbed the world's attention because it gravely damaged one of Italy's most precious and best-loved treasures, the Basilica di San Francesco in Assisi, just as the town was gearing up for the Holy Year 2000 celebrations. For most of the world, the earthquakes became the 'Assisi earthquakes'. Billions of lire poured in from the state, the Vatican, charities and other sources to restore the art, and a regional office of the Commissione dei Beni Culturali opened in Foligno to direct the flow. Priority was given to a 'Jubilee list' of art and monuments on the official pilgrimage route, but, even so, nearly a third of the entire budget in 1998 went to the big basilica; in Assisi everyone vowed it would reopen by Christmas 1999 and it did – an impressive feat, especially in Italy where projects on that scale usually take decades to complete. Just as impressive is the fact that San Francesco became the first major monument anywhere equipped with the latest anti-seismic technology woven into the more vulnerable sections of the walls and roofline: bundles of wires of 'shape-memory alloys' made of titanium and nickel. Invented in the aeronautics industry in 1951, the alloys are now used in shock absorbers – in this case, a very big shock absorber, which should give the basilica 50 percent more 'give', even improving on the flexibility it originally had.

Yet, for several years after the 1997 quake, some people in Assisi were still living in a 'container village' on the outskirts of town. Less famous towns sometimes had two or three container villages. The worst-hit places (Colfiorito, for instance, which was one of the epicentres) were all but abandoned except for the occasional stalwarts who refused to leave, living amid the rubble and ruined houses, where fallen walls revealed bright wallpaper or other poignant vignettes of the residents' former lives. Some of the smaller villages may never be rebuilt. But elsewhere there has been no lack of polemics over the way the government has handled the rehousing. Plenty of money was available for restoration and continues to be so, but a huge amount of it (in some cases, as much as half of a town's allotted sum) has gone into other pockets – not those of corrupt politicians, as happened in Naples after its big earthquake in 1983 – but to pay for the countless permits, licences and opinions by various state experts required even before the real work could begin. In the opinion of many residents, the bureaucrats were battening on Umbria's misfortune. Another unwelcome spin-off has been an alarming influx of organized crime, with mafia and *camorra* clans moving from Sicily and Naples into Umbrian towns such as Foligno and Spoleto to mop up lucrative building contracts.

So was art given precedence over people in Umbria? In many cases the answer is yes, although the result isn't quite as cold and heartless as it may sound. For a year or so after the earthquakes, tourists shied away from the region, partly because they were afraid of more tremors, but mostly because the key sights were closed. Tourism is a major source of income in Umbria and 1998 was an economic disaster for the area. So, by repairing and reopening the major attractions, most of them to anti-seismic specifications (and bringing visitors back in a big way), many argue that the overall result benefited everybody. The many Umbrians who work in the tourist industry were able to resume their jobs relatively quickly and, with this, a welcome degree of normality and vitality returned to the beleaguered region.

However, the situation is still critical in Nocera Umbra and the surrounding area, where the earthquakes struck first and most severely. At the time of writing, some public buildings, such as the Comune, bank and schools, are still housed in prefab buildings. The historical centre is closed to all but 10 families, for whom new flats have been built. The delay in Nocera's restoration cannot only be attributed to bureaucratic mismanagement, but also to its location and set-up: a village perched on a hill with narrow streets, through which machinery cannot easily pass, affected by long cold winters which grind building operations to a halt.

At the end of 2008 many things have changed, with the reopening of popular central monuments and churches. Umbria is no longer under the glare of the media spotlight, people have long returned to their everyday way of life and the region looks green again. Some locals feel that too much fuss was made about earthquakes which certainly brought fear and tragedy, but were not as bad as others that shook Italy in the 20th century.

All kinds of restoration projects on buildings not directly damaged by the earthquakes have been undertaken, on buildings and art that otherwise would have been left to crumble slowly. In these cases, local authorities benefited from the influx of expert restorers and of money, and from a heightened focus of attention on 'Art' in Umbria. Once work has been completed, visitors will find things in a much better state than they would have been had the earthquakes never happened. Assisi is a particular example. The damage was extensive, but the restoration has been so spectacular that those buildings will be in better condition than they have been for hundreds of years once the scaffolding comes down. Even the priceless frescoes inside the Basilica di San Francesco have shone again. Some 20 restorers were employed full-time working their way through trays of rubble, trying to piece together the world's most intricate jigsaw puzzle, including some pieces plundered by foreign tourists as souvenirs and later sent back with anonymous apology notes. Apparently they could, at a glance, distinguish fragments of colours enough to know which artist the minute pieces belonged to.

Another case is Spoleto, much of it currently under restoration and expected to remain that way until at least the end of the decade. But as the wraps start to come off some of the buildings, such as the superbly renovated town hall, the early signs are that the wait will be worth it. On that note, at least in the long-range view of things, the disaster may have been a blessing in disguise.

# Guelphs and Ghibellines

One medieval Italian writer claimed that the great age of factional strife in his nation began with two brothers of Pistoia, named Guelf and Gibel. Like Cain and Abel, or Romulus and Remus, one murdered the other, starting the seemingly endless troubles that to many seemed a God-sent plague, meant to punish the proud and wealthy Italians for their sins. Medieval Italy may in fact have been guilty of every sort of jealousy, greed and wrath – Perugia was near the top of the list on all three counts – but most historians trace the beginnings of this party conflict to two great German houses, *Welf* and *Waiblingen*.

To the Italians, what those barbarians did across the Alps meant little; the chroniclers pinpoint the outbreak of the troubles to the year 1215, when a politically prominent Florentine noble named Buondelmonte dei Buondelmonti was assassinated by his enemies while crossing the Ponte Vecchio. It was the tinder that ignited a smouldering quarrel all over Italy, and explains the often pathological behaviour of medieval Umbria.

The atmosphere of contentious city-states, each with its own internal struggles between nobles, a rich merchant class and commoners, crystallized rapidly into parties. In the beginning, at least, they stood for something. The Guelphs, largely a creation of the newly wealthy bourgeois, were all for free trade and the rights of the free cities; the Ghibellines from the start were the party of the German emperors, nominal overlords of Italy who had been trying to assert their control ever since the days of Charlemagne. Naturally, the Guelphs found their protector in the emperors' bitter temporal rivals, the popes. This brought a religious angle into the story, especially with the advent of the excommunicated Emperor Frederick II, who destroyed and rebuilt a number of villages in Umbria and set up court in Foligno in defiance of the tirades from Rome.

Everything about this convoluted history tends to confirm the worst suspicions of modern behavioural scientists. Before long, the labels Guelph and Ghibelline ceased to have any meaning at all. In the 13th and 14th centuries, the emperors and their Ghibelline allies helped the Church root out heretical movements like the Patarenes, while the popes schemed to destroy the liberty of good Guelph cities, especially in Umbria, and incorporate them into the Papal States. Black was the Ghibelline colour, white the Guelph, and cities arranged themselves like squares on a chessboard. When one suffered a revolution and changed from Guelph to Ghibelline, or vice versa, of course its nearest enemies would soon change the other way.

The English, like many uninvolved European nations, looked on all this with bewilderment. Edmund Spenser, in glosses to his *Shepheards' Calendar* (1579), wrote this fanciful etymology:

*When all Italy was distraicte into the Factions of the Guelfes and the Gibelins,
being two famous houses in Florence, the name began through their great
mischiefes and many outrages, to be so odious or rather dreadfull in the peoples
eares, that if theyr children at any time were frowarde and wanton, they would
say to them the Guelfe or the Gibeline came. Which words nowe from them (as
may thinge els) be come into our vsage, and for Guelfes and Gibelines, we say
Elfes and Goblins.*

# St Francis of Assisi

Francesco Bernardone was one of the most remarkable men who ever lived,
and, although he's now the patron saint of all Italy, he always remained closely
attached to his native Umbria, in life as well as death; nearly every town in the
region seems to have a legend about him, or at least a Franciscan church founded
in the early days of his movement. He lived in what the Chinese call interesting
times. His gentle spiritual revolution occurred amid the sound and the fury that
fills the chronicles of the 13th century. While the Guelphs and Ghibellines were
going at it tooth and nail and the Church was becoming increasingly worldly,
wealthy and ambitious, Francis taught that the natural world was a beautiful place,
and that there was tremendous joy in living an ordinary humble life in it in the
imitation of Christ.

Francis was born in 1182 to a merchant, Pietro Bernardone, and his Provençal wife,
Madonna Pica. Some say Pietro was the richest man in Assisi; he travelled often
through the south of France, buying and selling fine cloth, and although he named
his son Giovanni at the baptismal font he always called him Francesco after the
country he loved. At one point Francis accompanied his father on his annual
journey through Provence and up the Rhône to Bruges and Ghent, but most of all
he used his father's wealth to finance a merry and dissipated youth; according to
his first biographer, Tommaso da Celano, he was 'the first instigator of every evil,
and behind none in foolishness'. He was also a poet in the troubadour tradition. His
Francophile upbringing gave him an early taste for the cult of chivalry and mystic
love, imported from Provence and by 1200 all the rage among young Italians.

His conversion to saintliness did not happen overnight. In 1202, Francis joined the
cavalry of Assisi in one of its many wars against Perugia, but was captured and
spent a dismal year in a Perugian prison. He also suffered a long, severe illness. The
two events made him stop and think; he yearned for something more than the
carefree life he had been living. At first he thought it might be chivalry, so he joined
a band riding to join the Fourth Crusade. He got as far as Spoleto when he fell ill
again. He took this as a warning that he was on the wrong track, and changed his
allegiance from a temporal lord to a spiritual one.

Francis began to spend his time alone in the woods and meadows around Assisi,
reflecting on the world's vanity. A revelation came to him while attending Mass one
Sunday in 1205, as the priest read the words of the Gospel: '... and as ye go, preach,

saying, the kingdom of Heaven is at hand. Heal the sick, cleanse the lepers, raise the dead, cast out devils: freely have ye received, freely give.' Francis took this message literally: he would live like Christ, in poverty and humility. The story goes that he took his final decision before the Crucifix in the little church of San Damiano outside Assisi, which spoke to him, saying 'Repair my house, which you see is in ruins.' Francis sold his father's pack horse and merchandise in Foligno to do just that; when his angry father hauled him before the bishop of Assisi and reproached him, Francis stripped off his rich clothes and declared that henceforth his only father was his father in heaven.

It has been commented that much of Franciscan legend comes in exemplary packages too tidy to be taken as literal truth, but there is no doubt that this merchant's son who called himself 'God's Fool' and lived in total poverty, kissing lepers and preaching to the outcasts of the world, struck a chord in the hearts of many thirsting for something beyond the carrot-and-stick fare offered by the medieval Church. Although at first he was chased and stoned by the boys of Assisi as he begged for alms, Francis soon attracted a band of followers who lived with him in the Porziuncola, a chapel on the plain below Assisi, and wandered about the area preaching, doing odd jobs to support themselves or begging their bread.

His visit in 1210 to Pope Innocent III is part of Franciscan legend. Innocent was the man perhaps most responsible for the new worldly and militant direction of the Church, and he had little truck with reformers or anyone critical of its ambitions and corruption (in the previous year, he had declared the Albigensian Crusade against the other-worldly Cathars in southern France). His proud and wealthy court scoffed at the shabby Umbrian holy man, but that night Innocent dreamt that his church of St John Lateran – then the seat of the popes – was collapsing, and that this same Francis came along to hold up its walls.

Dream or not, it did occur to the pope that he might be able to harness the spiritual renewal that Francis preached within the institutions of the Church; unlike the Cathars and other heretics, Francis never attacked the papal hierarchy, explicitly at any rate, although his beliefs that a person could live by the Gospel in the 13th century and that the love of money was the root of all evil were harder to fit in the current scheme. Innocent nevertheless confirmed his First Rule for a simple lay order based on poverty, which Francis called the *Frati Minori*. As the movement quickly grew and the roads filled with begging friars, the Church tried to convince Francis to impose on it the discipline of a monastic rule. Francis resisted this, having no interest in organization; he never even took holy orders.

In the meantime, Francis spent his time travelling and preaching, mostly in Umbria, where many villages can show a humble stone in a cave where the saint rested his head or tell a legend of his sway over the birds and beasts. In 1219, he went further afield, as far as Spain in an unsuccessful attempt to reach Morocco, and then to the Holy Land and Egypt, accompanying the Crusaders. At Damietta, on the Nile, he preached to Sultan Malik el Kamil and was warmly received. The story goes that Francis was on an apostolic mission to convert the infidels, but it's just as likely he went to learn from them, especially from the Sufi mystics, not too surprising for a former troubadour, immersed in ideas of divine love that had come originally from the East during the first Crusades. One of the more intriguing parallels was a Sufi brotherhood very similar to the Friars Minor, founded some sixty years before Francis's birth by a holy man named Najmuddin Kubra, a wandering preacher with an uncanny influence over birds and animals.

Drawing on his troubadour days, Francis composed some of the first and finest vernacular verse in Italy, including the famous *Canticle of the Sun*, a poem in his native Umbrian dialect on the unity of all creation. His poetry became the foundation of a literary movement, based on Christian devotion: Tommaso da Celano, one of Francis's first followers and his autobiographer, composed the powerful *Dies Irae*, followed a few decades later by Jacopone da Todi (*see* p.193), who was, after Dante, the greatest poet of his century.

By 1221 Francis's extraordinary character and sanctity had inspired a movement of spiritual renewal that had spread across Italy and beyond. Unwilling to manage the growing organization, he turned the vicarship of the Friars Minor to Pietro Catani, who soon died, and then to Brother Elias. 'Henceforth I am dead to you,' he declared to the friars, and went to live in retreat with his early followers. But he wasn't quite dead; realizing that the movement was already slipping away from his intentions, he wrote a second Rule (1223) under Pope Honorius III that created the Franciscan order based on poverty as a supreme good, and confirmed it in his testament, urging his friars to remain 'wayfarers and pilgrims in this world'. It was at Christmas in the same year that he reconstructed a manger scene in Greccio (a village just south of Umbria), to emphasize the humble, human, child side of Christ as opposed to the stern arbitrator of the Last Judgement. The Italians were charmed and have been making their Christmas *presepi* ever since.

During the last three years of his life, Francis spent most of his time at the sanctuary of La Verna in Tuscany, where in 1225 he received the stigmata, which seemed to confirm his life as an imitation of Christ. Increasingly frail, he returned to Assisi a year later to meet his good Sister Death at age 44. In under two years he was canonized by Gregory IX, who as Cardinal Ugolino had been his friend and one of the Order's first protectors. At the same time, Gregory also did much to defuse Francis's dangerous legacy by declaring that his testament was not binding, and by directing the Franciscans down the path of the other new preaching order of the 13th century, the Dominicans. Huge churches, urban convents, university education and rich donations to be 'used' by the property-less friars soon came into being, explained away as necessary for the times. The order split into the 'Conventuals', who agreed, and the 'Spirituals', who wanted to hold on to their founders' prescription of poverty, the more extreme going off on paths of esoteric mysticism that would have probably appalled Francis as much as his order's prosperity.

But for the average Italian in the streets these intermural disputes took nothing away from the humane Christianity of love and charity exemplified by Francis and preached by his friars. His native Assisi quickly became a place of pilgrimage, and his native land was well on its way to becoming *Umbria mistica*.

# Landscapes and Nature

Other regions in Italy have taller mountains and more fertile valleys, others support a far greater variety of flora and enjoy a more temperate climate. Yet, when all is said and done, it is the landscapes of Umbria that exert the most lasting charm of the region. Would St Francis now be the patron saint of the Green Party if he had been born in the sun-baked prairies of Oklahoma? In the paintings of the Renaissance, the backgrounds of rolling hills and rocky peaked mountains, orderly cypresses, poplars and parasol pines, blue-green Lake Trasimeno and multi-towered towns in the distance are often more beautiful than the nominally religious subject in the foreground. Very early on, beginning with Giotto and his followers, Umbrian artists took special care to relate the figures in their composition to the architecture and the landscape around them, to the extent that for many art lovers, at any rate, the expression 'Holy Land' conjures lush scenes of Umbria rather than the decidedly more arid countryside around Jerusalem.

The beauty of the countryside may be natural, but it's no accident. Every Italian is born with an obsessive instinct to put in order, or *sistemare*, things; with a history of wars, earthquakes, foreign rulers and an age-old tendency to extremes of all descriptions, the race has had a bellyful of disorder and unpredictability. The tidy, ordered geometry and clipped hedges of an Italian garden are a perfect example of the urge to order nature; the Tuscans, in the vanguard of Italy in so many ways, were the first to order their entire territory. The vicious medieval wars between cities and the Guelphs and Ghibellines devastated the countryside and much of the forests; the Black Death in the 1300s depopulated the cultivated areas, offering a unique opportunity to arrange things just so.

The Valle Umbra has an air of exquisite civilization not unlike Tuscany, but in general Umbria is more dramatic than its Tuscan neighbour and, above all, less manicured; hills here tend to be steeper, the precious valleys narrower and its forests denser – just the sort of countryside sought by hermits and saints. Since the 19th century it has been celebrated for its greenness, the most mystical of colours, which suits its mystical nature. One feature of the Umbrian landscape, however, is as artful as Tuscany – its hill towns of pinkish-grey stone. From some vantage points you can see several at a time, like an archipelago of islands crowned with villages, one behind the other, vanishing into the bluish haze of the horizon, in autumn swirled in mists.

Close up, the flora and fauna that populate Umbria's hills are close cousins to those seen in northern Europe and America, only somehow they seem more splendid, like the saints in Perugino's paintings, for their lovely settings. There are a million varieties of buttercup, usually tiny ones like the *ranuncolo* and *bottoncini d'oro*, and of bluebell, called *campanella* or *campanellina*. Many of the common five-petalled pink blossoms in spring fields are really small wild geraniums (*geranio*), with pointed leaves like the anemone, and you'll see quite a few varieties of violets (*violette*) with round or spade-shaped leaves (a few species are yellow). A daisy, in Italian, is a *margherita*, and they come in all sizes. Tiniest of all are the wild pink and blue forget-me-nots (*non ti scordar di me*); you'll have to look closely to see them in overgrown fields.

The real star of the fields is the poppy, bright red and thriving everywhere in the spring as if the whole landscape was kissed with a dashing shade of lipstick. Dandelions and wild mustard are plentiful, along with white, umbrella-like bunches of florets called *tragosellino* or *podragraria*, similar to what Americans call Queen Anne's Lace. More exotic flowers include wild orchids, some with small florets growing in spiky shoots, and rhododendrons (in mountainous areas). The best wildflowers are up in the Sibillini mountains; the Piano Grande blooming in early summer is an unforgettable sight.

There are other plants to look out for. A dozen kinds of wild greens that go into somewhat bitter salads, anise, fennel, mint, rosemary and sage are common. The Umbrians beat the bushes with fervour every spring looking for wild asparagus and repeat the performance in autumn searching for truffles and mushrooms.

As for the animals, you can start with those two regional totems, the viper and the boar. The bad old viper, the only really unpleasant thing you may encounter in Umbria, proliferates especially where farmlands have been abandoned; he's brownish-grey, about a foot and a half long (never more than a yard), and has a vaguely diamond-shaped head. In spite of their retiring, shy nature, vipers are a nuisance only because they are so numerous, and because they object to being stepped on. If one bites you, you've got half an hour to find somewhere with the serum – a hospital or a *croce verde* in more remote villages. The boar, an equally shy creature, flourishes everywhere despite the Umbrian hunters' best efforts to turn him into salami or prosciutto. In summer, you may hear him nosing around the villages at night looking for water.

Beyond these, there are plenty of hares and rabbits, foxes and weasels, also polecats, badgers and porcupine (the latter is a local delicacy in the more remote corners of Umbria). Lynxes and deer were once common, and a few survive in the higher reaches of the Apennines; wolves, once almost extinct, are returning to higher altitudes, and brown bears apparently have migrated from the Abruzzo into the Sibylline mountains.

Many writers on Umbria comment on the silence of the country and the absence of birdsong. They are exaggerating, although it is true that Umbria has more hunters per capita and they do shoot anything that flies, but there are still quite a few thrushes, starlings, wrens, buzzards and such like, along with the white doves, ubiquitous in Umbria, that always make you think of Assisi and St Francis. Cuckoos unfailingly announce the spring, pheasants lie low during the hunting season, and an occasional owl can be heard in the country. Nightingales are common and in the evening you're quite likely to see bats.

The insect world is well represented, and if you spend time in the country you'll meet many (perhaps too many) of them: lovely butterflies and moths and delicate white feather-winged creatures; and rather forbidding black bullet bees and wasps that resemble vintage fighter planes. Beetles, in particular, reach disproportionate sizes, especially the *diavolo*, a large black or red beetle with long, gracefully curving antlers that sings when you trap it; Leonardo drew one in his notebooks, and rumour has it that they mate for life. On spring nights in the country, if you're lucky, the fireflies put on a magical kinetic display worthy of Times Square. There are enough mosquitoes, midges and little biting flies to be a nuisance, and, perhaps most alarming at first sight, the shiny black scorpion, who may crawl inside through the window or up drains – you may want to keep the plugs in – or come in with the firewood. Once inside they head for dark places like beds or shoes. One thwack with a shoe means curtains for a scorpion (they're actually quite soft), but you may start feeling sorry for the little critters. Most people we know have devised cunning scorpion traps and take their captives back to the woods. If you happen to be stung, it may be painful but is not deadly; the Italians recommend a trip to the doctor for treatment against an infection or allergic reaction.

# Food and Drink

04

In Italy, the three Ms (the *Madonna, Mamma* and *Mangiare*) are still a force to be reckoned with and, in a country where millions of otherwise sane people spend much of their waking hours worrying about their digestion, standards both at home and in the restaurants are understandably high. Everybody is a gourmet, or at least thinks he or she is, and food is not only something to eat but a subject approaching the heights of philosophy – two Umbrian businessmen once overheard on a train heatedly discussed mushrooms for over four hours. Although ready-made pasta, tinned minestrone and frozen pizza in the *supermercato* tempt the virtue of the Italian cook, few give in (although many a working mother wishes she could at times).

For the visitor this national culinary obsession comes as an extra bonus to the senses – along with Italy's remarkable sights, music, and the warm sun on your back, you can enjoy some of the best tastes and smells the world can offer, prepared daily in Italy's kitchens and fermented in its countless wine cellars. Eating *all'italiana* is not only delicious and wholesome, but now undeniably trendy. Foreigners flock here to learn the secrets of Italian cuisine and the even more elusive secret of how the Italians can live surrounded by such a plethora of delights and still fit into their sleek Armani trousers.

# Restaurant Generalities

**Breakfast** (*colazione*) in Italy is no lingering affair, but an early-morning wake-up shot to the brain: a *cappuccino* (*espresso* with hot foamy milk, often sprinkled with chocolate – incidentally first thing in the morning is the only time of day at which any self-respecting Italian will touch the stuff), a *caffè latte* (white coffee) or a *caffè lungo* (a generous portion of *espresso*), accompanied by a croissant-type roll, called a *cornetto* or *briosche*, or a fancy pastry. This repast can be consumed in any bar and repeated during the morning as often as necessary. Breakfast in most Italian hotels seldom represents great value.

**Lunch** (*pranzo*), generally served around 1pm, is the most important meal of the day for the Italians, with a minimum of a first course (*primo piatto* – any kind of pasta dish, broth or soup, or rice dish), a second course (*secondo piatto* – a meat dish, accompanied by a *contorno* or side dish – a vegetable, salad, or potatoes usually), followed by fruit or dessert and coffee. You can, however, begin with a platter of *antipasti* – the appetizers Italians do so brilliantly, ranging from warm seafood delicacies to raw ham (*prosciutto crudo*), salami in a hundred varieties, lovely vegetables, savoury toasts, olives, pâté and many many more. There are restaurants that specialize in *antipasti*, and they usually don't take it amiss if you decide to forget the pasta and meat and just nibble on these scrumptious hors-d'œuvres (though in the end it may well cost more than a full meal). Most Italians accompany their meal with wine and mineral water – *acqua minerale*, with or without bubbles (*frizzante* or *naturale*), which supposedly aids digestion – concluding their meals with a *digestivo* liqueur.

**Cena**, the evening meal, is usually eaten around 8pm – earlier in the north and later in the south. This is much the same as *pranzo* although lighter: a pizza and beer, eggs or a fish dish. In restaurants, however, they offer all the courses whatever the time of day, so if you have only a sandwich for lunch you can have a full meal in the evening.

In Italy the various terms for types of **restaurants** – *ristorante, trattoria* or *osteria* – have been confused. A *trattoria* or *osteria* can be just as elaborate as a restaurant, though rarely is a *ristorante* as informal as a traditional *trattoria*. Unfortunately the old habit of posting menus and prices in the windows has fallen from fashion, so it's often difficult to judge variety or prices. Invariably the least expensive eating place is the increasingly scarce *vino e cucina*, a simple establishment serving simple cuisine for simple everyday prices. It is essential to remember that the fancier the fittings the fancier the bill, though neither of these points has anything at all to do with the quality of the food. If you're uncertain, do as you would at home – look for lots of locals.

People who haven't visited Italy for years and have fond memories of eating full meals for under a pound will be amazed at how much **prices** have risen, especially since the arrival of the euro; though in some respects eating out in Italy is still a bargain, especially when you figure out how much all that wine would have cost you at home. In many places you'll often find restaurants offering a *menu turistico* – full, set meals of usually meagre inspiration for a reasonable set price. More imaginative chefs often offer a *menu degustazione* – a set-price gourmet meal that allows you to taste their daily specialities and seasonal dishes. Both of these are cheaper than if you had ordered the same food *à la carte*.

As the pace of modern urban life militates against traditional lengthy home-cooked repasts with the family, followed by a siesta, alternatives to sit-down meals have mushroomed. Many office workers now behave much as their counterparts elsewhere in Europe and consume a rapid snack at lunchtime, returning home after a busy day to throw together some pasta and salad in the evenings.

The original Italian fast food alternative is known as the 'hot table' (*tavola calda*), a buffet serving hot and cold foods, where you can choose a simple prepared dish or a whole meal, depending on your appetite. The food in these can occasionally be truly impressive, though nowadays they are becoming harder to find among the growing number of international and made-in-Italy fast food franchises. However, bars often double as *paninotecas* (these make sandwiches to order), and if everywhere else is closed, you can always try the railway station bars – these will at least have sandwiches and drinks. Some of the station bars also prepare *cestini di viaggio*, full-course meals in a basket to help you survive long train trips.

The *rosticceria* is another very varied alternative to a restaurant meal – hot and cold food to take away, and usually of better quality than the *tavola calda*. Rarely do they have anywhere to sit down. Pastas, rice, roasted meats (always including spit-roasted chickens), veg, dessert and drinks are always good value.

For information on snacks and picnics, *see* pp.50–1.

# Umbrian Specialities

Regional traditions are strong in Italy, not only in dialect but in the kitchen. Umbrians are no exception and firmly maintain their distinctive cuisine even when you wish they wouldn't – especially in the case of the tasteless bread, a hangover from the salt wars, described by astonished visitors as being as 'tasty as chewy water' and 'scarcely distinguishable from a cricket bat'. It often comes stamped with the name of the bakery on it, like a brick. For a historically poor area, Umbria offers good, honest, traditional dishes, which are often humble and rarely elaborate.

The truth is that, although beans and *coratella* (lambs' intestines) often appear on the menu, most people when dining out want to try something different, from the recent concoctions of Italian nouvelle cuisine, or *cucina nuova*, or perhaps a recipe from the Middle Ages or Renaissance. Some of the country's finest restaurants are in Umbria, although its dishes may not be as diverse as in Tuscany.

## Food

Umbria's cooking is simple, honest, hearty and excellent. It may not officially rank among the great culinary regions of Italy, but it rarely disappoints, either; it is not elaborate but the local ingredients are very good – in the case of truffles, they are transcendent. Although Umbria boasts one of Italy's top gourmet restaurants in Baschi, on the whole the region is gastronomically conservative and not so sure about this new-fangled *cucina nuova*, much less the *cucina* from anywhere else in Italy, and even less anything non-Italian. This devotion to Umbrian food can reach astonishing proportions: Umbrian teenagers on their summer language courses in England who had to be flown home after two days because they were starving to death; adventurous Umbrian diners who dared to enter a Chinese restaurant, but could only eat the rice; our Umbrian landlord who went to Dalmatia on his honeymoon, found the pasta overcooked and returned to Terni, swearing he would never leave again as long as he lived.

Umbria produces excellent olive oil (*see* box, above right), which it now treats like wine, divided into several growing regions. It grows wheat, which it makes into delicious fresh pasta as well as dried pasta sold nationwide (Buitoni is one of several firms in Perugia). It is known for its game dishes, especially wild boar, its wild mushrooms (best April–June and October–November) and various kinds of cold cuts made from the acorn-fed pigs of Norcia, so renowned that all over Italy a pork butcher is known as a *norcino*. But, because of the long centuries of poverty, many specialities were born of thrift; some of these have died out, while others have become trendy.

Dense, heavy, salt-free Umbrian bread, potential murder weapon that it is, has the one great virtue of being made to order for *bruschetta*, a favourite **antipasto** now made familiar by Italian restaurants around the world, although in Umbria it seems to taste best, grilled over an open fire, covered with the region's exquisite olive oil and rubbed with garlic; a fancier version has chopped tomatoes and basil. For any

## Deluxe Virgins

Some day, on a trip to one of the fancier Italian food shops, you may pause near the section devoted to condiments and wonder at the beautiful display of bottles of unusually dark whiskies and wines, with corks and elegant labels – why, some is even DOC, though much is far more costly than the usual DOC vintages. A closer look reveals these precious bottles to be full of nothing but olive oil. Admittedly, *olio extra vergine di oliva* from Umbria makes a fine salad dressing. Its delicate, fruity fragrance derives from the excellent quality of the ripe olive and the low acidity extracted from the fruit without any refinements. The finest, Extra Virgin, must have less than 1 percent acidity (the best has 0.5 percent acidity). Other designations are Soprafino Virgin, Fine Virgin and Virgin (each may have up to 4 percent acidity), in descending order of quality.

As any Italian will tell you, it's good for you – and it had better be, because Umbrian chefs have put it in nearly every dish for centuries. The only difference is that it now comes in a fancy package at a fancy price, a victim of the Italian designer label syndrome. Not only does the oil have corks, but the trend in the early 1990s was for some of the smarter restaurants to offer an olive oil list similar to a wine list. Many of these, perhaps fortunately, have gone out of business.

special occasion, out come the *crostini*, thin slices of toast with a piquant pâté spread of chicken livers (or spleen), or anchovies, capers and lemons, or truffles mixed with mushrooms. The other traditional Umbrian *antipasto* is a platter (*affettati*) of prosciutto, salame, sliced stuffed rabbit and capocollo (cured neck of pork, rolled in pepper).

Umbrians are more than fond of their pasta, with good reason – *tagliatelle ai funghi* (with wild porcini mushrooms), or *al tartufo* (with grated truffles); *tortellini con panna* (with cream sauce); *ciriole* or *pici* or *umbricelli* or *strangozzi* (various names for fat, home-made spaghetti) with various sauces, of which wild asparagus (*asparago selvatico*) holds pride of place in April and May (it's also excellent in omelettes). Other pasta sauces you may see are *sugo alle rigaglie*, made of chicken livers and other innards, with onion and parsley, or *alla ternana* (a rich tomato sauce with pecorino cheese), or *all'amatriciana*, from nearby Rieti province, made with tomatoes, bacon, black pepper and pecorino, or its close cousin, *spaghetti col rancetto*, from Spoleto. In autumn many restaurants serve *pappardelle al cinghiale*, thick pasta with a rich sauce made from wild boar, red wine, juniper berries, tomatoes and so on. In northern Umbria look for *strascinati*, homemade macaroni served with sausage, eggs and cheese; Amelia is famous for its *manfricoli all'arrabbiata*, homemade pasta with a spicy hot tomato sauce. The real test of an Umbrian chef is eggs with truffles, a difficult dish to time correctly but superb when successful; risotti with truffles or mushrooms are also delicious.

Menus usually include some kind of **soup**. Spelt (*farro*) was long regarded as a poor man's wheat, but now is specially cultivated organically for its authentic taste in minestrone; the lentils of Castelluccio, once regarded as a poor kind of protein, are now in demand (in Umbria they make them into a soup with garlic, celery and olive oil). Another soup, one you're more likely to see in a home than in a restaurant, is *pancotto*, made of stale bread, olive oil, tomatoes, onions and often peppers, served cold in the summer. You may also see *baggiana*, a soup of fava beans, tomatoes and basil (especially in the north) or the archetypal *pasta con ceci*.

The average restaurant in Umbria rarely offers exceptional **secondi**. Most Umbrians are content with grilled chops, salad and fried potatoes. The meats –

lamb, pork or veal – are of fine quality, especially the lamb, often served in a pile of small chops with a lemon (*agnello alla scottadito*: 'finger-burning lamb'). *Fritto misto* is an interesting alternative, where lamb chops, liver, sweetbreads, artichokes and courgettes (*zucchini*) are dipped in batter and deep-fried. Otherwise look for *arista di maiale* (pork loin with rosemary and garlic), *anatra* (duck, often served with truffles), *piccione* (stuffed wild pigeon), *palomba* (wood pigeon) or *cinghiale* (boar) – either in sausages or *stufato* (stewed) or *alla cacciatora*. Umbrians are rather too fond of their *girarrosto*, a great spit of tiny songbirds and pork livers. The one chicken dish the region is famous for is Orvieto's *gallina ubriaca*, 'drunken' in white wine and slowly cooked with raw ham, tomatoes and garlic.

In landlocked Umbria, **fish** is rare outside the fancy restaurants that have it brought in daily from the coast, although you can usually get trout and occasionally freshwater crayfish (*gamberi*) especially in the Valnerina and by Lake Piediluco. A couple of restaurants by Lake Trasimeno specialize in the lake's tench, perch, eel and carp. You'll have to be lucky or persistent, however, to find the classsic *regina alla porchetta* (a big carp, stuffed with garlic, fennel and lard, wrapped in rosemary, tied up with reeds and roasted on a spit, or more often baked in the oven). The thick local fish soup, *tegamaccio*, is made with onions, garlic and lots of tomatoes.

Umbria is not known for its **cheese**, but its best, the fresh ewe's milk *caciotta*, comes from Norcia and is often on sale in the *norcinerie*; another is tangy *pecorino*, made by the Sard shepherds who immigrated to the region. Although most Umbrians prefer fruit to sweet desserts, they have no lack of **sweets** for other times of the day, and especially for special occasions and holidays. Typical sweets include Perugia's *torciglione*, shaped like a coiled serpent, made of flour and almond paste; Terni's *panpepato* (a rich, spicy, dense cake full of nuts and candied fruit); *frappe* or *cenci* or *strufoli* (deep-fried strips of dough, served with honey, lemon rind or sugar, made for carnival), *castagnaccio* (chestnut cake, with pine nuts, raisins and rosemary), *crostate* (fruit tarts), *torcolo* (ring-shaped cake with pine nuts and candied fruit, or perhaps a *gelato ai Baci* (made with Perugia's famous hazelnut chocolates). In Assisi, the shops sell *rocciata*, a spicy strudel filled with a mixture of almonds, walnuts, prunes, figs, raisins and honey, and *pane di San Francesco*, a hard cake made with pine nuts, currants, honey and aniseed. Tozzetti, made with almonds or hazelnuts, are favourite *vin santo* dunkers.

## Picnics, Snacks and *Porchetta*

There are several alternatives to sit-down meals. Little shops selling pizza by the slice (*pizza al taglio*) are common in city centres; some, called *gastronomie*, offer other take-out delicacies as well. At any delicatessen (*pizzicheria*), grocer's (*alimentari*) or market (*mercato*) you can buy the materials for picnics; some places will make the sandwiches for you. Common snacks you'll encounter include *panini* of cheese, tomatoes and prosciutto (or other meats); and *tramezzini*, little sandwiches on plain, square white bread that are always much better than they look. In and around Perugia the favourite snack is *torta al testa*, a pizza-like flat bread cooked on a hot stove, filled with prosciutto or sausage or cheese.

The traditional sandwich of Umbria, however, is nothing so dainty, but a hard roll filled with fat slices of warm *porchetta* (roast whole pig stuffed with fennel and garlic and pepper, complete with all the fat and gristle). Often it is *girarrosto* (cooked on a spit) or roast in the oven. You can often find it in the *norcinerie*, or in roadside vans. The fact that these roadside vans resemble those used by itinerant prostitutes has led at least one near-sighted hungry Umbrian into a comedy of errors, but you really do have to try hard to confuse them.

## Umbria's Totem Tubers

Umbria's most valuable cash crop has neither seeds nor a planting season, and adamantly refuses to grow in straight rows. An aura of mystery surrounds their very nature; according to legend they are spawned by lightning bolts flickering among the oaks. Truffles they are, *tartufi*, and although they look a lot like granulated mud on your pasta, these earthy, aromatic and aphrodisiac tubers that are actually a weird type of fungi are the most prized gourmet delicacy in Italy. Even in their natural state they aren't much to look at, bulbous lumps from the size of a pea to a baby's fist, and they're very picky about where they grow. Umbria is one of their favourite spots – here are the proper calcareous soils, oak and beech forests and exposures, in particular around Spoleto and Norcia, and most especially in the Valnerina around Scheggino. This is the realm of the highest-quality black truffle (*Tuber melanosporum vittadini*), which in Europe grow here, and in Perigord in France, and almost nowhere else. The even rarer white truffle (*Tuber magnatum pico*), mostly found in Piemonte, deigns to grow around Gubbio, and is avidly sought from October to December. The black truffle season is considerably longer, extending into March, and in summer you can find *scorzone* – a lower-quality version which is nevertheless very good and sells at a fraction of the usual price. Out of season you can find them bottled in oil (never buy fresh except in season – they just won't be good) but they are absolutely heavenly when fresh from the ground and offer a perfectly legitimate reason for visiting Umbria in the off season (serious eaters might want to aim for the February gastronomic fair in Norcia).

Except for saffron, gram for gram truffles are the most expensive comestible in the world. Prices for a good white truffle can easily top a staggering €2,300 a kilo, while the more common black truffles are half as much, but still make a dent in the pocketbook. Not only are they resistant to cultivation, but they're fiendishly hard to track down. The vast majority are still brought to market by secretive truffle-hunters and their keen-nosed, specially trained hounds, who learn to love the smell as tiny pups, because of the truffle juice rubbed around their mother's teats. They are gathered during the night, when the truffles smell the strongest, or perhaps because the best truffles are always on someone else's land. Beware: truffle-hunting requires not only a dog and a special digging implement called a *vanghetta*, but also a licence. And competition can be deadly – on more than one occasion, the season has been marred in Umbria by a psycho truffle-dog poisoner. Fortunately, a little *tartufo* goes a long way, and Italians will travel far to look, dreamy-eyed, at glass jars of them at Umbria's truffle fairs.

Profits are such that imitations have made considerable headway in recent years. Beware synthesized truffle aromas, which are nothing like the real thing, or cheap low-grade black truffles imported from China that lack the pungent, aromatic intensity of the Umbrian-grown. Also you'd do well to steer clear of one local truffle product – the nubby black bottles of Tartufo liqueur, which tastes as vile as it looks.

# Wine

Most Italian wines are named after the grape and the district they come from. If the label says DOC (*Denominazione di Origine Controllata*) it means that the wine comes from a specially defined area and was produced according to a certain traditional method; DOCG (the G stands for *Garantita*) means that a high quality is also guaranteed – a badge worn only by the noblest wines. *Classico* means that a wine comes from the oldest part of the zone of production; *Riserva*, or *Superiore*, means a wine has been aged longer.

Umbria has been a wine region ever since the Etruscans planted the first cuttings from the Greeks, but through much of its history the main concern was to produce wine rather than good wine. The naturally fertile soil brought forth luxuriant vines, which were often planted alongside outcrops and simply trained over the trees. The one exception to the generally mediocre plonk was the still-reigning king of Umbrian vines, **Orvieto** and **Orvieto Classico**, a delicate wine, dry with a slightly bitter aftertaste; Orvieto Classico comes from the old *zona* around the Paglia river.

Orvieto, like nearly all of Umbria's wine, is a blend that flies in the face of modern trends towards single varietal wines. The white grapes of Umbria are *grechetto* (according to legend, introduced by the ancient Greeks), *trebbiano toscano* and the great Byzantine *malvasia*; reds, which have radically improved in the last two decades, are predominantly *sangiovese, sagrantino* and *ciliegiolo*. Even the excellent **Sagrantino di Montefalco**, recently elevated to DOCG status, has lots of *sangiovese* in it; it comes as the dry, garnet Sagrantino, with the aroma of blackberries, or the sweet Sagrantino Passito, made from raisins. Adanti, one of the top makers, also produces a dry, velvety *rosso*; other names of repute are Rocca di Fabbri, Decio Fongoli, Arnaldo Caprai, Antonelli, Val di Maggio and Scaccia Diavoli.

Among the finest and most innovative DOC wines are those of **Torgiano**, from a small zone near the village south of Perugia; it produces magnificent dry, full-bodied reds that can take years of ageing, especially its famous Rubesco di Torgiano (*sangiovese, montepulciano, canaiolo* and *ciliegiolo*), and the light and lively Torre di Giano, made of *trebbiano* and *grechetto*.

Umbria's other DOC wines are grown on the western hills of the region; most are very drinkable, and many are economical as well. **Colli del Trasimeno** wines come from the hills around Umbria's largest lake (a garnet, slightly tannic red wine and deep, straw-coloured, dry and mellow whites); **Colli Perugini** from the hills of Perugia (dry ruby red, fruity light white, and a dry, intense rosé); **Colli Amerini**, from the Amelia region (the three main colours, with very good blended reds, a not terribly exciting Novella or new wine, and Malvasia); the **Colli Martiri** between

Montefalco and Todi (light reds and aged *riserve*, and whites based on *grechetto*); and **Colli Altotiberini** from around Umbertide (a pleasant dry white, reds based on *sangiovese* and merlot, and a pale, fresh rosé).

One of the more unusual wines is the dessert wine **Vernaccia di Cannara**; only made in Cannara, it's unlike every other *vernaccia* in Italy, in that it's red. The most famous dessert wine in the region, however, is *vin santo*, a rich, deep, unctious golden wine made from semi-dried grapes; it's sweet and strong (14 percent), and holy only because priests are so fond of it. Although some producers make it commercially, the best is still homemade in small quantities; you know you're in with the locals when they serve you a glass from their precious cache, with the traditional hard biscuit or crunchy waffle (*cialda*).

# Italian Menu Reader

## Antipasti

These before-meal treats can include almost anything; these are among the most common.

*antipasto misto* mixed antipasto
*bruschetta* garlic toast (sometimes with tomatoes)
*carciofi (sott'olio)* artichokes (in oil)
*frutti di mare* seafood
*funghi (trifolati)* mushrooms (with anchovies, garlic and lemon)
*gamberi ai fagioli* prawns (shrimps) with white beans
*mozzarella (in carrozza)* cow/buffalo cheese (fried with bread in batter)
*olive* olives
*prosciutto (con melone)* raw ham (with melon)
*salame* cured pork sausage
*salsicce* sausages

## Minestre (Soups) and Pasta

*agnolotti* ravioli with meat
*cacciucco* spiced fish soup
*cannelloni* meat/cheese rolled in pasta tubes
*cappelletti* small ravioli, often in broth
*crespelle* crêpes
*fettuccine* long strips of pasta
*frittata* omelette
*gnocchi* potato dumplings
*lasagne* sheets of pasta baked with meat and cheese sauce
*minestra di verdura* thick vegetable soup
*minestrone* soup with meat, vegetables and pasta
*orecchiette* ear-shaped pasta, served with turnip greens
*panzerotti* ravioli with mozzarella, anchovies and egg
*pappardelle alla lepre* pasta with hare sauce
*pasta e fagioli* soup with beans, bacon and tomatoes

*pastina in brodo* tiny pasta in broth
*penne all'arrabbiata* quill-shaped pasta with tomatoes and hot peppers
*polenta* cake or pudding of corn semolina
*risotto (alla milanese)* Italian rice (with stock, saffron and wine)
*spaghetti all'amatriciana* with spicy pork, tomato, onion and chilli sauce
*spaghetti alla bolognese* with ground meat, ham, mushrooms, etc.
*spaghetti alla carbonara* with bacon, eggs and black pepper
*spaghetti al pomodoro* with tomato sauce
*spaghetti al sugo/ragù* with meat sauce
*spaghetti alle vongole* with clam sauce
*stracciatella* broth with eggs and cheese
*tagliatelle* flat egg noodles
*tortellini* pasta caps filled with meat and cheese
  *al pomodoro* with tomato sauce
  *con panna* with cream
  *in brodo* in broth
*vermicelli* very thin spaghetti

## Carne (Meat)

*abbacchio* milk-fed lamb
*agnello* lamb
*animelle* sweetbreads
*anatra* duck
*arista* pork loin
*arrosto misto* mixed roast meats
*bistecca alla fiorentina* Florentine beef steak
*bocconcini* veal mixed wih ham and cheese and fried
*bollito misto* stew of boiled meats
*braciola* chop
*brasato di manzo* braised beef
*bresaola* dried raw beef
*capretto* kid
*capriolo* roe buck
*carne di castrato/suino* mutton/pork
*carpaccio* thinly sliced raw beef

*casseuola* pork stew with cabbage
*cervello (al burro nero)* brains (in black
  butter sauce)
*cervo* venison
*cinghiale* boar
*coniglio* rabbit
*cotoletta* veal cutlet
  *alla milanese* fried in breadcrumbs
  *alla bolognese* with ham and cheese
*fagiano* pheasant
*faraona* guinea fowl
  *alla creta* in earthenware pot
*fegato alla veneziana* liver with onions
*lepre (in salmi)* hare (marinated in wine)
*lombo di maiale* pork loin
*lumache* snails
*maiale (al latte)* pork (cooked in milk)
*manzo* beef
*osso buco* braised veal knuckle
*pancetta* rolled pork
*pernice* partridge
*petto di pollo* boned chicken breast
  *alla fiorentina* fried in butter
  *alla bolognese* with ham and cheese
  *alla sorpresa* stuffed and deep fried
*piccione* pigeon
*pizzaiola* beef steak in tomato and oregano
*pollo* chicken
  *alla cacciatora* with tomatoes and
  mushrooms, cooked in wine
  *alla diavola* grilled
  *alla Marengo* fried with tomatoes, garlic
  and wine
*polpette* meatballs
*quaglie* quails
*rane* frogs
*rognoni* kidneys
*saltimbocca* veal scallop with prosciutto and
  sage, cooked in wine and butter
*scaloppine* thin slices of veal sautéed in butter
*spezzatino* pieces of beef/veal, usually stewed
*spiedino* meat on a skewer/stick
*stufato* beef and vegetables braised in wine
*tacchino* turkey
*trippa* tripe
*uccelletti* small birds on a skewer
*vitello* veal

## Pesce (Fish)

*acciughe or alici* anchovies
*anguilla* eel
*aragosta* lobster
*aringa* herring
*baccalà* dried salt cod
*bonito* small tuna
*branzino* sea bass
*calamari* squid
*cappe sante* scallops
*cefalo* grey mullet

*coda di rospo* angler fish
*cozze* mussels
*datteri di mare* razor (or date) mussels
*dentice* dentex (perch-like fish)
*dorato* gilt head
*fritto misto* mixed fried delicacies,
  mainly fish
*gamberetto* shrimp
*gamberi (di fiume)* prawns (crayfish)
*granchio* crab
*insalata di mare* seafood salad
*lampreda* lamprey
*merluzzo* cod
*nasello* hake
*orata* bream
*ostriche* oysters
*pesce spada* swordfish
*polipi/polpi* octopus
*pesce azzurro* various small fish
*pesce di San Pietro* John Dory
*rombo* turbot
*sarde* sardines
*seppie* cuttlefish
*sgombro* mackerel
*sogliola* sole
*squadro* monkfish
*stoccafisso* wind-dried cod
*tonno* tuna
*triglia* red mullet (rouget)
*trota* trout
*trota salmonata* salmon trout
*vongole* small clams
*zuppa di pesce* mixed fish in sauce or stew

## Contorni (Side Dishes, Vegetables)

*asparagi* asparagus
  *alla fiorentina* with fried eggs
*broccoli* broccoli
*carciofi (alla giudia)* artichokes (deep-fried)
*cardi* cardoons/thistles
*carote* carrots
*cavolfiore* cauliflower
*cavolo* cabbage
*ceci* chickpeas
*cetriolo* cucumber
*cipolla* onion
*fagioli* white beans
*fagiolini* French (green) beans
*fave* broad beans
*finocchio* fennel
*funghi (porcini)* mushrooms (boletus)
*insalata (mista/verde)* salad (mixed/green)
*lattuga* lettuce
*lenticchie* lentils
*melanzane* aubergine/eggplant
*patate (fritte)* potatoes (fried)
*peperoncini* hot chilli peppers
*peperoni* sweet peppers

*peperonata* stewed peppers, onions, etc.
(similar to ratatouille)
*piselli (al prosciutto)* peas (with ham)
*pomodoro(i)* tomato(es)
*porri* leeks
*radicchio* red chicory
*radice* radish
*rapa* turnip
*rucola* rocket
*sedano* celery
*spinaci* spinach
*verdure* greens
*zucca* pumpkin
*zucchini* courgettes

## Formaggio (Cheese)
*bel paese* soft white cow's cheese
*cacio/caciocavallo* pale yellow, sharp cheese
*caprino* goat's cheese
*fontina* rich cow's milk cheese
*groviera* mild cheese (gruyère)
*gorgonzola* soft blue cheese
*parmigiano* Parmesan cheese
*pecorino* sharp sheep's cheese
*provolone* sharp, tangy; *dolce* is less strong
*stracchino* soft white cheese

## Frutta (Fruit, Nuts)
*albicocche* apricots
*ananas* pineapple
*arance* oranges
*banane* bananas
*cachi* persimmons
*ciliege* cherries
*cocomero* watermelon
*datteri* dates
*fichi* figs
*fragole (con panna)* strawberries (with cream)
*lamponi* raspberries
*limone* lemon
*macedonia di frutta* fruit salad
*mandarino* tangerine
*mandorle* almonds
*melagrana* pomegranate
*mele* apples
*mirtilli* bilberries
*more* blackberries
*nespola* medlar fruit
*nocciole* hazelnuts
*noci* walnuts
*pera* pear
*pesca* peach
*pesca noce* nectarine
*pinoli* pine nuts
*pompelmo* grapefruit
*prugna/susina* prune/plum
*uva* grapes

## Dolci (Desserts)
*amaretti* macaroons
*cannoli* crisp pastry tubes filled with ricotta,
cream, chocolate or fruit
*coppa gelato* assorted ice cream
*crema caramella* caramel-topped custard
*crostata* fruit flan
*gelato (produzione propria)* ice cream
(homemade)
*granita* flavoured ice, often lemon or coffee
*monte bianco* chestnut pudding
with cream
*panettone* sponge cake with candied fruit
and raisins
*panforte* dense cake of chocolate, almonds
and preserved fruit
*saint honoré* meringue cake
*semifreddo* refrigerated cake
*sorbetto* sorbet/sherbet
*spumone* a soft ice cream
*tiramisù* layers of sponge, mascarpone,
coffee and chocolate
*torrone* nougat
*torta* cake, tart
*torta millefoglie* layered pastry and custard
cream
*zabaglione* eggs and Marsala wine,
served hot
*zuppa inglese* trifle

## Bevande (Beverages)
*acqua minerale* mineral water
*con/senza gas* with/without fizz
*aranciata* orange soda
*birra (alla spina)* beer (draught)
*caffè (freddo)* coffee (iced)
*cioccolata* chocolate
*gassosa* lemon-flavoured soda
*latte (intero/scremato)* milk (whole/skimmed)
*limonata* lemon soda
*succo di frutta* fruit juice
*tè* tea
*vino* wine
*rosso* red
*bianco* white
*rosato* rosé

## Cooking Terms (Miscellaneous)
*aceto (balsamico)* vinegar (balsamic)
*affumicato* smoked
*aglio* garlic
*alla brace* on embers
*bicchiere* glass
*burro* butter
*cacciagione* game
*conto* bill
*costoletta/cotoletta* chop

*coltello* knife
*cucchiaio* spoon
*filetto* fillet
*forchetta* fork
*forno* oven
*fritto* fried
*ghiaccio* ice
*griglia* grill
*in bianco* without tomato
*magro* lean meat/pasta without meat
*marmellata* jam
*menta* mint
*miele* honey
*mostarda* candied mustard sauce
*olio* oil
*pane* bread
*pane tostato* toasted bread
*panini* sandwiches (in roll)
*panna* cream

*pepe* pepper
*piatto* plate
*prezzemolo* parsley
*ripieno* stuffed
*rosmarino* rosemary
*sale* salt
*salmì* wine marinade
*salsa* sauce
*salvia* sage
*senape* mustard
*tartufi* truffles
*tavola* table
*tazza* cup
*tovagliolo* napkin
*tramezzini* finger sandwiches
*umido* cooked in sauce
*uovo* egg
*zucchero* sugar

# Planning Your Trip

# When to Go

## Climate

The climate in Umbria is temperate, but considerably cooler up in the mountains; the higher Apennines have enough snow for **skiing** until April. **Spring**, especially May, when it rains less, is pleasantly warm, as fields and gardens brim with wildflowers. **Summers** are hot and humid; in August most of the city dwellers abandon their cities to the tourists and head for the sea or the mountains.

**Autumn**, too, is a classic time to visit; in October and November, before the winter rains begin, while the air is clear, the colours of the countryside are brilliant and rare. The hills of Umbria are never less than beautiful but in October they're extraordinary – and it's the **truffle season**. **Winter** can be an agreeable time to visit the many indoor attractions of the cities and avoid the crowds; it seldom snows but may rain for days at a time.

Umbria is not called the 'green heart of Italy' for nothing: it can be hung over with mists for weeks on end, which, depending on how you look at it, can be terribly romantic or a big bore. The mountains also get a lot of rain, with 80–120mm possible in a year.

## Average Maximum Temperatures in °C (°F)

|  | Jan | April | July | Oct |
|---|---|---|---|---|
| Perugia | 5 (40) | 11 (52) | 24 (75) | 13 (55) |
| Terni | 5 (40) | 13 (55) | 25 (77) | 15 (59) |

## Average Monthly Rainfall in Millimetres (Inches)

|  | Jan | April | July | Oct |
|---|---|---|---|---|
| Perugia | 60 (2½) | 70 (2¾) | 30 (1) | 115 (4½) |
| Terni | 68 (2⅔) | 85 (3½) | 43 (1½) | 123 (4¾) |

## Festivals

Although festivals in Umbria are often more show than spirit (though there are several exceptions to the rule), they can be very lively occasions. Some are great costume affairs, with roots dating back to the Middle Ages, and there are quite a few music festivals, antique fairs, and, most of all, festivals devoted to regional food and drink. Dates can vary, so be sure to ring the local tourist offices to check (*see* relevant chapters for phone numbers). *See* below for an annual calendar of the major events.

## National Holidays

*See* p.74.

## Calendar of Events

### January

**24** Feast of San Feliciano, procession with a traditional fair, Foligno.

**27** Feast of Sant'Emiliano, with a procession of lights, Trevi.

### February

**Carnival** Celebrated in private parties nearly everywhere.

**International gastronomic festival of the black truffle**, Norcia.

*Bruschetta* festival, Spello, with a parade of olive-pickers and garlic toast feast, set to music.

**14** St Valentine's Day, with a fair, fireworks and music, Terni (plus romantic concerts all month).

**End of month** Truffle and Valnerina food fair, Norcia.

### April

**First 3 weeks** Huge antiques fair, Todi.

**Holy Week** Religious rites, torchlight processions and so forth, Assisi.
Umbria jazz, gospel and soul festival, Terni.

**Holy Thursday and Good Friday** Trial of Jesus and re-enactment of Christ's Passion, Sigillo (Perugia).

**Good Friday** Evening procession and Passion of the Dead Christ, a 13th-century tradition against haunting, ancient penitential chants, Gubbio.

Passion of the Dead Christ, dating from the 16th century, Bevagna.

**30** *Cantamaggio*, parade of illuminated floats, Terni.

**30 April–5 May** Feast of San Pelligrino, Gualdo Tadino (Perugia).

**End of month** *Corso dell'Anello*, medieval Tournament of the Ring, Narni.

## May

**Early May** *Calendimaggio*, Assisi.

**1st week** Kite festival, even-numbered years only, Castiglione del Lago.

**15** *Corsa dei Ceri*, race of tower shrines, Gubbio.

**17–21** Giostra della Quintana, medieval joust, Foligno.

**21–22** Feast of Santa Rita, Cascia.

**Last Sunday** Palio della Balestra, crossbow competition against Sansepolcro, in medieval costume, Gubbio.

**Pentecost** *La Palombella*, Orvieto.

**Late May–early June** Processions, Orvieto.

**1st Sun after Corpus Domini** Flower carpets in the streets, Spello.

## June

**June–July** International ceramics competition, Gualdo Tadino.

**2nd half of June** *Corso del Bove*, Montefalco. *Mercato della Gaite*, old-fashioned fair, Bevagna.

**June–July** Festival of the Two Worlds, a feast of contemporary culture with music, theatre and dance, Spoleto.

**Sunday nearest 21st** *L'Infiorata*, flower festival, Città della Pieve.

**End June–early July** *Festa delle Acque*, with fireworks, Piediluco.

## July

**All month** Umbria Jazz Festival, in and around Perugia and Terni.

Gubbio festival, with classical plays and concerts.

**3rd Sunday** *Palio delle Barche*, boat race in medieval costume, Passignano.

## August

**All month** Folkloric and religious festivals, Assisi.

**1st 3 weeks** Festival with theatre and music concerts, Corciano.

**14** *Palio dei Quartieri*, flag-tossing and crossbow contest, Gubbio.

**15** *Palio dei Terzieri*, archery contests and costumes, Città della Pieve.

**August–September** Festival of Chamber music, Città di Castello.

Sacred music festival, Perugia.

Todi festival, with all kinds of music, ballet, film, culture.

Experimental opera festival, Spoleto.

## September

**2 weeks** Festival of Peace, Assisi.

**All month** Baroque music and theatre festival, Foligno.

**2nd Sunday** Giostra della Quintana, jousting competition, Foligno.

Crossbow contest with Gubbio in Sansepolcro.

**2nd week** National horse festival, Città di Castello.

**14–15** San Manno fair, Foligno.

**22–24** Festival of the Portals, re-enactment of events in costume, Gualdo Tadino (Perugia).

**End Sept–early Oct** *Giostra dell'Arme*, jousting and fine dining, San Gemini.

## October

**All month** Eurochocolate festival, Perugia. Wine festivals.

**1** *Palio dei Terzieri*, historical parade and cart race, Trevi.

**3–4** Feast of San Francesco, religious and civic rites held in honour of Italy's patron saint, Assisi.

**31 Oct–2 Nov** *Festa del Bosco*, a festival of edibles from the woods, Montone.

**Oct/Nov** Antiquarian festival, Perugia.

## November

**1–5** *Fiera dei Morti*, All Souls' Fair, at the Pian di Massiano, Perugia.

**11** Feast of San Martino, with wine and chestnuts, Sigillo (Perugia).

**2nd weekend** Truffle festival, Città di Castello.

**24** Offering of candles, with processions in 14th-century costume, Amelia.

## December

**Last 2 weeks** 'World's largest Christmas tree', Gubbio.

**24** Christmas cribs and also Franciscan rites, Assisi.

**29–early Jan** Umbria Jazz Winter, with music and bands, Orvieto.

# Tourist Information

For information before you travel, contact the Italian National Tourist Office (*www.italiantourism.com*) in your own country.

## Italian Tourist Offices Abroad

**UK**: Italian State Tourist Office, 1 Princes St, London W1B 2AY, t (020) 7408 1254, *www.italiantouristboard.co.uk*; Consulate General of Italy in London, 38 Eaton Place, London SW1X 8AN, t (020) 7325 9371, *www.conslondra.esteri.it.*

**USA**: 630 Fifth Ave, Suite 1565, New York, NY 10111, t (212) 245 4822; 12400 Wilshire Blvd, Suite 550, Los Angeles, CA 90025, t (310) 820 1898; 500 N. Michigan Ave, Suite 2240, Chicago 1, IL 60611, t (312) 644 0996.

**Australia**, Level 4, 46 Market St, Sydney NSW 2000, t (02) 92 621666.

**Canada**: 175 Bloor St East, Suite 907, South Tower, Toronto, Ontario M4W 3R8, t (416) 925 4882.

**New Zealand**: c/o Italian Embassy, 34 Grant Rd, Thorndon, Wellington, t (044) 947170.

## Tourist Offices in Umbria

The main regional tourism office in Umbria is found in Perugia:

**Azienda di Promozione Turistica (APT)**, Via Mazzini 6, 06100 Perugia, t 075 572 8937, *www.regione.umbria.eu*, *info@iat.perugia.it.*

The city/provincial tourist offices (given in the area chapters) often have websites and will usually provide lists of villas and farmhouses for rent, plus B&Bs and *agriturismi* (*see* p.68).

# Embassies and Consulates

If you have a choice, use the consulate in Rome.

**UK**: Via XX Settembre 80a, Rome, t 06 4220 0001; Lungarno Corsini 2, Florence, t 055 284133.

**Ireland**: Piazza Campitelli 3, Rome, t 06 697 9121.

**USA**: Via Vittorio Veneto 119a, Rome, t 06 46741; Lungarno Amerigo Vespucci 38, Florence, t 055 2669 5232.

**Canada**: Via Zara 30, Rome, t 06 445981.

**Australia**: Via Alessandria 215, Rome, t 06 852721.

**New Zealand**: Via Zara 28, Rome, t 06 441 7171.

# Entry Formalities

## Passports and Visas

To get into Italy you need a valid passport. **EU citizens** do not need visas. Nationals from the **USA, Canada, Australia** and **New Zealand** do not need visas for stays of up to 90 days. For longer, you must get a *permesso di soggiorno*. For this you need to state your reason for staying and prove both a source of income and medical insurance.

The Italian law states you must register with the police within 24 hours of arrival. If you check into a hotel this is done automatically; otherwise you should go to the local police station (in practice few people do this). If you need advice on the forms, call the Rome Police Office for visitors, t (06) 4686, ext. 2987.

## Customs

EU nationals over 17 can import an unlimited quantity of goods for personal use. Arrivals from non-EU countries have to pass through Italian customs, which are usually benign, unless you're carrying more than 150 cigarettes or 75 cigars, 1 litre of hard liquor or 3 bottles of wine, a couple of cameras, one movie camera, 10 rolls of film for each, one tape-recorder, one radio, one record-player, one canoe less than 5.5m and one TV (though you'll have to pay for a licence for it), or sports equipment not for personal use. Pets must have a bilingual Certificate of Health from your vet. US citizens may return with $400 worth of merchandise – keep your receipts.

There are no limits to the amount of money you may bring into Italy, and no one is likely to check how much you leave with.

# Disabled Travellers

Access-for-all laws in Italy have improved the once-dire situation: the number of ramps and stairlifts has increased dramatically in the past decade, and nearly every hotel has one or two rooms with facilities for the disabled, though older ones may not have a lift, or not one large enough for a wheelchair.

## Disability Organizations

### In Italy

**Centro Studi Consulenza Invalidi**, Via Gozzadini 7, 20148 Milan, **t** 02 4030 8339. Ask for the annual accommodation guide, which is called *Vacanze per Disabili*.

**CO.IN (Consorzio Cooperative Integrate)**, Via Enrico Giglioli 54A, 00169 Rome, **t** 800 271027, **t** 06 2326 7504, *www.coinsociale.it*. The tourist information centre (Mon–Fri 9–5) offers advice and information on accessibility.

### In the UK and Ireland

**Holiday Care Service**, Enham Place, Enham Alamein, Andover SP11 6JS, **t** 0845 124 9971, *www.holidaycare.org.uk*. Information on accommodation, transport, equipment hire, services, tour operators and contacts.

**Irish Wheelchair Association**, Blackheath Drive, Clontarf, Dublin 3, **t** (01) 818 6400, *www.iwa.ie*. Provides travel advice and information.

**RADAR (Royal Association for Disability and Rehabilitation)**, 12 City Forum, 250 City Rd, London EC1V 8AF, **t** (020) 7250 3222, *www.radar.org.uk*. Provides information and books.

**RNIB (Royal National Institute of Blind People)**, 105 Judd St, London WC1H 9NE, **t** 020 7388 2525, *www.rnib.org.uk*. The mobility unit has a 'Plane Easy' audio-tape with advice for visually impaired flyers, and also advises on finding accommodation.

### In the USA and Canada

**American Foundation for the Blind**, 11 Penn Plaza, Suite 300, New York, NY 10001, **t** (212) 502 7600, *www.afb.org*. Provides information for visually impaired travellers.

**Fedcap**, 211 West 14th St, New York, NY 10011, **t** (212) 727 4200. Summer tours for members.

**SATH (Society for Accessible Travel and Hospitality)**, 347 5th Ave, Suite 605, New York, NY 10016, **t** (212) 447 7284, *www.sath.org*. Travel and access information. The website has good links and a list of online publications.

### Internet Sites

**Access-Able Travel Source**, *www.access-able.com*. Information for older and disabled travellers.

**Access Ability**, *www.access-ability.org/travel.html*. Information on travel agencies.

**Emerging Horizons**, *www.emerginghorizons.com*. An online newsletter for disabled travellers.

Service stations on the *autostrade* have equipped restrooms, but you could get very stuck in the middle of a city – Florence, visited by zillions of tourists, lacks accessible loos. Local tourist offices (listed in the text) are helpful, and may even find someone to give you a hand, while the national tourist office (*see* p.60) can offer tips for difficult hill towns.

Italian churches are a problem, with their long flights of steps in front, designed to impress on the would-be worshipper the feeling of going upwards to God.

## Insurance and EHIC Cards

National health services in the UK and Australia have **reciprocal healthcare agreements** with Italy (you need a European Health Insurance or **EHIC card**, which has replaced the old EIII forms; see *www.dh.gov.uk* or pick up a form at a post office), but this only allows for state-provided 'necessary' care, so you should also take out your own insurance to cover the gap. Note that you will be expected to pay for all medicine and treatment in the first instance

– the cost can be claimed back later, provided that you have the correct documentation. Make sure you get a receipt.

Other nationals should check their current policies to see if they're covered abroad for mishaps such as cancelled flights and lost baggage, and under what circumstances, and judge whether they need an additional policy. Travel agencies sell policies, as well as insurance companies, but they're not cheap. First check whether your credit card company or bank account gives you some kind of cover. *See* also **Health and Emergencies**, p.73.

## Money

The **euro** is divided into 100 **cents**. There are banknotes in denominations of 5, 10, 20, 50, 100, 200 and 500, and coins in denominations of 1 and 2 euros, and 1, 2, 5, 10, 20 and 50 cents.

You can withdraw cash from most **ATMs**/ cash dispensers with any of the common debit or credit cards; your bank may charge a small fee, but it won't work out any more expensive than normal commission rates. It's worth having a backup (e.g. travellers' cheques) in case your card is rejected; also remember to bring some euros with you for when you arrive.

**Credit and debit cards** are accepted by most hotels, resort-area restaurants, shops and car-hire firms, although some may take exception to American Express. Italians are wary of plastic, though, and you may be asked for some ID when paying by card.

For **banking hours**, *see* p.74.

# Getting There

## By Air from the UK and Ireland

Rome is the closest major international airport to Umbria; Alitalia operates connecting flights to Perugia from Rome and Milan. British Airways and Alitalia fly several times a day to Rome Fiumicino airport, and British Airways also have direct flights there from Manchester and Birmingham. Of the low-cost airlines, Ryanair flies to Rome Ciampino airport from Luton, Stansted, East Midlands and Liverpool and from Stansted to Perugia; Jet2 flies to Rome Fiumicino from Manchester and Leeds Bradford; and easyJet flies to Rome Ciampino from Gatwick (twice daily) and Bristol.

Milan can be reached direct with British Airways or Alitalia; bmibaby, Ryanair and easyJet also fly there from various UK airports. Other possibilities include a Ryanair flight to Ancona in the Marche, with frequent train links to Umbria, or direct flights from London Heathrow to Florence with Alitalia. If you wish to fly to Bologna (just over the Apennines), easyJet depart from London Stansted, Alitalia from London Heathrow and British Airways from London Gatwick.

From **Ireland**, there are direct flights from Dublin and Cork on either Alitalia or Aer Lingus to Milan and Rome, from where you can pick up a connecting flight to Perugia. Ryanair flies from Dublin to Rome Ciampino. Both airlines also fly to Bologna. Keep your eye open for bargains and charters advertised in the newspapers.

See the airlines' own websites for special offers, or visit UK flight websites, including: *www.cheapflights.co.uk, www.flightline.co.uk, www.airflights.co.uk, www.lastminute.com* and *www.flightsdirect.com.*

## By Air from the USA and Canada

From the USA, the major carriers fly to Rome or Milan. Your travel agent may be able to find a much cheaper fare from your home airport to your Italian airport by way of London, Brussels, Paris, Frankfurt or Amsterdam. From Canada, only Alitalia flies direct to Italy (from Toronto/Montréal to Rome/Milan).

For **Apex fares**, you need fixed arrival and departure dates and to spend at least a week in Italy but no more than 90 days. Some Apex fares must be purchased at least 14 days (sometimes 21) in advance, and there are penalties if you change dates. At the time of writing the lowest midweek Apex between New York and Rome in the off-season was around $700, rising to about $900 in summer; from Canada, low-season fares are about $900–1,250. Some carriers, including Alitalia, offer **promotions** that might include car hire or discounts on hotels, domestic flights or excursions; ask a travel agent for details. Under-2s usually travel free, and both BA and Alitalia offer cheaper tickets on some flights for students and under-26s.

It may be worth catching a cheap flight to London (New York–London fares are always competitive) then flying on using a British low-cost carriers such as easyJet and Ryanair (*see* box opposite). Prices are rather more from Canada, so it's best to fly from the USA.

For **discounted flights**, check the small ads in newspaper travel pages (e.g. *New York Times, Chicago Tribune, Toronto Globe & Mail*). Numerous travel clubs and agencies also specialize in discount fares but may require annual membership. You could also try some of the US **cheap flight websites** including: *www.priceline.com* (bid for tickets), *www.expedia.com, www.hotwire.com, www.bestfares.com, www.travelocity.com, www.cheaptrips.com, www.courier.org* (courier flights) and *www.ricksteves.com.* Other websites are listed in the box opposite.

### Transport from the Airports

There are frequent trains from Rome to the region of Umbria. For further details of **train connections** from the various Italian airports, *see* p.65. Also of interest are **Sulga buses**, which will take you directly from Rome's Fiumicino airport to Perugia in about

## Direct Flights from the UK and Ireland

**Aer Lingus**, Ireland, t 0818 365 000;
UK t 0870 876 5000, *www.aerlingus.com*.
**Alitalia**, t 0870 544 8259, *www.alitalia.com*.
**British Airways**, UK t 0844 493 0787;
Ireland t 1890 626 747, *www.ba.com*.
**Ethiopian Airlines**, t (020) 8987 7000,
*www.ethiopianairlines.com*.

### Low-cost Carriers

**easyJet**, t 0905 821 0905, *www.easyJet.com*.
**jet2.com**, t 0906 302 0660, *www.jet2.com*.
**FlyGlobespan**, t 0871 271 9000, *www.flyglobe-span.com*.
**Meridiana**, t 0871 222 9 319,
*www.meridiana.it*.
**My Travel**, t 0871 664 7970, *www.mytravel.com*.
**Ryanair**, UK t 0871 246 0000, Ireland t 0818 303030, *www.ryanair.com*.
**Thomson**, t 0871 231 4691,
*www.flights.thomson.co.uk*.

## Direct Flights from the USA and Canada

**Alitalia**, US t 800 223 5730, *www.alitalia.com*.
**British Airways**, t 800 AIRWAYS, *www.ba.com*.

## Discounts and Youth Fares

### From the UK and Ireland

**Budget Travel**, 134 Lower Baggot St, Dublin 2,
t (01) 631 1111, *www.budgettravel.ie*.
**Italflights**, 125 High Holborn, London WC1V 6QA,
t (020) 7405 6771.
**Trailfinders**, 194 Kensington High St, London
W8 7RG, t (020) 7938 3939; 4–5 Dawson St,

Dublin 2, t (01) 677 7888, *www.trailfinders.co.uk*;
plus branches in other major UK cities.
**United Travel**, 12 Clonkeen Rd, Deansgrange,
Blackrock, Co. Dublin, t (01) 219 0600,
*www.unitedtravel.ie*.
 Besides saving 25% on regular flights,
under-26s can fly on special discount
charters. Contact:
**STA**, 52 Grosvenor Gardens, Victoria, London
SW1W 0AG, t 0871 468 0649, *www.statravel.co.uk*. There are several other branches in
London, and many in other major UK towns
and cities.
**USIT Now**, 19–21 Aston Quay, Dublin 2,
t (01) 602 1906, *www.usitnow.ie*. Ireland's no.1
specialist student travel agent, with other
branches around the country.

### From the USA and Canada

 It's also worth looking at the websites
*www.xfares.com* (carry-on luggage only) and
*www.smartertravel.com*.
**Airhitch**, 481 Eighth Ave, Suite 1771, New York,
NY 10001-1820, t (212) 247 4482 or t 877
AIRHITCH, *www.airhitch.org*.
**STA**, t 800 781 4040, *www.statravel.com*. There
are branches at most universities and at 30 3rd
Avenue, New York, NY 10003, t (212) 473 6100,
and 920 Westwood Boulevard, Los Angeles, CA
90024, t (310) 824 1574.
**TFI Tours**, 1270 Broadway Suite 409, New York,
NY 10001, t (212) 736 1140 or t 800 745 8000,
*www.tfitours.com*.
**The Last Minute Club**, 1300 Don Mills Rd,
Toronto, Ontario M3B 2W6, t (416) 441 2582.
**Travel Cuts**, 187 College St, Toronto, Ontario
M5T 1P7, t (416) 979 2406, *www.travelcuts.com*.
Canada's largest student agency, with branches
in most provinces.

4 hours, via the city's Tiburtina (train) station
(t 075 500 9641 or freephone t 800 099661;
*see* timetable at *www.sulga.it*).

## By Train

 By Eurostar from London, the journey time
to Perugia is about 19–20hrs. Services run
daily and return fares cost around £280. The
journey involves changing trains and stations
in Paris and in Rome.
 Travelling by train and ferry takes about
22 hours and costs around £189 for a second-
class return (including the couchette). There
are also Motorail links from Denderleeuw in

Belgium to Bologna (contact Rail Choice,
*see* p.64, for more details).
 Eurostar tickets, booking for onward
journeys to destinations in Italy, and tickets
and passes within Italy, can be bought from:

**Rail Europe**, t 08448 484064, *www.raileurope.co.uk* (USA t 888 382 7245, Canada
t 800 361 7245, *www.raileurope.com*).

 In an age of low-cost airlines, rail travel is
not much of an economy unless you can take
advantage of student, youth, family and
young children or senior citizen discounts,
although it is less environmentally harmful.

**Interail** (UK) or **Eurail** (USA/Canada) passes offer unlimited travel for all ages throughout Europe for a variety of timeframes. Various youth fares and inclusive rail passes are also available within Italy if you're planning on doing a lot of train travel solely in Italy; you can organize these before leaving home with: **Rail Choice, t** 0870 165 7300, *www.railchoice.co.uk.*

The **Trenitalia Pass**, available to non Italian residents, allows 1st- or 2nd-class travel on all Trenitalia trains for 4–10 days (consecutive or non-consecutive) within a two-month period. It can be obtained at main Italian stations, or in travel agencies abroad. The versions are: Basic for over-26s, Youth for under-26s, and Saver for groups of 2–5. Prices for Basic 2nd-class tickets are €174 for 4 days, €282 for 10 days. You need to pay supplements if you take an Italian Eurostar (*see* opposite), book a couchette or bed on an overnight train, or take an Artesia train.

For more passes and discounts, contact **Rail Europe** or **Rail Choice** (for both, *see* above).

## By Coach

The coach is the last refuge of aerophobic bargain-hunters. The journey time from London to Florence is around 30hrs; the return full fare is around £115. There are discounts for students, senior citizens and children as well as off-peak travel.

**National Express/Eurolines, t** 08717 818181, *www.eurolines.co.uk.*

## By Car

Driving to Italy from the UK is a rather lengthy and expensive proposition, and if you're only staying for a short time compare your costs against Alitalia's or other airlines' fly-drive scheme. No matter how you cross the Channel, it is a good two-day drive – about 1,600km from Calais to Perugia.

**Eurotunnel trains, t** 08705 353535, *www.eurotunnel.com,* shuttle cars and their passengers through the Channel Tunnel from Folkestone to Calais on a simple drive-on-drive-off system (journey time 35mins). Eurotunnel runs 24 hours a day, year round, with a service at least once an hour through the night. Standard return fares range from £104 to £349, but special offers can bring them as low as £49 one way. **Ferry**

information is available from any travel agent or direct from the ferry companies.

You can cut many of the costly motorway tolls by going to Calais, travelling through France to Basle, Switzerland, and from there through the Gotthard Tunnel over the Alps. In the summer you can save the expensive tunnel tolls, and see some marvellous scenery, by taking one of the mountain passes instead.

To bring your car into Italy, you need your car registration (log book), valid driving licence and valid insurance (a Green Card is not necessary, but you'll need one if you go through Switzerland). If your driving licence is of the old-fashioned sort without a photograph, the AA strongly recommends that you apply for an international driving permit as well (available from the AA or RAC).

Make sure everything is in excellent working order; it's not uncommon to be stopped, checked and fined by the police. Spare parts for some non-Italian cars are difficult to come by.

Foreign-plated cars are no longer entitled to free breakdown service from the **Italian Auto Club (ACI)**, *www.aci.it,* but their prices are fair. Freephone ACI on 803116 or **t** 02 661 65116 (or **t** 06 491115 from outside Italy) to find out the current rates (*see* also p.66).

Current motorway tunnel tolls are:

**Fréjus Tunnel,** *www.tunneldufrejus.com,* from Modane (France) to Bardonècchia. Prices from €30.50 one way.

**Gran San Bernardo,** *www.sitrasb.it,* from Bourg St Pierre (Switzerland) to Aosta. Prices from €18.70 one way.

**Mont Blanc Tunnel,** *www.tunnelmb.com.* €30.50 one way.

For more information on driving in Italy, contact a motoring organization:

**AA, t** 0800 085 7253, *www.theaa.com* (UK).

**AAA, t** 800 222 4357, *www.aaa.com* (USA).

**RAC, t** 0870 572 2722, *www.rac.co.uk.*

# Getting Around

Italy has an excellent network of airports, railways, highways and byways, and you'll find getting around fairly easy – unless one union or another goes on strike (*sciopero,* pronounced SHO-PER-O). There's always a day or two's notice of one, and they usually last only 12 or 24 hrs, but this is long enough to throw a spanner in the works if you have to catch a plane, so keep your eyes and ears open for advance warnings. That said, they rarely happen in the main holiday season.

## By Train

**FS information from anywhere in Italy**: t 892021, *www.trenitalia.com*.

Italy's national railway, the FS (**Ferrovie dello Stato**) is well run and often a pleasure to ride. There are also several private rail lines around cities and in rural districts. We have tried to list them all in the Getting Around sections of the area chapters in this book. Some of these private companies don't accept Interail or Eurail passes.

**Train fares** have increased greatly over the last five years or so and only those without extra supplements can still be called cheap, although they are still inexpensive by British or US standards. Possible FS unpleasantnesses you may encounter, besides a strike, are delays and crowding (especially at weekends and in summer).

**Reserve seats** in advance (*fare una prenotazione*); the fee is small and can save you hours of standing. For upper-echelon trains (Italian Eurostars and some Intercities), reservations are mandatory. Check when you buy your ticket in advance that the date is correct; tickets are only valid the day they're purchased unless you specify otherwise.

**Tickets** are sold at stations and many travel agents (and many also online); it's wise to buy in advance as queues can be long. Make sure you ask which platform (*binario*) your train leaves from; the big permanent boards posted in the stations are not always correct.

Always **stamp your ticket** (*convalidare* or *obliterare*) in the not-very-obvious machine at the head of the platform before boarding – failure to do so may result in a fine. If you get on a train without a ticket you can buy one from the conductor, for an added 20%. You can also pay a conductor to move up to 1st class as long as places are available.

There is a strict **hierarchy of trains**. *Regionales* travel shortish distances, and tend to stop at all stations. There are only a few *Espressi* left

and they are in poor condition; most serve the long runs from the south of Italy. *Intercity* trains link Italian cities, with minimum stops. Some carry an obligatory seat reservation requirement (free); all require a supplement. The 'Kings of the Rails' are the swish, super-fast (Florence–Rome 90mins) *Eurostars*. These make very few stops, offer 1st- and 2nd-class carriages, and carry a supplement that includes an obligatory seat reservation. For the **Trenitalia pass** for non-residents, *see* p.64.

**Refreshments** on routes of any great distance are provided by buffet cars or trolleys; you can usually get sandwiches and coffee from vendors along the tracks at intermediary stops. Station bars often have a good variety of takeaway travellers' fare. Bring a bottle of mineral water, as there's no drinking water on the trains.

Italy's stations also offer other facilities. All have a *deposito*, where you can leave your bags for hours or days for a fee. The larger ones have porters (who charge about €3 per piece) and luggage trolleys. Major stations have an *albergo diurno* ('day hotel', where you can shower, get a shave and haircut, etc.), information offices, currency exchanges open at weekends (not at the best rates), hotel reservation services, kiosks with foreign papers, restaurants, etc. You can also book a hire car to pick up at your destination, through Avis, Hertz or Maggiore (listed where relevant in the area chapters).

## By Coach and Bus

**Intercity coach travel** is often quicker than train travel and a bit more expensive. You will find regular coach links only where there's no train to offer competition. In many regions, buses are the only means of public transport and are well used, with frequent departures.

Coaches almost always depart from near the train station, and tickets usually need to be bought before boarding. Country bus lines are based in provincial capitals; we've done our best to explain the connections even for the most out-of-the-way routes, as well as listing coach companies in the relevant areas.

**City bus routes** are well labelled; all charge flat fees for rides within the city limits and immediate suburbs (around €1). Tickets must be purchased before you get on, from a tobacconist's, a newspaper kiosk, many bars, or ticket machines near the main stops. Once you're on, you must 'obliterate' (punch) your ticket in the machines at the front or back of the bus; controllers stage random checks, with fines for cheats of about €40.

## By Car

The advantages of driving in Umbria generally outweigh the disadvantages. Before you bring your own car or hire one, consider the kind of holiday you're planning. If it's a tour of the major towns and cities, you'd really be best off not driving at all: parking is impossible. In nearly every other case, however, a car gives you the freedom and possibility of making your way through the delightful open countryside and stopping at the smaller towns and villages.

Be prepared to spend a very long time looking for a place to park in any town bigger than a peanut, and face drivers who look at motoring as if it were a video game. The Italians, whether 21-year-old madcaps or elderly nuns, turn into aggressive starfighters once behind the wheel; their mission is to reach their destination in a certain allotted time (especially around lunch or dinner, if they think the pasta is already on the boil), regardless of minor nuisances such as other cars, road signs, traffic signals, solid no-passing lines, or blind curves on mountain roads. No matter how fast you trip along on the *autostrade* (Italy's toll motorways, official speed limit **130km/80 miles** per hour), someone will pass you going twice as fast.

If you aren't intimidated, buy a good road map of Italy or a detailed one of the region you're travelling in (the Italian Touring Club produces excellent ones). Most petrol stations close for lunch in the afternoon, and few stay open late at night, though you may find a 'self-service' one where you feed a machine nice, smooth bank notes or a credit card. *Autostrada* tolls are high – the website *www.autostrade.it* will help you calculate the cost for your journey. The rest stops and petrol stations along the motorways are open 24 hours. Other roads – from *superstrade* on down through the Italian grading system – are free of charge. The

Italians are good about signposting, and roads are fairly well maintained. Some highways seem to be built of sheer bravura – suspended on cliffs, crossing valleys on enormous piers – feats of engineering that will remind you, more than almost anything else, that this is the land of the ancient Romans. Beware that you may be fined on the spot for speeding, a burnt-out headlamp, etc.; if you're especially unlucky you may be slapped with a *super multa*, or superfine, of €130–260 or more. You may even be fined for not having a portable triangle danger signal (these can be picked up at the border or from an ACI office). It is now law a) to keep headlights dipped on the *autostrada* and in any rural area *at all times* and b) to carry a bright orange fluorescent jacket in the car at all times and to put it on if you break down.

The **Automobile Club of Italy (ACI)** (Via Marsala 8, Rome, **t** 02 661 65116, *www.aci.it*) is a good friend to the foreign motorist. Besides having bushels of useful information and tips, they can be reached from anywhere by calling free on **t** 803116 – also use this number if you have an accident, need an ambulance, or simply have to find the nearest service station. If you need major repairs, the ACI can make sure the prices charged are according to their guidelines.

**Hiring a car** is fairly simple if not particularly cheap (around €40 a day for a smallish car, €300 for a week). Italian car rental firms are called *autonoleggi*. There are both large international firms through which you can reserve a car in advance, and local agencies, which often have lower prices. Air or rail travellers should check out possible discount packages.

Most companies will require a deposit amounting to the estimated cost of the hire, and there is 19% VAT added to the final cost. Petrol is as expensive as in the UK. Rates become more advantageous if you take the car for a week with unlimited mileage. If you need a car for more than three weeks, leasing is a more economic alternative. The National Tourist Office has a list of firms in Italy that hire caravans (trailers) and campers.

### By Taxi

Taxi tariffs from town to town start at €4.50; then add €1 per km (there's a minimum charge of €4.50). Each piece of baggage will cost extra, and there are surcharges for trips outside the city limits, trips between 10pm and 6am, and trips on Sundays and holidays.

### By Motorbike and Bicycle

The transport of choice for many Italians, motorbikes, mopeds and Vespas can be a delightful way to get between cities and see the countryside. You should only consider this, however, if you've ridden them before – Italy's hills and traffic make it no place to learn. Helmets are compulsory. A *motorino* (moped) costs from about €30/day to hire; scooters are somewhat more (from about €50).

Italians are keen cyclists, racing drivers up the steepest hills; if you're not training for the Tour de France, consider the hilliness of the region before planning a bicycling tour – especially in the summer months. Bikes can be transported by train in Italy, either with you or within a couple of days; apply at the luggage office (*ufficio bagagli*). Hire prices range from about €15/day; to buy one, you'll pay upwards of €130, either in a bike shop or through local classified ads. If you bring your own bike, check with your airline first about their policies on transporting them.

# Where to Stay

## Hotels

Umbria is endowed with hotels (*alberghi*) of every description, from the spectacular to the humble. These are rated by the government's tourism bureaucracy on a five-star scale. Ratings take into account such features as a restaurant on the premises, plumbing, air-con, etc., but not character, style or charm. Use the stars, included here, as a quick reference only. Hotels may stay at a lower rating than they've earned, so a three-star could be as comfy as a four-star.

**Breakfast** is often included in the room rate. You might find that **half- or full board** is obligatory, particularly in high season at hotels in seaside, lake or mountain resorts, spas or country villas. Otherwise, meal

## Hotel Price Ranges

Categories are based on a standard double room (en suite where available) in high season.

| | | |
|---|---|---|
| *luxury* | €€€€€ | over €230 |
| *very expensive* | €€€€ | €150–230 |
| *expensive* | €€€ | €100–149 |
| *moderate* | €€ | €60–99 |
| *inexpensive* | € | under €60 |

arrangements are optional. In the majority of cases hotel food is bland, just as it is anywhere else.

### Prices

Prices listed above are for **double** rooms in **high season**. Taxes and service charges are included in the given rate. If rooms are listed without bath, it simply means the shower and lavatory are in the corridor. For rooms without bath, subtract 20–30%. Prices are by law listed on the door of each room and printed in hotel lists available from local tourist offices. They may cost up to 50% less in the **low season**. In resorts, hotels may close down for several months of the year.

For a **single**, count on paying two-thirds of a double; to add an extra bed in a double adds 35% to the rate. Taxes and service charges are included in rates. **Non-en suite rooms** (i.e. sharing toilets and bathrooms in the hall) are about 20–30% cheaper.

A booking is valid once a **deposit** has been paid; different establishments have different policies about **cancellation charges** after a certain time. If you come in summer without reservations, call around for a place in the morning or put yourself at the mercy of one of the tourist office **hotel-finding services** (we've listed these in the area chapters).

The National Tourist Office (*see* p.60) has lists and booking information for motels and five- and four-star hotels and chains. Besides classic hotels, there's an increasing number of alternatives, nearly always in historic buildings, which in Umbria are classified as *residenza d'epoca* or country houses.

### Inexpensive Accommodation

Bargains are few and far between in Italy. Most cheaper places are around railway stations. In small towns the tourist office may have a list of *affitta camere* (**rooms to** rent), which vary from basic accommodation in someone's house to more upmarket places. Besides youth hostels (see p.68), there are **city-run hostels** with dorm-style rooms, which are open to all. In some cities **religious institutions** let extra rooms. Rural monasteries and convents sometimes take guests (bring a letter of introduction from your local priest or pastor).

## Youth and Student Hostels

You'll find hostels in Perugia, Assisi, Gubbio, Magione, Trevi, Sigillo and Poggiodomo. The regional head office is the **Ostello della Pace**, Via di Valecchie 177, Assisi, **t** 075 816767. You can nearly always buy an **IYHF card** on the spot. There are no age limits, and senior citizens are often given added discounts.

Accommodation is usually a bunk in a single-sex room, plus breakfast, and costs around €10 per day. Curfews are common, and you usually can't check in before 5 or 6pm. You can book in advance by sending your dates along with the number of guests (by sex) to the individual hostel, including international postal coupons for the reply. Avoid spring, when noisy school groups descend on hostels for field trips.

The **Centro Turistico Studentesco e Giovanile** (CTS; www.cts.it), with offices in most Italian cities (and one in London), can also book cheap accommodation for students.

## Self-catering Holidays: Villas, Farmhouses and Flats

Renting a villa, farmhouse, cottage or flat is becoming increasingly popular in Umbria. The **Internet** has made finding a place easier than ever, with companies providing detailed listings and photos. Another place to look is the Sunday papers; or, if you're set on a particular area, write to its tourist office (or see its website) for a list of local rental agencies. These should provide photos to give you an idea of what to expect; make sure all pertinent details are in your rental agreement to avoid misunderstandings later.

In general **minimum lets** are for one week; rental **prices** (generally per week) usually include insurance, water and electricity, and sometimes linen and maid service. Don't be surprised if when you arrive the owner 'denounces' (denunciare) you to the police;

according to Italian law, all visitors must be registered upon arrival. Common problems are water shortages, unruly insects and low kilowatts. Most companies offer **packages** with flights and car hire. Book as far in advance as possible for summer.

## Rural Self-catering or *Agriturismo*

For a breath of rural seclusion, gregarious Italians head for **working farms**, offering accommodation (sometimes self-catering) that often approximates to French *gîtes*. The real pull may be cooking by the hosts, using homegrown produce. This branch of the Italian tourist industry is run by **Agriturist** (www.agriturist.it). Prices, compared with the over-hyped villas, are still reasonable. Local tourist offices will have information on such accommodation in their areas. The APT (see p.60) publishes an annual listing, or contact:

**Agriturist Umbria**, Via Savonarola 38, Perugia, **t** 075 32028, www.agrituristumbria.com.

**Terranostra Umbria**, Via Settevalli 131/F, Perugia, **t** 075 506761.

**Turismo Verde Umbria**, Via Mario Angeloni 1, 06100 Perugia, **t** 075 500 2953, www.turismoverde.it.

**Umbria in Campagna**, Strada San Cristoforo 16, Amelia, **t** 333 453 7711, www.umbriaincampagna.com (a farmers' co-operative).

## Camping

Most official campsites are near the mountains or lakes; there is usually one within commuting distance of major tourist centres. Details are published in the Italian Touring Club's *Campeggi e Villaggi Turistici*, sold in Italian bookshops (€20), or ask for a free abbreviated list from:

**Centro Internazionale Prenotazioni Federcampeggio**, Via Vittorio Emanuele 11, Calenzano (Florence), **t** 055 882391, www.federcampeggio.it.

Request a booking form to reserve a space – in summer tents and caravans are packed cheek to cheek. Fees vary enormously, so check with the individual sites. You may camp outside official sites with landowners' permission. Caravans are expensive to hire: the National Tourist Office and local branches have lists of firms.

# Specialist Tour Operators

For **specialist holidays and courses for foreigners**, *see* p.76.

## In Italy

**Amber Road Tours**, Via delle Cantoncelle, 06049 Spoleto, t 0743 224946, *www. amberroadtours.com*. Specialized tours, concentrating on out-of-the-way areas.

**Corymbus Viaggi**, Via Massetana Romana 56, 53100 Siena, t 0577 271653, *www.corymbus. it*. Wine and classical tours.

## In the UK

**Abercrombie & Kent**, St George's House, Ambrose St, Cheltenham, Glos GL0 3LG, t 0845 070 0610, *www.abercrombiekent.co.uk*. City breaks in all major cities.

**Ace Study Tours**, Babraham, Cambridge CB2 4AP, t (01223) 835055, *www.study-tours.org*. Cultural tours through Tuscany and Umbria.

**Arblaster & Clarke Wine Tours**, Farnham Rd, West Liss, Petersfield, Hants GU33 6JQ, t (01730) 893344, *www.arblasterandclarke.com*. Tuscan wine tours, truffle hunts and cooking tours.

**ATG Oxford**, 69–71 Banbury Road, Oxford OX2 6PJ, t (01865) 315678, *www.atg-oxford.co.uk*. Offers walking, wildflower, garden and cycling tours; also arranges truffle hunts and painting courses.

**Inntravel**, Whitewell Grange, near Castle Howard, York YO60 7JU, t (01653) 617949, *www.inntravel.co.uk*. An award-winning firm, particularly strong on walking holidays.

**Kirker**, 4 Waterloo Court, 10 Theed St, London SE1 8ST, t (020) 7593 1899, *www.kirkerholidays. com*. City breaks and tailor-made tours.

**Martin Randall Travel**, Voysey House, Barley Mow Passage, Chiswick, London W4 4PH, t (020) 8742 3355, *www.martinrandall.com*. Imaginative cultural tours with expert guides – art, archaeology, history, architecture, music, 'Medici Villas and Gardens', and opera in Macerata and Pesaro.

**Prospect Cultural**, 79 William Street, Herne Bay, Kent CT6 5NR, t (01227) 743307, *www. prospecttours.com*. Art tours and specialist holidays devoted to local cultural figures.

**Ramblers**, Lemsford Mill, Lemsford Village, Welwyn Garden City, Hertfordshire AL8 7TR, t (01707) 331133, *www.ramblersholidays.co.uk*. Walking holidays.

**Real Holidays**, 66–68 Essex Rd, Islington, London N1 8LR, t (020) 7359 3938, *www.realhols.co.uk*. Quirky holidays.

**Sherpa Expeditions**, 131a Heston Rd, Hounslow, Middlesex TW5 0RF, t (020) 8577 2717, *www.sherpa-walking-holidays.co.uk*. Walking and cycling holidays in Tuscany and Umbria.

**Specialtours**, 2 Chester Row, London SW1 9SH, t (020) 7730 2297, *www.specialtours.co.uk*. Cultural tours.

**Tasting Places**, Unit 40, Buspace Studios, Conlan St, London W10 5AP, t (020) 8964 5333, *www.tastingplaces.com*. Cookery courses near Orvieto.

## In the USA and Canada

**Abercrombie & Kent**, 1411 Opus Place, Executive Towers West II, Ste 300, Downers Grove, IL 60515-1182, t 800 554 7016, *www.abercrombiekent.com*. City breaks and walking holidays.

**Bike Riders**, PO Box 130254, Boston, MA 02113, t 800 473 7040, *www.bikeriderstours.com*. Cycling tours with stopovers at elegant hotels.

**Randonnée Tours**, 203-1338 West 6th Ave, Vancouver, BC V6H 1A7, t (604) 730 1247 or t 800 242 1825, *www.randonneetours.com*. Self-guided cycling vacations.

**Stay & Visit**, 7256 South Tamiami Trail, Sarasota, FL 34231, t 877 222 4857, *www. stayandvisit.com*. Run by an Italian family, with good introductory tours.

# Self-catering Operators

## In Italy

**The Best in Italy**, Via Ugo Foscolo 72, Florence, t 055 223064, *www.thebestinitaly.com*.

**Castello di Reschio**, Count Benedikt Bolza, t 075 844362, *www.castellodireschio.com*. Medieval castle surrounded by exclusive farmhouses/villas for rent.

**Cuendet**, Strada di Strove 17, 53035 Monteriggioni, Siena, t 0577 576330, *www.cuendet.com*.

**Euro Casa**, Piazza Silvio Pellico 1, Marchiano della Chiana, Arezzo, t 0575 845348, *www. eurocasa.com*.

**Houses of Charme**, Piazza Baronale 4, 05020 Montoro, t 0744 793051, *www.vacation-rentals-italy.net*.

**Rent Tuscany**, Via L. da Vinci 9, 53044 Chiusi, Siena, t 0578 2337, *www.renttuscany.com*.

## In the UK

**CV Travel**, Skyline House, 200 Union Street, 2nd Floor, London SE1 0LX, t (020) 7401 1039, *www.cvtravel.net*.

**Home in Italy**, 15 Northfields Prospect, Northfields, London SW18 1PE, t (020) 7404 4911, *www.homeinitaly.com*.

**Individual Travellers**, Spring Mill, Earby, Barnoldswick, Lancs BB94 0AA, t 08700 780193, *www.individualtravellers.com*.

**Interhome**, Gemini House, 10–18 Putney Hill, London SW15 6AX, t (020) 8780 6633, *www.interhome.co.uk*.

**Owners' Syndicate**, Skyline House, 200 Union Street, London SE1 0LX, t 020 7401 1086, *www.ownerssyndicate.com*.

**Simply Travel**, Columbus House, Westwood Way, Westwood Business Park, Coventry CV4 8TT, t 0871 231 4050, *www.simply-travel.co.uk*.

**Travel à la Carte**, 4A, 36 Queens Road, Newbury, RG14 7NE, t (01635) 33800, *www.anotheritaly.co.uk*.

## In the USA and Canada

**At Home Abroad**, 405 East 56th St 6H, New York, NY 10022-2466, t (212) 421 9165, *www.athomeabroadinc.com*.

**Hideaways International**, 767 Islington St, Portsmouth, NH 03801, t (603) 430 4433 or t 877 843 4433, *www.hideaways.com*.

**Homebase Abroad**, Two Hooper Street, Marblehead, MA 01945, t (781) 639 4040, *www.homebase-abroad.com*.

**Italian Villas**, 5530 St. Patrick Street, Suite 2210, Montreal, Quebec, t 877 993 0100, *www.italianvillas.com*.

**Rent Villas**, 9452 Telephone Rd, Ventura, CA 93004, t 800 726 6702, *www.rentvillas.com*.

**Via Travel Design**, 7458 Devon St, Philadelphia, PA 19119, t 888 477 2740, *www.viatraveldesign.com*.

# Practical A–Z

06

# Conversions: Imperial–Metric

## Length (multiply by)
Inches to centimetres: 2.54
Centimetres to inches: 0.39
Feet to metres: 0.3
Metres to feet: 3.28
Yards to metres: 0.91
Metres to yards: 1.09
Miles to kilometres: 1.61
Kilometres to miles: 0.62

## Area (multiply by)
Inches square to centimetres square: 6.45
Centimetres square to inches square: 0.15
Feet square to metres square: 0.09
Metres square to feet square: 10.76
Miles square to kilometres square: 2.59
Kilometres square to miles square: 0.39
Acres to hectares: 0.40
Hectares to acres: 2.47

## Weight (multiply by)
Ounces to grams: 28.35
Grammes to ounces: 0.035
Pounds to kilograms: 0.45
Kilograms to pounds: 2.2
Stones to kilograms: 6.35
Kilograms to stones: 0.16
Tons (UK) to kilograms: 1,016
Kilograms to tons (UK): 0.0009
1 UK ton (2,240lbs) = 1.12 US tonnes (2,000lbs)

## Volume (multiply by)
Pints (UK) to litres: 0.57
Litres to pints (UK): 1.76
Quarts (UK) to litres: 1.13
Litres to quarts (UK): 0.88
Gallons (UK) to litres: 4.55
Litres to gallons (UK): 0.22
1 UK pint/quart/gallon =
1.2 US pints/quarts/gallons

## Temperature
Celsius to Fahrenheit:
multiply by 1.8 then
add 32

Fahrenheit to Celsius:
subtract 32 then multiply
by 0.55

# Italy Information

## Time Differences
Country: + 1hr GMT; + 6hrs EST
Daylight saving from last weekend in March
to end of October

## Dialling Codes
**Italy country code** 39

**To Italy from:** UK, Ireland, New Zealand 00 /
USA, Canada 011 / Australia 0011 then dial 39
and the full number including the initial zero
**From Italy to:** UK 00 44; Ireland 00 353; USA,
Canada 001; Australia 00 61; New Zealand 00
64 then the number without the initial zero
**Directory enquiries:** 12
**International directory enquiries:** 176

## Emergency Numbers
**Police:** 112/113
**Ambulance:** 118
**Fire:** 115
**Car breakdown:** 116

## Embassy Numbers in Italy
**UK:** 06 4220 0001; **Ireland** 06 697 9121;
**USA:** 06 46741; **Canada** 06 445981;
**Australia** 06 852721;
**New Zealand** 06 441 7171

## Shoe Sizes

| Europe | UK | USA |
| --- | --- | --- |
| 35 | 2½ / 3 | 4 |
| 36 | 3 / 3½ | 4½ / 5 |
| 37 | 4 | 5½ / 6 |
| 38 | 5 | 6½ |
| 39 | 5½ / 6 | 7 / 7½ |
| 40 | 6 / 6½ | 8 / 8½ |
| 41 | 7 | 9 / 9½ |
| 42 | 8 | 9½ / 10 |
| 43 | 9 | 10½ |
| 44 | 9½ / 10 | 11 |
| 45 | 10½ | 12 |
| 46 | 11 | 12½ / 13 |

## Women's Clothing

| Europe | UK | USA |
| --- | --- | --- |
| 34 | 6 | 2 |
| 36 | 8 | 4 |
| 38 | 10 | 6 |
| 40 | 12 | 8 |
| 42 | 14 | 10 |
| 44 | 16 | 12 |

# Children

Children are still the royalty of Italy: pampered, often spoiled, probably more fashionably dressed than you are, and never allowed to get dirty. If you're bringing your own *bambini* to Italy, they'll be warmly received. Many **hotels** offer slight discounts and have play areas, and most larger cities have permanent **Luna Parks** (funfairs).

Other activities young children enjoy are the **Bomarzo Monster Park** in Lazio, close to the Umbrian border, and **Città della Domenica** in Perugia. If a **circus** visits town while you're there, you're in for a treat; it will either be a sparkling showcase of daredevil skill or a poignant, family-run, modern version of Fellini's *La Strada*.

# Crime and the Police

**Police/Emergency, t 113**

Cities attract a fair amount of petty crime – pickpocketing, white-collar thievery (check your change) and car break-ins – but violent crime is rare. Stay on the inside of the pavement and hold on to your property; pickpockets most often strike in crowds; don't carry too much cash and don't keep what you have in one place; be extra careful in stations, don't leave valuables in hotel rooms, and park in garages, guarded car parks, or well-lit streets, with any temptations out of sight.

Purchasing small quantities of cannabis is legal, but 'small quantity' isn't specified and if the police dislike you already, it may be enough to get you into big trouble.

Once the scourge of Italy, political terrorism has declined drastically in recent years, mainly thanks to special squads of the *Carabinieri*, the black-uniformed national police, technically part of the Italian army. Local matters are usually in the hands of the *Polizia Urbana*; the nattily dressed *Vigili Urbani* concern themselves with directing traffic and handing out parking fines. You probably will not have anything to do with the *Guardia di Finanza*, the financial police, who spend their time chasing corrupt politicians and their friends (unless they happen to catch you leaving a bar or restaurant without a receipt).

## Restaurant Price Categories

Categories are based on an average complete meal, Italian-style with house wine, for one.

| | | |
|---|---|---|
| *very expensive* | €€€€ | over €45 |
| *expensive* | €€€ | €30–45 |
| *moderate* | €€ | €20–29 |
| *inexpensive* | € | under €20 |

# Eating Out

When you leave a restaurant you will be given a receipt (*ricevuta fiscale*) that, according to Italian law, you must take with you out of the door and carry for at least 300m. If you aren't given one, the restaurant is probably fudging its taxes and thus offering you lower prices. There is a slim chance the tax police may have their eye on both you and the restaurant; if you don't have a receipt they could slap you with a heavy fine.

**Prices** quoted for meals are for a complete meal with house wine for one person. We have divided restaurants into price categories (*see* box above).

When you eat out, mentally add to the bill (*conto*) the bread and cover charge (*pane e coperto*, €1–3), and a 15% service charge. This is often included in the bill (*servizio compreso*); if not, it will say *servizio non compreso*. Extra tipping is at your own discretion; *see also* p.78.

For further information about eating in Italy, including local specialities and a menu vocabulary, *see* **Food and Drink**, pp.45–56.

# Electricity

For electric appliances you need a 220AC adaptor with two round prongs on the plug. American appliances need transformers too.

# Health and Emergencies

**Health Emergencies, t 118**

Minor illnesses and problems that crop up in Italy will usually be handled free of charge in a public hospital **walk-in clinic** (*ambulatorio*). If you need minor aid, you'll find that Italian **pharmacists** are highly trained and can probably diagnose your problem; look for a *farmacia* (all have a list in the window detailing which are open during the night and holidays). In extreme cases, you should head for the Pronto Soccorso (**Accident and Emergency**) of the nearest hospital.

Italian doctors are not always great linguists; contact your embassy or consulate (*see* p.60) for an **English-speaking doctor**. For **insurance and EHIC cards**, *see* p.61.

## Internet

Internet access has become much more widespread in Italy in recent years. Nearly all hotels and B&Bs now have their own website, which simplifies booking, and offer free Internet access (increasingly Wifi) for guests. Most resorts and towns have at least one Internet point of some kind; ask for a list at the tourist office. Costs vary widely: in some cities there is free access for those under 26 or for students.

## Maps and Publications

The maps throughout this guide are for orientation only; it is worth investing in a good, up-to-date regional map before you arrive in Italy, ideally from one of the following bookshops:

**Stanford's**, 12–14 Long Acre, London WC2E 9LP, **t** (020) 7836 1321, *www.stanfords.co.uk*. There are also branches in Bristol and Manchester.

**The Travel Bookshop**, 13–15 Blenheim Crescent, London W11 2EE, **t** (020) 7229 5260.

**The Complete Traveller**, 199 Madison Ave, New York, NY 10016, **t** (212) 685 9007.

Excellent touring maps produced by Touring Club Italiano, Michelin and the Istituto Geografico de Agostini are available at major bookshops in Italy or sometimes on newsstands. Italian tourist offices can often supply good area maps and town plans.

Books are more expensive in Italy than in the UK, but some good bookshops stock English-language books.

## Opening Hours

Most of Umbria closes down at 1pm until 3 or 4pm, to eat and properly digest the main

## National Holidays

Most museums, banks and shops are closed on the following national holidays:

**1 January** New Year's Day (*Capodanno*).

**6 January** Epiphany; better known to Italians as the day of *La Befana* – a kindly witch who brings *bambini* the toys that Santa Claus or *Babbo Natale* somehow forgot.

**Easter Monday**

**25 April** Liberation Day.

**1 May** Labour Day – lots of parades, speeches, picnics, music and drinking.

**2 June** *Festa della Repubblica.*

**15 August** Assumption (*Ferragosto*); the biggest holiday of all – woe to the innocent traveller on the road or train!

**1 November** All Saints (*Ognissanti*).

**8 December** Immaculate Conception of the Virgin Mary.

**25 December** Christmas Day.

**26 December** *Santo Stefano.*

meal of the day, although things are now beginning to change in the cities. Many more shops in the centre of town now stay open during lunch.

Afternoon working hours are from 4 to 7, often from 5 to 8 in the hot summer months. Bars are often the only places open early afternoon. In any case, don't be surprised if you find anywhere in Italy unexpectedly closed (or open for that matter), whatever its official stated hours.

### Museums and Galleries

Most major museums open 9am–7pm; Sun afternoons and Mon they often close. Where possible we have given opening hours for individual museums; but note that they can change at short notice, particularly in summer.

With two works of art per inhabitant, Italy has a hard time financing the preservation of its national heritage; it's as well to enquire at the tourist office about what's open and what's 'temporarily' closed before setting off on a wild-goose chase.

Entrance charges vary wildly; expect to pay €2–5 for museum entrance; expensive ones can be as high as €9.50 if there is a special exhibition. State museums and monuments are free to under-18s and over-60s (bring ID). One week a year – usually in late spring – all state museums are free of charge for the *Settimana dei Berri Culturali*.

## Banks and Shops

**Banks** are open Mon–Fri 8.30–1/1.20 and 3–4 or 4–5 except local and national holidays (*see* opposite). For **post offices**, *see* below.

**Shops** are generally open Mon–Sat 8–1 and 3.30–7.30. In bigger towns some supermarkets and department stores now open all day, but this varies from region to region. Food shops shut on Wed afternoons in winter, and Sat afternoons end June–beginning Sept; Sun opening is becoming more usual, particularly in the centre of town.

## Churches

Italy's churches have always been a prime target for art thieves and as a consequence are usually locked when there isn't a sacristan or caretaker. All churches, except the really important cathedrals and basilicas, close in the afternoon at the same hours as shops, and the little ones tend to stay closed.

Don't do your visiting during services, and don't come to see paintings and statues in churches during the week preceding Easter – you'll probably find them covered with mourning shrouds.

Always have a pocketful of coins to feed the light machines in churches, or what you came to see is bound to be hidden in ecclesiastical gloom.

## Packing

You simply cannot overdress in Italy. Whether or not you want to try to keep up with the natives, however, is your own affair and your own heavy suitcase – you may do well to compromise and just bring a couple of smart outfits for big nights out. It's not that the Italians are very formal; they simply like to dress up with a gorgeousness that adorns their cities just as much as those old Renaissance churches and palaces. The few places with dress codes are the major churches and basilicas (no shorts or sleeveless shirts), and the smarter restaurants.

After agonizing over fashion, remember to pack small and light: transatlantic airlines limit baggage by size (two pieces are free, up to 1.5m, in height and width; in 2nd class

you're allowed one of 1.5m and another up to 110cm). Within Europe limits are by weight: 20 kilos (44lbs) in 2nd class, 30 kilos (66lbs) in 1st, though allowances are substantially less for low-cost carriers. You may well be penalized for anything bigger. If you're travelling mainly by train, you'll especially want to keep bags to a minimum: jamming big suitcases in overhead racks isn't much fun.

Never take more than you can carry, but do bring the following: any prescription medicine you need, an extra pair of glasses or contact lenses, a torch (for dark frescoed churches and hotel corridors), a travel alarm (for those early trains) and a pocket Italian–English dictionary (for flirting and other emergencies). You may also want to invest in earplugs.

## Photography

Film and developing are very expensive in Italy, so a digital camera is handy. You're not allowed to take pictures in most museums, or in some of the churches. Most cities now offer 1hr processing if you need your pictures in a hurry.

## Post Offices

t 803160, *www.poste.it*.

City post offices usually open Mon–Sat 8.10–6; elsewhere it's Mon–Sat 8.10–1.25.

The postal service in Italy used to have an extremely poor reputation, but has improved in the last couple of years. First-class mail, *posta prioritaria* (€0.62), is supposed to get to an address in Italy within 24hrs and to EU countries within 36. You can use registered delivery, *raccomandata*, for a €2.80 supplement. Stamps (*francobolli*) may also be purchased at tobacconists (*tabacchi*, identified by blue signs with a white T). Airmail letters to and from North America can quite often take up to two weeks. This can be a nightmare if you're making hotel reservations and are sending a deposit – emailing or telephoning ahead is far more secure if time is short.

Mail can be sent to you care of your hotel or addressed *Fermo Posta* (*poste restante*:

general delivery) to the central post office where you are staying. When you go to pick up mail at the *Fermo Posta* window, take your passport as proof of ID. You will need to pay a nominal charge.

The Italian post has recently made the process of sending parcels a lot easier. You no longer have to wrap things in a certain way; the post offices have boxes if you want to use them. Whether they will be sent as a *lettera* or *pacco* depends on size, weight and contents. *Posta prioritaria* is good for parcels up to 2kg.

# Shopping

'Made in Italy' has long been a byword for style and quality, especially in fashion and leather, but also in home design, ceramics, kitchenware, jewellery, lace and linens, glassware and crystal, chocolates, hats, straw-work, art books, engravings, handmade stationery, gold and silverware, a hundred kinds of liqueurs, wine, aperitifs, coffee machines, gastronomic specialities and antique reproductions, as well as the antiques themselves. If you're looking for the latter and are spending a lot of money, be sure to demand a certificate of authenticity – reproductions can be very, very good.

There's a large antiques market at Assisi in late April and early May, and a smaller one held in Perugia on the last Sunday of each month. Ceramics are an old tradition in Gubbio, Deruta, Ficulle, Gualdo Tadino and Città di Castello. Wine and olive oil, porcini mushrooms, jars of truffles and other 'gastro?nomic' specialities are available almost everywhere.

Italians don't like department stores, but there are a few chains – COIN stores often have good buys on almost the latest fashions. Standa and UPIM have a reasonable selection of clothes, houseware, etc., and often super?markets in their basements. Most stay open all day, but some take the same break as other Italian shops – 1pm to 3 or 4pm.

Non-EU nationals should save their receipts for Customs on the way home.

## Specialist Holidays and Courses for Foreigners

The **Italian Cultural Institute**, 39 Belgrave Square, London SW1X 8NX, t (020) 7235 1461, *www.icilondon.esteri.it*, or 686 Park Ave, New York, NY 10021, t (212) 879 4242, *www.iicnewyork.esteri.it*, is the main source of information on courses for foreigners in Italy, including Italian state scholarships and language courses for business students. Graduate students should also contact their nearest Italian consulate to find out about scholarships – many go unused each year.

**Worldwide Classroom**, *www.worldwide.edu*, also has a database of educational organizations around the world.

### Language Courses

One obvious course to take in the linguistically pure land of Dante is Italian language and culture: there are summer classes at the Università per Stranieri in Perugia, and special classes in August for teachers of Italian.

**Università per Stranieri**, Ufficio Relazioni con lo Studente, Palazzo Gallenga, Piazza Fortebraccio 4, Perugia, t 075 57461, *www.unistrapg.it*. Month-long courses in Italian year-round, attracting up to 4,000 students a year.

### Art Courses

In Spoleto, the Centro Italiano Studi di Alto Medioevo, in the Palazzo Ancaiani, offers classes on medieval art in April. Perugia's Accademia delle Belle Arti Pietro Vanucci, Piazza San Francesco al Prato 5, has painting and sculpture courses.

Shipping goods is a risky business unless you do it through a very reputable shop. Note well that the attraction of shopping in Italy is limited to luxury items; for less expensive clothes and household items you'll always do better in Britain or America. Prices for clothes, even in street markets, are often ridiculous. Bargains of any kind are rare, and the cheaper goods are often very poor quality.

Italian clothes are lovely, but if you have a large-boned Anglo-American build, you may find it hard to get a good fit, especially on trousers or skirts (Italians are a long-waisted, slim-hipped bunch). Shoes are often narrower than the sizes at home.

# Sports and Activities

## Gliding

Gliding and hang-gliding are big in Umbria, where the hills provide the proper updraughts; Monte Subasio by Assisi and Castelluccio are centres for the sport, but the Parco Naturale di Monte Cucco is the best organized – there's a club, the Centro di Volo Libero, at Sigillo, near Gualdo Tadino, t 0759 220693. The little airports at Foligno, t 0742 670201, and Perugia, S Egidio, t 075 592141, also offer gliding.

## Golf

There's a golf course near Lake Trasimeno (Circolo Golf Perugia, Loc. Santa Sabina, Ellera Umbra, t 075 517 2204); another north of Perugia at Antognola; and a third at Panicale, south of Lake Trasimeno, the Golf Club Lamborghini, Loc. Soderi, t 075 837 582.

## Horse-riding

Horse-riding is increasingly popular, and Agriturist has a number of villa and riding holidays on offer. The National Association of Equestrian Tourism (ANTE) is very active here. Umbria's riding centre is at Montebibico, near Spoleto (Centro Ippico La Somma, t 0743 54370, *www.lasomma.it*), with day and longer excursions available. For more information, write directly to the local Agriturist office (*see* 'Where to Stay', p.68).

## Hunting

The most controversial sport in Italy pits avid enthusiasts against a burgeoning number of environmentalists who oppose it. The Apennines, especially in Umbria, are boar territory, and in the autumn months the woods are full of hunters. Pathetically tiny birds, as well as ducks and pigeons, are the other principal game.

## Medieval Sports

Some ancient sports are still popular, and not entirely as a tourist attraction – the rivalries between neighbourhoods and cities are intense. Gubbio and Sansepolcro stage two annual crossbow matches against each other. Narni and Foligno have annual jousts.

## Potholing

Monte Cucco near Gualdo Tadino has the most important of the 865 caves in Umbria; the Centro Nazionale di Speleologia Monte Cucco is in Costacciaro, t 075 917 0400. For information on other subterranean excursions in the region, contact the Gruppo Speleologico CAI Perugia, Via Santini 8, t 075 584 7070, *www.speleopg.it*.

## Rowing, Rafting, Canoeing

Rowing is the big sport at Umbria's Lake Piediluco, site of the Federazione Italiana di Canottaggio and an international championship, while the upper Tiber and River Nera, below the Cascata delle Marmore, are the place to hire a raft or canoe.

## Skiing

In Umbria there's downhill skiing in the Monti Sibillini, at Forca Canapine on the border of the Marches; many people also head south of the border into Lazio to the big ski complex at Terminillo, east of Rieti. Cross-country skiiers head up to Castelluccio above Norcia, or Monte Cucco, or Monte Serra above Gualdo Tadino.

## Tennis

Each *comune* has at least one or two courts that you can hire by the hour, and many hotels have them too.

## Walking

There are a number of marked paths in the mountains, especially in the natural parks; the local Club Alpino Italiano (CAI) offices can suggest routes. In Perugia, you'll find them at Via della Gabbia 9; in Spoleto, at Via Pianciani 4; in Terni, at Via Fratelli Cervi 31.

# Telephones

Public phones for **international calls** may be found in the offices of Telecom Italia, Italy's telephone company. They are the only places where you can make **reverse-charge (collect)** calls (*a erre*), but be prepared for a wait, as they go through the operator in Rome. **Rates** for long-distance calls are among the highest in Europe (they're lowest after 11pm).

Direct international calls may be made by dialling the **international prefix** (for the UK 0044, Ireland 00353, USA and Canada 001, Australia 0061, New Zealand 0064).

Calls within Italy are cheapest after 10pm. Most phone booths now take only **phonecards** (*schede telefoniche*) available in €3, €5 and €10 denominations at tobacconists and newsstands – you'll have to snap off the small perforated corner to use them. Avoid telephoning from hotels, which often add 25% to the bill.

You now have to dial the full **town prefix**, including the zero, to call anywhere in Italy, even the town you are in. In this book we have given all phone numbers with the full town prefix. To **call Italy from abroad**, dial **t** 0039 followed by the area prefix, including the initial zero, e.g. 0039 06 for Rome.

Note that **mobile phone** numbers do NOT begin with an '0'.

## Time

Italy is one hour ahead of UK time and six hours ahead of North American EST. Italian summer time runs from the last Sunday in March to the last Sunday in October; clocks change on those days.

## Tipping

If you're in a **bar**, leave the small change in the form of the copper-coloured coins if you were standing, and around 30–50 cents if you sat down. In **restaurants**, service is usually included (if not, leave 10%) but it's always nice to reward good service with a few euros.

For **taxis**, 10% is the norm.

## Toilets

Don't get confused by Italian plurals: *signori* (gents), *signore* (ladies).

There are very few holes in the ground left in Italy, but public loos only exist in places such as train and bus stations and bars; the latter are legally obliged to let you use their *bagno* without buying a drink. Stations, motorway stops and smarter cafés have toilet attendants who expect a small tip.

# Perugia, Lake Trasimeno, Assisi

*Perugia, capital of Umbria, is one of Italy's greatest art cities, an intensely atmospheric place sheltering some of Europe's most authentic medieval streets. What's more, Perugians have their own 'riviera' a hop and skip to the west, on the gentle shores of Lake Trasimeno with its bijou islands and mighty castles; Perugino was born just south of the lake in Città della Pieve and made these bluish-green landscapes his own. To the east, in view of Perugia's balconies, is lovely cream and pink Assisi, home of St Francis and Italy's finest collection of trecento painting.*

# 07

## Don't miss

**1** Modern jazz and medieval arches
Perugia **p.81**

**2** Colourful ceramics
Deruta **p.105**

**3** Islands and lakeside villages
Lago Trasimeno **p.106**

**4** Perugino's hometown
Città della Pieve **p.113**

**5** The restored Basilica of St Francis
Assisi **p.119**

*See map overleaf*

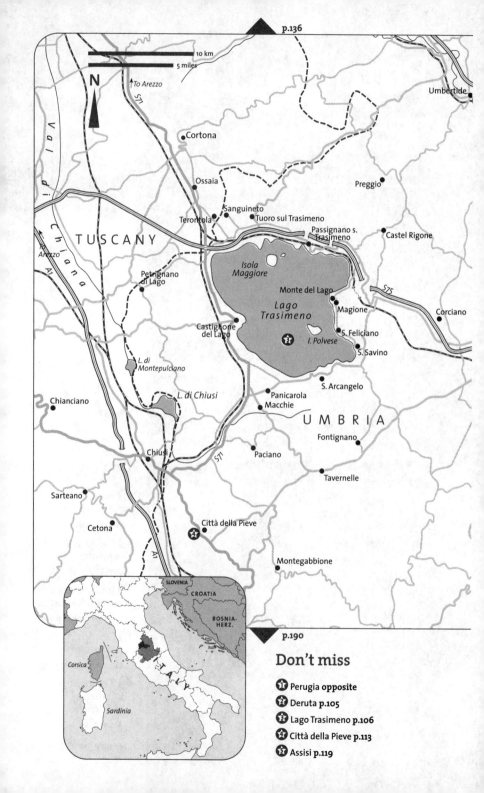

p.136

10 km

5 miles

N

↑To Arezzo

S71

Umbertide

Cortona

Ossaia

Preggio

Sanguineto

Tuoro sul Trasimeno

Terontola

Passignano s. Trasimeno

Castel Rigone

TUSCANY

Val di Chiana

F. Arezzo

A1

Isola Maggiore

Petrignano di Lago

Monte del Lago

S75

Magione

Corciano

Lago Trasimeno

Castiglione del Lago

S. Feliciano

I. Polvese

S. Savino

L. di Montepulciano

L. di Chiusi

S. Arcangelo

Chianciano

Panicarola

Macchie

UMBRIA

Fontignano

Paciano

Chiusi

S71

Sarteano

Paciano

Tavernelle

Cetona

A1

Città della Pieve

Montegabbione

p.190

SLOVENIA

CROATIA

BOSNIA-HERZ.

ITALY

Corsica

Sardinia

## Don't miss

⚝ Perugia **opposite**

⚝ Deruta **p.105**

⚝ Lago Trasimeno **p.106**

⚝ Città della Pieve **p.113**

⚝ Assisi **p.119**

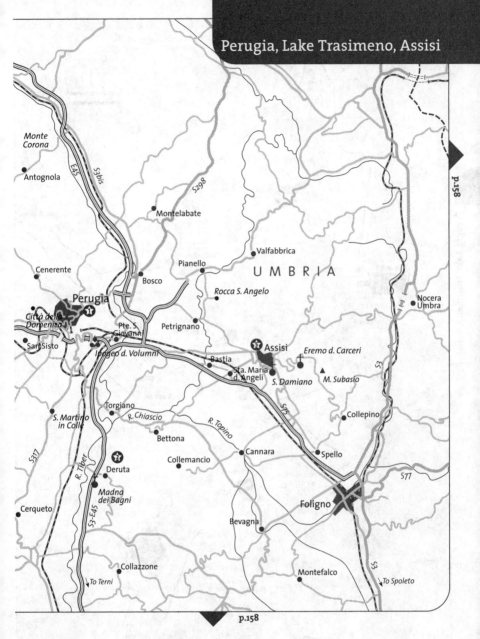

p.158

p.158

## ✪ Perugia    **Perugia**

*What a
town for
assassinations!*

H. V. Morton

Balanced on a commanding hill high over the Tiber, Perugia
(population 155,000) is a fascinating medieval acrobat able to
juggle adroitly several roles: that of an ancient hill town, a
magnificent *città d'arte*, a bustling university centre and a slick
cosmopolitan city famous for chocolates. It is a fit capital for

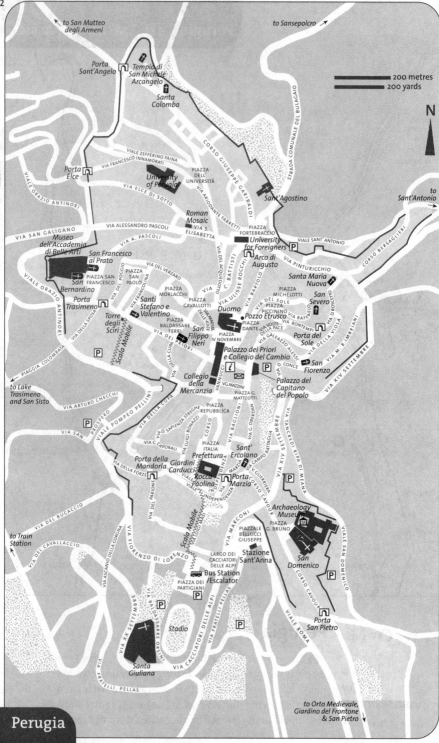

Perugia

# Getting to and around Perugia

## By Air

Perugia's airport, Sant'Egidio-Perugia (t 075 592141, *www.airport.umbria.it*), 12km east of the city towards Assisi, has Ryanair flights (*see* p.63) from London Stansted, plus connections with Milan (Malpensa; with Alitalia and Interstate), Rome (Fiumicino; with Interstate) and Reggio Calabria (with Interstate) and, from June to September, Olbia in Sardinia (with Air Vallee).

## By Train

As Perugia is on a hill, its two train stations are some distance from the centre. Regular city buses (nos.6, 7, 8 and 9) link the FS station with Piazza G. Matteotti or Piazza Italia in the centre; the more convenient FCU station (S. Anna, t 075 575 4038) is a short walk from Piazza dei Partigiani and the escalators up to the centre.

The main FS station, on Piazza V. Veneto, is about 3km from the centre in the lower suburb of Fontivegge; it has trains (t 892021, *www.trenitalia.com*) for Florence (154km/2hrs 30mins) and Arezzo (78km/90mins), via the Terontola junction on the northern shore of Lake Trasimeno; for Siena (147km/3hrs 30mins) another change is required, at Chiusi (a pain – the FS replaced several routes with direct buses). Another line passes through Assisi (26km/25mins), Spoleto (47km/70mins), Foligno and Terni on the way to Rome (3hrs), while the route to Ancona (3hrs) via Foligno stops at Nocera Umbra, Gualdo Tadino, Gubbio, Genga and Fabriano.

For other places in Umbria, the narrow-gauge Ferrovia Centrale Umbria (FCU), t 075 575401, *www.fcu.it*, is handy. Its main station here is Stazione Sant'Anna, halfway up the hill, off Piazza dei Partigiani. The FCU goes north to Città di Castello (45km/1hr) and Sansepolcro (60km/1Vhrs), south to Todi (41km/1hr) and Terni.

## By Bus

Perugia's bus station is near the FCU station in Piazza dei Partigiani, linked to Piazza Italia by steps and escalators. APM buses, t 075 573 1707, *www.apmperugia.it*, serve villages in Perugia province (roughly the northern two-thirds of Umbria). There are about 12 a day to Santa Maria degli Angeli (for Assisi), five carrying on to Spello and Foligno; others to Deruta and Todi; Torgiano and Bettona; Gubbio; Gualdo Tadino; the towns of Lake Trasimeno; one to Orvieto; and five a day to Città della Pieve and Chiusi (on the Florence–Rome line).

SSIT (t 075 573 1707; *www.spoletina.com*) has one or more buses a day to Nocera Umbra, Spoleto, and Norcia and Cascia; SULGA (t 075 5009641, *www.sulga.it*) has direct links to Rome and Fumicino airport; SENA (t 800 930 960, *www.sena.it*) goes to Siena, Ascoli Picero and the coast of the Marches; CONTRAM (t 800 037737, *www.contram.it*) to Macerata and Civitanova Marche; and Freccia dell'Appennino (t 800 930 960, *www.sena.it*) goes down the coast of the Marches to San Benedetto del Tronto and Porto Ascoli.

## By Car

Most of the city is closed to traffic, peripheral garages and car parks are few and usually charge by the hour. Car parks nearest the centre, at Piazza Italia, Piazza Pellini, the Mercato Coperto and Piazza dei Partigiani, are connected to the centre by elevator or escalator.

Small local car-hire firms may give better rates but tend not to be as flexible over pick-ups and drop-offs. The main operators are at the airport; some are at the train station too: Avis, t 075 692 9346, *www.avisautonoleggio.it*; Hertz, t 075 500 2439, *www.hertz.it*; Maggiore, t 075 500 7499, *www.maggiore.it*; and Europcar, t 075 692 0615, *www.europcar.it*.

For a taxi, call Radio taxi, t 075 500 4888.

## On Foot

Perugia's difficult topography has been mastered with ingenuity – stairs, elevators or escalators to carry you from one part to another. Many are on the edges, where beautiful parks have been strung along the cliffs to take advantage of unusable land – Perugia has one of the highest densities of green areas in Italy.

Umbria, with splendid monuments from the Etruscan era to the late Renaissance stacked next to one another; its gallery contains some of the region's finest art, but in the alleyways cats sleep undisturbed. Yet it is haunted by sinister shadows. Four medieval popes died in Perugia. One did himself in – stuffing himself with Lake Trasimeno eels – but for the other three the verdict was poison. Then there were the Baglioni, the powerful family that ruled the city for a time, so dangerous they nearly exterminated themselves. Even today, Perugia has the highest percentage of freemasons anywhere in Italy. Assisi, perfumed with the odour of sanctity, may only be over the next hill, but Perugia in the old days was as full of trouble as a town could be. As so often in medieval and Renaissance Italy, creativity and feistiness went hand-in-hand, and the Umbrian capital has contributed more than its share to Italian culture and art. Their biggest annual event is a jazz festival. Just as remarkable as the people is the stage they act on: the oldest, most romantically medieval streets and squares in Italy.

A strange thing happened to Perugia in the middle of its rough-house career. Like the great cities of Tuscany, it suffered in the political changes of the 1500s but claims the singular privilege of having been a part of the Papal States. Art, scholarship, trade and civic life quickly withered, and the town's penchant for violence was rocked to sleep under a warm blanket of Hail Marys. Now, a little more than 100 years after liberation, its people are famed for their politeness, urbanity and good taste; Perugians dress more sharply than Florentines for half the money and effort. They make their living from chocolates and ladies' shoes, and teaching Italian language and culture to foreigners. Maybe a few centuries under the pope was just what they needed.

## History

Gubbio, Perugia's longtime rival, liked to claim it was one of the first cities founded by Noah's sons after the flood. To top that, one of Perugia's medieval chroniclers records that Noah himself, at the age of 500 or so, pitched his tents on Perugia's mountain. That would have been news to the Etruscans, who had settled *Pieresa* by the 5th century BC and probably much earlier. Pieresa was the easternmost city of the Dodecapolis, and maintained its freedom until the Roman conquest of 309 BC.

Never entirely happy under Roman rule, the city staged several revolts. In the years after Caesar's assassination, it chose the wrong side with catastrophic results; Octavian's troops besieged it for seven months, and when after the capitulation an Etruscan diehard committed suicide rather than surrender, his funeral pyre started a conflagration that took the rest of the city with him. Some years later, Octavian, by then **Emperor Augustus**, rebuilt the city and renamed it after himself – *Augusta Perusia*.

Almost nothing is known of the city in the Dark Ages. Totila the Goth took it from the Byzantines around 545, after a (probably apocryphal) siege of seven years, but the Exarchs of Ravenna were still, with the Lombards, fighting for it 50 years later. Among the constantly changing alliances of medieval Italian states, Perugia found itself out of the turbulent mainstream, with no large and dangerous neighbours and a potential ally (when it suited Perugia) of pope, emperor or any Tuscan cities. As a result, the Perugians were almost always able to manage their own affairs. Mostly they spent their time subjugating neighbours: Lake Trasimeno towns in 1130, Città di Castello not long after, then Assisi and Spello. Foligno, another bitter enemy, fell in 1282.

Almost always a Guelph city, Perugia maintained a special relationship with Florence and the popes – it had allies, certainly, but friends never. Even fierce, factional cities such as Florence and Siena were careful to walk wide of this wildcat that was constantly molesting its neighbours when not itself convulsed in civil wars. Siena had its annual festive punch-up, the *Gioco del Pugno*, but the Perugians enjoyed spending their holidays at the *Battaglia de' Sassi*, the 'Battle of Stones', in Piazza del Duomo, usually causing a dozen or so fatalities each year. In religion, besides being a graveyard for popes, Perugia gave a cold shoulder to most of the early reformers. Even St Francis, who before he became a preacher spent a year in a Perugian dungeon, couldn't make the city mend its ways. One product of Perugian piety cannot be denied, but characteristically of the city it involved blood: the medieval mass-psychosis of the Flagellants or Disciplinati began here in 1259 with the hallucinations of a Franciscan hermit, Ranieri Fasani, who after years of private devotions was told by the saints and the Virgin to take the idea to the bishop of Perugia, who was impressed and ordered a two-week city-wide flagellation. This mode of penitence seemed right for the time: the Calabrian prophet Joachim da Fiore had pinpointed 1260 as the end of the second age of the world, which everyone interpreted as the apocalypse. Soon bands of Disciplinati were wandering from town to town in Umbria, singing *laude* or simple hymns to the tunes of the popular ballads of the day. Thousands joined in, and the movement spread to Tuscany and across Europe, meeting only occasional pockets of resistance: the king of Poland, for instance, turned the Disciplinati aside at his frontiers. After the initial fervour, the movement would survive in the 20th century, organized into lay confraternities by the Franciscans; you can often see them in paintings, in their specially designed hoods with bare backs.

In principle, Perugia belonged to the papal dominions, the 'Patrimony of St Peter', from the days of Charlemagne. Few popes, though, were able to exercise much control over such a volatile city. After 1303, the priors of the 10 major guilds established their rule, though noble families such as the Oddi and the Baglioni remained extremely influential. In 1304, Pope Benedict XI came to Perugia while mediating a dispute in Florence, only to be slipped some poisoned figs by a nun. In 1305, one of the five papal conclaves that took place in Perugia selected the Gascon Bertrand de Got as Pope Clement V. Perhaps not surprisingly, he wanted to get out of Perugia as soon as possible. But instead of Rome he took refuge in Avignon.

In the 1360s and 70s, when **Cardinal Albornoz** was raising armies and building castles to reassert papal authority over central Italy, Perugia revolted. Pope Urban VI paid a visit in 1387 to make up – a wild dove perched on his shoulder as he entered, taken as a good omen. At least he managed to get out of Perugia alive.

Unfortunately, the rebellion only took the lid off a cauldron of conflicting ambitions that was ready to boil over, and Perugia's three big factions – the nobles, *raspanti* (the wealthy merchant class) and commoners – leapt at each other's throats. In 1393, with the connivance of the pope, a noble named **Biondo Michelotti** seized power. Five years later (again the pope was involved), Michelotti was murdered on his wedding day by the abbot of San Pietro. In the resulting confusion, Giangaleazzo Visconti of Milan grabbed the city for a time (1400–2); there followed a period under the rule of King Ladislas of Naples (1408–14).

After Ladislas, celebrated Perugian *condottiere* **Braccio Fortebraccio** ('Arm Strongarm', the Popeye of the Renaissance, whose arms picture a bouquet of spinach and a helmet), won the city by defeating another *condottiere*, Carlo Malatesta of Rimini, at the battle of Sant'Egidio. Fortebraccio, soon master of all Umbria and 'Prince of Capua', had king-sized ambitions and potent friends – according to contemporary gossip he owned a crystal with a genie inside who gave him good advice. After conquering most of the Marches, Fortebraccio had dreams of ruling a united Italy, but his luck ran out in 1424, when he died at the hands of another Perugian during the siege of L'Aquila in Abruzzo.

In the aftermath, Pope Martin V took control of Perugia, although he could do nothing to stop the increasingly bloody feud between the noble clans of the **Oddi** and the **Baglioni**; the latter, with their legendary good looks, pet lions and tendency towards fratricide, blazed meteorically through Perugia's history like the House of Atreus and along the way sponsored some of the city's great Renaissance art. The first to take power, Malatesta I Baglioni, married the niece of Fortebraccio and manoeuvred to put Perugia under the Pope's suzerainty, and as a reward received the lordship of Perugia, Spello, Bettona, Torgiano, Cannara, Bastia and Collemancio. His eldest son, Braccio I, only killed a couple of cousins, but when his second son Guido came to power, the fight with the Oddi reached such a point that there was a pitched battle in Piazza IV Novembre that left 130 dead. After losing a second battle in 1488, the Oddi were expelled from the city, but only went as far as Lake Trasimeno where they stirred up more trouble, twice trying to capture Perugia; scores of their bodies and those of their supporters were left dangling from the windows of the Palazzo dei Priori.

In 1500, on the occasion of the great wedding of Guido's son and heir Astorre I, a group of Baglioni enemies plotted to kill the whole family in a single night. They managed to get seven out of eight; the eighth, **Giampaolo Baglioni**, escaped and spent the next few years killing all the conspirators, and the last surviving Oddi for good measure. After having eliminated all his enemies, he became the family's most successful ruler, fought for Julius II against Bologna, and later became a condottiere for Venice; but in 1520 an even bigger shark, the Medici pope Leo X, tricked him into coming to Rome, where he was imprisoned, tortured and beheaded.

His death set off a new round of bloody fighting for Perugia between his sons and nephew. The one who survived the demolition derby, Malatesta II Baglioni, distinguished himself by betraying Florence to the Medici and Charles V in the siege of 1530. Another, Rodolfo, murdered a papal legate in revenge for the death of his uncle Giampaolo, giving **Pope Paul III** the perfect excuse to visit Perugia. Over the centuries it had become customary for popes reasserting their authority to make a formal visit to Perugia; contemporaries record Paul, father of the Inquisition and one of the kinkiest, most corrupt of all popes, requiring all nuns in the city to queue up and kiss his feet, apparently leaving him 'very greatly edified'.

To put an end to Perugia's independence for ever, Paul needed yet one more provocation: he found it in 1538, raising the salt tax a year after promising not to. The Perugians revolted again, initiating the **Salt War**, but were crushed by a huge papal force of mercenaries and Spaniards. Government was handed over to officials entitled Preservers of Ecclesiastical Obedience; its trade ruined and its streets full of monks, nuns and Jesuits, Perugia began a precipitous economic decline not to be reversed until the Risorgimento. To this day, Perugians, indeed all Umbrians, eat bread made without salt, an unappetising hangover from the salt rebellion (Umbrians swear it tastes better).

### It's all in the Detail

Make sure you take time to notice the atmospheric street names while wandering around Perugia, including Via Curiosa ('Curious Street'), Via Perduta ('Lost Street'), Via Piacevole ('Pleasant Street') and Via Pericolosa ('Dangerous Street'). And look out for medieval details – carved symbols and coats of arms. One local peculiarity is the narrow Porta del Morte, 'Death's Door', used only to carry out the dead, and bricked up the rest of the time – where death has once passed, the superstition went, he might pass again. Or so the story goes; in most houses these doors were the only access to the upper floors, with ladders inside that could be pulled up in emergencies.

Until then, the only event in the conquered city was to be the Napoleonic occupation: the emperor's troops sent the hordes of monks and nuns packing but also packed much of Perugia's art – some of the best Peruginos included – back to the Louvre. In 1859, during the disturbances of the Risorgimento, Perugia rebelled once more against the pope. Pius IX sent his Swiss Guard to quell them – some 2,000 Switzers forced the city, burning, looting and butchering citizens in the streets. All of Europe heard, and although the Swiss succeeded in crushing the revolt, it backfired into a major propaganda weapon against the papacy. After that, the city's final liberation a year later was greeted with delirium. King Vittorio Emanuele's army had to protect the retiring Swiss Guards from massacre by the Perugians.

## Piazza IV Novembre

Magnificent, time-worn Piazza IV Novembre, once the setting for the 'War of the Stones' and countless riots and street battles, remains the heart and soul of Perugia, as well as the central node of its meandering streets. As in many Umbrian cities, the old town hall, symbol of the *comune*, entirely upstages the cathedral, but here, the two stare at each other over Italy's most beautiful medieval fountain, the 25-sided polygonal pink and white **Fontana Maggiore**, designed in the 1270s by Fra Bevignate. The occasion was the construction of Perugia's first aqueduct since Roman times, and the Priors commissioned Nicola Pisano and his son Giovanni to sculpt the 48 double relief-panels around the lower basin. Twelve of these portray that favourite medieval conceit, the *Labours of the Months*, each accompanied by its zodiacal sign; in between are scenes from Roman legend, Aesop's fables, and saints' lives, personifications of the sciences and arts – altogether a complete, circular image of the medieval world. Above them, the 12-sided upper basin has concave panels filled with 24 saints and figures from Perugia's history, most of them by Giovanni Pisano, with three water nymphs to keep them company. The more you look, the more you realize the subtlety and dynamism of Fra Bevignate's design, particularly the way in which the panels of the lower basin are never congruent, but pull the eye along.

**Palazzo dei Priori**
*houses Collegio del Cambio,* **t** *075 572 8599, collegiodelcambio@ libero.it, and Collegio della Mercanzia,* **t** *075 573 0366*

Surveying the piazza, high up on the wall of the **Palazzo dei Priori**, perch a Guelph lion and Perugia's totem, the famous brass griffin, an emblem visible at least once on every street in town. The scrap iron dangling beneath it is said to be chains and bolts from the gates of Siena, captured after a famous victory at Torrita in 1358 (this isn't true – the real war trophies, whatever they were, disappeared two centuries ago; these chains simply held them up). This stern, Gothic, asymmetrical complex, crowned with toothsome crenellations and pierced by beautiful, narrowly spaced windows, has been cleaned to look as sharp and new as when it was begun in 1297. Two later building phases left an elegant, slightly curved, elongated building, housing Perugia's finest art (*see* 'Galleria Nazionale', pp.90–2 and also the Collegio del Cambio (*see* p.92) and the Collegio della Mercanzia (*see* p.93).

**Sala dei Notari**
*t 075 577 2339; open Tues–Sun 9–1 and 3–7*

The whole first floor of the Piazza IV Novembre section is occupied by the **Sala dei Notari**, a remarkable room divided into bays by huge round arches, with interesting early 13th-century frescoes of Old Testament scenes along the top by a student of Pietro Cavallini. The other frescoes, painted in the 19th century, are the coats of arms of all the *podestà* and *capitani del popolo* who served Perugia from 1293 to 1443.

## The Cathedral of San Lorenzo

**Duomo di San Lorenzo**
*t 075 572 4853; open Tues–Sat 10–1 and 3–6; adm*

For all the attention they lavished on their Palazzo dei Priori, the Perugians never seemed much interested in their cathedral. After laying the cornerstone in 1345, they didn't add another stone for a decade. A century later, when the building was substantially completed, a papal legate tore part of it down to use the stone for his own palace. For the façade, they once stole half a marble facing destined for the cathedral at Arezzo, but not long after, the Aretini whipped them in battle and made them give it back. The cathedral's finest hour, perhaps, came during a fit of civic strife in 1488, when the Baglioni, fighting the Oddi, seized the building, turning it into a fortress, complete with cannon protruding from its Gothic windows. So much blood was spilled that the cathedral had to be washed out with wine and reconsecrated.

Despite its lack of a proper façade, this prim old dear of a building seems just right for its post on lovely Piazza IV Novembre. The side facing the Fontana Maggiore has a geometrical pattern, employing the warm pink marble quarried near Assisi that is everywhere in Umbria. Next to it a bronze statue commemorates the pleasure-loving Julius III, the only pope the Perugians ever liked. The unfinished pulpit on the façade was especially built for the charismatic revivalist San Bernardino of Siena, who preached to vast crowds in the piazza, finally persuading them to stop at least the *Battaglia de' Sassi* in 1425; Perugia, he claimed, was his favourite town, and judging by the church the Perugians gave him (*see* p.95), he was their favourite saint. The best feature of the façade, however, is the elegant travertine **Loggia di Braccio Fortebraccio**, added by the *condottiere* in 1423.

The Duomo's Baroqued interior is determinedly unimpressive, supported by columns badly painted to simulate marble. However, there are a few things worth picking out. In the first chapel on the right, the tomb of Bishop Baglioni (d. 1451) by Urbano da Cortona stands across from a saccharine *Descent from the Cross* by the

16th-century painter Federico Barocci of Urbino. In the **Cappella del Sacramento**, designed by Galeazzo Alessi, Perugia's top 16th-century architect, hangs Luca Signorelli's luminous and recently restored *Pala di Sant'Onofrio* (1484), one of his earliest and best works, showing the Madonna enthroned with saints and a pot-bellied angel tuning a lute. The presbytery has beautiful intarsia choir stalls by Giuliano da Maiano and Domenico del Tasso (1486–91).

On the left side, near reliefs of the *Eternal Father* and *Pietà* by Agostino di Duccio, is the **Cappella del Santo Anello**, housing the Perugians' most prized relic. This is nothing less than the wedding ring of the Virgin Mary. Many stories have grown up around this prodigy, a big onyx stone that, like a 1970s mood ring, changes colour according to the moral character of the wearer. A Perugian woman stole the ring from Chiusi in the Middle Ages, and the townspeople have never stopped worrying that the Chiusini might try to get it back: they keep it in 15 nested cases under 15 locks, spread the keys out among 15 notable and trustworthy citizens, and only take it out of the box on 29–30 July. The relic indirectly inspired Raphael's famous *Betrothal of the Virgin*; Raphael picked up the idea from a painting by Perugino that hung in this chapel before Napoleon spirited it off to France (now in the museum in Caen) – the emperor always had a weakness for doe-eyed Virgins and Perugino was one of his favourite painters.

Behind the cathedral, the cloister of the Canonica witnessed five conclaves of cardinals between 1124 and 1305. Among the popes elected here was Frenchman Clement V, who began the 'Babylonian Captivity' by moving the papacy to Avignon. In the cloister is the **Museo Capitolare della Cattedrale**, with a little art, some reliquaries and hymnals. If it's noon, the campanile bells, just over your head, will make sure you know it.

**Museo Capitolare della Cattedrale**
*t 075 572 4853; open Mon–Fri 10–1, Sat and Sun 10–1 and 4–6; adm*

**Galleria Nazionale dell'Umbria**
*Palazzo dei Priori, t 075 574 1410, www.gallerianazionale umbria.it; lift to the 3rd floor; open Tues–Sun 8.30–7.30; adm; ticket office on ground floor*

## Galleria Nazionale dell'Umbria

The elaborate **main door** (1326) of the Palazzo dei Priori is around the corner in Corso Vannucci, its lunette featuring statues of Perugia's patron saints, Louis of Toulouse, Lawrence and Ercolanus. Through this and up the lift, the Galleria Nazionale has the finest, largest collection of Umbrian (and many other) paintings anywhere, displayed with explanations in English. The mezzanine floor was left unsound by the earthquake, but the masterpieces are all accessible, displayed chronologically and thematically. The first rooms contain some striking early works, among them sculptures for a public fountain by **Arnolfo di Cambio** (1281) and others from the Fontana Maggiore by **Nicola and Giovanni Pisano**, which were replaced by copies. There's a pre-Giotto *Crucifixion* and other works of the **Maestro di San Francesco** from the 1270s. Nor are all the best works Umbrian – the Sienese, in particular, are well represented, with a fine polyptych by Vigoroso da Siena (*c*. 1290) and a sweet *Madonna* by **Duccio di Buoninsegna**.

Mesmerizing rooms of trecento and early quattrocento gold-ground Madonnas and Annunciations (by Ambrogio Maitani, Meo di Guido da Siena, Ottaviano Nelli, Puccio Capanna) culminate in **Beato Angelico**'s *Guidalotti Polyptych*, his pupil **Benozzo Gozzoli**'s *Pala della Sapienza Nuova* and **Piero della Francesca**'s *Polyptych of Sant'Antonio* (1465–70), painted for a Franciscan convent. Piero himself assembled works from two distinct periods to fulfil the wishes of the buyers, who thought the project was dragging on a bit. The *Annunciation* shows the painter at the height of his powers, creating an eerie stillness out of mathematical purity – on either side of Gabriel and the Virgin rows of arches recede into a blank wall. From the International Gothic wizards of the Marches come two works: **Gentile da Fabriano**'s *Virgin and Child* (1408), painted for Perugia's San Domenico – note how the wood of the Virgin's throne is alive and budding – and a *Madonna del Pergolato* (1445) by **Giovanni Boccati da Camerino**, master of angelic choirs, *putti*, flowers and perspective tricks.

The best Perugians of the same period, **Benedetto Bonfigli** and **Bartolomeo Caporali**, show perhaps less spirituality, but fancier clothes and a lilting lyricism. Bonfigli also contributes the sharp and meticulously drawn **Cappella dei Priori** frescoes (1454–80). These dedicated to two of Perugia's three patrons: the older frescoes, late Gothic in style, are on the life of St Louis of Toulouse, while the unfinished later frescoes on the life of St Ercolanus show a more mature, Renaissance handling of space. They also feature the best portraits of Perugia itself, bristling with towers – at the time it had around 500, astonishing even for such a belligerent city. Also beautiful are a bronze relief, the *Scourging of Christ*, by **Francesco di Giorgio Martini**, and some terracotta reliefs by **Agostino di Duccio**.

The next section features two Perugian painters of the next generation, **Pinturicchio** and **Perugino**. Both, when young, worked on the *Miracles of San Bernardino of Siena* (1473), a series of eight small panels with charming imaginary town settings. Although he refused to participate in the High Renaissance, Pinturicchio rarely fails to charm; his nickname, 'Rich Painter', derives from his use of gold and gorgeous colours, seen here in his *Pala di Santa Maria dei Fossi*. Perugino always maintained an ideal classical vision, touched with the 'sweetness' mastered by Raphael. At his worst, Perugino can be painfully unconvincing ('I'll give them their Virgin and Saints,' you can imagine him grumbling as he dabbed on another rolling eyeball). The gallery has about a dozen of these, many almost entirely by his assistants; there's an *Adorazione* featuring the most disdainful Magi ever, as well as Perugino at his finest, in the *Polyptych of Sant'Agostino*.

The mezzanine floor, up a spiral staircase, displays long galleries of numb gigantic canvasses from the 16th to 18th centuries (there's a particularly good one by **Pietro da Cortona**, the ultimate idealized *Nativity*). The wooden horse was a model for an equestrian monument to Orazio Baglioni. At the end, there's a surprise in the shape of an interesting collection of 19th-century views of the city by a local artist, Giuseppe Rossi, showing the Rocca Paolina and the old market square, along with some 19th-century engineers' plans for shoring up Perugia and keeping it from sliding into the valley.

On the first floor, you can look through the glass door to the **Sala del Malconsiglio** (Bad Counsel), so-called because in the 1360s the Priors decided here to release some prisoners – English mercenaries from Sir John Hawkwood's company. The next year, Hawkwood's men defeated Perugia at the Battle of Ponte San Giovanni. The Perugians learned their lesson; they were never nice to anyone again. It contains the original bronze lion and griffin from the façade of the palace; over the door (on the inside) there's an early lunette by Pinturicchio.

## Corso Vannucci and the Collegio del Cambio

To complement the excellent Piazza IV Novembre, Perugia has a truly noble main street. The **Corso Vannucci** is named after Pietro Vannucci, who, after all, was named Perugino after Perugia; it is always closed to traffic and the citizens stroll along it every evening in central Italy's liveliest *passeggiata*.

At Corso Vannucci 25, in the third and final annexe to the enormous Palazzo dei Priori (1443), Perugino received a major commission in 1499 to decorate the Collegio del Cambio, headquarters of Perugia's money-changers' guild. Money-changing, or banking, was not quite reputable owing to biblical injunctions against usury and the first challenge was to come up with an appropriate decorative scheme. The city's leading humanist, Francesco Maturanzio, proposed an array of Christian, Classical and secular virtues for the walls and planetary gods for the ceiling. Perugino dressed them in the *haute couture* of the time, creating one of the finest pure Renaissance rooms in all Italy. Among these beautiful figures, Perugino painted an unflattering self-portrait in the middle of the left wall, tight-lipped and stern and sceptical, over an inscription added by the grateful Perugini: 'If the art of of painting had been lost, he would have rediscovered it. If it had never been invented, he would have done so.' A tradition now scoffed at by scholars has it that Perugino's pupil Raphael, then 17, contributed the figure of Fortitude; more probable is the

**Collegio del Cambio**

*Corso Vannucci 25, t 075 572 8599; open Mon–Sat 9–12.30 and 2.30–5.30, Sun 9–1; joint adm with Capella di San Giovanni Battista and Collegio della Mercanzia (see opposite)*

legend that he served as the model for the figure of the prophet Daniel. The ceiling was later decorated with grotesques, not long after Raphael set the fashion for them in Rome with the discovery of Nero's Golden House; the magnificent woodwork is by Domenico del Tasso and Antonio Bencivenni da Mercatello (1493–1508), and the gilded terracotta statue of Justice (the money-changers' guild arbitrated in financial disputes) is by Benedetto da Maiano.

The frescoes on the life of St John the Baptist in the Bankers' chapel, the **Cappella di San Giovanni Battista**, are by another of Perugino's students, Giannicola di Paolo. Nor is that all; the adjacent **Collegio della Mercanzia** was the seat of the merchants' guild, one of the oldest and most important in Perugia; the Sala di Udienza is richly decorated with 15th-century carvings, panelling and inlays, perhaps by craftsmen from northern Europe.

**Cappella di San Giovanni Battista**
*t 075 572 8599; open Mon–Sat 9–12.30 and 2.30–5,30, Sun 9–1; joint adm with Collegio del Cambio (see opposite) and Collegio della Mercanzia*

**Collegio della Mercanzia**
*Corso Vannucci 15 bis, t 075 573 0366; open Mar–Oct and 20 Dec–6 Jan Tues–Sat 9–1 and 2.30–5.30, Sun 9–1; 1 Nov–19 Dec and 7 Jan–28 Feb Tues, Thurs and Fri 8–2, Wed and Sat 8–4.30, Sun 9–1; joint adm with Collegio del Cambio (see opposite) and Cappella di San Giovanni Battista*

## A Vanished Fortress and Underground Perugia

Continuing down the Corso Vannucci, past the hotels and formidable Perugian pastry shops, you pass from the Middle Ages to 19th-century neoclassical in the blink of an eye at **Piazza Italia**, dominated by the bulky, 1870s **Prefettura**, emblazoned with another griffin; behind it, the balustrades of the **Giardini Carducci** offer a magnificent view over the Perugian suburbs and the distant countryside.

To find out why there are no old buildings on this piazza, take the unobtrusive down escalator under the colonnades of the Prefettura, into a Perugia that for over 300 years was lost to view and almost forgotten. Only days after the end of the Salt War, Paul III found a way to intimidate the Perugians into obedience until Judgement Day while obliterating the Baglioni family at the same stroke. The quarter of town he demolished for his famous **Rocca Paolina** was the stronghold of the Baglioni, including all of their palaces, 138 houses that they owned and seven churches. Most buildings were not completely razed, however, because Paul's architect, Antonio da Sangallo the Younger, needed them to give the new fortress a level foundation.

The 16th century may have been the age of the Renaissance, but in Italy it was also the era of grudges; Paul III came to Perugia seven times over the next three years to make sure the fortress was sufficiently repressive, and to crown it off, he had the Rocca inscribed with large letters: *Ad repellandam Perusinorum audaciam* (To curb the audacity of the Perugians). From the beginning, the Perugians looked upon it as a loathsome symbol of oppression, of the grisly terror that came to Italy in the 1500s. No enemy ever attacked it, and throughout the centuries of papal rule, its only real use was as a prison – a prison from which few ever found their way out again. In the general revolutionary year of 1848, a pick was ceremoniously handed to Count Benedetto Baglioni to begin its longed-for demolition. This was far from complete when the papal forces returned, but as soon as Perugia was liberated from the murderous Swiss Guard in 1860, the Piemontese General Pepoli signed a decree giving the Rocca to the Perugians and they gleefully tore down the rest; the workmen, with their dynamite, were joined by the entire populace, including women and children, some armed with pickaxes, some with their bare hands.

In a way, it's a pity the Rocca Paolina no longer stands. The old paintings and prints in the Palazzo dei Priori depict a startlingly modern building, designed by one of the best Renaissance architects. After demolishing it, the Perugians built the neoclassical ensemble of the Piazza Italia and the Carducci Gardens to replace it; few even knew about the medieval streets underneath, until the city made use of them to create a quick pedestrian passage down to Piazza dei Partigiani – one of the most fascinating things to visit in Perugia. At the bottom of the first escalator, you'll be at the medieval street level, among the brick palaces of the Baglioni, all roofed over by the arches and vaults of Sangallo. There are many interesting corners to explore, including stretches of the **Rocca Paolina bastions**, where you can peek out through the pope's gun slits to look over the peaceful Viale Indipendenza below.

**Rocca Paolina bastions**
*open daily 8–7*

The entrance to the bastions from the outside is on Via Marzia, where you can also see the **Porta Marzia**, the best surviving piece of Etruscan architecture anywhere that isn't a tomb. Antonio da Sangallo was so impressed with it that he carefully reassembled it here after destroying Perugia's original walls. The five sculpted panels, now almost completely eroded, probably represented five gods, although the Perugians have a strange old story that they are a Roman family who died from eating poisonous mushrooms.

## Perugia's West End: Down Via dei Priori

On the Corso Vannucci side of the Palazzo dei Priori, a little archway leads into Via dei Priori and Perugia's quiet, lovely west end. The first sight is **San Filippo Neri**, rebuilt by Roman architect Paolo Marucelli from an earlier church in the 1630s, with façade awkwardly squeezed and only visible in its entirety from across the small square. Perugians still call this impressive pile the Chiesa Nuova; it's surely the showiest Baroque building in Umbria. Its interior, full of florid paintings, seems to be made of dirty ice cream, an echo of Rome out in the provinces. You can also see the high altarpiece of the Immaculate Conception, completed by Pietro da Cortona. The medieval Via della Cupa descends from here under a series of arches to the Etruscan walls and gate, **Porta della Mandorla**.

Further down Via dei Priori is charming **Santi Stefano e Valentino**, a vaulted medieval church: the altarpiece is a fine *Madonna* by 16th-century Perugian Domenico Alfani. Next, in the shadow of the 46m **Torre degli Sciri** (13th century), Perugia's tallest surviving tower fortress, **Santa Teresa degli Scalzi**, was an ambitious Baroque project that was never finished. In the little piazza by the **Porta Trasimena**, built in the Middle Ages on Etruscan foundations, the church of the **Madonna della Luce** has a good Renaissance façade, a round fresco of God the Father by Giovanni Battista Caporali and another of the Madonna and saints by Tiberio d'Assisi. The church commemorates a miracle: a barber, playing cards by his shop, swore so hard after losing a hand that a wooden Madonna in a nearby shrine shut her eyes and didn't open them for four days.

## Piazza San Francesco

Turning right at the Madonna della Luce, the street opens into the green lawn of **Piazza San Francesco**, originally outside the walls. San Francesco al Prato (1230), once the finest and most richly decorated church in Perugia, suffered a partial collapse in a mudslide in 1737 and a thorough looting by Napoleon's soldiers; the elegant façade remains, in patterns of pink and white stone. Part of it is now open to the elements.

Next door, the **Oratorio di San Bernardino** commemorates the 15th-century Franciscan from Siena who made such an impression on the Perugians; 'Little St Bernard' must have been a crafty preacher to affect these pirates. The oratory was begun in 1461, the year after the saint's canonization, and placed on this site because Bernardino always stayed at the convent of San Francesco when visiting. Agostino di Duccio (1418–81), that rare Florentine sculptor who decorated the Malatesta temple of Rimini, was commissioned to do the façade, turning the little chapel into Umbria's greatest temple of pure Renaissance art. Framed in rich pink and green marbles, Agostino's reliefs are exquisite: beatific angel musicians, scenes of miracles from the life of the saint and allegorical virtues: Mercy, Holiness and Purity on the left; Religion, Mortification and Penance on the right. One of the panels on the lower frieze portrays the original Bonfire of Vanities, held in front of the cathedral after a particularly stirring sermon from Bernardino – which may have given Savonarola in Florence the idea. Inside, the chapel altar is a late Roman sarcophagus, perhaps that of a Christian; it seems to tell the story of Jonah and the whale and was the tomb of the Beato Egidio of Assisi (d. 1262), the third person to follow St Francis. The Oratory also has two works from the church of San Francesco: one of Benedetto Bonfigli's gonfalons, depicting the Madonna sheltering Perugia from the plague (1464), and a copy of Raphael's *Deposition*, now in Rome's Galleria Borghese.

**Museo dell' Accademia di Belle Arti**

*closed for restoration and not expected to reopen in 2009, though some artefacts are on display at the museum in Palazzo della Penna (Via Podiani 11; t 075 571 6233; open Tues–Sun 10–1 and 4–7; adm): ask at tourist office (see p.101), call t 075 573 0631 or email info@abaperugia.org for latest information*

Just behind, the convent of San Francesco holds the **Museo dell'Accademia di Belle Arti**, displaying a huge collection of plaster models, starring Canova's *Three Graces*; there are also prints, and typically academic 18th- and 19th-century paintings.

## Old Streets Around the Cathedral

Quite a few old tales start with a child going around a church widdershins (counter-clockwise) and ending up in fairyland. Try it with Perugia's cathedral, and you'll find yourself transported immediately back to the Middle Ages, a half-vertical cityscape of dark, grim buildings and overhanging arches, some incorporating bits of Gothic palaces and Etruscan walls – a set no film director could possibly improve upon. And they are as old as they look. Many arches originally supported buildings over the street; medieval Perugia must have seemed like one continuous building, linked by arches and passageways.

### An Etruscan Well and the Arch of Augustus

**Pozzo Etrusco**

*t 075 573 3669; open April–Oct 10–1.30 and 2.30–6 (closed Mon, except April and Aug); Nov–Mar Tues–Sun 11–1.30 and 2.30–5; adm (ticket also valid for San Severo, see p.98, Museo delle Porte e delle Mura Urbiche and Porta Sant'Angelo, see p.97)*

At Piazza Dante 18, marvel at an example of ancient engineering, the 3rd-century BC **Pozzo Etrusco**, a monumental 35m-deep well and cistern (if the debris at the bottom is ever excavated, it may prove deeper). According to estimates, it held 95,000 gallons of water, enough to supply all of Etruscan *Perusia*. Via Ulisse Rocchi, leading down steeply to the northern gate, used to be called Via Vecchia and is the oldest street in town; Perugians have been treading it for at least 2,500 years.

The old north gate is formed of another fabulous relic of the city's past, the **Arco di Augusto**. The huge stones of the lower levels are Etruscan; above rises a perfectly preserved Roman arch built during the emperor's refounding of Augusta Perusia. The city's new name is inscribed with typical Imperial modesty: 'Augusta' in very large letters, 'Perusia' in tiny ones. The portico on the Roman bastion, making this gate one of the most beautiful in Italy, was added in the 16th century. The arch faces Piazza Fortebraccio and the 18th-century Palazzo Gallenga Stuart, home of the **Università per Stranieri** (*see* p.76), founded in 1921 for the study of Italian language and culture and attended by students from all over the world.

Another little walk, beginning back in Piazza IV Novembre, is down **Via Maestà delle Volte**, one of the most picturesque medieval streets in Perugia, covered with arches that once supported a large Gothic hall. It leads down to **Piazza Cavallotti**, where Roman houses and a road were discovered just under the pavement.

### The University and Borgo Sant'Angelo

Another itinerary through this ancient district begins behind the cathedral and take you into a jumble of medieval arches and asymmetrical vaults that lead down to Via Battisti. Near it, a long stairway descends through the Roman–Etruscan walls to the **Borgo Sant'Angelo**, Perugia's medieval suburb, once the centre of popular resistance to the Baglioni and the popes; it's now home to the city's famous university. Walk over the **Acquedotto**, which in the Middle Ages supplied water from Monte Pacciano to the Fontana Maggiore; much later, it was converted into a long stone footbridge over the housetops to the precincts of the **university**, founded in 1307 and still one of the most prestigious in Italy. The central university buildings are now on Via Ariodante Fabretti, in an Olivetan monastery liquidated by Napoleon in 1801. In the **Institute of Chemistry** on Via Pascoli you can see a 2nd-century **Roman mosaic** of Orpheus charming the wild animals with his lyre.

**Dipartimento
di Chimica**
*open Mon–Fri 8–7.45*

Beyond the university, Corso Garibaldi runs north through Borgo Sant'Angelo, passing bulky pink-and-white-checked **Sant'Agostino**, with its set of extravagantly carved choirstalls by Baccio d'Agnolo, from designs by Perugino. The fresco over the altar is by Giannicola di Paolo, a student of Perugino, but the real prize, a five-part altarpiece by the master himself, was looted by Napoleon. Its panels are scattered across France, save the *Madonna*, who took a cannonball on the nose in Strasbourg during the Franco–Prussian war. Further up Corso Garibaldi is a plaque commemorating the meeting of St Francis and St Dominic, founders of the two great preaching orders of the Middle Ages, both in Perugia to visit Pope Honorius III; contemporary accounts say they embraced and went their separate ways, without more than a word or two.

One of the many convents in this area is **Santa Colomba** at Corso Garibaldi 191 (ring the bell); its most famous nun, the Blessed Colomba of Rieti (1467–1501), was so wise that the magistrates of Perugia often consulted her; her cell has the lovely painting *Christ Carrying the Cross* by Lo Spagno, and mementos of her life.

At the end of Corso Garibaldi, one of the highest points in the city was graced in ancient times by a circular temple, dedicated to Venus or Vulcan. In the 5th century Christians converted it into a church, the **Tempio di San Michele Arcangelo**, replacing the outer circle of columns with a plain stone wall. Many legends grew up around this singular church in the Middle Ages – some writers referred to it as the 'pavilion of Roland'. Today, with tons of Baroque frippery cleared away, it has something like its original appearance. Some scholars doubt there really was a temple here: the 16 beautiful Corinthian columns do come in a wild variety of styles and heights and some were undoubtedly brought from other buildings. Still, this oldest church in Umbria casts its quiet spell.

**Tempio di San
Michele Arcangelo**
*t 075 572 2624;
open Tues–Sun
9–1 and 3.30–6.30*

**Porta Sant'Angelo**
*t 075 41670; open
April–Oct 10.30–1.30
and 3–6 (closed Mon,
except April and Aug);
Nov–Mar Tues–Sun 11–1
and 3–5; joint adm
with Pozzo Etrusco,
see p.96, and San
Severo, see p.98*

The tall **Porta Sant'Angelo** behind the church, a key point in Perugia's medieval defences, was built by Lorenzo Maitani in 1326 next to a castle tower added by Braccio Fortebraccio. Beyond it, enjoy a rare patch of countryside that has remained unchanged over the centuries; here the **church of San Matteo degli Armeni** has good restored 13th-century frescoes.

## On Perusia's Acropolis

Yet another excursion from the cathedral and Piazza Dante would be up Via del Sole, through another ancient part of the city to **Piazza Michelotti**, an attractive spot and the highest point in Perugia. Long before the Rocca Paolina, the popes built their fortress here; and, like the work of Paul III, this castle was destroyed by the Perugians. In the rebellion of 1375 the people besieged it; after bribing Sir John Hawkwood, the paid protector of the papal legate, they knocked down the walls with the aid of a fearsome homemade catapult called the *cacciaprete* (priest-chaser). Today it is surrounded by peaceful 17th-century houses.

From here, an arched lane leads to **San Severo**, founded in 1007 by Camaldolese monks; the story goes that this high ground was ancient *Augusta Perusia*'s acropolis, and the church was built over the ruins of a Temple of the Sun. One chapel survives the Baroque remodelling of the 1750s and contains a celebrated fresco, *Holy Trinity and Saints*, one of Raphael's very first solo efforts; underneath are more saints by his master Perugino, ironically painted a couple of years after Raphael's premature death when Perugino was in a noticeable artistic decline.

Via Bontempi leads around to another Etruscan gate, the **Porta del Sole**. Two churches near here, **San Fiorenzo** in Via Alessi and 14th-century **Santa Maria Nuova** on Via Pinturicchio (at the bottom of Via Roscetto), both have one of Benedetto Bonfigli's bizarre gonfalons – painted banners intended to be carried during mournful *misericordia* processions in the streets, invoking God's mercy during plagues, famines or the frequent attacks of communal guilt to which Perugians were always subject. The one in Santa Maria Nuova (1472) is badly damaged but shows a vengeful Christ raining down thunderbolts of plague on sinful Perugia, while the Virgin, SS. Benedict and Scholastica, and the Blessed Paolo Bigazzini try to placate his wrath.

East of Santa Maria Nuova, Corso Bersaglieri continues out to the gate of Porta Sant'Antonio, where the **church of Sant'Antonio** has a frescoed *Crucifixion* recently attributed to Raphael.

## To San Domenico

The streets southeast of the cathedral, while not quite as dramatic, are just as ancient and intractable as those to the north and west. If you care to climb a bit, a tour of this area will take you to such sights as the **Via delle Volte della Pace**, an ancient vaulted tunnel of a street just east of the cathedral, where Perugians

**San Severo**
*t 075 573 3864; open daily 10–12.30 and 4–7; joint adm with Pozzo Etrusco, see p.96, and Porta Sant'Angelo, see p.97*

signed their peace treaties (with fingers crossed behind their backs). One of the few breathing spaces in the crowded district is elongated **Piazza Matteotti**, former marketplace and field for burning witches, parallel to and below Corso Vannucci. In the old days it was called Piazza Sopramura, being actually built on top of a section of the Etruscan–Roman walls. The west side is shared by the post office and a Perugian institution, a brightly decorated kiosk with an eccentric owner who sells nothing but bananas. Opposite stand the 17th-century Gesù church and two splendid 15th-century buildings: the **Palazzo del Capitano del Popolo** and the **Palazzo dell'Università Vecchia**, built between 1453 and 1515 and used as the quarters of the university until 1811.

From Piazza Matteotti, Via Oberdan descends to Perugia's oddest church, **Sant'Ercolano** (1326), a tall octagon constructed on the old walls with a gigantic pointed arch in each facet, a double Baroque stair, a train-station clock and lace curtains in the upstairs window; the interior, which is in good if rotting Baroque, has a Roman sarcophagus for its altar.

From here, the city extends along a narrow ridge, following Corso Cavour to another colossal, ambitious, woefully unfinished church, **San Domenico**. Designed by Giovanni Pisano, it was rebuilt in 1632 by Carlo Maderno when the vaulting caved in, though one wall and the apse are original; the latter has the second-largest stained-glass window in Italy after Milan cathedral, dated 1411. The light streaming through is the main feature of the interior, but there is also the fine *Tomb of Pope Benedict XI* by a student of Arnolfo di Cambio. Poisoned figs did Benedict in a year after his election, during a visit in 1304, but surprisingly, the Perugians had nothing to do with it; prime suspects after the nun who served them to him included the Florentines and King Philip the Fair of France. The fourth chapel on the right holds a beautiful marble and terracotta dossal (1459) by Agostino di Duccio.

## The Museo Archeologico Nazionale dell'Umbria

**Museo Archeologico Nazionale dell'Umbria**
t 075 572 7141,
www.archeopg.arti.
beniculturali.it;
open Mon 10–7.30,
Tues–Sun 8.30–7.30;
adm

Housed behind San Domenico, in an equally grandiose yet unfinished convent, this displays excellent material from prehistoric and Etruscan Umbria. The prehistoric collection will get you in touch with Palaeolithic, Neolithic and Bronze Age Umbria, while a large part of the historic collection comes from the Etruscan cemeteries around Perugia: an incised bronze mirror (an Etruscan speciality, 3rd century BC); intricate gold filigree jewellery; sarcophagi; a famous stone marker called the *Cippus Perusinus*, with one of the longest Etruscan inscriptions ever found (151 words); and bronzes, armour and weapons. Among the funeral vases and urns is one portraying a hero who looks like a dentist about to examine a monster's teeth; another shows a procession, perhaps of a victor. Roman finds include inscriptions in honour of Augustus, rebuilder of Perugia, and a beautiful sarcophagus sculpted with the myth of Meleager.

## San Pietro

From San Domenico, Corso Cavour leaves the city at the elegant **Porta San Pietro** (1473),which was designed by Agostino di Duccio with help from Polidoro di Stefano. Changing its name to Borgo XX Giugno, the street continues to the end of the ridge, past the university's **Orto Medievale** at No.74, a botanical garden where each plant has a symbolic meaning, to an 18th-century park, the **Giardino del Frontone**.

**Orto Medievale**
*t 075 585 6432;
open Mon–Fri 8–5;
guided tours available
on request:
ortobot@unipg.it*

Facing it is the Benedictine **church of San Pietro**, which was founded in the 10th century and retains substantial parts of its original structure. This is the most gloriously decorated church in the whole of Perugia, with nearly every square centimetre inside covered with frescoes and canvases. During the sack by the Swiss Guards in 1859, the monks of San Pietro shielded the leaders of the revolt from the papal bloodhounds – the story goes that they cut down their bell ropes by night and used them to lower the fugitives down the cliffs to safety. The 12-sided bell tower is one of Perugia's landmarks. The façade has a rare fresco of the Trinity, which is a feminine word in Italian and is here represented by a three-headed woman. The basilican interior dates from the early 1500s and has a carved, gilded ceiling. Among acres of painting are the large canvases in the nave by a Greek student of Veronese, L'Alisense. Two paintings in the right aisle have been attributed to Perugino's pupil Eusebio da San Giorgio, a *Madonna and Two Saints* and a *St Benedict*.

The **Cappella di San Giuseppe** has some fine 16th-century works, the sacristy painting, *Five Saints*, by Perugino, all that remains of yet another altarpiece looted by Napoleon, as well as a *Portrait of Christ* by Dosso Dossi, and a bronze crucifix by Algardi. The best works, however, have to be the extraordinary 1520s choirstalls, which were sculpted and inlaid by Bernardino Antonibi of Perugia, Nicola di Stefano of Bologna and Stefano Zambelli of Bergamo. A pretty door in the choir gives on to a little balcony with a memorable view over Assisi and Spello. The left aisle boasts a *Pietà* by Fiorenzo di Lorenzo.

There's a tabernacle attributed to Mino da Fiesole in the **Cappella Vibi**; the nearby **Cappella Ranieri** has a *Christ on the Mount* by Guido Reni, *St Peter and St Paul* attributed to Guercino, and a *Judith* by Sassoferrato, who was also responsible for the several Raphael and Perugino copies in the church. Beyond the **Cappella del Sacramento**, with paintings by Vasari, is an *Adoration of the Magi* in the nave by Eusebio da San Giorgio and a *Pietà* by Perugino.

## On the Outskirts of Perugia

**Santa Giuliana**
*t 075 575 0511;
open Sun only
11–12 (Mass)*

Leaving Perugia, Via XX Settembre down to the train station passes 13th-century **Santa Giuliana**, with a delicate pink and white façade and beautiful campanile, one of Perugia's landmarks. Attributed to Gattapone, it is one of the few medieval churches in Perugia to survive essentially intact, with frescoes from the 1200s and 1300s and a cloister from 1375, now a military hospital.

**Ipogeo dei Volumni**
*t 075 393329 or freephone 800 961993; open July and Aug daily 9–12.30 and 4.30–7; rest of year daily 9–1 and 3.30–6.30; adm; max. 7 people at a time, max. visit 5mins*

Near Ponte San Giovanni, east of Perugia, signs lead to one of the best-preserved Etruscan tombs anywhere, the **Ipogeo dei Volumni**. Sheltered by a modern yellow building next to a gritty bypass and train tracks, it can be hard to find: the most painless way is from Perugia by taxi. Dating from the 2nd century BC, the hypogeum is characteristically shaped like an Etruscan house, with an underground 'atrium' under a high gabled roof carved in the rock, surrounded by small rooms, the main one holding the travertine urns containing the ashes of four generations of the family. The oldest, that of a man named Arnth, is a typical Etruscan tomb with a representation of the deceased on the lid; that of his descendant, the 1st-century AD Pulius Voluminius, demonstrates Perugia's rapid Romanization. Unlike most Etruscan tombs, the Volumni has unusual high reliefs in stucco, rather than paintings. There's also a well-laid-out necropolis nearby and a small but good museum attached.

## San Sisto: Perugia's chocolate suburb

Perugia holds a special place in the hearts of chocoholics: since 1907, it has been the home of the Perugina chocolate company, now owned by Nestlé but still making their famous chocolate and hazelnut *baci* (kisses), wrapped in little love notes, 24 hours a day, seven days a week. You can tour the factory, the **Stabilimento Nestlé Perugina**, and visit the company museum and, naturally, the gift shop as well. In 2005, the world's only School of Chocolate opened here, and if you come to Perugia in mid-October you can celebrate the sweet brown stuff at the Eurochocolate festival.

**Stabilimento Nestlé Perugina**
*Viale San Sisto, t 075 527 6796, www.perugina.it; open Mon–Fri 9–1 and 2–5.30; ring ahead for a tour in English*

Perugia, Lake Trasimeno, Assisi | Perugia

07

## Tourist Information in Perugia

**ⓘ Perugia >**
*Loggia del Lanari, Piazza Matteotti 18, t 075 577 2686, and Via Mazzini 6, t 075 572 8937, www.regioneumbria.eu or http://turismo. comune.perugia.it*

**Post office:** Piazza Matteotti, t 075 573 6977, www.poste.it.
**Churches:** open 8–12 and 4pm–sunset unless otherwise noted.

## Market Days in Perugia

**Food market:** Pian di Massiano, Sat mornings.

**Mercato della Terrazza**, near Kennedy escalator, off Piazza Matteotti, daily. The city's market with a view, selling clothes and shoes.

## Entertainment, Events and Festivals in Perugia

The main Perugian evening occupation remains the *passeggiata* down Corso Vannucci, with a stop for a bite at Bar Ferrari (No.43), full of Perugia's famous chocolate *baci* and other confections, or a refreshing ice cream at the Gelateria Veneta (No.20), before loitering in Piazza IV Novembre. For live music in every possible shade, from jazz to traditional Turkish and tango, try Il Contrappunto, Via Scortici 4/a, t 075 573 3667 (Tues, Thurs and Sat).

Numerous outdoor performances, including concerts and films, cater to the large student population in summer. See the monthly *Viva Perugia: What Where When* for the latest happenings.

If you're travelling with children, note that Perugia has a large funfair plus Umbria's modest but sincerely meant answer to Disneyland, Città della Domenica, just west of the city (t 075 505 4941, *www. cittadelladomenica.com; open 10–7 daily April–Sept; Sat and Sun Oct–Mar; adm*), with a miniature Africa, serpentarium and bumper cars.

## Festivals

Umbria Jazz Festival, tickets from booth in Piazza della Repubblica, *www.umbriajazz.com*, July. An excellent event that has drawn such luminaries as Stan Getz and Wynton Marsalis.

Teatro in Piazza festival, July and Aug. Performances in the city's cloisters and squares.

Tenera è la notte, July–Sept. Music in and around the city.

Sagra Musicale Umbra, Sept. Sacred music in Perugia's churches.

Marcia della Pace, 2nd Sun in Oct. The march for peace, when thousands of Italians walk the 10km from Perugia to Assisi.

Eurochocolate Festival, *www. eurochocolate.com*, mid-Oct. Tastings, events, exhibits and courses on sweets and chocolate.

Fiera dei Morti, Pian di Massiano, 1st wk Nov. The oldest fair in central Italy.

# Where to Stay in and around Perugia

## Perugia ✉ 06100

The tourist office can provide you with a list of nearby rooms to rent, B&Bs and *agriturismi*.

### Luxury (€€€€€)

*****Brufani Palace, Piazza Italia 12, t 075 573 2541, *www.brufanipalace. com*. A renovated, traditional 19th-century hotel which has recently doubled in size to provide some 80 rooms. There are fine views over the countryside, luxurious fittings, air conditioning, an attractive central courtyard and a private garage.

****Alla Posta dei Donini, Via Deruta 43, San Martino in Campo, t 075 609132, *www.postadonini.it*. Just outside Perugia, this 17th-century villa has stylishly furnished rooms, faultless service and a glorious pool. Look out for special offers to coincide with events such as Umbria Jazz.

### Very Expensive (€€€€)

****Giò Arte e Vini, Via R. d'Andreotto 19, t 075 573 1100, *www.hotelgio.it*. A memorable hotel dedicated to the art of wine-drinking, a short drive out of town. Each room has rustic Umbrian furniture, including a display case filled with bottles of wine; guests are encouraged to taste them and buy from the amply stocked cellars on departure. In the restaurant the sommelier chooses three wines each evening; for a surprisingly modest fee, diners can quaff to their heart's content. Dishes include tripe with potatoes, and wild boar with spelt polenta.

****Hotel Perusia e La Villa, Via Egubina 42bis, t 075 573 0973, *www.hotelperusia.it*. A stone's throw from the centre, this is a modern hotel with spacious rooms and a pool. The roof garden has terrific views and breakfast is served in a Renaissance villa opposite.

****Locanda della Posta, Corso Vannucci 97, t 075 572 8925, *www. locandadellaposta.com, novelbet@ tin.it*. An old place that once played host to Goethe, centrally located, with an ornate exterior, pleasant, renovated rooms and a garage.

****Perugia Plaza, Via Palermo 88, t 075 34643, *www.umbriahotels.com*. A large, prestigious hotel in greenery at the foot of the city, with a pool, sauna and fitness centre. Breakfast is included, and there's an excellent restaurant (€€) with very reasonable fixed-price menus. *Closed Mon*.

****La Rosetta**, Piazza Italia 19, t 075 572 0841, *www.perugiaonline. com/larosetta*. A deservedly popular option with cosy, quiet rooms from different periods (all with Internet access), a garden and a celebrated restaurant (€€€).

**Expensive (€€€)**
***Fortuna**, Via Bonazzi 19, just off Corso Vannucci, t 075 572 2845, *www.umbriahotels.com*. This has a good location just off Corso Vannucci, and more comfort than charm; all rooms have bath and TV, and there's a garage.

**Moderate (€€)**
**Priori**, Via dei Priori 40, t 075 572 3378, *www.hotelpriori.it*. A refurbished building in the historic centre, plus a suite in a 15th-century palace nearby. A buffet breakfast is included in the room rates.

**Inexpensive (€)**
**Aurora**, Viale Indipendenza 21, t 075 572 4819, *www.hotel-albergoaurora.eu*, *albergoaurorapg@virgilio.it*. Conveniently situated only a minute's walk from Piazza Italia, on the main road up from the station. Rooms are rather spartan, but comfortable enough for a short stay, the service is friendly and prices are reasonable.

**Centro Internazionale Accoglienza per la Gioventù**, Via Bontempi 13, t 075 572 2880, *www.ostello.perugia.it*. A hostel by the Duomo, with bunks. You don't need a youth hostel card. It's cash only. *Closed 15 Dec–15 Jan.*

**Sant'Ercolano**, Via del Bovaro 9, t 075 572 4650, *www.santercolano.com*. Tidy en-suite rooms in a quiet 17th-century building in the *centro storico*. Its friendly owners know the city well. Guests get a 10% discount at the nearby Iris restaurant.

★ Antica
Trattoria San
Lorenzo >>

## Cenerente ✉ 06070
****Castello dell'Oscano**, 9km northwest of Perugia, t 075 584371, *www.oscano.com* (€€€€€). A Neo-Renaissance establishment with antique-furnished rooms, a pool in a large park, and two restaurants. They also offer wine-tasting and cookery courses.

## Bosco ✉ 06080
****Relais San Clemente**, Passo dell'Acqua, Loc. Bosco, 10km east on road to Gubbio, t 075 591 5100, *www.relais.it* (€€€€). A 14th-century Benedictine abbey with lovely grounds, a pool, tennis and volleyball courts, luxurious, stylish rooms and a very good restaurant. Breakfast is included; half/full board available.

## Torgiano ✉ 06089
*****Le Tre Vaselle**, Corso Garibaldi 48, t 075 988 0447, *www.3vaselle.it* (€€€€€). Winner of 'Best Luxury Country Hotel' in the 2008 World Luxury Hotel Awards. Housed in an old *palazzo* and neighbouring houses, on the edge of Torgiano (*see* p.104), surrounded by vineyards and olive groves, it offers a pool, a sauna, a fitness suite... the list goes on. The restaurant, **Le Melograne** (€€€€), is among the top in Umbria, serving local fare with a creative twist.

# Eating Out in Perugia

## Perugia ✉ 06100
Some of the best restaurants are in the hotels listed in the previous section; try Perugia Plaza, La Rosetta and especially Giò Arte e Vini.

**Expensive (€€€)**
**Antica Trattoria San Lorenzo**, Piazza Danti 19a, t 075 572 1956. An elegant place in the centre, serving traditional fare with a creative spark: *maltagliati* with rabbit *alla cacciatore*, *pappa al pomodoro* with cod and cauliflower, and more. There's live jazz some evenings. Book ahead. *Closed Sun.*

**Il Falchetto**, Via Bartolo 20, t 075 573 1775. Umbrian specialities served in a medieval atmosphere near the cathedral, including homemade pasta with spinach and ricotta, risotto with *porcini*, prawns with brandy, and veal fondue. *Closed Mon and 15–30 Jan.*

**Osteria del Gambero**, Via Baldeschi 17, t 075 573 5461. A quattrocento *palazzo* offering good variations on Umbrian themes, including *porcini* soup and duck with vegetables and broad bean sauce. *Eves only, closed Sun, and part of Jan and June.*

**Osteria del Gufo**, Via della Viola 18, right by San Fiorenzo, t 075 573 4126. A seasonal menu that never lacks flair. Try *maltagliati* in a vegetable sauce, plus some ethnic dishes such as couscous, in a garden in summer. *Closed Sun, Mon, lunch and Aug.*

**Il Paiolo**, Via Angusta 11, t 075 572 5611. A Renaissance *palazzo* with good-value, tasty food, such as *taglierini* with smoked salmon, homemade *ravioloni* with *porcini*, and pork chop in apple vinegar. Pizzas are the real forte, though – try *del paiolo*, with truffles. *Closed Wed, and 1st half Aug.*

### Moderate (€€)

**La Bocca Mia**, Via V. Rocchi 36, t 075 572 3873. A place near the Etruscan Arch, with a reputation for desserts, not usually an Umbrian forte – the *pannacotta* and plumcake are especially good. Beforehand, try homemade *strangozzi* with truffles, spelt soup, or roast pork. *Closed Sun, Mon lunch, and 1–25 Aug.*

**Da Cesarino**, Piazza IV Novembre 4/5, t 075 572 8974. An old favourite serving reliable homemade pasta, traditional meat dishes and pizzas. *Closed Wed and Jan.*

⭐ **Del Borgo** >

**Del Borgo**, Via della Sposa 23/27, t 075 572 0390. A picturesque *trattoria* and *norcineria* (charcuterie specialist) with an exquisite array of *salumi* served with *torta al testo*. *Closed lunch.*

**Porta del Sole**, Via delle Prome 11 (extension of Via del Sole), t 075 572 0938. Good Neapolitan-style pizzas, served in a garden in warmer months. *Closed Mon and lunch.*

**La Taverna**, Via delle Streghe 8, t 075 572 4128. Just off the main drag of Corso Vannucci, this *trattoria* is a favourite with the locals. Its specialities include dried meats and a good range of classic pasta dishes.

### Inexpensive (€)

**Il Cantinone**, Via Ritorta 6, just left of cathedral, t 075 573 4430. Simple fare such as *spaghetti all'amatriciana*, beans and sausage, plus good *secondi* with meat, including *filetto tartufato* – fillet steak with a black truffle sauce. *Closed Tues.*

**Ceccarani**, Piazza Matteotti 16, t 075 572 1960. Well worth knowing if you fancy a feast *al fresco*. This bakery boasts a wonderful array of Perugia's best bread, baked in some 30 different ways. You'll be spoilt for choice for your picnic.

**Sandri**, Corso Vannucci, t 075 572 4112. One of the prettiest pastry shops in the whole of Italy, with a frescoed ceiling and divinely artistic confections; their window is always ablaze with colour, set to rival even the pinacoteca across the street. *Closed Mon.*

# Around Perugia: Torgiano, Deruta and Corciano

## Torgiano

Traditionally under Perugia's influence, Torgiano, situated 15km south of the capital, is practically synonymous with wine and the Lungarotti family; from the late 1970s, Dr Giorgio Lungarotti has made this minute DOC-growing area internationally famous. If Orvieto still rules the roost in Umbria's white wine league, Rubesco di Torgiano wins in the reds. The Lungarotti foundation runs an excellent **wine museum**, in the cellars of the 17th-century Palazzo Baglioni. Displays labelled in English as well as Italian trace the history of wine, techniques, rules and regulations; it also has a history of wine jars and vessels, a beautiful display of majolica,

**Museo del Vino**
*Corso Vittorio Emanuele;*
*t 075 988 0200,*
*www.lungarotti.it;*
*open daily 9–1 and 3–7; cantina by appt on t 075 988661; adm*

from Deruta, Faenza and Montelupo, and a wine library, with books going back to the Renaissance.

For accommodation in Torgiano, *see* p.103.

## Deruta

 Deruta

If there's room in your suitcase, buy a plate in the tiny hill town of Deruta (population 7,500), 5km south of Torgiano. Along with Gubbio, Deruta has been Umbria's centre for ceramics and majolica since the 13th century, and still has 200 ceramic workshops. Its location, on the fringe of Perugia's *contado*, brought it some hard knocks from Perugia's enemies over the centuries. During the height of its fame in the 1500s, Deruta was sacked twice, by Cesare Borgia and Braccio Baglioni, but it picked itself up and carried on making ceramics.

There are dozens of ceramics shops, particularly in the lower part of town. One of the biggest is **Maioliche Sberna**, where you can watch ceramics being made and painted in the workshop, or try **Ubaldo Grazia**, which has been in the same hands for 25 generations and is said to be the 13th oldest company in the world. Admire works of past artisans in the **Museo Regionale della Ceramica**, in a former convent; there are examples from Deruta's golden age in the early 1500s, church floor tiles, devotional plaques and a majolica font.

In Piazza dei Consoli (note the miniature copy of Perugia's Fontana Maggiore, minus the reliefs), the 14th-century **church of San Francesco** has patches of Sienese and Umbrian frescoes, while the medieval Palazzo Comunale holds the **Pinacoteca**, with paintings and a gonfalon by Nicolò Alunno, painted on both sides. There's also a detached fresco by Fiorenzo di Lorenzo, one of his best works, of the Plague Saints Rocco and Romano standing over Deruta (1478).

Another church, **Sant'Antonio Abate**, has a fresco by Bartolomeo Caporali of the All-Protecting Virgin, who also features in the **Madonna dei Bagni**, 3km south along the SS3bis in Frazione Casalina. This is full of quaint ceramic votive plaques made in the 17th and 18th centuries, showing pratfalls, sinking ships and exorcisms, all with happy endings thanks to the Madonna.

Closer to Perugia, to the west of the Tiber, a country chapel outside **San Martino in Colle** has a fresco of the Madonna and Child, restored and attributed to Pinturicchio.

## Corciano: Town of Cashmere

On its hill midway to Lake Trasimeno, pretty Corciano is protected by a nearly intact castle and 13th-century walls. Controlled by Perugia into the 15th century, it has small-scale versions of all the essential buildings of a *comune*, neatly labelled with ceramic

**Maioliche Sberna**
*t 075 971206;
call for opening hrs*

**Ubaldo Grazia**
*Via Tiberina 181,
t 075 971 0201,
www.ubaldograzia.it*

**Museo Regionale
della Ceramica**
*Largo San Francesco;
t 075 971 1000,
www.museoceramica
deruta.it; open
April–Sept daily 10–1
and 3.30–7;
Oct–Mar Wed–Mon
10–1 and 3.30–7; joint
adm with Pinacoteca*

**Pinacoteca**
*t 075 971 1000; open
Sat and Sun 10–1 and
3.30–7; joint adm with
Museo della Ceramica*

**Madonna
dei Bagni**
*t 075 973455;
open by appt*

plaques, which gives it a slight museumish air. To visit the small museums here, call the **Comune di Corciano** several days ahead.

**Comune
di Corciano**
*t 075 518 8254/5*

There's a convenient car park outside the walls near the pink-and-white striped **San Francesco**, which was founded after St Francis' visit in 1211 (the Corcianese got a headstart on his church, sure he was going to be canonized). Perugino left one of his finest late works, the *Assumption* altarpiece (1513) in 13th-century **Santa Maria**; it also has one of Bonfigli's strange gonfalons, dedicated to the Madonna della Misericordia, here defending Corciano from outrageous fortune. These days, Corciano and nearby Solomeo are famous for their numerous cashmere factory outlets.

**Pieve del Vescovo**
*t 075 505 8611; open
for pre-booked visits
last Fri of month*

The big castle just north of Corciano at **Pieve del Vescovo** was restored in the late 1500s by Galeazzo Alessi, as a residence. There's an even more impressive work by the same architect just north of the main road: the **Villa del Cardinale**, built for Cardinal Fulvio Della Corgna, now owned by the state (there are plans to open it to the public). It has a very imposing gate and a lovely Renaissance garden.

Corciano is best known, these days, for its **cashmere factory** outlets. One of the most famous designers, Brunello Cucinelli, has a boutique in Solomeo near Corciano, a village he is slowly restoring.

## Lake Trasimeno

**ⓘ Lago
Trasimeno**

The fourth largest lake in Italy, Trasimeno (45km in circumference) has a subtle charm. Sleepy, placid and shallow, almost marshy in places, and large enough to create its own soft microclimate, it shimmers like a mirror embedded in gentle rolling hills covered with olives and vineyards. The Etruscans of *Camars* (Chiusi) coveted the lake for its fish and the fertility of its shores, and around the time of their famous king Lars Porsena, the bad guy in Macaulay's *Horatio at the Bridge*, they founded Perugia to control it. In the 12th and 13th century, wars were fought for its eels. Napoleon took one look at it and wondered how to drain it.

Hans Christian Andersen, drawing on his own travels, put Trasimeno in one of his fairytales, *The Galoshes of Fortune* – how beautiful it was, but how poor the people were (in the 1830s), and how wretched their lives were among the swarms of biting flies, mosquitoes and malaria. A post-war dose of American DDT wiped out the latter, and the lake has since become a modest resort – the Umbrian Riviera.

Never one to fully cooperate with humanity, Trasimeno, once prone to flooding, is now doing its best to become a peat bog. A few fishermen skim over its waters, seeking eels, tench, shad and carp. Ducks, cormorants and kingfishers love it, and waterlilies float among the reeds. And, as the tourist office reminds visitors,

# Getting to and around Lake Trasimeno

Lake Trasimeno lies 37km south of Arezzo, 13km south of Cortona, 69km east of Siena, and 30km west of Perugia. By **car**, you can approach it along the A1 from the north; take the Val di Chiana exit for the spur of the *autostrada* that skirts the northern shore en route to Perugia. Coming from the south, taking the Chiusi exit off the A1 will bring you out near the SS71 to Castiglione del Lago.

Perugia is the main **bus** terminus for the area; connections from Cortona and Siena are less frequent. A fairly frequent bus service runs around the north shore (Tuoro–Passignano–Magione–San Feliciano–San Savino–Perugia) and around the southern shore (Perugia–Magione–San Arcangelo–Panicarola–Macchie–Castiglione del Lago). Contact APM buses (**t** 075 506781, freephone **t** 800 512141, *www.apmperugia.it*).

**Train** travel can be a bit awkward: Castiglione del Lago is a stop on the main Florence–Rome line but not for fast trains (*Intercity* and *Eurostar*), so check before setting out. Florence–Perugia *Regionale* trains and Rome–Perugia *Interregionale* and *ES* trains also pass through. On the main Florence–Rome line, you can change at Terontola for Perugia and the north-shore towns of Tuoro sul Trasimeno and Passignano; coming from Siena, change at Chiusi for Castiglione.

You can hire **bikes** in Castiglione from Marinelli, Via B. Buozzi 26, **t** 075 953126, *mfstefano@libero.it*, in Passignano from Eta Beta Modelismo, Via della Vittoria 58, **t** 075 829401, or in Tuoro from Balneazione Tuoro, Loc. Punta Navaccio, **t** 334 979 4208 (mobile), April–Sept, or from Marzano, Via Console Flaminio 59, **t** 075 826269.

Castiglione, Tuoro and Passignano, the lake's ports, are linked by **boat** to one another as well as to Isola Maggiore and Isola Polvese. Connections are frequent in summer but only once or twice daily in winter; for times, call **t** 075 827157 or ask at tourist offices (*see* pp.112 and 113).

some 20 percent of the world's artistic heritage listed by UNESCO lies within two hours of its quiet shores.

## Magione and Trasimeno's East Shore

From Perugia it's 30km to Trasimeno; snub the *autostrada* to visit **Magione**, a little industrial centre known for its copper- and brassware. Like any place within Perugia's radius, it spent much of the Middle Ages fighting: there's a ruined 13th-century **Torre dei Lombardi**, and on the edge a striking **Castello dei Cavalieri di Malta** of 1420, built by Bolognese architect Fieravante Fieravanti and still owned by the Knights of Malta, now based in Rome. The knights had inherited an 11th-century Templar hospital here, of which a few traces remain. Their church, **San Giovanni**, was damaged in the last war, and rebuilt and frescoed in a traditional manner by Perugian futurist Gherardo Dottori in 1947. On the main road, the little 13th-century **church of the Madonna delle Grazie** has a lovely fresco, *The Madonna Enthroned*, by Andrea di Giovanni da Orvieto.

Long before the knights, this was the birthplace of missionary Fra Giovanni di Pian di Carpine ('of the hornbeam plain', as the area under Magione was known), sent in 1245 by Innocent IV to convert the Mongols; though his preaching failed to make an impact, he returned from Karakorum after 20 years and wrote the *Historia Mongolorum*, the first eyewitness account of China and the Far East, which was much studied by later missionaries and Marco Polo. Some scholars suspect the Venetian merchant never visited Kubla Khan but cribbed much of his *Travels* from Fra Giovanni. Needless to say, this doesn't go down well in Venice.

**Castello dei Cavalieri di Malta**
*t 075 843547; open in summer for guided tours (call for times)*

07 Perugia, Lake Trasimeno, Assisi | Lake Trasimeno

Three of Trasimeno's prettiest beaches are between Magione's lakeside *frazioni*. One of these *frazioni*, **Montecolognola**, high on a hill blanketed with olives, has another castle built in the late 13th century by the beleaguered residents of Magione, and lovely views over the lake. Montecolognola's parish church has 14th- to 16th-century frescoes, another of 1947 by Gherardo Dottori and a pretty majolica altarpiece made in Deruta.

Further south are picturesque **Monte del Lago**, near the impressive but ruined **Castello di Zocco** (1400) with its five towers and **San Feliciano**. The latter village is home to the fascinating little

**Museo della Pesca**

t 075 847 9261,
museodellapesca@
tiscali.it; open Feb–Oct
daily 10.30–1
and 4–7; adm

**Museo della Pesca**, dedicated to the lake's fishermen, and enjoys magical sunsets over the water and **Isola Polvese**, the largest of Trasimeno's three islands, reached in summer by boats from San Feliciano. The large village that stood on Polvese was abandoned in the 17th century because of malaria; today, only the 14th-century castle and an older monastery still stand. Now owned by the province, Polvese has olive groves, lush vegetation and hundreds of nesting birds; a path encircles it and takes about an hour to walk, and there's a little beach and summer snack bar.

**Oasi la Valle**

t 075 847 6007,
www.oasilavalle.
provincia.perugia.it;
open June–Sept daily
9–1 and 4–8; Oct–May
Tues–Sun 9–1 and 3–6;
guided tours for min.
6 people by advance
booking; adm

South of San Feliciano, the **Oasi la Valle**, run by an environmental group, is the most important bird-watching area on Trasimeno, hosting an impressive number of migratory visitors, especially in spring. It's here that the Romans dug a 7km underground emissary to drain the lake when levels reached the flood stage, diverting it through streams and into the Tiber; a second emissary was built in 1423 by Braccio Fortebraccio. Leonardo da Vinci, who visited in 1503, suggested diverting its flow into the Tiber, Arno and Chiana. As the shore grew swampier, his proposal received serious consideration, until yet another emissary was dug here in 1896. You can walk along it, and a museum on the site tells the whole soggy story.

## The North Shore: Castel Rigone, Passignano and Isola Maggiore

To the north of Magione, a road ascends to **Castel Rigone**, a dramatically poised fortress hill town that was founded in 543 by Rigone, lieutenant of Totila the Goth. It has spectacular views over the lake and a delightful Renaissance church, the restored **Madonna dei Miracoli**, which was built in 1494 by Perugia as a votive for the Virgin who spared the city from a plague. In the form of a Latin cross, it has a doorway with a relief by a student of Michelangelo, Domenico Bertini da Settignano (who, like most Renaissance artists, had a nickname – Topolino or 'Mousey' – the same as the Italian for Mickey Mouse). It has a fine interior and a gilded high altar by Bernardino di Lazzaro, a chapel with *ex votos* dedicated to the miraculous Madonna, and a sweet statue of St Anthony Abbot and his pet pig.

The lake's busiest resort, **Passignano sul Trasimeno** is on its own promontory midway between Perugia and Cortona. In the 1930s this was the HQ of the Società Aeronautica Italiana, which made zippy seaplanes and boats, until it was bombed in the war. Within Passignano's walls is an attractive old quarter around the 14th-century castle; below lies a beach with windsurf hire. Near the cemetery, the **Pieve di San Cristoforo** dating from the 11th century has restored frescoes from the 1300s; 1.5km northeast, the **Madonna dell'Olivo** is an elegant Renaissance church with a beautiful high altar and a fresco attributed to Bartolomeo Caporali. The town is at its liveliest for the **Palio delle Barche** on the third Sunday of July, when young Passignanesi dressed in medieval costume carry their boats shoulder-high through the streets and launch them on to the lake for a race.

Passignano is the nearest port to **Isola Maggiore** (20mins), Trasimeno's second-largest island, with a charming 15th-century village inhabited by fishermen and women famous for lace-making. In 1211, St Francis came to the then-deserted island to spend Lent alone. He made a lasting impression by throwing back a pike a fisherman had given him, only to be followed doggedly across the lake by his grateful 'Brother Fish' until the saint blessed him. Francis took only two loaves of bread to sustain himself, and when the fisherman returned to the island to pick him up, he was amazed to see that only one loaf had been half eaten in 40 days.

A footpath encircles the island, passing the Franciscan convent, built to commemorate the saint's visit and converted in the late 19th century into a neogothic folly by Senator Giacinto Guglielmi from Rome, now crumbling gently into a romantic ruin (a village custodian shows people round). The 13th-century **church of San Michele Arcangelo** has frescoes and an excellent *Crucifixion* by Bartolomeo Caporali (*c.* 1460).

## Tuoro sul Trasimeno

West of Passignano, Tuoro sul Trasimeno grew up in the late Middle Ages near the **Castello di Montegualandro**, a haven for citizens while their town was attacked by every army crossing the Italian peninsula or heading south to Rome. Visit the battlefield by car or foot, along the signposted **Percorso Storico Archeologico della Battaglia**, dotted with viewing platforms; along the way explanatory notes and maps help bring the Roman disaster to life. Near the first platform, note the pretty portal of the Romanesque **Pieve di Confini**. Tuoro has decorated its lake shore with Pietro Cascella's **Campo del Sole** (1985–9), a contemporary 'solar temple' garden of 27 pillars in locally quarried sandstone, each about 3.6m high and sculpted by a different artist, arranged in a wide spiral like a forest of idols to a preposterous god.

### The Battle of Trasimeno

Tuoro's first battle was the worst. Two years into the Second Punic War, Hannibal was on a winning streak, having defeated the Romans on the rivers Ticino and Trebbia – victories that had rallied the local Gaulish and Ligurian tribes to his banner. As it made its way south towards Rome, this swollen army got bogged down in the disease-ridden marshland of the Arno, at the cost of thousands of troops and all the exasperated elephants who had survived the march over the Pyrenees and Alps. Meanwhile, the Roman Senate sent Consul Gaius Flaminius, a bold populist politician (builder of the Via Flaminia), and an army of 25,000 to destroy the Carthaginians once and for all. With Flaminius in pursuit through the Valdichiana, Hannibal led his army, reduced to 40,000, to Trasimeno. Finding a perfect place for an ambush just west of Tuoro, in a natural amphitheatre closed off by the lake (the water level was considerably higher then), he arranged his troops in the hills, determined to risk all to defeat the Romans and convince the restive Etruscan cities to join him.

Believing Hannibal was at least a day's march in front, Flaminius failed to send scouts ahead; the morning of 24 June 217 BC was foggy and, according to chroniclers, he ignored a number of auguries pointed out by his Etruscan soothsayers. He marched straight into Hannibal's trap, along the narrow shore passage at Malpasso. In a panic, unable to get into battle formations, 15,000–16,000 legionaries (including Flaminius) were drowned or slaughtered within hours; those who got away found a safe haven in Perugia. The blood of the dead, which legend says ran in a river for three days, is recalled in the name of the hamlet Sanguineto, their whitened bones in the hamlet of Ossaia (from *ossa*, bones). Hannibal slew all the Roman prisoners but freed the various Italic tribes, hoping to gather support.

After Trasimeno, the Roman military machine grimly threw even more legions to their death against Hannibal at Cannae, before changing strategy and giving the Carthaginians the run of southern Italy for 15 years, harassing Hannibal while refusing to fight him before ultimately defeating him in Africa. The long-term effects of the war are felt to this day: as small farmers fled, they lost their income and had to sell their land to pay their debts. Snapped up cheap by a few rich men, it marked the beginning of the feudal *latifondo* system that condemned the once prosperous south of Italy to grinding poverty.

**La Dogana** near here was the Customs House between the Papal States and the Grand Duchy of Tuscany, and has plaques to the famous folk who passed this way.

## Castiglione del Lago

Among the silvery olive groves that soften the west shore juts the picturesque promontory of Castiglione del Lago (population 13,500), setting for the lake's biggest town, a cheerful, mostly modern place dating back to the Etruscans. Emperor Frederick II destroyed it for being an ally of Guelph Perugia, then ordered Fra Elia Coppi to lay out a new town, neatly in six streets, served by three gates and three squares. Afterwards, it kept siding with Cortona, causing no end of friction with Perugia until 1490, when it came once and for all under the Baglioni family, who in their brief period of glory hosted here such luminaries as Machiavelli and Leonardo da Vinci. Eventually the town was recovered by the popes; one, Julius III, gave it to his sister. In 1550, her son, celebrated *condottiere* Ascanio della Corgna and husband of Giovanna Baglioni, became the first in a series of dukes to rule the lake as an independent duchy, until 1648, when it passed into the Grand Duchy of Tuscany before returning to the popes the next century.

**Palazzo Ducale**
*t 075 951099; open
21 Mar–April daily
9.30–1 and 3.30–7; May
and June daily 10–1 and
4–7.30; July and Aug
daily 10–1.30 and
4.30–8; Sept and Oct
daily 10–1.30 and
3.30–7; Nov–20 Mar
Sat, Sun and hols
9.30–4.30; adm*

During Castiglione's ruritanian interlude, the great architect Vignola designed the ducal Palazzo della Corgna or **Palazzo Ducale**. Many rooms retain their fetching late Renaissance frescoes by Niccolò Pomarancio and the Roman school; one scene shows the battle of Trasimeno, another the battle of Lepanto, in which Ascanio distinguished himself. Like the great *condottiere* Federico da Montefeltro (*see* p.149), Ascanio was something of a humanist and so had his study decorated with frescoes on the Life of Caesar. From the palace, a covered walkway, fortified in case of surprise attack, allowed direct access to the mightiest of all the castles on the lake, the pentagonal Rocca del Leone designed in 1247 by Friar Elia Coppi with a sturdy triangular keep and four outer towers.

Also worth seeing, in the 19th-century **church of the Maddalena**, is a lovely painting, *The Madonna and Child with SS. Anthony Abbot and Mary Magdalene* (1500), by Eusebio da San Giorgio.

## The South Shore

**Strada del Vino**
*for details and a list
of wineries contact:
Associazione Strada
del Vino, Colli del
Trasimeno,
c/o Comunità Montana,
Via Sante Alighierri 2,
06063 Magióne;
t 075 847 411,
www.montitrasimeno.it*

Much of this shore is patterned by vines producing the grapes that go into Colli del Trasimeno, a local DOC wine and there's a **Strada del Vino**, literally a wine route, which takes you through some of the best vineyards with tastings en route.

In **Panicarola**, the most famous producer was Ferruccio Lamborghini, who declared an ambitious intention to make wines as fine as his sports cars – his father had been a farmer, and the first motors young Ferruccio built were for his tractors. He died in 1993, before quite succeeding, but you can still buy a Lamborghini to call your own.

## Tourist Information around Lake Trasimeno

Ask at Castiglione del Lago tourist office about **joint tickets** to the main attractions of Castiglione del Lago, Città della Pieve and Isola Maggiore.

In addition to Castiglione del Lago and Tuoro, there are **summer tourist offices** at Isola Maggiore, Magione, Rossignano and San Feliciano.

**Market Day**
Weds, Castiglione del Lago.

## Activities

**Sailing**: Club Velistico, Viale Brigata Garibaldi 3a, Castiglione del Lago, t 075 953035; and Loc. Darsena, Passignano, t 075 829 6021.

**Waterskiing**: Scuola Federale Sci Nautica, Punta Navaccia, Via Navaccia 4, Tuoro sul Trasimeno, t 075 826357. (*closed Nov–Feb*).

Sci Club Trasimeno, Castiglione del Lago, t 075 965 2836.

## Where to Stay and Eat around Lake Trasimeno

Not many Italians think of Trasimeno as a beach resort: the shallow water is warm and muddy. There are several modest holiday hotels around Castiglione, Passignano and Magione, and plenty of *agriturismi* (the local tourist offices can send you complete lists).

Medieval Perugians were so fond of fish from Trasimeno that Nicola

Pisano jokingly sculpted some on his famous fountain in front of their cathedral. Today, the catch isn't really big enough to send far outside the lake area, and it tastes pretty muddy, but you can try some at the unpretentious restaurants by the lake.

## Montesperello di Magione ✉ 06063

(★) Relais Il Cantico della Natura >

Relais Il Cantico della Natura, t 075 841699, www.ilcanticodellanatura.it (€€€). A 42-hectare organic agriturismo in an ancient olive grove, with orchards and woods with lake views. Rooms have canopy beds. Walk, mountain bike or ride horses over the hills, swim in the pool, and enjoy hearty meals.

## Isola Maggiore ✉ 06060

(★) Da Sauro >

***Da Sauro, Via Guglielmi, t 075 826168, www.hoteldasauro.it (€€). The best place in Umbria to get away from it all, gracious and uncomplicated, with basic but comfortable rooms. The island's only hotel, it has a private beach on the lake and a beautiful garden. The brilliant restaurant (€€) specializes in fish from the lake: eels, carp and more, along with traditional Umbrian dishes. Breakfast is included, and half and full board are available.

(i) Tuoro sul Trasimeno >

*Pro Loco, Via Ritorta 1, t 075 825220, www.proloco tuorosultrasimeno.it*

(★) I Capricci di Merion >

## Tuoro sul Trasimeno ✉ 06069

I Capricci di Merion, Via Pozzo 21, t 075 825 002, www.capriccidimerion.it (€), A few delightful antiques-filled rooms in a Liberty-style palazzo built for harp-playing Lady Merion by her lover. Surrounded by vines and olive trees, the saltwater pool has a double hydro-massage. The restaurant is excellent.

## San Feliciano ✉ 06060

*Da Settimio, Via Lungalago Alicato 1, 7km south of Magione, t 075 847 6000, dasettimio@tiscali.it (€€). Peaceful en-suite rooms and a simple restaurant in a lakeside hamlet.
**Montalcino**, Loc. Montalcino, San Feliciano, t 335 625 7939 (€€–€). This stone-built restaurant in the hamlet of Montacino, just outside San Feliciano, has views of the lake and a rich menu of traditional dishes from ingredients produced by the owners.

In June and Sept, a dinner buffet is served including starters, pasta, main course and dessert for a bargain price, but you must book in advance.
**Rosso di Sera**, Via Fratelli Papini 81, t 075 847 6277 (€€). An osteria serving delicious lake fish and land dishes. Try the seasonal soups, bollito and mustard, rock bass, pigeon with leek cake, and eels. Closed Tues, lunch exc Sun, and 20 days in Jan.

## Castel Rigone ✉ 06060

****Relais La Fattoria, Via Rigone 1, t 075 845322, www.relaislafattoria.com (€€€€). Pretty 1600s farm buildings with a pool, luxury rooms and a restaurant serving good filetto di persico (perch) and spaghetti al sugo di Trasimeno (with a sauce of mixed lake fish); half and full board are available. There is horse-riding and golf nearby. Restaurant closed 3wks Jan.
**L'Acquario**, Via Vittorio Emanuele 69, t 075 965 2432, www. castiglionedellago.it/acquario (€€). A classy place featuring pike, carp, eel and tench in imaginative ways, plus good meat dishes – the fat home-made pici with goose is excellent.

## Passignano sul Trasimeno ✉ 06065

***Villa Paradiso, Via Fratelli Rosselli 5, t 075 829191, www.bluhotels.it (€€€€). A large, comfortable option with a rustic feel, boating a pool, a kids' area and a restaurant.
***Lido, Via Roma 1, t 075 827219, www.umbriahotels.com (€€€). Well-equipped rooms on the water, a pool with hydromassage, a solarium, a garden, and a restaurant on a terrace with a lake view, specializing in fish (half board is available). Breakfast is included, and there's a minimum 3-night stay. Closed Nov–Feb.
*Del Pescatore, Via San Bernadino 5, t 075 829 6063, www.delpescatore.com (€€). Holiday apartments refurbished in 2006, furnished in a country style, with iron beds. The attractive trattoria serves lake fish and more; try eel with green beans, and roast carp. Closed Tues.
*Florida, Via 2 Giugno 2, t 075 827228 (€). Good simple en-suite rooms and a welcoming atmosphere.

**Da Luciano**, Via Lungolago 3, t 075 827210 (€€). A lakeside restaurant serving fish for more than 40 years. Booking is strongly advised. *Closed Wed and 3wks Jan.*

**Il Fischio del Merlo**, San Donato 17a, t 075 829283 (€€). Creative cuisine based on seafish and Chianina beef served up in a lovely rustic room. Booking is advisable. *Closed Tues and 3wks Nov.*

(i) **Castiglione del Lago >**
*Piazza Mazzini 10, t 075 965 2484, www.lagotrasimeno.net*

**Castiglione del Lago** ✉ 06061

**\*\*\*Duca della Corgna**, Via Buozzi 143, t 075 953238, www.hotelcorgna.com (€€). A comfy, relaxing option in a wood, with en-suite rooms and a pool. There's a summer restaurant (with half board).

**\*\*\*Miralago**, Piazza Mazzini 5, t 075 951157, www.hotelmiralago.com (€€). A small, basic but comfortable choice with pretty lake views. Half board is available. *Closed Jan and Feb.*

**\*\*\*Trasimeno**, Via Roma 174, t 075 965 2494, www.hotel-trasimeno.it (€€). Basic rooms, a pool, and a fish restaurant.

**La Cantina**, Via Vittorio Emanuele 69, t 075 965 2463 (€€). Smoked eel, carp wrapped in *porchetta* (a typical local dish) and pizzas. Local products are sold. *Closed Mon in winter.*

**Monna Lisa**, Via del Forte 2, t 075 951071 (€€). Specializes in re-creating fish and meat dishes from ancient times, including those from *cucina povera*, the peasant cuisine on which much Umbrian cooking is based.

# South of Lake Trasimeno

These hills and their towns are known for their magical views over Lake Trasimeno and their souvenirs of Perugino, who made this loveliness part of his artistic vocabulary. Italian writers have often commented that Città della Pieve looks more Sienese than Umbrian – the Tuscan border and interesting towns such as Chiusi and Montepulciano are only a few kilometres away.

⭐ **Città della Pieve**

### Città della Pieve

From Castiglione del Lago, it's 27km to handsome red-brick Città della Pieve (population 6,500). Etruscans and Romans were here; in the Middle Ages it became *Castrum Plebis*, then *Castel della Pieve*. Perugia considered it within the western borders of its turf and in the 1320s built the square fortress to defend it. In 1503, Cesare Borgia sacked it, then, typically, had colleagues, the Duke of Gavina and Piero Orsini, strangled for conspiring against him. Later it was ruled by Ascanio della Corgna and his heirs until 1601, when the Church picked it up and Clement VIII made it a bishopric, changing its name to Città della Pieve.

But Città della Pieve is best known as the birthplace of **Perugino** (Pietro Vannucci, *c.* 1446–1523), who, to Vasari, committed the sin of not being born in Tuscany. If there is anything to the Vasari's *Lives of the Artists*, Perugino was perhaps the most bitter artist of the Renaissance. Born into a desperately poor family, he was transformed by success into an untrusting miser, riding from job to job with saddlebags full of money he was afraid to leave anywhere else. About midpoint in his career, he became an atheist, yet he cranked out two decades of richly rewarded, often vacuous,

Madonnas and religious scenes with lyrical soft-tinted Trasimeno backgrounds, before dying, unconfessed and unabsolved – very rare then – rejecting a future with the angels he depicted for others.

Perugino did leave several paintings in his home town, of which the greatest is a lovely fresco, *The Adoration of the Magi* (1504), painted for a charitable confraternity in the **Oratorio di Santa Maria dei Bianchi**, just within the walls. It portrays the birth of the Saviour in an Arcadian spring, with the view from Città della Pieve towards Lake Trasimeno in the background and an elegant Renaissance garden party – a world that seems hardly to need a redeemer. Two letters from Perugino on display show he demanded 200 florins for his work but settled for much less, partly as he was painting for his fellow citizens.

**Oratorio di Santa Maria dei Bianchi**
*open by appt on*
*t 057 829 9375*

Via Vannucci leads uphill to the cluster of monuments in Piazza Plebiscito. The undistinguished **Duomo** was built in the 1600s to replace the far older **SS. Gervasio e Protasio**, the *pieve* (parish church) that gave the town its name; 9th-century sculptural work is embedded in the façade. There are more works by Perugino, as well a crucifix attributed to Pietro Tacca. The second chapel has one of Domenico Alfani's finest works, the *Madonna and Child and Saints*.

**Duomo**
*open daily 9.30–7*

Standing next to the Duomo is the lofty **Torre del Pubblico**, built in the 12th century but heightened in 1471; in the same piazza are the trecento **Palazzo dei Priori** and **Palazzo della Corgna**, designed in 1551 by Perugian architect Galeazzo Alessi; inside are good 16th-century frescoes by Pomarancio and Salvio Savini and a little sandstone obelisk, brought here from the convent of San Francesco. Near the piazza is what locals claim is the narrowest lane in Italy, **Vicolo Bacciadonne** ('Kiss-the-Women Lane'; you're almost compelled to do so, to get past).

**Palazzo della Corgna**
*t 057 829 9375; open May–Sept daily 9.30–1 and 4–7.30; Oct–Apr Sat, Sun and hols 10–12.30 and 3.30–6; adm*

Just off Piazza Pretorio is the brick **Palazzo Bandini**, remodelled in the 16th century by Galeazzo Alessi; carry on to the Porta Romana and **Santa Maria dei Servi**, frescoed by Perugino with a famous *Deposition* of 1517, damaged when monks erected a *cantoria* in front. The Porta Romana is linked by walls to the Perugian **Rocca**, built by Ambrogio and Lorenzo Maitani in 1326. Opposite is 13th-century **San Francesco**, redone in the 18th century, now a popular shrine to Fatima. It has two good paintings, Domenico Alfani's *Virgin and Saints* and a *Pentecost* by Niccolò Pomarancio. Next door, the **Oratorio di San Bartolomeo** has a large fresco of the Crucifixion (1342) by Sienese painter Jacopo di Mino del Pellicciaio, surrounded by weeping angels – hence its nickname, *Pianto degli Angeli*.

**Santa Maria dei Servi**
*often locked; custodian at Santa Maria dei Bianchi has key*

**Oratorio di San Bartolomeo**
*open daily 10–12 and 4–7*

## Panicale and Around

**Panicale** is famous for its enchanting, and strategic, view over Trasimeno, which in the Middle Ages made it sought by Chiusi and Perugia; even so, in 1037, it became an independent *comune*, one of

Italy's first. In the 14th century it produced sweet early Renaissance master Tommaso Fini (or Masolino da Panicale), who painted with Masaccio in Florence; it also produced Giacomo Paneri, a fierce and brutal *condottiere* known as Boldrino di Panicale, who was briefly lord of the town. Another native, who tips the balance on the side of art, was the poet Cesare Caporali, born in 1530.

An old walled town built on a natural terrace 'in a spiral', Panicale has pretty squares. The asymmetrical Piazza Umberto I is home to a charming fountain of 1473 and the 14th-century **Palazzo Pretorio**, with peculiar carvings and coats of arms. Nearby is the late-18th-century stuccoed **Teatro Cesare Caporali**, restored in 1991. Further up, the handsome semi-fortified Baroque **Collegiata di San Michele** has an *Adoration of the Shepherds* by Gian Battista Caporali (1519).

Panicale's most important treasure is in **San Sebastiano**, just outside the walls. Here Perugino left one of his finest frescoes: a formal, dream-like *Martyrdom of St Sebastian* (1505), a geometrical composition with antique ornamentation, with four superbly costumed and codpieced archers powerfully poised to shoot the saint; in the background is a faithful rendition of Panicale's lovely lake view. The same church contains Perugino's *Madonna*, a detached fresco from the church of Sant'Agostino.

Just to the west of Panicale, **Paciano** is a well-preserved medieval village on a spur of Monte Petrarvella, wrapped in 14th-century walls, towers and gates. The **Confraternità del Santissimo Sacramento** has a fresco of the Crucifixion (1425) by the first reputed teacher of Perugino, Francesco di Castel della Pieve. Another church, **San Giuseppe**, keeps the communal gonfalon from the workshop of Benedetto Bonfigli (*c.* 1480). Outside the walls, the **Madonna della Stella** (1574) is a simple Renaissance church with frescoes by Scilla Pecennini.

Near the lignite-mining village of **Tavernelle**, just off the SS220, the tiny *frazione* of **Mongiovino Vecchio** has a well-preserved castle overlooking a stately domed Renaissance temple, the **Sanctuario di Mongiovino**. Begun in 1513, this is an early but characteristic shrine to Mary. With its fine octagonal cupola, it has been attributed to Michelangelo or Bramante; a more likely candidate is Rocco di Tommaso from Vicenza, who made the finely sculpted doorways. Inside are cinquecento frescoes by Niccolò Pomarancio and the Flemish painter Heinrich van den Broek (aka Arrigo Fiammingo).

Perugino died of the plague in nearby **Fontignano** in 1523; his tomb, and the fresco he was working on when he died, an almost primitive *Madonna and Child*, are in the **Annunziata**, the parish church, plus a photo of another fresco he made for the church, the *Adoration of the Shepherds*, now in the National Gallery in London.

## Side notes

**Teatro Cesare Caporali**
*tours of theatre and San Sebastiano by arrangement with tourist office (see p.116), t 075 837319*

**San Sebastiano**
*tours of church and Teatro Cesare Caporali by arrangement with tourist office (see p.116)*

**Confraternità del Santissimo Sacramento**
*t 075 830120; ask over road at No.12 to visit*

**Annunziata**
*ask at tourist office, t 075 600276, about guided tours*

ⓘ **Panicale »**
*Piazza Umberto I,*
*t 075 837 8017*

ⓘ **Città della Pieve ›**
*Piazza del Plebiscito 1,*
*t 057 829 9375,*
*www.prolocopieve.it*

## Shopping South of Lake Trasimeno

### Market Day

Sat, Città della Pieve.

## Where to Stay and Eat South of Lake Trasimeno

### Città della Pieve ✉ 06062

**\*\*\*Al Poggio dei Papi**, Loc. San Litardo, just outside town, t 057 829 7030, *www. alpoggiodeipapi.com* (€€). A comfy, modern hotel with a restaurant, an Olympic-size pool, a gym and a tennis courts. Rooms are rustically styled. Half and full board are available.

**Da Bruno**, Via Pietro Vannucci 90–92, t 057 829 8108 (€€). A restaurant serving good, unpretentious food. *Closed Mon.*

### Panicale ✉ 06064

**Vannucci**, Via Icilio Vanni 1, t 0578 298063, *www.hotel-vannucci.com* (€€€€). A revamped option, now quite luxurious, with a sauna, a Jacuzzi and a pool in the private walled garden.

**\*\*\*Le Grotte di Boldrino**, Via V. Ceppari 43, t 075 837161, *www.grottediboldrino.com* (€€). A sweet little hotel with 19th-century furnishings, home to the best restaurant in town, serving gourmet Italian dishes and specialities based on lake fish (half board is available).

# Assisi

Less than half an hour east of Perugia and visible for kilometres around, Assisi (population 26,000) sweeps the flanks of Monte Subasio in a broad curve, like a pink ship sailing over the green sea of a valley below. This is Umbria's most famous town and one of its loveliest, but there's more to it than St Francis. Occupied from the Iron Age, it emerged as an ancient Umbrian town in the 6th century BC, one that maintained its cultural distinction into the 1st century BC. As wealthy Roman *Asisium*, it produced the poet Sextus Propertius and first heard of Christianity from St Rufino in 238.

Part of the Lombard duchy of Spoleto, the city came into prominence again in the Middle Ages as another of Umbria's battling *comuni*, one firmly on the side of the Ghibellines, though in 1198 it rebelled against the duke of Spoleto and defied its nominal lord, Emperor Frederick Barbarossa.But Assisi saved most of its bile for incessant wars with arch-rival Perugia; St Francis in his chivalry-obsessed youth had joined in the fighting. The 13th century, which saw his great religious revival, was also the time of Assisi's greatest power and prosperity, leaving behind a collection of beautiful buildings any Italian city could be proud of, and one of Europe's greatest hordes of 13th- and 14th-century frescoes in the Basilica di San Francesco.

Although Cardinal Albornoz nominally put Assisi under the Church's thumb and rebuilt the Rocca Maggiore to keep it there, the city was controlled by various *signori* until the early 16th century, when the papal pall descended like a curtain at the end of a play. Even pilgrimages declined dramatically after the Council of Trent began the Counter-Reformation. Another pall that fell over Assisi was taste. In 1786, Goethe, on his way to view the Temple of

# Getting to and around Assisi

Assisi is a 23km/30min **train** ride (**t** 892021, *www.trenitalia.it*) from Perugia or Foligno, where you have to change from Rome (177km/2hrs 30mins) or Terni. The station is on the plain, a block from the suburban Basilica of Santa Maria degli Angeli, and there are regular linking buses every 20mins to Piazza Unità d'Italia.

There are also convenient **buses** direct from Perugia, Bettona and Gualdo Tadino (APM, **t** 075 573 1707, freephone **t** 800 512141, *www.apmperugia.it*); Rome and Florence (SULGA, **t** 075 30799, *www.sulga.it*); 1 a day from Norcia and Cascia (SSIT, *www.spoletina.com*); and several from Bevagna, Montefalco, Foligno and Spello (APM or SSIT). The bus stops are in Piazza Matteotti, Largo Properzio, Piazza Unità d'Italia, S. Maria degli Angeli and Piazza Garibaldi.

There are three **car parks** on the fringes of town: in Piazza Unità d'Italia below the Basilica of San Francesco, at the Porta Nuova at the east end of town, and an underground lot at Piazza Matteotti, by the Duomo. A series of little buses, the A and B, do the run between Piazza del Comune and Piazza Matteotti every 20mins or so (tickets sold at newsstands, bars and tobacconists).

There is **car hire** by Hertz, Via V. Veneto 4, **t** 075 500 2439, *www.hertz.it*; **bike hire** by Angelucci Cicli, Via Becchetti 31, **t** 075 804 2550, *www.angeluccicicli.it*.

---

Minerva, walked past the Basilica of St Francis, dismissing it as 'a Babylonian tower'. Nevertheless, it was Francis who in the long term made all the difference to Assisi (*see* p.39). Pilgrimages began again in the 19th century with the revival of interest both in the saint and the artists who decorated his shrine – Ruskin, who went into ecstatic overdrive at the medieval purity of the frescoes and used to dream he was a Franciscan friar, was the locomotive drawing the first train of English-speakers. Five million pilgrims and tourists crowded Assisi's narrow streets for Francis's 800th birthday year in 1982 and, although now surpassed by the new shrine of the miracle-working Padre Pio in Puglia, Assisi remains the third most-visited pilgrimage site in Italy. On any given summer day, you'll see coachloads of tourists and stands peddling ceramic friars and plastic medieval torture instruments, intermingled with flocks of serene Franciscans and enthusiastic, almost bouncy nuns from Africa or Missouri or Bavaria, having the time of their lives visiting a place that, much more than Rome, is the symbol of a living faith. And it's true that something simple and good and joyful has survived in Assisi in spite of the odds. The city has hosted unusual demonstrations that could never have happened anywhere else – Pope John Paul II's hosted his interfaith World Day of Prayer in 1986, with Tibetan lamas, Zoroastrians and American Indian medicine men, and the 1988 Umbria Jazz Festival, when gospel choirs from New Orleans sang in the upper church of San Francesco – the friars only let them sing for 15 minutes at a time, fearing the rhythm might bring down the roof and Giotto's frescoes, but providence saw that the building came to no harm, and by the end the Franciscans were clapping with everyone else.

Where gospel singing failed, earthquakes succeeded. In 1997 they brought the roof down, killing two friars and two technical experts who were examining the damage caused by the first shock of the day. The medieval builders had given the basilica the flexibility to withstand earthquakes, but restorers over the centuries had been too lazy to haul out the rubble that they had created, and it accumulated, tons of it, in the essential breathing space between the pricelessly frescoed ceiling vaults and the walls; ultimately, the weight proved too great.

The upper church reopened in 1999 after extensive restoration and structural reinforcements. To ensure that a similar disaster never recurs, the foundations have been reinforced to withstand earth tremors of 12 on the Richter Scale. The two collapsed arches have been repaired but are blank. Technicians have painstakingly pieced the frescoes back together; much of what they worked with was just fine rubble. The other frescoes in the nave were virtually unscathed and the façade has been beautifully restored.

The *palazzi* on the east side of Piazza del Comune were all badly damaged, but have since been repaired, as have most of the buildings in Piazza S. Rufino and surrounding area. In fact, apart from the odd crane, visitors can now see the city, and to a lesser extent the whole region, in better condition than ever. As a result of the quake, even buildings that were not damaged have been restored, as it was deemed a good time to do the work and funds were there. The social effects of the quake have not been addressed with such vigour, however, and many feel that, for the sake of tourism, art was given precedence over people (*see* pp.36–8).

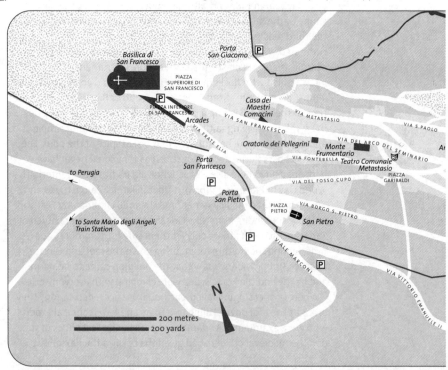

*I would give all the churches in Rome for this cave.*

Hippolyte Taine (19th-century French critic)

**🟢 Basilica Patriarcale di San Francesco**

*t 075 819001, www.sanfrancescoassisi.org; open Easter–Nov daily 6am–6.45pm (upper basilica 8.30–6.45); Nov–Easter daily 6am–6pm (upper basilica 8.30–6); info office, Piazza San Francesco, t 075 819 0084, open Mon–Sat 9–12 and 2–5.30, Sun 2–5; no shorts/bare shoulders*

## Basilica of San Francesco

Though the medieval popes were mistrustful of the spontaneous, personal approach to faith preached by Francis and his followers, they realized that this powerful movement would be better off within the Church than outside. In transforming the Franciscans into a respectable, doctrinally safe arm of Catholicism, they had the invaluable aid of Francis's successor, Brother Elias, Vicar-General of the Order, a worldly, businesslike, organization man, epicurean and friend of Emperor Frederick II. Elias's methods caused the first split within the Franciscans, between those who enjoyed the growing opulence of the new dispensation and those who tried to keep to the poverty preached by their founder.

This monumental building complex, begun the day after Francis's canonization in 1228, when Pope Gregory IX laid the cornerstone, was one of the biggest causes of contention. Nothing could have been further removed from the philosophy and intentions of Francis himself; on the other hand, nothing could have been more successful in perpetuating his memory and his teaching than this great treasure house of art.

From the beginning, the popes were entirely behind the effort. They paid for it with a great sale of special indulgences across Europe, and the basilica belongs to the Vatican (though thanks to a clause in the Lateran Treaty of 1929, signed by Mussolini and

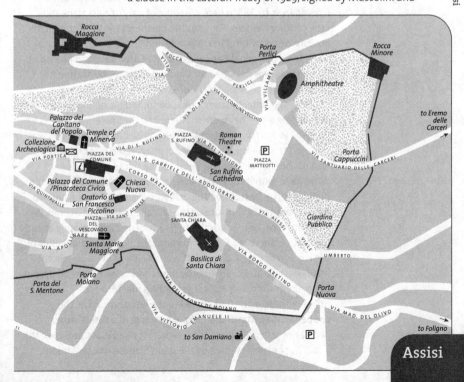

Assisi

renewed in 1989 by the late Socialist prime minister Bettino Craxi, the Italian State is responsible for the upkeep – including all earthquake repairs). There's a story that Brother Elias supplied the design – the lower basilica does have an amateurish, clumsy form. The beautiful campanile dates from 1239; the completed basilica was consecrated by Innocent IV in 1253. Behind it, visible for kilometres around, on huge buttressed vaults, is the enormous convent built by Sixtus IV in the 15th century. Now a missionary college, it, too, was damaged by the quake, though part of it is being used as a fresco hospital.

## The Lower Church

The usual approach to the basilica is by way of the Lower Church from the **Piazza Inferiore di San Francesco**, lined with arcades where medieval pilgrims bought their souvenirs before returning home. Because of its partially underground location on a hill, the Lower Church has no façade, but it does have a rather grand Renaissance portico of 1487, which protects a fine Gothic portal. Brother Elias, or whoever was responsible, designed the church to hold the saint's body, and with its low dark vaults, dimly illuminated through stained glass, it certainly resembles a crypt (it's a good idea to bring a torch). It is confusing at first in its overwhelming detail, and perhaps even a bit claustrophobic if it's crowded, yet tucked in here are some of Italy's finest 13th- and 14th-century frescoes. Those in the **narthex**, as you enter, are 17th-century works by Girolamo Martelli and Cesare Sermei.

The large polygonal **Cappella di Santa Caterina** at the far end of the narthex was designed for Cardinal Albornoz by Matteo Gattapone and frescoed by Andrea de' Bartoli. The Cardinal's nephew, appointed governor of Spoleto, and his nephew's son were buried here after they were murdered by the Spoletines. The Cardinal (d. 1367) was entombed here as well, before his body was removed to safer keeping in Toledo; you can see him on the left wall of the chapel, kneeling before three saints.

The **nave**, with its original pavement, gently slopes down to the high altar. The frescoes on the walls are the oldest in the basilica, dating back to 1253 and are by the so-called Master of St Francis, who may have been an Umbrian painter. Their iconography already identifies Francis as a Christ figure: on the right wall are scenes of the Passion of Christ, on the left wall the life of St Francis. Both were unfortunately damaged as new chapels were opened up, but as compensation, some of these contain masterpieces.

One of these is the first chapel to the left of the nave, the **Cappella di San Martino**, a unique example of a total Gothic decorative scheme, where the frescoes, stained glass, and even the inlaid floor were designed by the great Sienese master Simone

Martini (*c.* 1315–20). Martini's courtly International Gothic-style poses are a serious artistic challenge to Giotto and the other great precursors of the Renaissance. This master of line and colour, whom Berenson called the 'most lovable painter of the pre-Renaissance', creates here a wonderful, elegant narrative on the *Life of St Martin*, the 4th-century Gaulish soldier and wastrel who ended up as a bishop and split his cloak to give half to a beggar seems a perfect foreshadowing of St Francis.

Next to the chapel is the stair down to the **crypt**, built in 1925 for the bones of St Francis and four of his closest followers. These were discovered only in 1818. At first Francis had been buried in the church of San Giorgio (now incorporated into the church of Santa Chiara), but Brother Elias, worried that the Perugians would come to steal the saint's body, made off with it himself during the canonization ceremonies and then hid it here with exceeding care behind tons of stone. His fears were not unfounded; when Francis was returning from La Verna to die in Assisi, the wicked Perugians (who never listened when Francis came to preach) were lying in wait to kidnap him along the road, and would have succeeded had Brother Elias not thought to direct Francis on a longer route.

The **Cappella della Maddalena** on the right contains frescoes on the life of Mary Magdalene, attributed to Giotto and his assistants (*c.* 1309). The scenes were commissioned by the then Bishop of Assisi, who is shown being crowned with a mitre by St Rufino. There's also a scene of the Magdalene sailing to Marseille, not a subject you often see outside France. The barrel-vaulted transept on the west end (the usual east end of a church, but topography forced Brother Elias to lay it out backwards) is even more lavishly decorated. In the crossing over the high altar, known as the **Quattro Vele**, are four beautiful allegorical frescoes, *Poverty*, *Chastity*, *Obedience* (the three Virtues of St Francis) and the *Glory of St Francis*. *The Marriage of St Francis with Lady Poverty* is one of the most striking images ever to come out of the 13th-century religious revival; Obedience has her finger to her lips, extolling silence. Long attributed to Giotto, these are now attributed to two of his students, one from Tuscany and one an Umbrian now known as the Maestro delle Vele.

The **left transept** has a remarkable fresco cycle on the Life of Christ, among the best in the basilica, by Pietro Lorenzetti of Siena (*c.* 1320–30). Lorenzetti, a contemporary of Martini, could be just as decorative and elegant, as in the *Entrance in Jerusalem*, but he could also achieve a powerful degree of drama and emotion, as in his *Crucifixion* and the immensely sombre and harrowing *Descent from the Cross*. These frescoes are his masterpieces; it may be that working among the likes of Cimabue and Giotto inspired Lorenzetti to make the imaginative breakthrough in composition

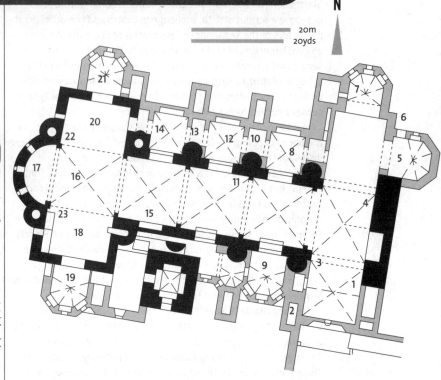

N

20m
20yds

1 Cerchi Tomb with big porphyry vase (13th century)

2 Cappella di San Sebastiano, frescoes by Girolamo Martelli (1646) and the *Madonna della Salute*, the only known work by 15th-century painter Ceccolo di Giovanni

3 *Madonna with Saints* by Ottaviano Nelli (1422)

4 Tomb of John Brienne, Latin Emperor of Constantinople (and friend of St Francis)

5 Cappella del Sacramento, with two 14th-century tombs

6 Cemetery cloister

7 Cappella di Santa Caterina, frescoes by Andrea de' Bartoli of Bologna (1360s)

8 Cappella di Santo Stefano, frescoes by Dono Doni (1574)

9 Cappella di San Martino by Simone Martini (c. 1320)

10 Cappella di San Lorenzo, frescoes by Andrea de' Bartoli

11 Stairs to the crypt

12 Cappella di Sant'Antonio di Padova, frescoes by Cesare Sermi (1610), early 14th-century stained glass

13 Cappella di San Valentino, with a pavement tomb of Friar Ugo of Hartlepool, one of the first English Franciscans (d. 1302)

14 Cappella della Maddalena, frescoes by Giotto and assistants (c. 1309)

15 *Coronation of the Virgin* by Puccio Capanna (1337), over a Cosmati work pulpit

16 The *Quattro Vele* (*Poverty, Chastity, Obedience* and the *Glory of St Francis*)

17 *The Last Judgement* by Cesare Sermei (1623)

18 Frescoes of the Passion by Pietro Lorenzetti (c. 1320)

19 Cappella di San Giovanni Battista, triptych by Lorenzetti (c. 1320–30)

20 Frescoes by Cimabue, Giotto, Martini, Lorenzetti

21 Cappella di San Nicola, frescoes by Giotto and assistants

22 Steps to the chapterhouse

23 Stairs to terrace and treasury

and meaning, here leaving all the typical Sienese decoration behind to convey the depths of tragedy and despair.

In the **right transept**, Giotto's assistants frescoed the childhood of Christ and the posthumous miracles of St Francis (1315–20), while the *Crucifixion* here is believed to be by Giotto himself. Cimabue's famous *Madonna and Child, with Angels and St Francis* (1280) is one of the most famous images of the saint, and believed to be an accurate likeness. This is a sole survivor of the frescoes that Cimabue and the Master of St Francis painted in the transepts, before they were redone in the 1300s. A serious-looking female saint nearby, by Simone Martini, is believed to be St Clare. Martini also painted *Madonna and Child and Two of the Wise Men*. This transept also has Pietro Lorenzetti's first contribution to the church, the graceful *Madonna della Tramontana* ('of the sunset') with *St Francis and St John*, a fresco in a painted frame. The polygonal **Cappella di San Nicola** has frescoes on the life of St Nicholas by Giotto and his assistants.

In 1995, the contents of the 'secret sacristy' were put on display in the **chapterhouse**: Pope Honorius III's Bull approving the Order's Rule (1223), the saint's tunic, cowl, girdle and sandals, an ivory horn given to Francis by the Sultan of Egypt which he would blow to assemble his followers, the *Laud to the Creator* and *Benediction of Brother Leone* on parchment, in the saint's own hand, and a chalice and paten used by Francis and his followers. The Crucifixion fresco on the wall here is by Puccio Capanna (1340).

**Museo-Tesoro della Basilica**

*t 075 819 001, centrodf@tiscali.it; open April–Oct Mon–Sat 9.30–5.30; Nov–Mar by appt; adm*

From the transepts, stairs lead up to a terrace and the Sala Gotica, home of the **Museo-Tesoro della Basilica**, which went on tour when the building was damaged by the quake, but reopened for Easter 2000. This contains many beautiful things that somehow escaped being pillaged or pinched through the centuries: a Venetian cross in rock crystal, a French ivory Madonna from the 13th century; a 15th-century Flemish tapestry with St Francis and an altar frontal with a scene by Antonio del Pollaiolo (both presented to the basilica by Sixtus V), the ornate Chalice of Nicholas IV (1290), and much more. Since 1986, the treasury has also contained the **Mason Perkins Collection**, donated by the art historian, who gathered together many works by Pietro Lorenzetti, Lorenzo Monaco, Taddeo di Bartolo and other trecento masters.

## The Upper Church

In complete contrast to the Lower Church, the Upper Church with its big rose window and false front gable (beautifully restored after the earthquake) is strikingly bright and airy and vibrant, and filled with frescoes that emphasize its perfectly balanced proportions. Architecturally, this is Gothic reduced to its basics. The medieval Italians, who never took to the style imported from the north and regarded all the flamboyant vaults and spires and buttresses as barbaric, nevertheless did appreciate the possibilities that the style offered over Romanesque, especially the opportunity the new techniques provided in creating a single open space. The Upper Church, whoever designed it, became the great prototype of Italian Gothic, the model for countless Franciscan and Dominican churches: here all the features emphasized by northern architects are minimalized to provide a perfect framework for the frescoes in a revolutionary synthesis of art and architecture. The space, the simplicity and the easy to 'read' illustrations were just what a popular preaching order required. Although the frescoes tend to steal all the thunder, give a few minutes to the beautiful 13th-century **stained glass**, considered the finest in medieval Italy.

Two bands of frescoes run in narrative bands along the nave. The **lower register**, on the life of St Francis (*c.* 1290–95), constitutes perhaps the longest-raging controversy in the history of art. Vasari in the 16th century attributed them to Giotto, and the Italian faction is convinced that they are the climax of his early career, painted some two decades before his work in the Lower Church, while most foreign scholars, faced with the stylistic differences between these and Giotto's uncontroversial surviving fresco cycle in the Arena chapel in Padua (1305), believe that Giotto didn't paint them at all, but that they are the work of three or four of his followers. What convinces most Italian scholars that the San Francesco frescoes were at least partially by Giotto is the artist's mastery of composition; Giotto amazed his contemporaries with his ability to illustrate the physical and spiritual essentials of a scene with simplicity and drama, cutting to the core of the matter. Although the controversy may never be resolved to everyone's satisfaction, one thing is certainly true: even if the man recognized in his own lifetime as the greatest painter since antiquity didn't actually apply brush to wall, his guiding spirit is certainly here, not least in the frescoes' humane qualities that have made them posterity's image of Francis.

The scenes are perfectly integrated in the four bays of the nave, all knit together with a *trompe l'œil* cornice. They begin in the fourth bay on the right, with *Francis honoured by the simple man*, who lays down his cloak and foretells the saint's destiny (note Assisi's Temple of Minerva in the background), followed by 2. *Francis gives his cloak to a poor knight* (with Assisi in the background). 3. *He dreams of a palace full of arms*. 4. *The voice in San Damiano tells Francis to 'Rebuild my Church'*. 5. *He renounces the world before the bishop of Assisi and his father*, who in his anger and disappointment has to be restrained. 6. *The Dream of Innocent III*, a memorable scene, in which Francis supports the falling Church. 7. *Innocent III approves Francis's Rule*. 8. *The Fiery Chariot*, from a vision of one of the saint's followers. 9. *Fra Leone dreams of the throne reserved for Francis in heaven*. 10. *The demons are expelled from Arezzo by Fra Silvestro*. 11. *Francis meets the Sultan of Egypt and offers to undergo the Ordeal by Fire*. 12. *Francis in Ecstasy*. 13. *The creation of the first Christmas crib at Greccio*.

On the inner wall of the façade: 14. *Francis brings forth a spring for a thirsty man*. 15. *Francis preaches to the birds*.

Then around on the left wall of the nave: 16. *The knight of Celano dies, as foretold by the saint*. 17. *Francis preaches to Pope Honorius III*. 18. *He appears in two places at the same time*. 19. *He receives the stigmata, from a six-winged cherub*. 20. *The death of Francis*. 21. *The saint appears to the Bishop of Assisi and Fra Augustine*. 22. *Girolamo of Assisi accepts the truth of the stigmata*. 23. *Francis mourned by the Poor Clares*. 24. *Coronation of Francis*. 25. *He appears to Gregory IX in a dream*. 26. *He heals a wounded man*. 27. *He revives a devout woman*. 28. *He releases Pietro d'Alife from prison*. The last three scenes are generally ascribed to the Master of Santa Cecilia, who was famous for his lively figures, warm colours and very meticulous architectural scenes.

The **upper register** of frescoes, of Old Testament and New Testament scenes, were commissioned in 1288 to celebrate the election of Nicholas IV, the first Franciscan pope. Badly damaged in places and much harder to see, they are usually attributed to the Roman painters Pietro Cavallini and Jacopo Torriti, and to Cimabue's followers (including, some say, the young Giotto, who may have painted those with the most striking architectural compositions, *Isaac blessing Jacob* and *Esau before Isaac*). Giotto is also generally credited with the *Four Doctors of the Church*, in the vault of the first bay, part of which collapsed in the earthquake, along with the arch. Some of the frescoes have been reconstructed.

The transepts were painted with a famous cycle of frescoes by Giotto's master, Cimabue, though the works had oxidized into mere shadows or negatives of their former selves even before the earthquake turned them to crumbs. In the left transept are scenes of the Apocalypse and the famous *Crucifixion*, a faded masterpiece of 1277 that still radiates some of its original drama and feeling. The earthquake shattered two bays of the vault and arch, and took Cimabue's *St Matthew* from the Four Evangelists in the crossing. The bays have since been reconstructed from the hundreds of thousands of coloured pieces of the Cimabue and other frescoes, using a hyper-colour-sensitive computer programme.

## To the Piazza del Comune

**San Pietro**

*t 075 812311; open daily 7.30–7*

Entering Assisi along the main road from the car park, you may have noticed the Romanesque–Gothic façade of **San Pietro**, with three rose windows, just inside the gate of the same name. This

Benedictine church was built in the 1200s, although Assisi's chroniclers date the original building to Palaeochristian times.

From the tidy lawn of the Upper Church, Via San Francesco, the main street, leads into the *centro storico*, passing fine medieval houses and the rather unexpected **Museo degli Indios dell'Amazzonia**, with ethnographic items collected by Capuchin missionaries in the Amazon. In the same building, Amazonian fish and plants are on show as the **Mostra Etnologica**.

**Palazzo Vallemani**, on the left, houses the **Pinacoteca**, with detached frescoes, including a scene of 13th-century knights from the Palazzo del Capitano del Popolo that probably caught the fancy of the young Francis, and others by Tiberio d'Assisi; there's also a rather sleepy collection of Umbrian paintings, including a *Madonna della Misericordia* by L'Alunno.

At No.11, the **Oratorio dei Pellegrini** is a 15th-century gem, all that survives from a pilgrims' hospice, frescoed on the façade and altar wall by Matteo da Gualdo. The frescoes on the walls are by another Umbrian, Pierantonio Mezzastris (1477), with scenes of miracles on the road to Compostela and the life of St Anthony Abbot (with the friendly camels). The Oratorio is currently home to works from the **Museo Comunale di Nocera Umbra**, closed by the earthquake.

At No.3, the portico belonged to **Monte Frumentario**, built in the 13th century as a hospital, one of Italy's first, later converted into a granary. Next to it, a 16th-century **fountain** still warns that the penalty for washing clothes here is one *scudo* and confiscation of laundry. Via San Francesco then passes through an arch from the city's Roman walls and continues as the Via del Arco del Seminario, named for the former missionary college on the left. Further up, the 19th-century **Teatro Comunale Metastasio** is now a cinema.

Near here is the **Museo e Foro Romano**, in the crypt of the now-vanished church of San Niccolò (1097); it has a small collection of urns, statues and bits of Roman frescoes. The collection was founded in 1793 by the local Accademia Properziano del Subasio and hasn't changed much. A passage leads from the museum into the ancient **Roman forum** (or the sacred area of *Asisium*), excavated in the 19th century, under the modern Piazza del Comune. Here you can see bases of statues, a platform that may have been an altar, an inscription to the Dioscuri, steps to the temple of Minerva and the remains of a fountain.

## Piazza del Comune

Long Piazza del Comune, medieval centre of Assisi, is embellished with 13th-century buildings of the old *comune*: the lofty **Torre del Popolo** and the **Palazzo del Capitano del Popolo**, the **Palazzo del Podestà** (now the Palazzo del Comune) and a genuine Roman **temple of Minerva** from around the 1st century BC, with Corinthian

---

**Museo degli Indios dell'Amazzonia**
*t 075 812280; open Easter–14 Jan daily 10–12 and 3–6; donations welcome*

**Pinacoteca**
*t 075 815 5234; open Nov–Feb daily 10.30–1 and 2–5; March–May and Sept–Oct daily 10–5; June–Aug daily 10–6.30; joint adm with Museo e Foro Romano (see below)*

**Oratorio dei Pellegrini**
*t 075 812267; open Mon–Sat 10–12 and 4–6*

**Museo e Foro Romano**
*Via Portica 1, t 075 815 5234; open daily Nov–Feb 10–5, March–May and Sept–Oct 10–6, June–Aug 10–7; adm with Pinacoteca (see above)*

**Tempio di Minerva**
*t 075 812268; open daily 7–7*

columns and travertine steps. Goethe came to Assisi to see this and nothing else. It has the best-surviving Roman temple front on the Italian peninsula, as good as any ruin in Rome for helping your imagination conjure up the classical world. But only the *pronaos* (entrance hall) and façade remain; inside is some eccentric Baroque belonging to the church of Santa Maria della Minerva.

**Chiesa Nuova**
*t 075 812339; open daily summer 8.30–12 and 3–6, winter 8.30–12 and 3–5*

Left of the palazzo, the **Chiesa Nuova** was constructed in 1615 by Philip III of Spain on property owned by St Francis's father. In an adjacent alley, the **Oratorio di San Francesco Piccolino** is believed to mark the saint's birthplace.

## Upper Assisi: the Cathedral, the Castle and Around

**Cattedrale di San Rufino**
*t 075 812283; open daily Aug 7–7, rest of year 7–1 and 2.30–6*

Most visitors labour under the impression that the Basilica of St Francis is Assisi's cathedral: the real **Cattedrale di San Rufino** is up Via di San Rufino from Piazza del Comune. Set over a piazza (another candidate for the Roman forum), it has a huge campanile and the finest Romanesque façade in Umbria, designed by Giovanni da Gubbio in 1140 and adorned with fine rose windows and the robust medieval carvings of animals and saints that Goethe so disdained. In the central lunette, God the Father sits enthroned in the circle with San Rufino on the right and Mary, nursing the infant Christ, on the left. The three monumental figures in the rectangular niche above appear to hold up the church. Inside is the porphyry font where Saint Francis and Saint Clare were baptized, as well as Emperor Frederick II, born nearby in Jesi, in the Marches. It is an amazing coincidence that these two major protagonists of the 13th century should have been baptized in the same place: the holy water must have had a special essence in it. Both Francis and Frederick were profoundly influenced by the East and were among the first poets to write in vernacular Italian rather than Latin. The interior was restored in the 16th century, when the beautiful carved wooden choir was added.

**Museo Capitolare**
*t 075 812712; open (inc crypt) Mar–Oct daily 10–1 and 3–6; adm*

Off the right nave is the small **Museo Capitolare**, with Romanesque capitals, codices, frescoes, paintings by Matteo da Gualdo and a beautiful triptych by L'Alunno (1470). You can explore the ancient **crypt**, dating from an earlier, 11th-century church, with a few frescoes and a 3rd-century Roman sarcophagus decorated with reliefs of the myth of Endymion, where St Rufino was buried. Don't miss the barrel-vaulted Roman cistern under the campanile, with an inscription in the Umbrian dialect. The Umbrii worshipped springs, and this is believed to have been a sacred fountain. The inscription names the *marones*, or officials who were in charge of building projects, not unlike the Roman *aediles*.

**Rocca Maggiore**
*t 075 815 5234; open daily Sept–Feb 10–4.30, Mar 10–5.30, April, May, Sept, Oct 7–7; June–Aug 7–8; adm*

From the cathedral, it's a bracing walk up to the **Rocca Maggiore**, the well-preserved castle, built in 1174 and used by Conrad von Luetzen (who cared for the orphan Emperor Frederick II). Destroyed and rebuilt on several occasions, once by Cardinal Albornoz, it has great views of Assisi, the Valle Umbra, the Rocciciola (an inaccessible fortress built by Albornoz) and the surrounding countryside.

East of the cathedral, you can visit more of Roman *Asisium* – the **theatre** in Via del Torrione, by the cathedral, and the remains of the **amphitheatre**, off Piazza Matteotti and Via Villamena. The **Porta Perlici** near the amphitheatre dates from 1199 and there are some well-preserved 13th-century houses on the Via del Comune Vecchio. The **Giardino Pubblico**, with its pavilions and fishponds, is a fine place to have a picnic. *Asisium* had up-to-date plumbing; you might be able to pick out the Roman drain between the amphitheatre and the Giardino Pubblico, built to carry off water after the amphitheatre was flooded for mock sea-battles.

## Basilica di Santa Chiara

**Basilica di Santa Chiara**
*southeast of Piazza del Comune by way of Corso Mazzini, t 075 812282; open daily winter 6.30–12 and 2–6, summer 6.30–12 and 2–7*

Saint Clare's basilica, built in 1265 , is a pink-and-white striped beauty with a lovely rose window, supported by huge flying buttresses added a century later that not only keep it from falling over but create a memorable architectural space below. It stands on the site of the old church of San Giorgio, where Francis attended school and where his body lay for two years awaiting completion of his own basilica. The shadowy **interior** has frescoes in the transepts by followers of Giotto, damaged and hard to see; by the altar are scenes from Clare's life by the late 13th-century Maestro di Santa Chiara. On the right, the **Oratorio del Crocifisso** contains the famous *Crucifix of San Damiano* (*see* p.129), a 13th-century triptych by Rinaldo di Ranuccio and reliquaries of St Clare, with some of her garments and golden curls. The adjacent **Cappella del Sacramento** has fine Sienese frescoes; these two chapels were part of San Giorgio. Clare's body, rediscovered in 1850 under the high altar, shrivelled and darkened with age, lies like a never-kissed Snow White in a crystal coffin, down in the neogothic crypt.

### The Patron Saint of TV

Born in 1194, Chiara Offreduccio was 17 when she ran away from her wealthy, noble family to become a disciple of St Francis at the Porziuncola. By 1215, she was abbess of a Franciscan Second Order, the Poor Clares or Clarisse, based on the primitive rule of St Francis. Whatever the later church mythology, rumours were never lacking that there was more to her relationship with Francis than practical piety. Gentle and humble, she once had a vision of a Christmas service in the Basilica of St Francis while at San Damiano, more than 1km away – a feat that led Pope Pius XII in 1958 to declare her the patron saint of television. Like Francis, Clare lived on alms and is reputed to have twice saved Assisi from the army of Frederick II. Her rule of poverty was only confirmed by Pope Innocent IV while she lay on her deathbed, two days before she died in 1253. She was canonized two years later but, as in the case of Francis, her desire for her followers to live in absolute poverty was denied when Pope Urban IV approved a new Rule for her Order (1264). Still, it did offer something of an alternative for women in an age where many were forced into arranged marriages or convents if there wasn't enough dowry to go around; two Umbrian women who followed in Clare's footsteps were the great 13th-century mystics, the Blessed Angela of Foligno and St Clare of Montefalco.

## Piazza Vescovado and Around

**Santa Maria Maggiore**
*t 075 813085; open daily Easter–Nov 8.30–7, Dec–Easter 8.30–6.30*

**House of Sextus Propertius**
*visitors need permission from Soprintendenza Archeologica in Perugia, t 075 57411*

From Santa Chiara, Via Sant'Agnese leads down to Piazza Vescovado and the **church of Santa Maria Maggiore** (1163), with a pink-and-white checked façade. This was Assisi's first cathedral, built on the site of the Roman temple of Apollo, traces of which are visible in the 9th-century crypt. Nearby, the reputed **house of Sextus Propertius**, Roman poet of love (46 BC–AD 14), was found, with wall paintings. Between here and Piazza Unità d'Italia, Via Fontebella has wrought-iron dragons and a pretty fountain.

# Around Assisi

## San Damiano

**San Damiano**
*t 075 812273; sanctuary open daily summer 10–12 and 2–6 (vespers 7pm), winter 10–12 and 2–4.30 (vespers 5pm); no bare legs and shoulders – they're very strict on the dress code here*

Many of the key events of Francis's life took place in the countryside around Assisi. San Damiano is a short drive or a pleasant 2km walk from Santa Chiara down Via Borgo Aretino, through the Porta Nuova. It was in this simple, asymmetrical Benedictine priory (1030) that the Crucifix spoke to Francis in 1205, commanding him to 'rebuild my church'. Francis took the injunction literally and sold his father's horse and cloth to raise the money – the priest at San Damiano refused to take it, so Francis threw it out of the window and returned to restore the church. He brought Clare to San Damiano in 1212, when restoration was complete, and here she and her followers passed their frugal, contemplative lives (forbidden to beg, they nearly starved). Sitting in the garden on one of his visits, Francis composed his superb *Cantico della creature*, the 'Canticle of All Things Created', in 1224.

Enter the church through the Cappella di San Girolamo, with a fine fresco by Tiberio d'Assisi, *Madonna and Child, with SS. Francis, Clare, Bernardino and Jerome* (1517); the next chapel has a wooden crucifix of 1637 by Fra Innocenzo da Palermo. Frescoes in the church record events that happened here (one shows the saint's father chasing him with a stick). The crucifix over the altar is a copy of the original, now in Santa Chiara. In the convent are a fresco of the Crucifixion by Mezzastris, the room where St Clare died, and the tiny cloister with frescoes by Eusebio da San Giorgio (1507) of the Annunciation and St Francis receiving the stigmata.

In 1870, when the Papal States were united to the new Kingdom of Italy, Lord Ripon, a Catholic convert, bought San Damiano to stop it becoming state property and let it to the friars on the condition they did nothing to restore it. Lord Lothian, who inherited it, returned it to the Franciscans in 1983.

## The Eremo delle Carceri and Monte Subasio

**Eremo delle Carceri**
*t 075 812301; www.eremocarceri.it; open daily 6.30–sunset; guided tours 9, 11.30, 2.30 and 5.30*

Another Franciscan shrine more true to the spirit of the saint than the great basilicas is the peaceful **Eremo delle Carceri**, in a beautiful setting on the edge of a ravine, deep in the woods along the road up Monte Subasio, a spectacular walk or drive 4km east of Assisi (leave via the Porta dei Cappuccini). This 'Hermitage of the Prison' was Francis's retreat, where he and his followers strove to live like the first Umbrian saints, walking through the woods and meditating. In 1426 Bernardino of Siena founded the small convent here where a handful of friars still live a traditional Franciscan existence on the alms they receive.

By the little triangular courtyard are two small chapels, the **Cappella di San Bernardino**, with tiny stained-glass windows, and the **Cappella di Santa Maria delle Carceri**, with a fresco, *Madonna and Child and St Francis*, by Tiberio d'Assisi. A steep stair leads down to the **Grotto di San Francesco**, with one of the saint's beds hollowed from the rock, and the very old ilex down in the ravine, where the birds are said to have flocked to hear him preach, as a faded fresco on the cave recounts.

From the Eremo delle Carceri it's 7.5km up the Collepino road to the distinctive bald summit of **Monte Subasio** (1,289m), centre of a regional park, with superb views over the high Apennines to the east and a network of walking paths. In summer you can continue a further spectacular 10km over the mountains on an unpaved road to the medieval village of **Collepino**, above Spello (*see* p.161).

## Santa Maria degli Angeli

The real centre of early Franciscanism was the oratory called the Porziuncola ('the little portion'), where angels were wont to appear, down on the plain near the train station. Francis, in return for the use of the oratory, owed a yearly basket of carp from the Tescio river to the Benedictines, which is still faithfully paid by the Franciscans. In 1569, a monumental basilica, **Santa Maria degli Angeli**, by Galeazzo Alessi, was begun to shelter the Porziuncola. Only completed in 1684, it is an excellent piece of nostalgic Baroque, though it was mostly reconstructed after an 1832 earthquake; the grandiose façade was only added in 1927. You certainly can't miss it, rising over a modern suburb and Assisi's train station: Santa Maria degli Angeli is the eighth largest church in the world. On its flank it is graced by a suitably enormous **fountain**, donated by the Medici in 1610 and designed for pilgrims to wash away the dust from the road.

**Basilica Patriarcale di Santa Maria degli Angeli**
*t 075 80511; open daily 6.15–12.50 and 2.30–7.30*

The side chapels are mostly decorated with early Baroque works. Beneath the dome, the **Cappella della Porziuncola** has an entrance dolled up with frescoes from the 19th century on the pardon of St Francis. The rugged stone oratory can be seen inside, with a superb altarpiece on the life of St Francis (1393) by Ilario da Viterbo, this artist's only known work (but undergoing restoration). One of the very few benefits of the 1997 earthquake was the revealing of the decoration on the oratory's roof. The chapel also has the stone marking the tomb of Pietro Cattani (d. 1221), who was appointed first Vicar of the Order when the pope encouraged Francis, who had no interest in organization or discipline, to step down, or rather sideways, since he considered the position as only the first among equals. On the back wall there's a fine 15th-century fresco of the Crucifixion.

St Francis died in the infirmary cell, which is now the tiny **Cappella del Transito**. His last concerns were for 'his lady Poverty'; he insisted on being laid out on the bare earth, and would have died naked had not the bishop of Assisi insisted that as the tunic he wore was borrowed, he could truly leave the world with no possessions. Through the gate you can see some unusual frescoes by Lo Spagna of the saint's oldest companions, along with a statue of St Francis by Andrea della Robbia. The rope the saint used to belt his habit is displayed in a case. There are more early Baroque chapels in the transept, and in the south transept, off a corridor, the entrance to the **crypt**, part of the excavations in 1968 that revealed the foundations and some of the walls of the first Franciscan convent. It also has a very beautiful altarpiece by Andrea della Robbia (you may have to find the sacristan to unlock it).

The garden contains the roses that Francis is said to have thrown himself on while wrestling with severe temptation, staining their leaves red with blood, only to find that they lost their thorns on contact with his body. Still thornless, they bloom every May. Francis's own cell at the Porziuncola was covered by St Bonaventura with the frescoed **Cappella del Roseto**, which has some of Tiberio d'Assisi's finest frescoes, one showing the famous scene in the garden. There's also an old pharmacy and, in the

**Museum**
*t 075 805 1430; open daily April–Oct 9–12 and 3–6, Nov–Mar 3–6*

**Museo Etnografico Universale**
*open Mon–Fri 9–12 and 3–6, Sat 9–12*

refectory of the old convent, a **museum** which has a portrait of St Francis by an unknown 13th-century master, another that has been attributed to Cimabue, and a crucifix (1236) by Giunta Pisano; there's also a **Museo Etnografico Universale**, in Via de Gasperi, displaying items relating to Franciscan missionary work.

A 14km Via di San Francesco is being built from the Porziuncola to the Basilica di San Francesco, linking the sites associated with the saint along the way. It is paved with bricks inscribed with the name and city of any benefactor who contributes €42.50.

# West of Assisi

## Bastia Umbria and Around

A prosperous industrial centre, **Bastia Umbria** began as an island, the *Insula Romana*, before the valley was drained. Once surrounded by walls, it was a hot potato contested by Perugia and Assisi. Its unattractive environs fend off most visitors, but the *centro storico* has a pretty 14th-century church with a triptych by L'Alunno and frescoes by Tiberio d'Assisi and students of Bartolomeo Caporali.

North of Bastia and the village of **Petrignano** (famous for its animated *presepio* at Christmas), the valley of the Chiascio is guarded by the splendidly sited **Rocca Sant'Angelo**; nearby, the **Convento di Santa Maria della Rocchicciola** (ring bell next to church for the sisters to let you in) has frescoes by Bartolomeo Caporali and Lo Spagna, and a crucifix by Matteo da Gualdo.

## Bettona

Southwest of Assisi, Bettona is a compact, nearly elliptical hill town wrapped in olive groves. It was big enough to have a long history as Vettona, an Etruscan city – it is the only Umbrian town east of the Tiber with Etruscan origins – and later as a Roman *municipium*. At the north end of the walls, the huge golden stones of the original Etruscan fortifications (4th century BC) are visible, and 1km west is the simple, barrel-vaulted **Ipogeo Etrusco** (key held at Vigili Urbani at Municipio in Piazza Cavour) from the 2nd century BC, with funerary urns *in situ*.

**Pinacoteca Comunale**
*t 075 987 306; open Mar–May, Sept–Oct daily 10.30–1 and 2–6; June–July daily 10.30–1 and 3–7; Aug daily 10.30–1 and 3–7; Nov–Feb Tues–Sun 10.30–1 and 2.30–5; adm*

Up in Bettona itself, central Piazza Cavour has a fountain and the 14th-century **Palazzo del Podestà**. Within this and an adjoining palazzo is the **Pinacoteca Comunale** with two minor paintings by Perugino, detached frescoes by Fiorenzo di Lorenzo and Tiberio d'Assisi, Dono Doni (*Adoration of the Shepherds* with a predella on the life of San Crispolto, first bishop of Bettona), ceramics from Deruta and wooden chests. In 1987, the most important works were stolen and found their way to Jamaica where they were recovered; they came back to Bettona in 1990. At the museum ask to visit the **Oratorio di Sant'Andrea** in the same piazza, with a fresco of the Passion by Giotto's school; opposite, **Santa Maria Maggiore** has a gonfalon by Perugino and works by L'Alunno, currently in the museum while the church is being restored. For accommodation here, *see* p.134.

For accommodation here, *see* p.134.

**ⓘ Assisi >**
*Piazza del Comune 12, t 075 8138680; open Mon–Sat 8–2 and 3–6; Sun 10–1 and 2–5 in summer, 9–1 in winter; Largo Properzio, t 075 816766 (closed Wed and Nov–Easter), www.regioneumbria.eu or www.comune. assisi.pg.it*

## Tourist Information in Assisi

**Post office**: Largo Properzio 4, t 075 813114, *www.poste.it*.

**Churches**: open daily 7–12 and 2 until sunset unless otherwise stated. All churches and major sights now open.

## Festivals in Assisi

**Calendimaggio**, *www.calendimaggiodiassisi.it*,
1st Thurs–Sat in May. Assisi's medieval May Day celebrations, commemorating Francis's troubadour past with song, dance, torchlight parades, lovely costumes and contests between lower and upper Assisi.

**Easter week.** Religious celebrations, including a mystery play on the Deposition from the Cross (Holy Thursday), and processions through town (Good Friday and Easter Sunday).

**Antiques fair**, *www.assisiantiquariato.it*, April and May.

**Festa del Perdono** (Feast of Forgiveness), Porziuncola, 1–2 Aug. Indulgences given out in commemoration of St Francis, who had a vision of Christ asking him what would be most helpful for the soul, and suggested offering forgiveness to anyone who crossed the threshold of the chapel.

**St Francis's Day**, 3–4 Oct. Religious ceremonies, singing and dancing.

**Marcia della Pace**, 2nd Sun Oct. A peace walk begun in 1963, from Perugia to Assisi.

## Shopping in Assisi

Assisi overflows with little ceramic friars, crossbows, local ceramics and glass, and textiles, and there are serious art galleries too.

**Enoteca Hispellum**, Corso Cavour 35, t 074 265 1766. A place to sample and buy local cheeses, wines, biscuits, honeys, jams, sauces and spreads.

### Market Day

Saturday, Piazza Matteotti.

## Where to Stay in and around Assisi

### Assisi ✉ 06081

Book ahead for Calendimaggio (*see* above), Easter, July and August. There's a hotel booking service at Via Cristofani, t 075 816566, *caa@krenet.it* (*closed Sat and Sun*). Or the tourist office has a long list of rooms in religious or private houses.

### Very Expensive (€€€€)

★★★★**Le Silve**, Armenzano, 10km from centre on Monte Subasio, t 075 801 9000, *www.lesilve.it*. A 10th-century former hostel combining antique furnishings with all modern comforts, including a pool and sauna. There's a restaurant serving homemade Umbrian fare; half and full board are available. *Closed Dec–Feb.*

★★★**Dei Priori**, Corso Mazzini 15, t 075 812237, *www.assisi-hotel.com* (*€165*). A gracious, well-restored 18th-century *palazzo* off the main piazza, with a restaurant. Breakfast is included. Half/full board available.

**Fontebella**, Via Fontebella 25, t 075 812883, *www.fontebella.com*.

A 17th-century *palazzo* with quite elegant rooms with modern bathrooms (breakfast included), a restaurant, a garden and a garage.

### Expensive (€€€)

★★★★**Subasio**, Via Frate Elia 2, t 075 812206, *www.hotelsubasio.com*. A traditional, formal hotel linked to the Basilica of St Francis by a portico, counting among its past guests the King of Belgium and Charlie Chaplin. Many rooms have countryside views from vine-shaded terraces, and there are a private garage and an attractive medieval-vaulted restaurant. Breakfast is included in the rates.

★★★**Giotto**, Via Fontebella 41, t 075 812209, *www.hotelgiottoassisi.it*. Very pleasant, modern rooms near the basilica, a restaurant, a garden, and a garage. Breakfast is included. Full board available.

**La Terrazza**, Via Fratelli Canonichetti, t 075 812368, *www.laterrazzahotel.it*. A comfortable and welcoming family-run hotel in a peaceful setting just outside the centre. The sunsets are gorgeous. Half board available.

### Moderate (€€)

★★★**Il Palazzo**, Via San Francesco 8, t 075 816841, *www.hotelilpalazzo.it*. A 13th-century building in the centre. Simple rooms with antiques.

★★★**Umbra**, Via degli Archi 6, t 075 812240, *www.hotelumbra.it*. A charming family-run inn near Piazza del Comune, with a walled garden. Rooms can be small, but many have balconies. The restaurant serves creative cuisine grounded in Umbrian tradition. *Restaurant closed Sun.*

★★**Country House**, Via di Valecchie 41, 1km from west gate of Assisi, t 075 816363, *www.countryhousetreesse. com*. Lovely rooms with antiques, most en suite. Evening meals can be prepared for guests, and there's a splendid pool, a solarium and garden terraces, plus parking.

★★**San Giacomo**, Via S. Giacomo 6, t 075 816778, *www.hotelsangiacomoassisi.it*. A reliable, welcoming option in the historic centre, with a restaurant.

### Inexpensive (€)

★★**Ideale per Turisti**, Piazza Matteotti 1, t 075 813570, *www.hotelideale.it*. A decent little hotel close to the

(★) **Le Silve >**

amphitheatre, with a garden in which to enjoy good breakfasts in summer.

**Pallotta**, Via S. Rufino 4, t 075 812307, www.pallottaassisi.it. Basic rooms in a medieval palace, plus a good trattoria serving homemade pasta and popular with the locals. Parking can be difficult.

**Sole**, Corso Mazzini 35, t 075 812373, www.assisihotelsole.com. A large hotel with some en-suite rooms and a good restaurant. Closed Wed.

*Anfiteatro Romano, Via Anfiteatro Romano 4, t 075 813025. A good, quiet little place near Piazza Matteotti, with a restaurant. One room is en suite.

**Brigolante Guest Apartments**, Costa di Trex 31, 6km from centre at foot of Mt Subasio, t 075 802250, www.brigolante. com (€80 p/n). A working farm with apartments sleeping 2–4, with washing machines. Guests get a basket of local produce and can buy fresh meat, veg, eggs and cheese. Lets are by the week.

**Il Morino**, Via Spoleto 8, Bastia Umbria, 2km west of town, t 075 801 0839, www.ilmorino.com. A guesthouse on a working farm. Two of the basic rooms have balconies with views. Bikes are loaned and reasonably priced dinners served. Half and full board available.

**St Anthony's Guest House**, Via G. Alessi 10, t 075 812542. One of the most pleasant religious houses, run by American sisters. Breakfast is included, good cheap lunches are available. There's an 11pm curfew. Closed Nov–Feb.

## San Gregorio ✉ 06086

***Castel San Gregorio**, Via S. Gregorio 16, 12km northwest of Assisi, t 075 803 8009 (€€). Rooms in a restored 13th-century castle with a garden. Half and full board available.

## Bettona ✉ 06084

**Relais La Corte Di Bettona**, Via Caterina 2, t 075 987114, www.relaisbettona.com (€€€€). Unexpected contemporary style in sleepy Bettona (see p.132), in a former medieval hospital for orphans. The good restaurant (€€) serves Umbrian dishes with the odd twist; half board available.

# Eating Out in and around Assisi

## Assisi ✉ 06081

### Expensive (€€€)

**Buca di San Francesco**, Via Brizi, t 075 812204. This is something of an institution. Meals are served in the elegant stone-walled dining room or in the pretty garden. Closed Mon and first 2wks of July.

**San Francesco**, Via S. Francesco 52, t 075 812329. Fine cuisine and views from a veranda overlooking the basilica; try strangozzi with truffles. Closed Wed and 1–15 July.

### Moderate (€€)

**Al Camino Vecchio**, Via S. Giacomo 7a, t 075 812936. A good stopping-off point before or after visiting the Basilica, this has parking nearby. Set favourites include pasta dishes such as lasagne and a good maialino or roast pork. Closed Tues.

**Il Medio Evo**, Via Arco dei Priori 4, t 075 813 068. Local/global fare in a medieval setting. Try guinea fowl with grapes. Closed Mon, Jan, 3wks July.

**Nuova Osteria Piazzetta dell'Erba**, Via S. Gabriele dell'Addolorata, t 075 815352. This cheerful restaurant has a good central position. It offers dishes such as caramelle di pasta fresca con pere e pecorino (fresh pasta cushions stuffed with pear and sheep's cheese) and petto di faraona ai mirtilli (wood?cock cooked with blackcurrants). The set menu is good value. Closed Mon.

**Osteria Pozzo della Mensa**, Via Pozzo della Mensa 11b, t 075 815 5236. A Roman pillar is embedded in the walls of this attractive restaurant, with an upstairs terrace. Try the ravioli stuffed with truffles and porcini mushrooms or the wild boar casserole.

**La Stalla**, Via Eremo delle Carceri 8, Fontemaggio, t 075 812317. A lovely country trattoria on the way to the Eremo delle Carceri (see p.129). Hearty fare includes polenta with sausages. Closed Mon exc Easter and summer.

### Inexpensive (€)

**La Bottega della Pasticceria**, Via Portica 9. Strudels, chocolate and nut breads.

# Northern Umbria

Route SS3bis and Umbria's private railway, the FCU, follow the upper Tiber valley into a green landscape of tobacco farms, olive groves and rolling hills, enclosed by large stretches of forest and mountains – some of the most underpopulated countryside in Italy. To the west near Tuscany is arty Città di Castello; to the east stern, grey Gubbio is a drop of pure Umbrian essence up in the rugged mountains. In between are frescoes by Signorelli at Morra, a garden maze at Castello Bufalini in San Giustino, and lovely hill towns such as Monte Santa Maria Tiberina, Citerna and Montone. The mountains along the border of the Marches, meanwhile, form one of Umbria's beautiful natural parks.

# 08

## Don't miss

⭐ **Expressive junk-based art**
Collezione Burri, Città di Castello **p.140**

⭐ *Madonna del Parto* **painting**
Museum in the old school, Monterchi **p.144**

⭐ **A race between wax saints**
Gubbio **p.150**

⭐ **Awesome views**
Monte Ingino **p.152**

⭐ **Meadows and beech forests**
Parco Naturale del Monte Cucco **p.152**

*See map overleaf*

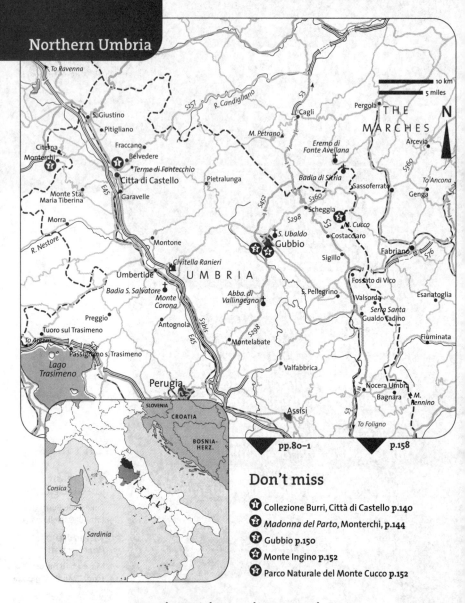

pp.80–1

p.158

## Don't miss

- ⭐ Collezione Burri, Città di Castello **p.140**
- ⭐ *Madonna del Parto*, Monterchi, **p.144**
- ⭐ Gubbio **p.150**
- ⭐ Monte Ingino **p.152**
- ⭐ Parco Naturale del Monte Cucco **p.152**

# Umbertide and Around

Approaching Umbertide from Perugia, the SS3bis is fairly straight and fairly dull, but there are a couple of possible detours in the nest of villages between it and the road to Gubbio. The most important town is **Montelabate**, where the large church of Santa Maria (1325) has an 11th-century crypt and some good frescoes, a *Madonna and Saints* by Bartolomeo Caporali and a *Crucifixion* by Fiorenzo di Lorenzo. It also has a pretty cloister from an earlier church. You might also stop in **Civitella Benazzone**, where the medieval Abbazia Celestina has been restored, and the parish church has paintings by Benedetto Bonfigli and Domenico Alfani.

Midway between Perugia and Città di Castello, **Umbertide** (population 14,000) on the Tiber was an Etruscan and Umbrian trading post. Known as *Pitulum* by the Romans, then Fratta until 1863, it changed its name in its enthusiasm for the new Kingdom of Italy, in honour of Umberto, son of Vittorio Emanuele II. It's sprawling and industrial, with a small *centro storico* that survived the Allied bombs that blew the rest of town to smithereens; Piazza 25 Aprile commemorates that day.

The main landmark, the **Rocca**, with fat crenellated towers, was built by the Perugians in the 1300s and houses the **Centro per L'Arte Contemporanea**, which has temporary exhibitions. There are three churches in Piazza San Francesco, outside the original walls. **Santa Croce** is a small museum with an excellent *Deposition* (1515) by Luca Signorelli and Niccolò Pomarancio's *Madonna and Child and Angels* (1577). Next door, **San Francesco** has good, if damaged, 17th-century frescoes. Like so many Umbrian towns, Umbertide has a geometrical Renaissance temple dedicated to Mary outside the walls, the octagonal Santa Maria della Reggia, begun in 1559.

Just east of Umbertide, the magnificent 15th-century castle **Civitella Ranieri** lords it high over a wooded park; it is privately owned but occasionally open in the summer. At the foot of Monte Corona (693m), 3km south of town, the Badia di San Salvatore was founded by wandering hermit saint Romualdo in 1008 for his Camaldolesian monks. Remodelled in the 18th century, and partly un-remodelled in the 20th, it has an unusual campanile that doubled as a defensive tower. The bare stone interior has traces of 14th-century frescoes and the nave is supported by an interesting hotchpotch of capitals and columns. The 8th-century stone ciborium was brought here from another church. The scenery from here towards Lake Trasimeno is lovely, especially around the medieval village of Preggio.

**Centro per L'Arte Contemporanea**
*t 075 941369;*
*open Tues–Sun*
*summer 10.30–12.30*
*and 4.30–7.30,*
*winter 10.30–12.30*
*and 4–7; adm*

**Santa Croce**
*t 075 942 0147;*
*open Fri–Sun and hols*
*summer 10.30–1 and*
*3.30–6, winter 10.30–1*
*and 3–5.30; adm*

## Montone

Northeast of Umbertide, the prettiest village is fortified hilltop **Montone**, on the road to Pietralunga. Founded in the 9th century, its strategic position high over the Tiber Valley made it a prize fought over by Perugia, Città di Castello and Gubbio. It was the birthplace of Andrea Braccio, better known as Braccio Fortebraccio (1368–1424), who grew up in Perugia only to be exiled from there with other members of the nobility in 1393. It became his lifelong ambition to return, and over the next 23 years he made himself one of the most feared *condottieri* in Italy, serving Ladislas King of Naples and the anti-pope John XXIII, at times taking Rome and the

Romagna, but in 1416 finally realizing his goal of returning to Perugia as its lord and master. It's worth making the trudge up to the top of the village, where one of the towers of the citadel makes a fantastic belvedere over the region.

Today a quiet, evocative village, Montone's Gothic church of **San Francesco** (1305) and its convent have recently been arranged as a **Museo Comunale**. The church has fine frescoes, including *St Anthony Abbot* by Bartolomeo Caporali and a damaged cycle on the life of St Francis. Among the paintings in the convent there's Caporali's *Madonna del Soccorso*, with a charming scene of Montone, and paintings by local 16th-century artist Vittorio Cirelli, who let his imagination run wild in a fantastical *Immaculate Conception*, and a remarkable life-sized wooden sculptural group of the Deposition of the Cross from the 1200s. On the ground floor, the **Museo Etnografico** has a fascinating display not of Umbrian farm tools, but of artefacts from East Africa, collected by a local resident.

**Museo Comunale**
*t 075 930 6535; open April–Sept Fri–Sun 10.30–1 and 3.30–6; Oct–May Sat and Sun 10.30–1 and 3–5.30*

Further up the valley, the *condottiere* Braccio Fortebraccio's castle, the magnificent **Rocca d'Aries**, has been well restored by its owner, the Region of Umbria. Further up the narrow road to the northeast is **Pietralunga**, a remote medieval village and a good base for exploring the mountains and forests, and for communing with the boars, foxes and other wildlife.

## Morra

Tobacco is king west of the Tiber. Morra, on the banks of the torrential Nestore, is the village to aim for. The story goes that Luca Signorelli, a native of nearby Cortona, fell in love when passing through in 1508 and decided to stay awhile, picking up the commission to fresco the 15th-century **Oratorio di San Crescentino**, on a hill outside town. The master worked with assistants, but his hand is easily identifiable in the *Flagellation*, *Crucifixion* and *Christ between Two Angels* (look out for the trademark Signorelli bottoms). Unfortunately, most of the other frescoes aren't as well preserved (they were restored in the 1970s) but they are beautiful; don't miss the older Gothic frescoes in the 13th-century sacristy.

**Oratorio di San Crescentino**
*t 075 855 4705; open Mon–Sat 2.30–6.30, Sun and hols 9.30–1 and 2.30–6.30; adm; knock at modern house next door for custodian*

## Where to Stay and Eat in and around Montone

**ⓘ Umbertide ›**
*Via Cibo, t 075 941 7099, www.comune. umbertide.pg.it*

### Umbertide ✉ 06019

**\*\*\*Rio**, SS. Tiberina, t 075 941 5033, *www.hotelrio.org* (€€€). Comfortable modern rooms (breakfast included in rates), a classy restaurant and landscaped grounds.

**\*\*Capponi**, Piazza 25 Aprile 19, t 075 941 2662, *www.hotelcapponi. com* (€€). A simple central option with a restaurant serving good-quality dishes at very reasonable prices. *Restaurant closed Sun.*

**\*\*Moderno**, SS. Tiberina, t 075 941 3759, *hotelmoderno@hotmail.com* (€€). Comfortable if basic rooms and a restaurant (half board is available).

**Country Hotel Poggiomanente,** SS219, Uscita E45, **t** 075 925 2000, *www.poggiomanente.com* (€€). A great deal of care has gone into converting this beautiful old stone mill and furnishing the rooms, all of them different. Lovely gardens and a pool make this an excellent base. Price includes breakfast. The owners also have apartments at the pleasant **Agriturismo Aqua Sorgiva** (€€), a few hundred metres from the hotel, which also has its own pool.

**Ristorante Poggiomanente**, SS219, Uscita E45, **t** 075 941 7388 (€€). Run by the same family as the Country Hotel Poggiomanente, but housed in a separate building, this restaurant has a well-earned reputation for fine Umbrian cooking, with dishes such as *tagliatelle al sugo d'oca* (in goose sauce) and *suino al finocchio selvatico* (pork roasted with wild fennel).

**Montone** ✉ 06060

**Ristorante Erba Luna**, Piazza Fortebraccio 4, **t** 075 930 6405 (€€€). Sophisticated versions of traditional Umbrian cuisine on the main square, with views over the valley. *Closed Tues.*

ⓘ **Montone »**

*Pro Loco,*
*Via San Francesco 1,*
**t** *075 930 6427,*
*www.montone.info*

# Città di Castello

Set on a plateau overlooking the Tiber valley, Città di Castello (population 38,000) is the most important city in northern Umbria, and one that has a marked Tuscan air. It started as the ancient Umbrian *Tifernum* and prospered under the early Roman Empire, when as *Tifernum Tiberinum* it controlled much trade in the upper Tiber valley. Totila and his Goths knocked it flat; the Early Christian bishops rebuilt it into a fortress town called *Castrum Felicitatis* ('Happy Castle').

In the 1400s and 1500s, under the enlightened tyranny of the Vitelli family, the city hired some of the best Renaissance artists (Raphael among them). In the 20th century, it was the birthplace of one of Italy's best-known post-war artists, Alberto Burri, who has left it an impressive collection of his works. Although bombed during the war, Città di Castello has recovered well, and today the Tifernati, as they are still known, make their living from textiles, printing and tobacco, but recall their love of culture in Umbria's second most important art museum.

## The Duomo and its Museum

Within its Renaissance walls, Città di Castello is a neat rectangle, still roughly following the streetplan of ancient *Tifernum*. The **Duomo**, with exactly one-half of a harmonious Baroque façade, was rebuilt in 580, and several more times. Much of what you see is from the 1400s, though parts of the original Romanesque cathedral remain – especially the 11th-century round campanile, inspired by the ancient towers of Ravenna (and just as tilted). Two handsome Gothic reliefs decorate the north portal. Inside, the single nave has a panelled wooden ceiling: the best painting is a mystical, dramatic altarpiece of the Transfiguration in the fourth chapel by Florentine Mannerist Rosso Fiorentino, who took refuge

## Getting to and around Città di Castello

Città di Castello has a station on the FCU Sansepolcro–Terni **train** line, or take the FS train to Arezzo then the bus. There are also daily **buses** to Urbino, Gubbio and Perugia.

**Parking** within the walls can be a nightmare; there are some car parks outside the walls – the free one to the north on Viale Nazario Sauro (Parcheggio Enrico Ferri) is close to an **escalator** taking you up into town.

here when he fled the sack of Rome in 1527. Much of the rest of the decoration is by local artists: one, 17th-century Giovanni Battista Pacetti (Lo Sguazzino or 'Splashy'), painted a view of his home town in the third chapel. The lower church was the ancient crypt and contains the bodies of Città's patrons, saints Florido and Amanzio.

**Museo del Duomo**
*t 075 855 4705;
open Tues–Sun 10–1
and 3–6.30; adm*

The rarest prize in the excellent **Museo del Duomo** is the **treasure of Canoscio** – beautiful 6th-century liturgical silver, probably hidden by the priest when Totila and the Goths came, and found 1,400 years later in 1932. The enamelled and gilded 12th-century altar frontal, showing Christ, the Evangelists and scenes from the Life of Christ, is said to have been donated by Pope Celestine II. There's a beautifully worked 14th-century crozier and 15th-century paintings, including a *Madonna* by a follower of Signorelli, a rich collection of liturgical items, two angels attributed to Giulio Romano and a small *Madonna and Child* and *St John the Baptist* by Pinturicchio.

### Near the Duomo

The triangular Piazza Gabriotti by the Duomo faces a small park where the papal fortress once stood; here too is the trecento **Palazzo dei Priori** (or Comunale) designed by Angelo da Orvieto, a handsome but unfinished building in sandstone. Opposite, the

**Torre Civica**
*open Tues–Sun
10–12.30 and
3–6.30; adm*

**Torre Civica** from the same century once held the city's medieval prisons, and has magnificent views over the valley from the top of its rickety old stair.

From a 14th-century **loggia**, Corso Cavour leads past the covered market, with an 18th-century print shop on top and a pretty 1890s

**Laboratorio
e Collezione
Tela Umbra**
*t 075 855 4337; open
Tues–Sat 9–12 and
3.30–5.30, Sun and hols
10.30–1 and 3–5.30; adm*

Art Nouveau bank. Civic life focused on Piazza Matteotti, which is overlooked by the very austere **Palazzo del Podestà** with double clocks on the façade, also by Da Orvieto. In Piazza Costa, cloth is woven on traditional looms at the **Laboratorio e Collezione Tela Umbra**, founded in 1908 by Baron Leopoldo Franchetti. The adjacent **museum** tells the history of weaving.

**★ Collezione
Burri**
*Via Mazzini,
t 075 855 4649, www.
fondazioneburri.org;
open Tues–Sat 9–12.30
and 2.30–6, Sun 10.30–
12.30 and 3–6; adm*

### Collezione Burri

Rather than nod off with all its art under its belt, 20th-century Città di Castello produced one of Italy's best known contemporary artists, Alberto Burri (1915–95). Burri was a doctor who ended up a prisoner of war in Texas in 1943; there he turned to art to express the carnage he had witnessed, using whatever he could find. On his return to Italy, he continued to explore the evocative power of discarded materials and junk, most famously his sacking soaked in red paint that resembled giant bandages, and his carefully composed pieces of twisted metal and charred wood. Burri was one of the great precursors of Abstract Expression and junk art in the USA, and of Italian Arte Povera; in later years he explored colour and other materials. This collection in the quattrocento Palazzo Albizzini comprises numerous works from 1943 to 1983.

Burri's large-scale works are exhibited in the tobacco-drying shed he used as a studio, the **Seccatoi Tabacchi**, to the south of town in Via Francesco Pierucci.

**Seccatoi Tabacchi**
*open Tues–Sat 9–12.30 and 2.30–6, Sun 10.30–12.30 and 3–6; adm*

## The North End of Town

The ruling Vitelli family could not have enough palaces; the Collezioni Burri is near their largest spread, the elegant **Palazzo Vitelli a Porta Sant'Egidio** built in 1540 by Giorgio Vasari, the writer and workmanlike painter from nearby Arezzo. It has a beautiful façade facing a huge garden, and an interior lavishly frescoed by Cristoforo Gherardi (Il Doceno) and Prospero Fontana; it's now owned by a bank and used for concerts.

Also along Via Albizzini is 13th-century **San Francesco** with its 18th-century interior. Vasari designed the elaborate Cappella Vitelli and painted the altarpiece; both are outdone by the fancy wrought-iron grille by local craftsman Pietro di Ercolano. There's a majolica of St Francis receiving the stigmata by the Della Robbia workshop, and a German-made wooden polychrome *Pietà* from the 1400s. The *Betrothal of the Virgin* (1504), Raphael's early masterpiece, was painted for this church. Napoleon put it in the Brera, and the Brera won't give it back; Città di Castello still hasn't got over it, and grudgingly shows a copy, a bittersweet consolation prize. In the adjacent piazza is an 1860 monument celebrating the end of the Papal States.

Via San Bartolomeo heads north, passing a smaller Palazzo Vitelli on the way to the **Biblioteca Comunale** and **Museo Civico**. This contains fossils from the Pleistocene era, when the Tiber was a lake, and a small archaeological collection. Around Via XI Settembre are three convents of closed orders of the Clarisse; at No.21, the nuns at **Santa Veronica** will show on request their pretty cloister and a small museum dedicated to their order and to St Veronica Giuliani (d. 1727), who lived here for 50 years in a state of almost continuous mystical experience and vision. Nearby, the non-conventual **church of Santa Maria delle Grazie** has a fresco of the Transition of the Virgin by Ottavino Nelli and a highly venerated painting, *Madonna della Grazie*, by Giovanni di Piemonte, a collaborator of Piero della Francesca; unfortunately, it's kept locked up and shown only twice a year (2 February and 26 August).

**Biblioteca Comunale/ Museo Civico**
*t 075 855 5687; open Mon, Tues, Thurs and Sat 9–12.45 and 3–6.45, Wed and Fri 9–1*

## The Pinacoteca Comunale

**Pinacoteca Comunale**

*Via della Cannoniera 22 (from behind Duomo, take Via di Modello/Via C. Battisti south), t 075 852 0656; open Tues–Sun mid-Sept to mid-July 10–1 and 2.30–6.30, mid-July–mid-Sept 10–6.30; adm*

This contains Città di Castello's only surviving Raphael, a half-ruined processional standard of 1503, but there are plenty of other attractions, beginning with the building itself. The Palazzo Vitelli alla Cannoniera (one of five Vitelli *palazzi* in town) was built in the 1520s by Antonio da Sangallo the Younger and Pier Francesco da Viterbo, decorated with *sgraffito* by Giorgio Vasari – a lovely façade, facing the inner gardens. The 16th-century frescoes inside (on the stairs) are the work of Cola dell'Amatrice and Doceno.

The star of the early paintings is a beautiful restored 14th-century *Maestà* by an anonymous painter known as the Master of Città di Castello. Nearby hangs a fine *Madonna and Child* by Spinello Aretino. The next room has another *Madonna* by the Sienese Andrea di Bartolo, as well as some early choirstalls; after that there's a residual Gothic Venetian view of the same subject by Antonio Vivarini. Lorenzo Ghiberti, master of Florence's baptistry doors, puts in a rare guest appearance with an equally Gothic-style golden reliquary of St Andrew (1420). The other highlight in this room is a Florentine *Madonna and Two Angels* by Neri di Bicci. In the next room is a *Coronation of the Virgin* from the workshop of Domenico Ghirlandaio; the *Head of Christ* is usually attributed to Giusto di Gand, a Flemish painter who worked in Urbino.

The next room has the Raphael standard, followed by altarpieces by local boy Francesco Tifernate and five marquetry sacristry cupboards. Many of these rooms contain frescoes by Doceno and reproductions of other works he produced during his stay. The most powerful painting in the museum is a *San Sebastiano* by Luca Signorelli and his workshop – a fascinating work with fantasy Roman ruins and a surreal treatment of space. There's also a good comical kitsch piece, an anonymous *Quo Vadis?*, a strange Virgin by a follower of Pontormo, and works by Raffaellino del Colle.

The sculpture collection includes early medieval woodcarving, or mixtures of painting and wooden sculpture, especially the altarpiece of the Crucifixion with the Virgin Mary and the Magdalene, the Sun and Moon – the wooden crucifix has disappeared, but the work is strangely suggestive without it. Here, too, is a fine 14th-century Sienese relief on the Baptism of Christ and works by Della Robbia.

## San Domenico

The first street left of the museum, Largo Muzi, leads up to the huge preaching church of San Domenico, finished in 1424. The façade was never finished but it has a handsome door on the left; the gloomy interior has good 15th-century frescoes and choirstalls. Signorelli's *San Sebastiano* used to hang in the Renaissance chapels by the altar, along with Raphael's *Crucifixion*, which is now in the National Gallery in London; it's replaced here by a copy.

(i) Città di
Castello >
*Via Sant'Antonio 1,*
*t 075 855 4817,*
*and Piazza Matteotti,*
*t 075 855 4922,*
*www.regioneumbria.eu*
*and www.cdcnet.net*

## Tourist Information in Città di Castello

It's worth noting that entrance to any museum within Città di Castello gets you a discount on admission to others, so you should make sure to keep your ticket.

### Market Days

**Food and general market**, Thurs and Sat, Piazza Gabriotti.

**Fleamarket**, 3rd Sun of month, Piazza Matteotti and surrounding streets.

## Where to Stay in Città di Castello

### Città di Castello ✉ 06012

****Tiferno**, Piazza R. Sanzio 13, **t** 075 855 0331, *www.hoteltiferno.it* (€€€€). A plush option occupying a 17th-century palace, with comfortable rooms (a buffet breakfast is included in rates), a billiards room, a garage, and one of the best restaurants in town, where you can feast on the likes of ravioli with shrimp in orange sauce or pigeon with grapes.

***Europa**, Via V.E. Orlando 2, **t** 075 855 0551, *www.gita.it* (€€€€). A good option if you want to be in town, with pleasant rooms. Rates include breakfast, and half and full board is offered. Note that rates nearly halve outside high season.

(★) Ristorante
da Meo >>

***Hotel delle Terme**, Fontecchio, **t** 075 852 0614, *www.termedifontecchio.it* (€€). A large, pleasant hotel offering all modern comforts, thermal treatments, a fine open-air pool, a restaurant, and a pizzeria with a beautiful terrace. Breakfast is included and half board is available.

****Umbria**, Via Sant'Antonio 6, **t** 075 855 4925, *www.hotelumbria.net* (€). Modest rooms in the centre, with half or full board if you wish.

## Eating Out in Città di Castello

This is one place in Umbria with good bread; try the *pane nociato* with walnuts.

**Amici Miei**, Via del Monte 2, **t** 075 855 9904 (€€). Good salmon with chard, and wild boar with beans and sage. *Closed Wed and 2wks Nov.*

**Il Bersaglio**, Via V.E. Orlando 14, just outside walls, **t** 075 855 5534 (€€). Game, truffles, mushrooms and local wines. *Closed Wed and 2wks July.*

**Ristorante da Meo**, Fraccano, on SS257 10km east of town, **t** 075 855 3870 (€€). A small restaurant of the kind fast disappearing from Italy: choose from a limited but excellent menu of the day – usually a pasta dish followed by meat grilled over the fire in front of you – and be pleasantly surprised by the bill. *Closed Wed.*

# Around Città di Castello

Centro
Tradizioni
Popolari
*Villa Cappelletti;*
*t 075 855 2119; open*
*Tues–Sun summer*
*8.30–12.30 and 3–7,*
*winter 8.30–12.30*
*and 2–6; adm*

Just 2km south of Città di Castello, at **Garavelle**, the Centro Tradizioni Popolari is a fascinating folk museum in an Umbrian farmhouse, furnished as it would have been a century ago, with blacksmith's forge, oil press, wine cellars and farm instruments.

Just to the east, Città di Castello has its own spa, the **Terme di Fontecchio**, where Pliny the Younger came to take the alkaline sulphurous waters. The current spa (Mar–Dec) dates from the 19th century. There's fine scenery along the SS257, especially 5km east of Città di Castello at the hill of **Belvedere**, site of the **Santuario della Madonna del Belvedere**, an octagonal domed Baroque church with a quirky façade and a venerated terracotta *Madonna and Child*.

West of Città di Castello, **Monte Santa Maria Tiberina** is a lovely medieval hill town in a sublime lofty setting. Once inhabited by the

Etruscans, the village was made an independent marquisate for the Del Monte family by Emperor Charles IV in 1355. A favour to the French earned them the right to call themselves the Bourbon del Monte; they ruled their little Ruritania until 1798, when Napoleon, who had no patience for anachronisms, especially with the name Bourbon on, snatched it away. Today, fewer than 150 souls live here, but you can see what remains of the Del Monte family's medieval castle and some of their tombs in the parish church.

## Monterchi

**🏛 Museum**
*Via della Reglia,*
*t 0575 70713; open daily*
*9–1 and 2–7; adm*

Just 2km from Citerna in Monterchi, stop at the small **museum** in the old school to see Piero della Francesca's magnificent and recently restored *Madonna del Parto*, a rare portrayal of a weary, pregnant Virgin, painted in the tomb of a nobleman and forgotten for centuries. The rareness of the scene is emphasized by the fact that the Mother of God stands in an exotic tent, the flaps held open by two solemn angels to allow a glimpse of the sacred mystery; it is not only great art, but also a popular icon for expectant mothers in the vicinity.

## Colle Plinio

If you take the old road from Città di Castello, follow the signs east towards Pitigliano, continue over the bridge and take the first road left, you'll come to **Colle Plinio**, where in the 1970s excavations revealed the remains of the 1st-century AD villa of Pliny the Younger. Although not open to the public, you can look through the fence at the baths and wine cellar.

## Citerna

Head west from Città di Castello along the SS221 towards Arezzo to reach this gem of a hill town that has aged like fine wine. On the border of Tuscany, peacefully set over the Tiber valley on a densely wooded hill, **Citerna** was a Roman town, rebuilt by the Lombards, fought over by its neighbours and restored after a quake in 1917. One unusual feature is the partly vaulted medieval passageway circling much of the lower town. Further up, **San Francesco**, rebuilt in 1508, is the chief repository of art, with a late, rather worn fresco by Luca Signorelli and helpers, the *Madonna and Child, St Francis and St Michael*. The altars are decorated with Della Robbia ceramics that seeped over the Tuscan border, and there are fine altarpieces by Raffaellino del Colle, the *Christ in Glory* and the *Madonna and St John the Evangelist*, plus a *Deposition* by Pomarancio.

**San Francesco**
*if locked, ask at*
*Via Garibaldi 27, just*
*down from church*

The nearby **Casa Prosperi** has an extraordinary carved 16th-century fireplace. Up past pretty Piazza Scipioni, the dark 18th-century church of **San Michele Arcangelo** has more colourful Della Robbia work, a *Crucifixion* by Pomarancio and a bell from a church destroyed in the quake, signed and dated 1267. In the last war,

**Casa Prosperi**
*ask at bar on piazza*
*for someone with a key*

**San Michele**
**Arcangelo**
*ask at same bar for key*

Citerna's castle on top of the town was blown up by the Germans, leaving the walls and brick tower, which offer a spectacular view as far as La Verna in Tuscany, where St Francis received the stigmata. A fountain by the walls commemorates the saint, who visited in 1224.

### San Giustino

**Castello Bufalini**
*t 075 856 115; open 1 June only*

Further up the Tiber valley, San Giustino has the lovely **Castello Bufalini**, begun in the 1200s as a fortress by the *comune* of Città di Castello, which gave it in 1487 to the noble Bufalini family, to finish (and pay for) the impressive walls and star-shaped moat. A century later, when war seemed unlikely, Giulio Bufalini converted it into an seigneurial villa, on plans by Vasari, with a loggia and courtyard. He also planted one of the most beautiful Italian gardens in Umbria inside the moat, with a maze, geometric hedges, fountains and parterres. In 1989, the Bufalini donated the castle to the State; the gardens and ground floor, with rooms of antiques frescoed by 16th-century painter Cristofano Gherardi, have been restored.

### Borgo Sansepolcro

**Museo Civico**
*t 0575 732218; open daily Oct–May 9.30–1 and 2.30–6, June–Sept 9–1 and 2.30–7.30; adm*

Over the border in Tuscany, at the terminus of the FCU rail line, Borgo Sansepolcro was part of Umbria until 1441, when Pope Eugenius IV gave it to Cosimo dei Medici to pay back the 25,000 gold florins he owed him for the expenses of the Council of Basle. Which is why the art books so often classify its favourite son, Piero della Francesca, as a member of the Umbrian school. Two of his paintings are in the town hall's **Museo Civico**. The *Resurrection*, an intense, almost eerie depiction of the triumphant Christ rising from his tomb over sleeping soldiers and a dead landscape, shares pride of place with the *Misericordia Polyptych*, a gold-ground altarpiece dominated by a giant-sized Madonna, sheltering under her cloak members of the confraternity who commissioned the picture. Other works in the museum are by Luca Signorelli, Pontormo and Matteo di Giovanni; more Renaissance painting can be seen in Sansepolcro's Romanesque Duomo.

# Gubbio

In a way, Gubbio (population 33,000) is what Umbria has always wanted to be: stony, taciturn and mystical, a tough mountain town that fought its own battles until destiny and the popes caught up with it, and also a town of culture, one with its own school of painters. For a city more than 2,500 years old, it still seems like a frontier town, an elemental place that sticks in the memory, with its green mountainside, rushing stream, straight rows of rugged grey-stone houses. On its windy slopes, the hard-edged brilliance of the Italian Middle Ages is clear and tangible.

## Getting to and around Gubbio

Around 10 daily APM **coaches** (**t** 800 512141, *www.apmperugia.it*; Fontevegge station, **t** 075 501 0485, Fossato di Vico station, **t** 075 919230) follow the beautiful SS298 to Perugia (40km/1hr) from the central Piazza Quaranta Martiri (where schedules are posted). There are also buses to the closest **train** station, 20km southeast at Fossato di Vico, on the FS Foligno–Ancona line to Rome and a Città di Castello–Arezzo–Florence line. The bus and train info office at Via della Repubblica 13, **t** 075 922 0066, sells bus tickets.

Gubbio is also one of the few Italian hill towns that a stick-in-the-mud geologist might recognize. Everyone has heard of the theory that the dinosaurs became extinct after a large meteor struck the earth 65 million years ago and raised so much dust that it blocked out the sun. Some of the strongest evidence for the theory was discovered just outside Gubbio, in the Camignano valley towards Scheggia, where there's a layer of sedimentary rock dense with the rare minerals of meteorites. It's thin but chronologically correct, and thick enough to have done the dirty deed.

### History

Gubbio was a city of the ancient Umbrii, perhaps even their political and religious centre. In Roman times, it flourished as *Iguvium* and, according to legend, was where Rome exported its lunatics, which has left a lingering influence on the populace. Mad or not, the Eugubini, as the natives are known, certainly weren't stupid; when unsolicited visits by the Goths, Huns and Avars left the place a mess, the survivors moved their town to a more defensible site on the nearby hillside.

As soon as the wall was up, they began annoying their neighbours; the chronicles describe a tough, querulous medieval *comune*. In the 1150s, 12 Umbrian cities under Frederick Barbarossa combined to attack it; the city was saved by its bishop, later Sant' Ubaldo, who persuaded the emperor to grant it independence. The chroniclers also claimed for Gubbio a population of 50,000 – probably double the real figure but still quite large for a medieval town. As in every other city, there was continuous conflict between the *comune* and ambitious nobles. One of them, Giovanni Gabrielli, became *signore* of the town in 1350, but only four years later Cardinal Albornoz and his papal army snatched it away. In 1387 it fell to Urbino's dukes of Montefeltro, who ruled it well until their line became extinct in 1508. Gubbio remained part of the duchy of Urbino until 1624, when it became part of the Papal States.

One famous visitor in 1206–7 was St Francis, who found Gubbio plagued by wolves; one was ravaging the countryside and terrorizing the populace. Ignoring fears for his safety, he went and had a word with the wolf, brought it to town and made it promise to stop terrorizing Gubbio in exchange for regular meals – an agreement sealed with a shake of the paw. The wolf kept the bargain and is immortalized in a bas-relief over the door of a church on Via Mastro Giorgio. A few years ago, in another church, workmen discovered the skeleton of a giant wolf under a slab. In recent years some of its descendants have been sighted after a long absence, in the forests of northern Umbria.

Gubbio saw some terrible fighting in the Second World War. In 1943, after the Italian surrender, Umbria was occupied by the Germans, who were harried by partisans, based in the mountains above Gubbio. Though most of Umbria fell relatively quickly to the British and Commonwealth forces as they advanced north after the liberation of Rome on 4 June, the fighting was intense and progress slow in the north. Meanwhile, a number of vicious reprisals on innocent villagers took place around Gubbio, while the Germans took positions and pounded the allies; the battle for Gubbio took three weeks, only ending on 25 July.

All of Gubbio's churches are now open. The earthquake damage in 1997 was relatively minor compared to that of 1982.

## Gubbio, From the Bottom Up

Most people approach Gubbio from the west, passing open pastureland – once the centre of Roman *Iguvium*. In the middle stands a large, well-preserved 1st-century AD **Roman theatre and antiquarium** used for summer performances of classical Greek and Roman drama and Shakespeare. From here, you get the best view of Gubbio: stone houses climb the slope in neat parallel rows, and the tall Palazzo dei Consoli on its vast platform dominates the centre.

**Roman Theatre and Antiquarium**
*t 075 922 0992; open daily April–Sept 8.30–7.30, Oct–Mar 8.30–5.30*

Gubbio proper is entered via big green **Piazza Quaranta Martiri**, named for the 40 citizens gunned down on this spot by Nazis in reprisals for partisan activities. On the west end of the square, behind its unfinished façade, mid-13th-century **San Francesco**, with an octagonal campanile and a distinctive Gothic design with a triple apse, is the work of Perugian architect Fra Bevignate. Inside are good frescoes, especially the damaged series on the life of the Virgin in the left apse, painted in 1408–13 and one of the greatest works by Gubbio's greatest painter, the International Gothic master Ottaviano Nelli. There is also a copy of Daniele da Volterra's *Deposition* on the third altar; right of the altar are 14th-century frescoes on the life of St Francis. The oldest frescoes from the 1200s are high up in the main apse. In the restored cloister are bits of polychrome Roman mosaics found in Gubbio and more frescoes.

**San Francesco**
*visits by appt on t 075 927 3460*

On the other side of the piazza is the **Loggia dei Tiratoio** (Weaver's Loggia), an arcade dating from 1603 under which newly woven textiles could be stretched to shrink evenly – it's one of few such loggias to survive. The nearby church, **Santa Maria dei Laici**, dates from the 14th century and is usually locked; it contains an *Annunciation*, the last painting of Baroque master Federico Barocci.

## Piazza Grande and the Palazzo dei Consoli

From Piazza dei Quaranta Martiri, Via Piccardi ascends past picturesque medieval lanes on the banks of the Camignano, a rushing torrent in spring and winter. Many of the houses and modest *palazzi* date back to the 13th century, here and there adorned with carved doors or windows, or 'Death's doors' as in Perugia. At the top is the magnificent **Piazza Grande** (or Piazza della Signoria), occupying a balcony hovering over a steep drop, with a stunning view of the town.

King of the piazza is the beautiful, huge Palazzo dei Consoli, one of Italy's most remarkable public buildings, begun in 1332 by Gubbio's master architect Gattapone, with a bit of help from Angelo da Orvieto (*consolo*, a word derived from the Roman *consul*, was a common title for an officer of a free medieval *comune*). Supported on the hill by a remarkable substructure of arches, it's graced with an elegant loggia, a slender campanile, square Guelph crenellations and asymmetrically arranged windows and arches. It faces the Palazzo Pretorio (now the *municipio*) designed by the same architect to make the piazza a set-piece.

**Museo Archeologico Comunale**
*t 075 927 4298; open daily April–Oct 10–1 and 3–6, Nov–Mar 10–1 and 2–5; adm*

The **Palazzo dei Consoli**, now the Museo Archeologico Comunale, boasts treasures from the 16th century BC to the 19th century AD. On the first floor, the vast barrel-vaulted Sala dell'Arengo, where assemblies were held, is cluttered with fascinating archaeological odds and ends, tombstones, sarcophagi and crossbows. There's a Roman inscription – Governor Gnaeus Satirus Rufus bragging how much he spent to embellish the town – and a collection of seals and coins from the days when Gubbio minted its own. One unique treasure, the bronze **Eugubine tablets**, have by far the most important inscriptions ever found in the Umbrian language and were discovered in the 15th century near the Roman theatre. Partly written in the Etruscan alphabet and partly in the Latin, these codes of religious observances and rituals for Gubbio's priests are also a rare survival of a religious how-to textbook, with details on sacrifices (including human enemies) and how to read the future in a liver or in the flight of birds.

Medieval Gubbio made its living from ceramics; in the 16th century, this tradition produced a real artist, **Mastro Giorgio Andreoli**, who discovered a beautiful ruby and golden glaze for majolica plates (you'll notice the absence of red in most painted ceramics; it's very hard to do). Mastro Giorgio's secret died with him, and it was long one of Gubbio's deepest regrets that it had not a single example of his work to show. When it became known that Sotheby's had a plate by Mastro Giorgio to auction in 1991, the townspeople purchased it by public subscription. With another piece bought in 1996, it is displayed in the loggia; they show the fall of Phaeton and Circe, and keep company with ceramic works made over the centuries, including red terracotta pharmaceutical jars. There are also fine views over Gubbio.

**Pinacoteca**

*opening times as for Museo Archeologico Comunale (see opposite)*

The **Pinacoteca**, up the stairs on the *piano nobile*, is as quirky and charming, though there are few first-rate pieces: a 13th-century diptych in a Byzantine portable altar; painted crucifixes; a detached 17th-century fresco on St Francis and the Wolf; a *Tree of Jesse* by a cinquecento Gubbio artist; the quattrocento *Madonna del Melograno* by Pier Francesco Florentini; a *Flight into Egypt* by Rutilio Manetti; and an anonymous 1600s work, *Last Night of Babylon* – one of the best crazy paintings in Italy. Some rooms remain in their 1500s state. The rooms of the Pinacoteca are an attraction in themselves; some haven't been remodelled since the 1500s.

**Museo Archeologico**

*open daily 10–1 and 3–6*

The lower floor of the *palazzo* houses the **Museo Archeologico**, with an Umbrian and Roman collection of bronzes and ceramics, other architectural odds and ends, and a Byzantine sarcophagus.

## To the Duomo and Palazzo Ducale

From Piazza Grande, stepped **Via Galeotti**, one of the city's most resolutely medieval lanes, leads up to the winding Via Ducale and Gubbio's Duomo. On the way, note the old cellar under the cathedral housing the **Botte dei Canonici**, a house-sized 1500s barrel that once held 40,000 litres of wine – a masterpiece of the cooper's art, made without nails. On top, the 14th-century **Palazzo dei Canonici** houses the **Museo Diocesano**, with a damaged 14th-century fresco of the Crucifixion and a beautiful 16th-century Flemish cope, magnificently embroidered and presented to the cathedral by Pope Marcellus II, a native of Gubbio.

**Museo Diocesano**

*t 075 922 0904; open daily summer 10–7, winter 10–6; closed 15 May; adm*

The 13th-century **Duomo**, refitted with a simple front in the 1400s, is remarkable for the unusual pointed wagon stone vaulting of the nave, a Eugubine speciality, and for its stained-glass windows. Local talent is well represented in the side chapels; in the presbytery is a *Nativity* attributed to one of Pinturicchio's talented students, Eusebio di San Giorgio. The high altar is a Roman sarcophagus. Note the 16th-century choirstalls, painted to resemble intarsia by Benedetto Nucci, and the 1556 carved throne (real) by Girolamo Maffei.

⭐ **Corse dei Ceri**

From the Duomo, you can walk up and up to the sanctuary of Sant'Ubaldo, following the route run in the **race of the Ceri** (*see* p.150), but it's much easier to take the *funivia* (*see* p.152).

**Palazzo Ducale**

*Via Federico da Montefeltro, t 075 927 5872; open Tues–Sun 8.30–7.30; adm*

Opposite the cathedral, the **Palazzo Ducale** was designed in the 1470s for that great patron of artists and humanists, the *condottiere* Federico da Montefeltro, Duke of Urbino, by Sienese architect Francesco di Giorgio Martini. Gentlemanly Federico was a paragon among Renaissance rulers (he received the Order of the Garter from Edward IV); he took a paternalistic interest in the welfare of his subjects and frequently travelled to keep an eye on things. He also liked to lodge in style and built at least a dozen

## The *Corsa dei Ceri*

Gubbio has retained some exceedingly medieval festivals that fill its solemn streets with colour and exuberance. On the last Sunday in May, crossbow-men from Sansepolcro come to compete in the *Palio della Balestra*, a fiercely fought contest dating back to 1461, with a procession, flag-throwing and music to warm things up. An even older custom is the Good Friday procession and a representation of the Passion, performed at the little church of Santa Croce della Foce just outside the city walls, with medieval chants and music played on wooden instruments called *battistrangoli*. Oldest of them all, however, is the *Corsa dei Ceri*, held every 15 May, the day before the feast of Sant'Ubaldo, the town's patron saint. Although first documented a couple of years after Ubaldo saved the city from Emperor Frederick and his Umbrian allies, over centuries the festival has taken on the uninhibited trappings of a pagan celebration that may have predated the good bishop's heroism. The *ceri* (candles) are three tall, wooden, octagonal towers some 13ft high, each topped by a wax saint representing one of the three guilds of Gubbio – Sant'Ubaldo (the builders), San Giorgio (the artisans) and Sant'Antonio Abate (the farmers).

The *ceri* are brought down from the sanctuary into Gubbio on 1 May. On 15 May, following a mass, the three wax saints are brought out of the church of the Muratori and taken in a procession to the *ceri* in Piazza Grande, where they are affixed to the top of the 'candles'. A second procession then begins at Porta Castello and heads up to Piazza Grande, where the *ceri* are taken around town by their colourfully costumed teams. This is followed by a big fish banquet for participants and officials in the Palazzo dei Consoli. At 4.30 in the afternoon, there's another procession led by the bishop, in which the *ceri* are baptized with a jug of water. The race begins at 6, starting in Piazza Grande; 10 bearers hoist the supports of their respective *cero* on their shoulders and race pell-mell through the crowds up the streets (Via XX Settembre, Via Colomboni, Via Appennino to Porta del Monte, where they rest before continuing to the mountain-top church of Sant'Ubaldo). At intervals, the teams are replaced by fresh men – a neat trick done without slowing the remarkably quick pace. Ubaldo invariably wins (and what could be more Italian than a fixed race?). In the evening, the wax saints are returned to their home in the Muratori with the last procession of the day, by candlelight.

In 1943 during the German occupation, all-women teams carried the *ceri* (each weighs around 450lbs) and successfully made it all the way up to Sant'Ubaldo, for pride and to spite the Nazis – an experiment that hasn't been repeated since. Since the war, the *ceri* have become the symbol of Umbria, represented by the three red stripes on the region's coat of arms.

palaces in the northern Marches as homes from home. His Gubbio address was one of the most stylish – a compact version of his famous palace in Urbino. The elegant, serene little courtyard in particular evokes its great model, with *pietra serena* details and the initials FD (Federico Duca). The palace was stripped of its furnishings before it was purchased by the State in 1957, but some fireplaces remain, along with fine stairways, windows and original terracotta flooring, one wooden ceiling, a few 15th-century intarsia doors and photos of the beautiful intarsia work of the little *studiolo* or ducal study, made by Giuliano da Maiano, now in New York. Some rooms have detached frescoes and paintings. Downstairs, examine the plumbing and old kitchen, foundations of a Lombard palace from the 10th century. Upstairs, the loggia has a handsome frieze in *pietra serena* and lovely views onto the Palazzo dei Consoli.

## Gubbio's West End

From Piazza Grande, Gubbio's main street, Via dei Consoli, leads past ceramic shops to the very medieval western quarter. Near

Piazza Giordano Bruno, the **Bargello** (1302), the first public building here, was a police station and governor's office; its round 16th-century **Fontana dei Matti** (Fountain of the Mad) was Gubbio's main water source and has the power to make you *loco* if you run around it three times. Here, too, is **San Domenico**, an earlier Romanesque church taken over by the Dominicans in the 1300s. After an 18th-century remodelling, only bits of the trecento frescoes remain, along with an exceptional Renaissance intarsia reading stand.

Vias Vantaggi and Gabrielli lead from here to the 13th-century **Palazzo del Capitano del Popolo**, a no-nonsense Romanesque structure with a privately run **museum of torture instruments**. Nearby is one of the equally austere city gates, **Porta Metauro**, and a medieval tower fortress belonging to the Palazzo Gabrielli. **Santa Croce della Foce**, just outside the gate, is the site of the medieval Good Friday representation of the Passion.

Just inside Porta Metauro is the entrance to the **Parco Ranghiasci-Brancaleoni**, which sweeps up to the Palazzo Ducale. Laid out as an English garden in 1841 by Francesco Ranghiasci (who married an Englishwoman), it was restored by the *comune* and offers the greatest possible contrast to the grey-stone streets of the city. It has a pretty covered bridge, neoclassical pavilions and a café.

## The East End

**Porta Romana**
*t 075 922 1199; open daily 9–1 and 3.30–7.30; adm*

At the east end of town, the 13th-century Porta Romana is now a museum devoted to medieval gates, with a collection of old keys and a drawbridge mechanism, as well as a collection of Gubbio ceramics, which includes some from the workshop of Mastro Giorgio. Near the gate, two 13th-century churches contain works by Ottaviano Nelli. The deconsecrated Santa Maria Nuova has his joyous, worldly *Madonna del Belvedere* and frescoes by his followers. Just outside the gate, **Sant'Agostino** has more frescoes by Nelli and his pupils: the *Life of St Augustine* in the triumphal arch and apse and, on the fifth altar on the right, *Sant'Ubaldo and Two Saints*. The *funivia* here ascends to Monte Ingino (*see* p.152).

**Santa Maria Nuova**
*visitors need permission from Soprintendenza Archeologica in Perugia, t 075 57411*

Back within the Porta Romana, the **Arco di San Marziale** marks the site of the ancient Umbrian gate. Via Dante leads down to a giant 18th-century tabernacle of Sant'Ubaldo at the crossroads with Corso Garibaldi. Nearby, the **Palazzo Accoramboni** was the birthplace in 1557 of Vittoria Accoramboni. By age 16 she was not only married but having an affair with Duke Paolo Giordano Orsini, who killed her husband to marry her (twice), before she was killed aged 28 by Orsini ruffians. Papal involvement and other sordid details made it juicy enough for the London stage – John Webster's play on Vittoria's life, *The White Devil*, appeared in 1608.

From Corso Garibaldi, Via V. Armanni descends to **San Pietro**, with four Corinthian columns on the façade and a Renaissance interior.

The first altar has a *Martyrdom of St Bartholomew* by Sienese painter Rutilio Manetti; the fourth has a *Visitation* by Giannicola di Paolo; the fifth was decorated by Raffaellino del Colle. In the left transept is a 13th-century wooden statue of the *Deposition*.

Below San Pietro is the **Porta Vittoria**: if you follow Via della Piaggiola from here, you pass **Santa Maria della Piaggiola**, with an ornate Baroque interior used for concerts; there's a *Madonna and Child* by Ottaviano Nelli on the altar, repainted. Another Baroque church just over the bridge to the right, **Santa Maria del Prato** (1662), is a copy of Borromini's San Carlino alla Quattro Fontane in Rome.

If you continue along Via della Piaggiola, it's about 2km to the spot where Francis met with the wolf on Via Frate Lupo: the isolated **Chiesa della Vittorina** was built in the 13th century and the charming interior has another odd nave with pointed Gothic vaults and early frescoes, undisturbed by remodelling in the 1500s. A bronze statue (1973) of the saint and wolf marks the encounter.

**Chiesa della Vittorina**
*open Tues–Sun 9–12 and 4–7*

## Monte Ingino

⭐ **Monte Ingino**

You can make the stiff climb up Monte Ingino to the **sanctuary of Sant'Ubaldo** from the cathedral, but you'll make life much easier for yourself if you take the funivia from the Porta Romana instead. On display within the five-naved church, besides the ashes of the patron saint who saved Gubbio from the emperor, are the three *ceri* (*see* p.150). There's a café and restaurant too, and you can walk a bit further up for even more spectacular views from the **Rocca** (888m). At Christmas time, the entire slope of Monte Ingino is illuminated, using 12km of electric cable, to form 'the world's largest Christmas tree'.

**Funivia**
*t 075 927 3881, www.funivia gubbio.com; April and May Mon–Sat 10–1.15 and 2.30–6.30, Sun and hols 9.30–1.15 and 2.30–7; June Mon–Sat 9.30–1.15 and 2.30–7, Sun and hols 9–7.30; July and Aug daily 9–8; Sept Mon–Sat 9.30–1.15 and 2.30–7, Sun and hols 9.30–1.15 and 2.30–7.30; Oct daily 10–1.15 and 2.30–6; Nov–Feb Thurs–Tues 10–1.15 and 2.30–5; Mar Mon–Sat 10–1.15 and 2.30–5.30, Sun and hols 9.30–1.15 and 2.30–6*

## Excursions from Gubbio

Around Gubbio you can expect long stretches of empty space punctuated by an occasional half-ruined castle, monastery or the plainest of mountain villages. **Castel d'Alfiolo**, 6km to the south of Gubbio on the SS219, was converted from a family fortress to a Benedictine abbey in the 1100s; most of the buildings were redone in the 16th century, but the chapel and the main building conserve good stone carving from the 1200s.

Another abbey, the 13th-century **Abbazia di Vallignegno**, halfway down the road to Perugia, has been converted into an *agriturismo*, but you can still visit the church with its Roman sarcophagus.

To the east of Gubbio, the SS298 passes through a lovely gorge with old watermills on the way to the **Parco Naturale del Monte Cucco** on the border of the Marches. This is a popular spot with the Eugubini on summer weekends, with pretty mountain meadows and beech forests around Pian di Ranco; it's also one of the best places in Umbria in which to go hang-gliding, and in winter people

⭐ **Parco Naturale del Monte Cucco**
*t 075 917 7326, www.parks.it/parco. monte.cucco/index, parco.montecucco@ libero.it*

head up for the cross-country skiing. Descendants of Francis's Brother Wolf still roam on **Monte Cucco** (1,566m), one of Umbria's highest peaks. One of its flanks, Monte Cucco conceals one of the deepest subterranean systems in the world (922m) – the 20km-long **Grotte di Monte Cucco**, which is reached by a long iron stair (although it's currently off-limits to the public). The remains of gigantic prehistoric cave bears have been found here, and the innermost chambers are inhabited by a singular race of blind flies.

**Grotte di Monte Cucco**
*closed to public; for guided tours of other caves, contact CENS, t 075 917 0400 or t 075 917 0601, www.cens.it*

This mountainous region had a special pull on holy men of the 10th and 11th centuries. San Romualdo, a nobleman turned monk and the founder of the Order of the Camaldolese Benedictines, had a mystical vision of his vocation on Monte Sitria; the site is marked by the handsome Romanesque church of the **Abbazia di Santa Maria di Sitria**, above **Scheggia**, the last Umbrian town on the Via Flaminia. Romualdo, though a great wanderer who founded abbeys as far as the Pyrenees, was also the moving spirit behind the **Monastero della Fonte Avellana**, which is found off the SS360, just over the border in the Marches, in an isolated setting. Founded in 979, this was an important centre of learning during the Middle Ages (Dante was one of many famous visitors). Perhaps unique in Italy, it preserves the *scriptorium* in which codices and manuscripts were copied.

**Monastero della Fonte Avellana**
*open Mon–Sat 9–11.30 and 3–5, Sun 3–4*

## Shopping in Gubbio

Market day is Tuesday, in Piazza Quaranta Martiri.

Gubbio's artist-artisans still turn out some of the most beautiful **ceramics** in Italy, hand-painted in colourful, original floral designs, including plates in all sizes. On Via dei Consoli alone, try Fabbrica Ranimi, Fabbrica Mastro Giorgio, and No.44. Gubbio also has a longstanding tradition in **wrought-iron** work, harder to carry home.

## Where to Stay in Gubbio

**(i) Gubbio >**
*Via della Repubblica 15, t 075 922 0693 or t 075 922 0790, www.regioneumbria.eu*

### Gubbio ✉ 06024

Advance bookings are essential in July and August.

### Luxury (€€€€€)

****Park Hotel ai Cappuccini**, Via Tifernate, t 075 9234, *www.parkhotelaicappuccini.it*. An award-winning Franciscan monastery outside town, with a cloister and chapel, a pool, sauna and fitness centre, and an Umbrian restaurant.

### Very Expensive (€€€€)

****Relais Ducale**, Via Galeotti, t 075 922 0157, *www.mencarelligroup.com*. Three historic buildings in the medieval heart, linked by a lift. Rooms are sumptuous with beautiful views of town. It has a garage on the edge of town, accessed by a shuttle service.

### Expensive (€€€)

****Bosone**, Via XX Settembre 22, t 075 922 0688, *www.mencarelligroup.com*. A pretty *palazzo* off Piazza Grande, with a meal service (half and full board available) and a garage.

****Dei Consoli**, Via dei Consoli 59, t 075 922 0639, *www.urbaniweb.com*. Small, well-run hotel. The restaurant offers creative cuisine grounded in tradition. Half and full board available.

***Gattapone**, Via G. Ansidei 6, t 075 927 2489, *www.mencarelligroup.com*. A pleasant choice in the medieval centre, with a garden and garage. Half and full board available.

***San Marco**, Via Perugia 5, t 075 922 0234, *www.hotelsanmarcogubbio.com*. Modern comforts in a former

(★) Villa
Montegranelli >

(★) La Fornace
di Mastro
Giorgio >>

(★) Taverna del
Lupo >

convent, with a pretty garden terrace and a restaurant serving Umbrian cuisine. Breakfast is included. Half and full board available.

***Villa Montegranelli , Loc. Monteluiano, 4km from town, t 075 922 0185, *www.hotelvillamontegranelli.it*. An 18th-century villa overlooking town, with original features, including the *piano nobile* and private chapel, plus a garden and babysitting. The great restaurant serves Umbrian and Puglian fare (half/full board available).

Moderate (€€)

***Beniamino Ubaldi**, Via Perugina 74, t 075 927 7773, *www.rosatihotels.com*. Functional rooms in a seminarians' college just outside the walls, with a bar and restaurant (half and full board available), Internet access, parking and babysitting .

**Oderisi**, Via Mazzatinti 2, t 075 922 0662, *www.rosatihotels.com*. Good, well-furnished if basic rooms, all with bathroom.

*Locanda del Duca**, Via Piccardi 1, t 075 927 7753, *locandadelducaditraversi@ tin.it*. Simple rooms, all with bath, overlooking the river. The restaurant, which specializes in duck and lamb, has outdoor tables. Half/full board available. *Restaurant closed Wed.*

## Eating Out in Gubbio

Taverna del Lupo , Via Ansidei 21a, t 07 927 4368 (€€€). Excellent, traditional fare such as truffled *bresaola* in lemon sauce, and steak

with Parmesan and truffles, served in a medieval setting with a name recalling the legend of St Francis. *Closed Mon Oct–July.*

**Alla Balestra**, Via della Repubblica 41, t 075 927 3810 (€€). Homemade pasta, pizza, and meat, truffles and mushroom dishes. *Closed Tues.*

**All'Antica Frantoio**, Via Cavour 18, Largo Bargello, t 075 922 1780 (€€). Umbrian cuisine served in a 13th-century oil mill, plus wood-oven pizzas. *Closed Mon and 15–20 days Jan/Feb.*

**La Cantina**, Via Piccotti, t 075 922 0583 (€€). A pretty restaurant in the heart of town, the chef turns out an excellent steak sprinkled with grated truffles. *Closed Mon.*

**Federico da Montefeltro**, Via della Repubblica 35, t 075 927 3949 (€€). Memorable mushroom- and truffle-based dishes. *Closed Thurs, Feb.*

La Fornace di Mastro Giorgio , Via Mastro Giorgio 2, t 075 922 1836 (€€). A local classic in the workshop where the master ceramicist created his famous ruby glaze, serving esoteric Umbrian specialities. *Closed Tues, Wed lunch Nov–May and 3wks Jan.*

**Funivia**, Monte Ingino, t 075 922 1259 (€€). Fabulous views on clear days, accompanying delicious stuffed pigeon and other good-value treats. *Closed Dec–Feb exc Christmas holidays, and Wed exc summer.*

**San Francesco e Il Lupo**, Via Cairoli 24, t 075 927 2344 (€€). Local products, *porcini* and truffles, or pizza. *Closed Tues, 10 days in Jan and 10–25 July.*

# Down the Via Flaminia

The Via Flaminia (SS3) was a Roman road of conquest; even in the Dark Ages the Goths and Lombards kept it in repair, an important highway linking Ravenna, Spoleto and Rome. For all that, there's little to see on this mountainous stretch. **Sigillo** has some frescoes by the local painter Matteo da Gualdo in its church of Sant'Anna, and the remains of a small single-arch Roman bridge at the Ponte Spiano. **Fossato di Vico** was founded as a Roman station along the road, and is now divided into a quiet upper and very medieval quarter and a lower modern town. The upper town has an 11th-century church, San Pietro, and frescoes by an accomplished follower of Ottaviano Nelli in the little Santa Maria della Piaggiola, and one by Matteo da Gualdo of Pope Urban V in San Benedetto. Just west of the Flaminia from here is the pretty hill village of **San Pellegrino**, stalwart preserver of an old fertility rite of spring: on 30 April, two poplar trees are brought to the village and stripped of their branches like maypoles, before they are 'married'. The church has frescoes by Matteo da Gualdo and a triptych (1465) by the fine Marchesi painter Girolamo di Giovanni from Camerino.

Between Scheggia and Gualdo Tadino, the deciding battle in the bitter Greek–Gothic war took place in 552. The Goths, led by Totila, were coming up the road from the south, and were met here by Byzantine forces under the eunuch general Narses, at the time nearly 80 years old. The Goths were outnumbered, and Totila did everything he could to stall battle until reinforcements arrived, even to the extent of ordering his most skilled horsemen to put on a display of dressage to entertain the Byzantines. But Narses was not to be fooled. His troops completely outflanked the Goths; Totila was mortally wounded, and although enough Goths fled to fight one last showdown with the Greeks near Cumae, their show was over. As for the octogenarian eunuch, he continued to besiege, battle and consolidate the position of his Emperor Justinian in Italy for a further *nine* years.

## Gualdo Tadino

(i) **Gualdo Tadino**
*t 075 915021;*
*Pro Loco, t 075 912172*

This stern old town is under the steep slopes of Monte Serra Santa. The ancient Umbrian town of *Tarsinater* was mentioned in no uncertain terms in Gubbio's Eugubine Tables. The Romans, who called it *Tadinum*, refounded it down in the plain near the Flaminia; after it was destroyed by the Goths, the few surviving inhabitants took to the hills. The Lombards named it Gualdo di Nocera ('Nocera's wood'), and the present site was resettled in the 12th century. After a brief period of independence Gualdo was taken over by Perugia. It has suffered badly in earthquakes: the one in 1751 felled many public buildings and the 1997–8 one also pretty bad. Slowly, progress has been made and all the major churches and buildings have been restored. Almost everyone is now back in proper homes, but many of Gualdo's churches are still off limits and some of the historic buildings are still under scaffolding.

**Duomo**
*open to the public*
**Museo Regionale dell'Emigrazione**
*t 075 914 2445,*
*www.emigrazione.it;*
*open Tues–Sat 10–1 and 4–6.30; Sun and hols 4–6.30; adm*
**San Francesco**
*t 075 915 0263 or t 075 915 0223 to arrange a visit*

In Gualdo's main square, **Piazza dei Martiri della Libertà** (recalling the civilians killed by the Germans in the Second World War), is a squat but well-proportioned **Duomo** with a good façade and rose window of 1256 and three doors, with an inscription mentioning the restoration after the 1751 earthquake; the 16th-century fountain on its side is attributed to Antonio da Sangallo. The 13th-century **Palazzo del Podestà**, remodelled in Baroque times, houses the new **museum of emigration**; the earthquakes have caused many to emigrate from this region. Here, too, is the former **church** of San Francesco , a copy of the basilica in Assisi, with a luminous interior and frescoes by Matteo da Gualdo, a local boy of the late quattrocento given to brilliant colouring; others are by the school of Ottaviano Nelli. Another work by Matteo, a glowing triptych of the Virgin and Child with St Sebastian and St Roch, can be seen in the church of **Santa Maria dei Raccomandati** over on Piazza XX Settembre. Gualdo's castle, the **Rocca Flea** , was restored and improved by Emperor Frederick II, and is considerably larger than its name suggests. Restored before the quake as a **Museo Civico** , it contains Renaissance lustreware, archaeological finds and the town's painting collection, with a sumptuous polyptych by Niccolò Alunno and a *Coronation of the Virgin* by Sano di Pietro.

There's fine walking country in the mountains above Gualdo: take the road 8km east to **Valsorda**, a resort 3,333ft (1,015m) up and the base for the pilgrmage walk to the 12th-century sanctuary of **Santissima Trinità** on Monte Serra Santa, part of Monte Cucco park.

Gualdo has preserved four 13th-century gates, and in the last week of September, the townspeople from the four quarters, or 'gates', of Gualdo, don their medieval glad rags to play the *Giochi de le Porte* – archery and slingshot competitions and donkey races.

**Santa Maria dei Raccomandati**
*closed for restoration*

**Rocca Flea**
*t 075 916 078; open Oct–Mar Sat and Sun 10.30–1 and 2.30–5; April–May Thurs–Sun 10.30–1 and 3–6; June–Sept Tues–Sun 10.30–1 and 3.30–7*

**Museo Civico**
*same opening hours as Rocca Flea; adm*

**Santissima Trinità**
*open by request*

## Nocera Umbra

ⓘ **Nocera Umbra**
*for more information, contact Comune di Nocera, t 074 283 4011*

South of Gualdo Tadino, the hill town of Nocera Umbra was at the epicentre of the 1997–8 earthquake, but, although there's still some scaffolding, massive restoration work has done much to repair the damage.

Nocera was an ancient Umbrian town, and later the Roman *Nuceria Camellaria*. It became an important Lombard city (its three Lombard cemeteries yielded a number of treasures, now in Rome's Museo dell'Alto Mediœvo), and in the Middle Ages it was under the Trinci family of Foligno. In recent times, Nocera Umbra has been best known for the mineral water it ships all over Italy; it still has enough for spas in Bagni di Nocera and the Terme del Centino.

The **Pinacoteca** in the church of San Francesco has an excellent *Nativity* by Niccolò Alunno, works by Matteo da Gualdo, a 13th-century crucifix, and a set of Roman milestones. Further up is the recently restored 15th-century **Duomo**, and the tower of the castle, renovated after the earthquake and restored to its former height.

# The Valle Umbra

*Between Assisi and Spoleto spreads one of the largest patches of open country in the region. The sunny Valle Umbra, or Vale of Umbria, encompasses the valleys of the Teverone and the Topino (Little Mouse River) and has much in common with parts of southern Tuscany; the magnificent landscape seems almost consciously arranged by some geomantic artist to display each olive grove, vineyard, city and town to the best advantage. One Grand Tourist, the Abbé Barthélemy, wrote of the area, 'It is the most beautiful countryside in the world. I do not exaggerate.'*

# 09

## Don't miss

*See map overleaf*

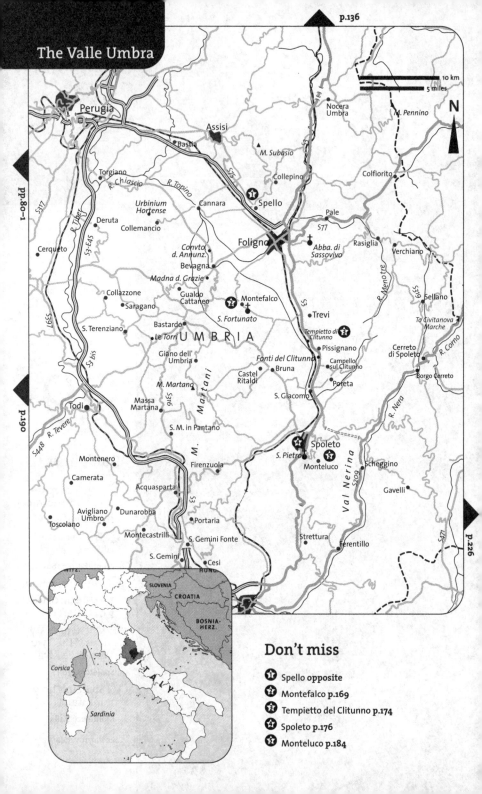

# The Valle Umbra

pp.80-1

p.190

p.226

10 km
5 miles

N

Perugia

Assisi

Bastia

M. Subasio

Nocera
Umbra

Colfiorito

M. Pennino

Torgiano

R. Chiascio

R. Topino

Cannara

Collepino

Spello

S75

Pale

S77

Rasiglia

Verchiano

Urbinium
Hortense

Deruta

Collemancio

Foligno

Abba. di
Sassovivo

R. Menotre

Cerqueto

Convto.
d. Annunz.

Bevagna

Madna d. Grazie

Sellano

S319

Collazzone

Saragano

Gualdo
Cattaneo

Montefalco

S. Fortunato

Trevi

Tempietto di
Clitunno

To Civitanova
Marche

R. Corno

Bastardo

Le Torri   U M B R I A

Pissignano

Cerreto
di Spoleto

S. Terenziano

Giano dell'
Umbria

Fonti del Clitunno

Campello
sul Clitunno

Borgo Cerreto

M. Martano

Castel
Ritaldi

Bruna

Poreta

Todi

Massa
Martana

S316

M.   Martani

S. Giacomo

R. Nera

S. M. in Pantano

Spoleto

Val Nerina

S209

Scheggino

Montenero

Firenzuola

S. Pietro

Monteluco

Gavelli

Camerata

Acquasparta

S3

Avigliano
Umbro

Dunarobba

Toscolano

Montecastrilli

Portaria

Strettura

Ferentillo

S. Gemini Fonte

S. Gemini

Cesi

R. Tevere

S448

R. Tevere

S3 bis

S3-E45

S317

S395

S75

SLOVENIA

CROATIA

BOSNIA-
HERZ.

Corsica

ITALY

Sardinia

# Don't miss

- Spello opposite
- Montefalco p.169
- Tempietto del Clitunno p.174
- Spoleto p.176
- Monteluco p.184

This area is littered with fascinating Roman and Lombard relics, thanks to that vital ancient thoroughfare, the Via Flaminia (SS3), the two branches of which joined in the remarkable but often overlooked town of Foligno before heading north to Gualdo Tadino. Besides some of Umbria's most beautiful hill towns, Spello, Montefalco and Trevi, the Valle Umbra is home to that unique relic of the Dark Ages called the Tempietto del Clitunno, and to glorious Spoleto, a genuine capital in those times, one of the most fascinating art towns in Italy, and now one of the trendiest, thanks to its famous Festival of the Two Worlds. For tourist information for the whole of this area, see *www.valleumbra.com*.

## Spello

 **Spello**

Lovely medieval Spello (population 8,000) could be Assisi's little sister, dressed in the same pink and cream Umbrian stone, lounging on the same sort of gentle hillside under Mount Subasio, overlooking the Valle Umbra. It has a similar history, first as an Umbrian settlement, then as the Roman city with a fancy name, *Splendidissima Colonia Iulia Hispellum*, or just *Hispellum* for short. The Lombards destroyed it, then made it part of the duchy of Spoleto. In the Middle Ages, as a *comune*, Spello fought to keep free of Assisi, the same way Assisi resisted domination by the Perugians. This earned it a thumping from Frederick II, and when he was dead Spello was swallowed up by Perugia. There's so much to see in nearby Assisi that relatively few tourists find their way up here, but like most little sisters, Spello has charms of her own.

### Pinturicchio *et al*

Spello has three excellently preserved Roman gates, including the main entrance to town, the **Porta Consolare**, with three arches and three worn statues from the time of the Roman republic, placed here in the 1600s after their discovery by the amphitheatre; in the Middle Ages, it was incorporated into the walls and given a tower.

From the gate, Via Consolare winds up into the centre, following the old Roman main street, passing an open chapel, the **Cappella Tega**, with faded Renaissance frescoes by L'Alunno. Where Via Consolare becomes Via Cavour stands Spello's chief monument, late-13th-century **Santa Maria Maggiore**, with its original Romanesque campanile and some 11th-century carving incorporated into its 17th-century façade. The interior was renovated at the same time, when it was given its fancy stuccoes and a hotchpotch of Baroque altars. The two holy-water stoups are ancient Roman columns, and there are two late, mediocre frescoes by Perugino on the pilasters either side of the apse, an excellent pulpit with grotesques of 1545 sculpted by Simone di Campione,

**Santa Maria Maggiore**

*t 0742 301792; open daily summer 8.30–12.30 and 3–7, winter 8.30–12.30 and 2.30–6*

# Getting to Spello

Spello is linked by **train** (station 1km from town) and **bus** to Assisi, Perugia and Foligno.

---

and fine inlaid choirstalls (1520), as well as a *baldacchino* by Tommaso di Rocco. Best of all is the **Cappella Baglioni**, commissioned in 1500 by Troilo Baglioni, scion of Perugia's gangster family, and brilliantly frescoed by Pinturicchio (you need €1 coins for the lighting). The three scenes, *Annunciation*, *Nativity* and *Dispute in the Temple*, are delightful, full of colour and incident, and include Pinturicchio's self-portrait hanging under the *Annunciation*. The floor is made of painted ceramics from Deruta (1516). More by Pinturicchio can be seen in the **Cappella del Sacramento**.

**Pinacoteca Civica**
*t 0742 301497, open Tues–Sun 10.30–1 and 3–6.30; adm*

The adjacent Palazzo dei Canonici contains the **Pinacoteca Civica**, a repository for art from Spello's churches: there's woodcarving from the 13th–14th centuries, including a fine *Madonna and Child* (1240) by an anonymous Umbrian sculptor; gold and silver work (a beautiful enamelled silver cross of 1398 by Perugian goldsmith Paolo Vanni); a portable diptych by Cola Petruccioli from the 1390s and Umbrian paintings by L'Alunno and his circle. Marcantonio Grecchi's *Madonna and Child with St Felice Vescovo and the Blessed Andrea Caccioli* includes a fine view of early 17th-century Spello.

**Sant'Andrea**
*open Mon–Sat 8–12.30 and 3–7, Sun 3–7*

There's yet more Pinturicchio (he spent 1501 in Spello) in nearby 13th-century **Sant'Andrea**: a large *Madonna, Child and Saints* to the right of the crossing he painted with another Perugino student, Eusebio di San Giorgio. There are also 13th–16th-century frescoes, and a high altar with a crucifix attributed to a follower of Giotto.

## Souvenirs of Roman *Hispellum*

Walking the narrow, cobbled streets, hidden archways and stairways of Spello is a joy, although they're a bit steep. Off the rather anonymous Piazza della Repubblica, the Romanesque **San Lorenzo** (*c.* 1160) has an unusual façade full of bits from Roman and early medieval buildings and some curious paintings within by a 16th-century artist from Brussels, Frans van de Kasteele. From here, ambitious climbers can continue up Via di Torre Belvedere to the top of Spello for the **belvedere** over the Vale of Umbria. There are ruins of the 14th-century **Rocca**, built by the indefatigable Cardinal Albornoz. The small **Roman arch** nearby was the entrance to *Hispellum*'s acropolis.

A circumnavigation of Spello's walls will show you the two other Roman gates: the **Porta Urbica** (near the Porto Consolare, close to a well-preserved stretch of walls dating back to the 1st century AD), and, best of all, the **Porta Venere**, a beautiful, almost perfectly preserved monumental gate from the time of Augustus, flanked by a pair of tall cylindrical towers.

## Outside the Walls of Spello

The Porta Venere is plainly visible from the road to Assisi and Perugia. Look the other way and you'll see the overgrown ruins of the **Roman amphitheatre**, perhaps more impressive when viewed from the belvedere in the city than ground level; it seated 15,000.

Just north of Spello is the charming, resolutely asymmetrical 12th-century Romanesque **church of San Claudio**. Already in bad shape in 1997, it was almost entirely destroyed by the quake and is still being restored. Just beyond, amid a lovely Italian garden, the **Villa Fidelia** was built in the 1500s but has been fiddled with; it contains the **Collezione Straka-Coppa**, with late Renaissance, Baroque and early-20th-century art, including a few big names (including a 16th-century *Madonna and Child* by Vincenzo Catena of Venice, Italy's first amateur painter), as well as silver and ceramics.

Beyond the 18th-century Porta Montanara 1km northeast of town, the cemetery **church of San Girolamo** (1474) has a portico and interior decorated by students and followers of Pinturicchio. Another road continues to the slopes of Monte Subasio and the walled medieval village of **Collepino**. Above town, Romanesque **San Silvestro**, founded by St Romualdo in 1025, has an interesting crypt and an altar carved from a Roman sarcophagus. From here, an unpaved road goes over Subasio to the Eremo delle Carceri (*see* p.129).

**Villa Fidelia**
*Via Flamina 72, t 0742 301866; open April–June and Sept Thurs–Sun 10.30–1 and 3.30–6; July and Aug daily 10.30–1 and 4–7; Oct–Mar Sat and Sun 10.30–1 and 3–6; adm*

## West of Spello: Cannara and Urbinum Hortense

The fertile plain of Foligno, along the banks of the Topino, was greatly appreciated in ancient times. Cannara was founded as a satellite of the large Roman town of Urbinum Hortense to the west but has survived the centuries in better nick; it is famous for its red onions (subject of a local festival) and its unique Vernaccia di Cannara, a sweet red dessert wine. There are two churches with good paintings of the Virgin, Child and saints by Nicolò Alunno: one in **San Matteo** (1786), the other in **San Giovanni**. The *municipio* has fresco fragments and other finds from Urbinum Hortense.

West of Cannara, in a beautiful setting, tiny walled **Collemancio** has a Romanesque church and Palazzo del Podestà in its core. From the public garden, a road leads up 0.5km to the ruins of Urbinum Hortense. Mentioned by Pliny the Younger, this has been partially excavated to unearth a temple, baths and a basilica.

## Festivals in Spello

**Bruschetta festival,** Feb.

**Corpus Domini,** 1st half June. An *infiorata* (flower carpets bedeck the town; best early mornings).

**Festa dell'Olivo,** early Dec. A festival celebrating local olive oil production.

## Where to Stay and Eat in and West of Spello

**Spello** ✉ 06038

★★★★**La Bastiglia**, Via dei Molini 17, t 0742 651277, *www.labastiglia.com* (€€€€). A charmingly restored mill

(★) Palazzo Bocci >

(★) Perbacco >>

with pleasant rooms, a beautiful terrace and views, Internet access, babysitting, parking, and a good restaurant. *Closed Wed.*

****Palazzo Bocci**, Via Cavour 17, **t** 0742 301021, *www.palazzobocci.com* (€€€€). A frescoed 17th-century building with elegant rooms, a hanging garden and a restaurant, **Il Molino**, just opposite, at Piazza Matteotti 6/7 (**t** 0742 651305). Under a vaulted ceiling, try characterful dishes featuring Norcia truffles, ceps, pulses and game. *Closed Tues and 10–24 Jan.*

***Del Teatro**, Via Giulia 24, **t** 0742 301140, *www.hoteldelteatro.it* (€€€). A quiet, cheerfully furnished hotel near the Teatro Comunale, with well-equipped, comfy rooms (breakfast included), wonderful views from the breakfast verandah, and parking.

***Altavilla**, Via Mancinelli 2, **t** 0742 301515, *www.hotelaltavilla.com* (€€€). Well-furnished rooms, a beautiful pool, a terrace and a restaurant with local cuisine (half/full board available).

***Il Cacciatore**, Via Giulia 42, **t** 0742 651141, *www.ilcacciatorehotel.com* (€€). Comfy rooms, most with splendid valley views, and a very popular restaurant serving beautifully prepared home-made pasta and other dishes at good prices (€€). *Closed Mon and Nov.*

****Il Portonaccio**, Via Centrale Umbra 46, **t** 0742 651313, *www. albergoilportonaccio.it* (€€). Decent rooms and room-service breakfasts.

**La Cantina**, Via Cavour 2, **t** 0742 651775 (€€). Seasonal dishes, BBQ meats and homemade pasta. *Closed Wed.*

## Cannara ✉ 06033

**Casa delle Volpi**, Vocabolo Ducale 50, **t** 0742 720361 (€€). Self-catering lodgings outside town, with a garden and views to Assisi. Breakfasts and dinners can be provided; cookery evenings are hosted. Min. 1-week stay.

**Perbacco**, Via Umberto I, **t** 0742 720492 (€€). *The* place to try Cannara's onions, especially in the delicious onion soup. Ask for directions when you book.

# Foligno

In Foligno (population 54,000), which ranks as Umbria's third city, the locals are wont to point out the exact centre of a billiard table in the centre of a bar in the centre of town, which is in the centre of Umbria, which is in the centre of Italy, which is in the centre of the Mediterranean, whose name means 'the middle of the world'. In September 1997, Foligno was in the middle again, this time of an earthquake. The whole world watched as its medieval Torre Comunale collapsed; the Folignati wept and vowed to rebuild it 'where it was, as it was' – the battle cry of major Italian restoration projects. All the townspeople are now back in their homes or new houses. The tower will take longer, and some *palazzi* are still under scaffolding, but most churches have now reopened.

Even before the disaster, not many people stopped for Foligno; in a sense, the centre has also been a victim of its post-war prosperity, and the ring of factories and modern suburbs that surrounds it is enough to discourage most travellers. But to pass by is to miss one of the most distinctive Umbrian towns, neither as archaic nor as cute as Assisi but memorable in its own way, a minor medieval capital with a pinch of grandeur and an air of genteel dilapidation and hopelessness that the tremors have aggravated.

# Getting to and around Foligno

Foligno, 36km/30mins from Perugia and 158km/2hrs 30mins from Rome, is one of the main **rail** junctions for eastern Umbria. **Buses** link it to Colfiorito, Montefalco, Bevagna, Trevi and Spoleto; FS bus services connect it to Assisi, Perugia and Siena 3 times a day. The bus station is on Viale Mezzetti.

There is underground **car parking** near Porta Romana, handy for the tourist office. You can hire **bikes** at Baltistelli, Via XX Settembre 88, **t** 0742 344059.

## History

Foligno was the ancient Roman *Fulginum*, near the junction of the branches of the Via Flaminia. This key location brought Christianity early to Foligno, thanks to St Felicianus, martyred in the 3rd century. In spite of its location on a plain, the city never disappeared in all the troubles that followed the crack-up of the Roman Empire: it survived attacks by the Saracens and Magyars to spring back up in the 12th century as a free *comune* with strong Ghibelline tendencies. St Francis was a frequent visitor; not long afterwards, it was the home of the Blessed Angela (1248–1309), a mystic whose direct communion with God and visions were recorded by her spiritual director in her autobiographical *Book of Divine Consolation*.

The Blessed Angela was 12 when the man suspected of being the Antichrist, the Emperor Frederick II, with his exotic Saracen army and dancing girls, held his parliament in Foligno, in defiance of the pope who had excommunicated him. This got the Folignati into trouble after his death, and the period of wars and civil disorders that followed resulted in the Trinci family assuming power in 1305. Their rule, which saw Foligno dominating Assisi, Spello, Montefalco, Bevagna and Trevi, lasted until 1439, when in a moment of upheaval Pope Eugenius IV sent in an army under Cardinal Giovanni Vitelleschi. Vitelleschi's family hated the Trinci and had no qualms about executing the last lord and his followers and instituting direct papal rule.

There was one bright spot before the town nodded off, when German printers brought their presses to Foligno in 1470, only six years after the first books were printed in Italy; the first printed edition of Dante's *Divina Commedia* – also the first printed book in the Italian language – came out in Foligno the following year.

### Piazza della Repubblica

Piazza della Repubblica marks the city centre, with the Duomo facing the **Palazzo Comunale** – a rare architectural catastrophe. This was a genuine 12th-century monument, until someone pasted a neoclassical façade on it in the early 1900s. The tower survived with its original lantern with Ghibelline crenellations as one of Foligno's proudest landmarks, before it collapsed in the quake. The Folignati can't leave well alone; in the 18th century they commissioned Luigi Vanvitelli, court architect to the Kingdom of

Naples, and the town's own Giuseppe Piermarini, designer of
La Scala in Milan, to modernize their already grandiose **Duomo**.
Fortunately, they didn't tamper with the two façades on either side
of the L-shaped piazza: the **east front** (1133) is pink and white in
Perugian style, with some 1900s Venetian mosaics and other
modern improvements, but the original **south front** remains,
featuring one of the finest portals in Umbria (1201). It's also one of
the least orthodox, a strange testament to the syncretic religious
and philosophical currents of that age. The reliefs include figures
of the zodiac, a medieval bestiary and long panels with geometric
patterns and grapevines. Frederick II appears left of the door, one of
only two existing likenesses in Italy. Two porphyry lions hold up the
doorway, and at the top of the arch, barely visible, is a Muslim star
and crescent. There are more fantastical animals above the portal
and a good rose window. The portal was brand-new when young
Francis of Assisi came here in 1205 and sold his father's stock of
cloth and a packhorse to raise money for the restoration of
San Damiano (*see* p.129). He wouldn't, however, recognize the
Duomo's interior, where the Cappella dell'Assunta is all that
remains of the 12th-century original. The best art is in the sacristy:
a painting of the Madonna and St John by Alunno and busts of
Bartolomeo and Diana Roscioli, recently attributed to Bernini.

**Palazzo Trinci**
*t 0742 357989; open
Tues–Sun 10–7; adm*

At the western end of the piazza, the much-altered **Palazzo Trinci**,
still has its elegant original Renaissance courtyard behind a
neoclassical façade. Nearly all the interior dates from the period
of Foligno's greatest *signore*, Ugolino III Trinci (ruled 1386–1415),
who commissioned a precocious humanistic cycle of late Gothic
frescoes, by Gentile da Fabriano and others, for the second floor.
They are an early example of the reawakening of interest in the
classical past, especially notable for being far from the centre of
action in Florence. The frescoes were undergoing restoration for
years before the quake and emerged unscathed. The palace **chapel**
has frescoes on the life of Mary (1424) by Ottaviano Nelli of Gubbio,
who also painted the heroic Roman figures in the Sala dei Giganti.
Frescoes in the loggia show the founding of Rome: most curious of
all is a half-completed fresco and *sinopia* (preparatory sketch), *Rhea
Silvia Being Buried Alive*; Rhea was the Vestal Virgin who gave birth
to Romulus and Remus. The **Sala delle Arti Liberali e dei Pianeti** has
allegorical figures of the liberal arts represented by women seated
on thrones, and allegories of the planets. The corridor, which gave
the Trinci access to the Duomo, has frescoes of ancient heroes and
the *Seven Ages of Man*. Ugolino also collected ancient art: there's a
rare high relief of the games in the Circus Maximus, busts of the
emperors and a statue of Cupid and Psyche.

**Pinacoteca
Comunale**
*open Tues–Sun 10–7;
joint adm with Palazzo
Trinci and other sights*

The building also houses the **Pinacoteca Comunale**, with an
*Annunciation* attributed to Gozzoli, works by Pierantonio

**Museo Multimediale dei Tornei delle Giustre e dei Giochi**

*t 0742 357697;*
*open Tues–Sun 10–7*

Mezzastris of Foligno and detached trecento frescoes. The newest museum, the Museo Multimediale dei Tornei delle Giustre e dei Giochi, also in Palazzo Trinci, has multimedia displays on Foligno's medieval pageant and similar jousts and tournaments elsewhere.

## Down Via Gramsci

Palazzo Trinci is only the first of a long line of Folignati palaces along Via Gramsci. Most of the noble residences were built in the 1500s and can now be seen restored after the earthquake and the preceding hundreds of years of neglect. The one nearest Palazzo Trinci, the 16th-century **Palazzo Deli**, is by far the most beautiful.

**Santa Maria Infraportas**

*open Mon–Sat 9–12 and 4–6, Sun 9–12*

**San Domenico**

*t 0742 344563; open for musical events Tues–Sat 10am–12.30pm*

**Nunziatella**

*t 0742 357989; open Tues–Sat summer 10–1 and 4–7, winter 10–1 and 3–6*

Foligno's other churches are well endowed with art: **San Niccolò** in Via Scuola d'Arti e Mestieri has works by Foligno's own Niccolò di Liberatore, known as Alunno; in Piazza San Domenico, Santa Maria Infraportas is one of Foligno's oldest churches, with unusual 12th-century windows and portico, and frescoes by Mezzastris and others; the large, deconsecrated San Domenico has good trecento frescoes, currently hidden by scaffolding.

There are more Renaissance palaces along Via Mazzini and Via Garibaldi, its northern extension, where the oratory known as the Nunziatella has a fresco by Perugino.

## Tourist Information in Foligno

ⓘ **Foligno >**
*Corso Cavour 126, t 0742 354459 or t 0742 354165, www. regioneumbria.eu, www.comune. foligno.pg.it*

Foligno is one of Umbria's **gliding and hang-gliding** centres (Aeroclub, Via Cagliari 22, **t** 0742 670201). Or you might like to **horse-ride** (Centro Ippico CO.GI.VE, Fraz. Verchiano, **t** 0742 632846).

### Market Days

Markets take place on Tuesday and Saturday on Via Nazario Sauro.

## Festivals in Foligno

**Giostra della Quintana,** *www.quintana. it,* 14–15 June, or nearest weekend. A 17th-century custom that involves knights from 10 districts jousting, plays in 300-year-old Umbrian dialect, a historic cooking competition, games, a fair, parades, outdoor taverns and so on.
**Rematch of Giostra,** 14–15 Sept.

## Where to Stay and Eat in Foligno

**Foligno** ✉ 06034

★★★**Le Mura**, Via Bolletta 29, **t** 0742 357344, *www.albergolemura.com* (€€). A comfortable modern hotel on the northwest of town, with a restaurant serving good *strangozzi* with pepper, tripe, lamb and veal (half and full board offered). *Closed Tues.*

★★★**Villa Roncalli**, Viale Roma 25, just south of centre, **t** 0742 391091 (€€). A stylish 17th-century villa with a shady garden, a pool, comfy rooms, and one of the city's finest restaurants (€€€) serving Umbrian dishes with gourmet flair, including ravioli and pigeon *allo spiedo*. Half board offered. *Closed Mon, 2wks Aug and 2wks Jan.*

★★**Albergo Valentini**, Via F. Ottaviani 19, near station, **t** 0742 353990 (€€). A pleasant family-run choice with parking and bike loan.

★ **Osteria Sparafucile >>**

Osteria Sparafucile, Piazzette Duomo 30, **t** 368 382 7246 (€€€). This bustling *trattoria* does a roaring trade, and deservedly so. Its affable owner does most of the cooking himself and prides himself on producing time-honoured local dishes cooked with the best ingredients in the Slow Food tradition. The menu changes daily.

**Da Remo**, Via Filzi 10, near station, **t** 0742 340522 (€€). A classic choice in a Liberty-style villa, four generations strong, serving typical Umbrian cuisine such as tasty *strangozzi* and roast kid simmered in Montefalco's Sagrantino wine. There's a garden for summer. *Closed Sun eve, Mon and Aug.*

**Osteria del Teatro**, Via Petrucci 6, **t** 0742 350745 (€€). An atmospheric, romantic restaurant in a 15th-century palace, with a vaulted ceiling, theatre posters, lovely wine cellars and a garden. The courgette fritters, deepfried sage, pumpkin ravioli and lamb and beef are recommended. *Closed Mon, Jan and Aug.*

**Barbanera**, Piazza della Repubblica, **t** 0742 350672 (€). An old *drogheria* with a wonderful old counter offering light snacks, coffees or *aperitivos*. *Closed Mon.*

## Up the Menotre Valley

Directly east of Foligno, follow the valley of the little Menotre river into the mountains, a beautiful but seldom-visited corner of Umbria that extends to the border with the Marches. This area was the worst hit by the quake. The collapsed buildings in villages have been cleared, but it will take a few years for the scaffolding, rubble and cranes to be removed. The villages are largely abandoned. Many families moved to Foligno or even Rome and most likely will not come back. While the state gave immediate compensation to victims, it has been slower to invest in rebuilding homes. In some cases, containers have been replaced by wooden chalets, and there is some new building outside the old villages. But overall, the area is very demoralized. The villagers had little before, and what little they had they lost. Modest roadside stalls sell the lentils, chick peas, red potatoes and onions indigenous to the region.

The SS77 from Foligno follows the valley but, just after crossing the Via Flaminia, a side road to the right (signposted Casale) heads 5km to the **Abbazia di Sassovivo**, an 11th-century Benedictine abbey with a remarkable cloister. The main road twists up into the mountains, passing interesting caves and a pretty waterfall on the Menotre at **Pale**, 8km from Foligno, a village wedged between the rocks. Paper has been milled here since the 13th century.

On the heights, just before the Marches border, the mountains level out to form the broad meadow or *valico* of **Colfiorito**, where the lofty green marshlands, 730m above sea level, are a favourite spot for migrating birds; other parts of the *valico* are used for growing beans and lentils. Most of the hamlets around its rim have been abandoned since the quake. The rugged roadside 11th-century church, **Santa Maria di Pistia**, has porticoes on two sides to accommodate the country fairs held here in the Middle Ages.

A side road turns off before Colfiorito (24km), heading south into pristine mountain scenery around **Rasiglia**, where the **Santuario della Madonna delle Grazie** has walls covered with well-preserved, colourful quattrocento frescoes, many painted as *ex votos*.

**Abbazia di Sassovivo**

*t 0742 340499; open daily sunrise–sunset*

# Bevagna

Under the Martani hills, on the original westerly route of the Via Flaminia, Roman *Mevania* has survived as Bevagna (population 2,400), a quiet, unspoiled, friendly town, where the main crops are flax and wine. Though low-key, it has some artistic gems. During its period as a free *comune* in the Middle Ages, before being taken over in 1371 by the Trinci family of Foligno, it built two of Umbria's best Romanesque churches. The quake left a number of people homeless; nearly all are back in their homes. It also damaged the churches, though there are fewer external signs of damage than elsewhere.

## Piazza Silvestri

Bevagna's pride and joy is perfect Piazza Silvestri, a medieval and theatrical *pièce de résistance* that shows that the Bevanati tried hard to keep up with their bigger neighbours. It has a Corinthian column, a fountain and the impressive Gothic **Palazzo Comunale** of 1270, restored after an earlier earthquake in 1832, with a charming little theatre inside. An archway connects it to the delightful **church of San Silvestro**, built by architect Maestro Binello (who signed his work) and being restored with the help of funds raised by Prince Charles. The simple façade incorporates bits of Roman buildings, an 1195 inscription to Emperor Henry VII and a frieze over the door. The interior is essentially Romanesque, and like many 12th-century buildings it features a raised presbytery, leaving room for twin pulpits (or *ambones)*, now vanished, on either side of the steps and a small crypt beneath. The real surprise is the style of the capitals – they're in the Egyptian order, representing papyrus leaves the way Ionic and Corinthian capitals recall the leaves of the acanthus. Such columns are common in this area, but their presence has never been explained: maybe they were copied from the ruins of some Roman-era temple to Isis or Serapis. They are slightly curved, in *entasis* to look straight.

Across the piazza, the late-12th-century church of **San Michele Arcangelo** has a few Egyptian capitals recycled from older buildings. Binello and Rodolfo built this about the same time as San Silvestro and to the same interior plan. St Michael and his dragon figure prominently on the façade, with some re-used Roman friezes, a Cosmatesque arch, and a menagerie of cows, cats and such, similar to the portal in Foligno (by the same architects). The crypt under the raised presbytery is supported by Roman columns. There are also two processional statues of Bevagna's patron saint Vincenzo, one of wood and the other of silver.

**Santi Domenico e Giacomo**

*open 11–12.30 and 3.30–6.30*

The third church on the piazza, **Santi Domenico e Giacomo**, has a Baroque interior with what must be the biggest alabaster window in Italy behind the altar. Of the original decoration, little remains but a radiant trecento *Virgin of the Annunciation* in the choir; there are also works by Bevagna-born artist Il Fantino ('the Jockey', Ascensidonio Spacco, d. 1646).

From here, Corso Matteotti follows the route of the old Via Flaminia, passing an 18th-century pharmacy and a *municipio* of the same period, home to the **Museo della Città**, with Roman artefacts and coins, busts and architectural fragments found in and around town, medieval manuscripts, a model of the Santuario della Madonna delle Grazie (*see* below), and works by Dono Doni and Il Fantino and an *Adoration of the Magi* by Corrado Giacinto.

**Museo della Città**
*t 0742 360031; open April, May and Sept daily 10.30–1 and 2.30– 6; June and July daily 10.30–1 and 3.30–7; Aug daily 10.30–1 and 3– 7.30; Oct–Mar Tues–Sun 10.30–1 and 2.30–5; adm; circuito cittadino ticket includes museum, theatre and mosaics, (see below)*

**Mosaic Romano**
*t 0742 360031, or ask at tourist office (see below)*

### The Rest of Town

There are more remnants of Roman *Mevania* a few blocks further up the Corso, at Via Crescimbeni, where a **Roman temple** was partly conserved when its columns were bricked in long ago. Nearby, at Via Porta Guelfa, is a **marine mosaic** with a big lobster, sea horses and Tritons, once part of the 2nd-century baths. A crescent of houses traces the curve of the **amphitheatre**, in Via dell'Anfiteatro, and a house at the end, in Via Dante Aligheri, has a fine **Roman frieze**.

At the highest point in town, 13th-century **San Francesco** holds the stone on which Francis stood when he preached to the birds at Pian d'Arca, north of here. Steps lead down to Piazza Garibaldi and Bevagna's best-preserved medieval gate, **Porta Cannara**.

### Around Bevagna

More bits of Roman *Mevania* can be seen off the old Via Flaminia to Foligno (the SS316): the fossil-like imprint of another amphitheatre in a field and two ruined tombs. Just north of Bevagna, the **Convento dell'Annunziata** has more works by Il Fantino and a pretty terracotta altarpiece of the Annunciation. A path from the convent leads down to a spring-fed lake.

Southwest of Bevagna is yet another 16th-century shrine to the Virgin Mary, the **Santuario della Madonna delle Grazie**, designed by Valentino Martelli with a comely octagonal dome and a pretty view, though the church is closed for restoration.

**Convento dell'Annunziata**
*closed for restoration at time of writing; call t 0742 361234 for latest information*

**Santuario della Madonna delle Grazie**
*closed for restoration*

### Festivals in Bevagna

**Mercato delle Gaite**, mid-June. A neo-medieval fair in which the four districts (*gaite*) vie to dress more authentically, and stalls sell food and drink.

### Where to Stay and Eat in Bevagna

**Bevagna** ✉ 06031
L'Orto degli Angeli, Via D. Alighieri 1, t 0742 360130, www.ortoangeli.it

(€€€€€). Modern comforts in a medieval atmosphere in the town centre. The Antonini Angeli Nieri Mongelli family home, it's filled with family antiques and pictures, and contains a 2nd-century temple to Minerva (forming one wall of the restaurant) and the ruins of a Roman theatre (part of the hanging garden). A 'residence' contains some luxurious guesthouses. There's also a restaurant (€€€) where you can enjoy Umbrian classics with a twist. *Closed Tues.*

ⓘ **Bevagna** ›
*Piazza Silvestri 1, t 0742 361667, www.comune. bevagna.pg.it*
★ **L'Orto degli Angeli** ›

***Palazzo Brunamonti**, Corso Matteotti 79, **t** 0742 361932, *www.brunamonti.com* (€€€). An old *palazzo* with 16 comfortable bedrooms with Internet access, and frescoed public rooms. *Closed 9–31 Jan.*

**Il Chiostro di Bevagna**, Corso Matteotti 107, **t** 0742 361987, *www.ilchiostrodibevagna.com* (€€). Simple but very charmingly furnished rooms with modern comforts, set in the frescoed cloister of the former Dominican convent.

**El Rancho**, Via Flaminia 53, **t** 0742 361913, *www.elrancho.it* (€€). Basic rooms and a beautiful pool amid trees, plus a restaurant offering tempting local dishes and products at down-to-earth prices, with the emphasis on truffles and wild boar (€20). You can eat outside in fine weather. *Closed Mon.*

**Da Nina**, Piazza Garibaldi 6, **t** 0742 360024 (€€). A simple but attractive lunch stop with a daily-changing menu featuring lots of truffles. *Closed Tues.*

# Montefalco

🔢 Montefalco

Only 7km from Bevagna but much higher in the hills, Montefalco (population 5,500) is another unspoilt gem. Dubbed the '*Ringhiera* (balcony) *d'Umbria*', the town offers splendid 360° views over to Assisi and Perugia and down the entire Valle Umbra as far as Spoleto. Another nickname, '*il lembo di cielo caduto in terra*' ('heaven's hem fallen to earth'), refers to its reputation as a factory for saints, extraordinary even by Umbrian standards; the celestial hosts count eight former Montefalconesi.

Until 1240 it was known as Coccorone; when Frederick II destroyed it and rebuilt it as a Ghibelline town, he named it after his imperial eagle. It later became part of the domain of the Trinci family, then part of the Church's; today, it is practically synonymous with its fine Sagrantino wines and woven textiles.

## San Francesco

Appropriately, the town of heaven's hem is capped by a monk's tonsure: the central, circular, partially arcaded **Piazza del Comune**, from which streets radiate down like spokes. One, Via Ringhiera Umbra, takes in the lovely Clitunno valley while descending to Montefalco's pride and joy: the frescoes in the deconsecrated 14th-century **San Francesco**, now a **museum**. Benozzo Gozzoli spent two years here (1450–52), painting the apse with the Life of St Francis. Montefalco's Franciscans did not let him put in many of his usual fancies, though there are a few moppet children grinning out from the corners. He does, however, indulge in his favourite cityscapes, including views of Montefalco (where Francis visited after preaching to the birds around Bevagna) and Arezzo (where he cast out the devils). Panels along the bottom of the apse show portraits by Gozzoli of great Franciscans – a distinguished company of saints, popes and philosophers, including Duns Scotus. The cycle makes a fascinating contrast to the earlier, much better frescoes in Assisi, but Gozzoli's rather facile, charming and sentimental figures

*San Francesco*

*t 0742 379598; open Mar–May, Sept and Oct daily 10.30–1 and 2–6; June and July daily 10.30–1 and 3–7; Aug daily 10.30–1 and 3–7.30; Nov–Feb Tues–Sun 10.30–1 and 2.30–5; adm*

## Getting to Montefalco

There are **2 trains** a day to/from Foligno, and SSIT **buses** (t 0743 212208, *www.spoletina.com*) to Montefalco from Bastardo, Bevagna and Perugia once a day, and from Foligno and Spoleto several times a day.

clearly struck a deep chord in the mid-15th century, because they were a model for a good deal of later Umbrian painting. Gozzoli also frescoed the first chapel, a triptych, *The Madonna and Saints and Crucifix*. The other Renaissance fresco here is by Perugino, a restored run-of-the-mill *Nativity* with Lake Trasimeno. The aisles contain fine trecento painting, including a vivid and unique *Temptations of St Anthony*; there is a fond painting by Tiberio d'Assisi of a local favourite and exemplar of spiritual first aid, the *Madonna del Soccorso*, in which Our Lady is about to whack a devil with a big club when he comes to snatch a child whose exasperated mother had exclaimed 'May the Devil take you!'

The **Pinacoteca**, also in the church, has an 18th-century statue of Foligno's Quintana Saracen, another *Madonna del Soccorso*, a *Madonna and Child* by the school of Melozzo da Forlì, and a lovely painting, *SS. Vincent, Illuminata and Nicolas of Tolentino*, by Antonizzo Romano; another section has an ancient marble statue of Hercules found in the town, a medieval lion and a Renaissance river god.

### The Rest of Town

**Sant'Agostino/ Sant'Illuminata**
*opening hours depend on priest*

Two other churches have frescoes by 14th–16th-century Umbrian painters –Sant'Agostino and Sant'Illuminata. Montefalco retains medieval walls, including two gates: **Porta Sant'Agostino**, with a fresco of the Virgin and saints, and **Porta Federico II**, with the eagle.

### Outside the Walls of Montefalco

**Santa Chiara da Montefalco**
*open daily 9.30–11.30 and 3.30–5.30*

Just outside the Porta Federico II, 17th-century Santa Chiara da Montefalco, built around a much earlier chapel of Santa Croce, has lovely frescoes of 1333 on the life of Saint Clare of the Cross (c. 1268–1308), a follower of St Francis, famous for her charity; after she died, her heart was found to be branded with the sign of the cross.

**San Fortunato**
*open daily 9.30–12 and 3.30–5*

The Franciscan convent of San Fortunato, just over 1km southeast of Montefalco's Porta Spoleto, enjoys a beautiful setting and still shelters a handful of friars; the thick ilex forest that surrounds it was planted as insulation against winter winds. The church, which is dedicated to Fortunatus (d. 400), a priest who was famous for his charity to the poor, was founded over a Roman basilica in the 5th century, rebuilt during the 16th and later Baroqued inside, although it preserves some interesting fresco fragments by Gozzoli: a lunette over the door, an *Adoration of the Child* and the *Enthroned St Fortunatus*. The cloister uses Roman columns and has a chapel frescoed by Tiberio d'Assisi on the life of St Francis.

## Where to Stay and Eat in Montefalco

### Montefalco ✉ 06036

This is perhaps best known for Sagrantino and Rosso di Montefalco red wines, both sold in shops around town and used widely in its cuisine.

****Villa Pambuffetti**, Viale della Vittoria 20, t 0742 379417, *www.villapambuffetti.com* (€€€€€). A 19th-century villa owned by a local noble family, with 15 rooms with antiques, a park with huge trees and an outdoor pool, and beauty treatments. Half board available.

***Ringhiera Umbra**, Corso G. Mameli 20, t 0742 379166, *www.ringhieraumbra.com* (€€). Basic rooms near Piazza del Comune, some en suite, and a restaurant serving local cuisine (half/full board available).

**Coccorone**, Vicolo Fabbri 7, off central square, t 0742 379535 (€€). An elegant, understated place with tempting homemade tagliatelle, *papardelli* and *strangozzi*, and beef cooked in Sagrantino wine sauce. *Closed Wed in winter.*

**Il Falisco**, Via XX Settembre 14, t 0742 379185 (€€). Local specialities such as beef fillet cooked in Sagrantino wine, and good gnocchi. It's tiny, so get here early. *Closed Mon.*

**Enoteca Federico II**, Piazza del Comune, t 0742 378902 (€). A pleasant spot to come for a snack and a glass of wine on the piazza. *Closed Wed.*

# Around Montefalco: Into the Monti Martani

At Montefalco begins a range of hills and lofty plateaux known as the Monti Martani, separating the Valle Umbra from the Tiber. This lies well off the tourist trails. Places such as **Gualdo Cattaneo**, west of Bevagna, knew their peak of importance under the Lombards (the name Gualdo comes from the German *wald* or wood). Its big cylindrical castle dates from 1494 – the work of Pope Alexander VI, built after his fiery son Cesare Borgia stormed through the area to show the Umbrians who was boss. When Gualdo's church was rebuilt in 1804, stonework from its 13th-century predecessor was preserved on its façade; the crypt is original as well. The apse has a fine *Last Supper* by Bevagna's early 17th-century master Fantino.

A pretty drive west of Montefalco is a market town bearing the unfortunate name of **Bastardo**, the gateway to other forgotten castles: **Le Torri** (a poor man's San Gimignano), Renaissance **Barattano** and a Lombard fort at **Saragano**.

Southeast of Bastardo, amid olive groves on the slopes of the Monti Martani, the walled village of **Giano dell'Umbria** is one of several in the area founded by Norman knights granted the land after fighting as mercenaries for Pope Gregory VII in the 1080s – the whole area extending to Castel Ritaldi was known as Normandia in the Middle Ages. Originally it consisted of two fortified villages, and it has two 13th-century churches on the same piazza but only a single Palazzo Pubblico; until the 1300s, Giano managed to remain independent in spite of being circled by all the local sharks. Of the churches, the Pieve has a Baroque interior and a restored painting by Andrea Polinori of the Madonna and Child (1620) who keeps company with a much-venerated *Madonna and Child* painted 300 years earlier.

Just north of Giano, the red-stone **Abbazia di San Felice** was founded by some of Umbria's early coenobitic monks. In the 8th century, the Benedictines moved in and rebuilt it, and since 1815 it has been reoccupied by a congregation dedicated to mission work. The Romanesque church, from the 12th century, has a handsome portal topped by a three-light window and an impressive apse with a gallery. Under the raised presbytery, the crypt has quaint old Roman and early medieval capitals and an ancient sarcophagus, holding the remains of the martyred bishop of Martana. San Felice's frescoed cloister is especially pretty.

**Castel Ritaldi** (14km south of Montefalco) has a castle from the 1200s. Just outside is the **Pieve di San Gregorio**, built in 1140, with a charming pink and white sculpted façade with elaborate interwoven designs inhabited by little monsters; it has been restored by funds raised in New York. Nearby **Bruna** has a Renaissance church in the shape of a trefoil, **Santa Maria della Bruna** (1510).

# Trevi and the Tempietto del Clitunno

No small town in Umbria makes a grander sight than Trevi (population 7,400), a nearly vertical village that's reminiscent of Positano on the Amalfi coast, hung on a steep and curving hillside draped with olive groves above the Via Flaminia. It has no connection with the fountain in Rome except that both were at the intersection of three roads or *tre vie*. Trevi, part of the duchy of Spoleto and seat of a bishop, was destroyed by the Saracens and Magyars. Briefly an independent *comune*, its strategic position made it a prize fought over by Perugia and Foligno. Joining the Papal States in 1439 brought it prosperity, at least in the short run, as well as the fourth printing press in Italy in 1470. These days, like its sister hill towns, it may look medieval but it dallies on the wild side of the international avant-garde.

## Two Churches, Two Art Museums

Trevi's credentials as a free *comune* in the Middle Ages are in its small but proud **Palazzo Comunale** in Piazza Mazzini, built in the 14th century, with later additions. From here, the stepped Via Beato Placido Riccardi leads up past the Piazza della Rocca, lined with quattrocento palaces; further up stands the domed cathedral, **Sant'Emiliano**. Emiliano, an Armenian monk, served in the 4th century as bishop of Trevi, and has been solemnly celebrated every 27 January since the Middle Ages with a procession of the Illuminata. His church has three Romanesque

# Getting to Trevi

There are **buses** to Trevi from Foligno several times a day (t 0743 212208, *www.spoletina.com*). There are also **trains**, from Spello, Assisi and Perugia several times a day, and from Spoleto, Terni, Narni and Rome, but you have to get a bus down the hill from the station.

apses and a 15th-century portal, with the good bishop and a pair of lions carved in relief. The interior was redone in the 19th century but contains a beautiful altar of 1522, carved by Rocco di Tommaso.

**Trevi Flash Art Museum**
*t 0742 381978; open Tues–Sun 3–7; adm varies by exhibition*

Next door, the **Palazzo Lucarini** hosts the Trevi Flash Art Museum, a joint endeavour between *Flash Art* magazine and the *comune*, with works by contemporary Umbrian, Italian and foreign artists.

For older stuff, make your way to **San Francesco**, a huge mid-14th-century church with original frescoes, on the site where Francis's preaching was drowned out by the braying of an 'indomitable ass'. 'Brother ass, do hush and let me preach to these people,' Francis said, and the animal 'put its head down on the ground and knelt, and remained silent until Francis had finished, much to the wonder of the people'. It has Renaissance tombs, a Roman sarcophagus with the remains of St Ventura (d. 1310) and one of Lo Spagna's finest works, the *Assumption with SS. Jerome, John the Baptist, Francis and Anthony of Padua*, where the Virgin ascends to heaven over Foligno. This was first in the chapel of the San Martino monastery (*see* below).

**Museo Civico/ Raccolta d'Arte di San Francesco**
*t 0742 381628; open April, May and Sept Tues–Sun 10.30–1 and 2.30–6; June and July Tues–Sun 10.30–1 and 3.30–7; Aug daily 10.30–1 and 3–7.30; Oct–Mar Fri–Sun 10.30–1 and 2.30–5; adm*

**Museo della Civiltà dell'Olivo**
*t 0742 381628; open April, May and Sept Tues–Sun 10.30–1 and 2.30–6; June and July Tues–Sun 10.30–1 and 3.30–7; Aug daily 10.30–1 and 3–7.30; Oct–Mar Fri–Sun 10.30–1 and 2.30–5; adm includes visit to San Francesco church*

**San Martino**
*open daily 8–12 and 4–sunset*

Access to the church is via its enormous convent, home to the Museo Civico or Raccolta d'Arte di San Francesco. There are good paintings by local artists, including an *Incoronazione di Maria* by Lo Spagna and scenes of the life of Christ from polyptychs by Giovanni di Corraduccio, a charming 15th-century painter from Foligno. The convent is also home to the Museo della Civiltà dell'Olivo. Trevi is famous for its olive oil: its conical hill is wrapped with majestic olive trees, including specimens believed to be well over 1,000 years old (especially the so-called Olivo da Sant'Emiliano, 3km south at Bovara). Olives, introduced by the Greeks in the bay of Naples, reached Umbria by the 5th century BC; like many Greek things, they were quickly adapted by the Etruscans and the rest is history.

## Around Trevi

Though the town has many churches, the best two are just outside. From Piazza Garibaldi, outside the gate to the *centro storico*, Via Ciuffelli leads to the 14th-century Capuchin monastery and church of San Martino. Over the door is a lunette by Tiberio d'Assisi, whose *St Martin and the Beggar* is inside; the other prize painting is Pierantonio Mezzastris' *Madonna*.

South of Trevi, in an olive grove, is the votive church of the **Madonna delle Lacrime**, built in 1487 to house a weeping statue of the Virgin – the first of many churches that went up during the great Marian renewal, inspired by the sermons of San Bernardino. The church, shaped like a Latin cross, has a fine sculpted portal by Giovanni di Gian Pietro of Venice; when the quake damage has been repaired, you'll be able to see the lovely frescoes: the *Adoration of the Magi* by Perugino, an anonymous *Madonna and Child* of 1483 and a *Deposition* by Lo Spagna. Many of the locally prominent Valenti family have impressive tombs from the 1500s and 1600s.

**Tempietto del Clitunno**

*t 0743 275085; open daily April–Nov 8.45–7.45, Dec–Mar 8.45–5.45; adm*

Though the Roman villas and temples that stood in sacred Clitunno (*see* below) are long gone, bits were reassembled in the mysterious little **Tempietto del Clitunno**, on the SS3 just south of Trevi (signposted). Two centuries ago this was believed to be a pagan temple converted to Christian use; Goethe dissented, believing it to be an original Christian work. For once this most misinformed of all geniuses got it right. The most recent studies put the Tempietto somewhere in the 6th century, or even as late as the 8th, making this obscure, lovely building in a way the last work of classical antiquity, Christian enough, but an architectural throwback to a world that was already lost.

The little track below the temple was the original Roman Via Flaminia; travellers between Ravenna and Rome would look up and see the beautiful façade, with its two striking coloured marble columns and ornate pediment in an exotic, half-oriental late Roman style. The entrance, however, is round the side, leading into the portico and from there to the tiny sanctuary decorated with Byzantine frescoes of the 700s: saints Peter and Paul flanking the altar, and, above, two unforgettable, very spiritual angels inspired by the great mosaics of Ravenna, gazing inscrutably out from the depths of the Dark Ages. The dedication remains intact, on the architrave: 'Holy God of the Angels who made the Resurrection'.

## The Fonti del Clitunno

**Fonti del Clitunno**

*t 0743 521141; open daily May–Aug 8.30–8; Sept 9–1 and 2–7.30; Oct–3 Nov 9–1 and 2–6.30; 4 Nov–Dec 10–1 and 2–5; Jan–14 Mar 10–1 and 2–4; 15 Mar–Apr 9–7; adm*

Still on the SS3, 2km south of the Tempietto, is Fonti del Clitunno, a famous beauty spot for some 2,300 years. Through the poetry of Virgil and Propertius, all of Rome knew about Clitumnus, its eponymous river god, and the snow-white oxen raised here to serve as sacrifices. It was one of the great sights of the Grand Tour; in the 19th century, it inspired Giosuè Carducci to write one of his best-known poems, baptizing Umbria green for evermore.

'*Salve, Umbria verde, e tu del puro fonte nume Clitumno! Sento in cuor l'antica patria e aleggiarmi su l'accesa fronte gl'ital iddii.*'

'Hail, green Umbria, and you, Clitumno, genius of the pure spring! I feel in my heart the ancient fatherland, and the Italic gods alighting on my fevered brow.'

A score of underground springs rise at the river's source, forming a landscape of astonishing crystal lagoons and islands, planted with weeping willows and poplars. Byron devoted a few stanzas of

*Childe Harold's Pilgrimage* to the place (Canto 4), but today the proximity of the busy Via Flaminia and the railway keep the springs from being quite the idyllic paradise evoked by the poets; still it comes pretty close if you come on a quiet weekday, late in the afternoon after the coach parties have moved on. Next to the park, part of the lagoon doubles as a delightful picnic ground and a well-stocked trout farm.

The village hanging on the steep slope above, **Campello sul Clitunno**, is built around the 16th-century **Chiesa della Bianca**, with frescoes by Lo Spagna. For a remarkable view over the Valle Umbra, take the steep little road up and up through the terraces of olives to the tiny **Castello** (or Campello Alto), hunkered down in the walls.

### South of Clitunno: San Giacomo

After Clitunno, the Via Flaminia passes under a grim square castle in **San Giacomo di Spoleto**, an outpost built in the 14th century by Cardinal Albornoz. Unlike the Cardinal's other Umbrian fortresses, this was later converted into a residential neighbourhood, with tiny lanes lined with little houses. Opposite the castle walls stands the **church of San Giacomo**, founded in the 13th century and redone in the 16th, the date of its beautiful carved doorway and frescoes. The best of these are by Lo Spagna and show miracles accredited to St James the Greater that occurred along the road to Compostela: a young man, unjustly hanged, is discovered still to be alive when his parents return to cut down his body. The parents hurry to tell the judge, who scoffs and says their son is as alive as the roast chickens on his table, whereupon the roast chickens fly away.

**09** The Valle Umbra | Around Trevi

## Where to Stay and Eat in Trevi

(i) Trevi >

*Piazza Mazzini 5,
t 0742 781150,
www.protrevi.com*

### Trevi ✉ 06039

In Oct try Trevi's famous black celery (*sedano nero*); every Thurs morning that month sees a market devoted to it.

***Il Terziere**, Via Salerno 1, t 0742 78359, *www.ilterziere.com* (€€€). A fine choice, with lovely views and delicious local cuisine (half and full board available).

*****La Cerquetta**, Via Flaminia 144, Loc. Parrano, t 0742 78366, *www. hotelcerquetta.com* (€€). Decent en-suite rooms and reliable Umbrian food at very honest prices; full board available. *Closed Sun.*

****Il Pescatore**, Via Chiesa Tonda 50, Loc. Pigge, t 0742 78483, *www. hotelilpescatore.net* (€). A peaceful

 Vecchio Molino >>

pensione a few km out of town with pleasant en-suite rooms, near a brook. Its excellent restaurant (€€) has an imaginative menu based on fish and truffles, and is very good value. Full board offered. *Closed Wed.*

**La Locanda di Fanfaluca**, Loc. Parrano, t 0742 780441, *www. locandadifanfaluca.com* (€€). Well worth the short drive from Trevi, this restaurant specializes in local ingredients. Try the *strangozzi al tartufo*. The meat dishes are also very good and the bread is homemade. Great value and a very pleasant atmosphere.

### Campello sul Clitunno
✉ 06042

**** Vecchio Molino, Via del Tempio 34, Loc. Pissignano, t 0743 521122, *www. vecchio-molino.it* (€€€). A former watermill close to the Perugia–Spoleto road but filled with the sound of gurgling water; two streams run through the garden. Bedrooms (breakfast included) are elegantly furnished in a traditional Umbrian style. *Closed Nov–Mar.*

**\*\*Fontanelle**, Via d'Elci 1, Loc. Fontanelle, t 0743 521091, *www.albergofontanelle.it* (€€). A lovely hotel surrounded by greenery. The bedrooms are basic but en suite, and they boast panoramic views. The restaurant (€€) serves good *bruschette*, *strangozzi* and specialities

based on local truffles, and half and full board are available.

**\*\*Ravale**, Via Virgilio, Loc. Ravele, Fonti del Clitunno, t 0743 521320, *www.ravale.it* (€€). Simple rooms and a restaurant-pizzeria (half and full board offered).

**Pettino da Palmario**, Loc. Pettino, northeast of town towards Colle Pian Fienile, t 0743 276021 (€€). A family-run *agriturismo* with simple but comfy double rooms and 2-person apartments in a rural setting, and a good reputation for its food (€€€). *Closed Tues and Mar.*

# Spoleto

 Spoleto

When composer Giancarlo Menotti was dreaming up the Festival of Two Worlds in the 1950s, he spent months travelling across central Italy looking for a pretty town where the best of modern culture could be displayed against a background that recalled the best of the past. Spoleto (population 36,000), a rather austere town of grey stone and cobbled streets, buried in one of the most obscure corners of darkest Umbria, was almost unknown then. But it has a remarkable past; after its prominence in classical times, it became the seat of one of the most powerful states in Italy at the very beginning of the Middle Ages. It remained splendid enough through the golden years of the high Middle Ages and Renaissance to acquire its share of lovely monuments, and then it pricked its finger on a spindle and dozed like Sleeping Beauty. Shelley called it 'the most romantic city I ever saw'.

After its long sleep, Spoleto was ready for Menotti, who died in 2007 leaving the Festival in the hands of his adopted son Francis. A bitter dispute ensued between Francis Menotti and Spoleto city council, which has now taken over the running of the event.

## History

Ancient *Spoletium*, one of the Umbrii's most important cities, was resettled as a Roman colony in 242 BC, only 24 years before an over-confident Hannibal came pounding at the gates, expecting an easy victory after his rout over the legions at Trasimeno (*see* p.110). But *Spoletium* remained loyal to Rome and repulsed the Carthaginians and their allies; Hannibal, who'd planned to go to Rome from there, was discouraged enough to make a fatal detour into the Marches.

Strategically located on the Via Flaminia midway between Rome and the late Imperial capital Ravenna, Spoleto was one of the rare towns to prosper in the twilight of the empire. King Theodoric built it up for the Ostrogoths; Justinian's general, Belisarius, did the same

# Getting to and around Spoleto

The Rome–Ancona **train** line follows the Via Flaminia to Spoleto. There are also some 12 trains daily from Perugia (63km/70mins). The station is a bit far from the centre, but there are regular connecting buses. The ticket office is at Piazza Polvani, t 0743 48516.

Spoleto has its own intercity **bus** company, Società Spoletina di Imprese Trasporti (SSIT, t 0743 212208, *www.spoletina.com*), with connections from Piazza Garibaldi on the west of town to Assisi, Terni, Perugia and nearby villages. Regular buses go to Norcia and Foligno; 1 a day to Rome and to Urbino in the Marches.

**Parking** in the centre is next to impossible; the best bet is to park at the Spoleto Sfera, a large new carpark as you drive into the city on Viale Martiri della Resistenza.

**Bikes** can be hired at Scocchetti Cicli, Via Marconi 82, t 0743 44728. For **car hire**, there are Avis, Loc. S. Chiodo 164, t 0743 46272, *www.avisautonoleggio.it*, and Hertz, Via Cerquiglia 144, t 0743 47195, *www.hertz.it*.

for the Byzantines; the Goths under Totila made it into a fortress, while the Lombards, arriving in 569, made it the base of their power, a duchy that in the 700s controlled most of central Italy.

In 890, after Charlemagne, Duke Guido III made an armed play for the Imperial Crown, but had to be content with crowning himself King of Italy at Pavia. After Guido and his son Lamberto, the duchy fell into decline, and in the 11th century the popes began to lean on Spoleto, claiming authority through that famous forgery, the 'Donation of Constantine'. Not until 1198, though, was Innocent III successful in capturing the city, and in 1247 it became part of the papal domains once and for all. But not without occasional complications: in 1499 Spoleto was briefly ruled by Lucrezia Borgia, a 19-year-old just married to the second of three husbands by her scheming papal father. By all accounts, Lucrezia ruled well but was sent off two years later to marry a bigger fish – Alfonso d'Este of Ferrara. Under the popes, it became a favourite with the papal nobility, who filled it with palaces and used it to entertain celebrities: chronicles record lavish banquets laid on for Queen Christina of Sweden in 1655 and for Maria Casimira, widow of the hero John Sobieski, in 1699.

Spoleto is only heard of again some three centuries later, thanks to Giancarlo Menotti and the late Thomas Schippers, who bestowed on the town their **Festival of Two Worlds** (*see* p.185).

## Remnants of Roman *Spoletium*

Like Perugia, Spoleto is a city of many ages, jammed together cheek-by-jowl in a fascinating collage of time and space. Thanks to the festival, the 20th century gets its say, too: if you arrive in Spoleto by train, you'll be greeted by a huge iron sculpture, the *Teodolapio* by Alexander Calder, a relic of the 1962 festival now used to shade a taxi stand. Buses from the station leave you at central **Piazza della Libertà**, which is also the usual approach if you arrive by car. Just across from the tourist office, the open side of the piazza overlooks the **Roman theatre**, built in the 1st century AD. In the 1950s it was restored as a venue for concerts and ballets

**Teatro Romano**
*open daily 8.30–7.30; joint adm with Museo Archeologico (see p.179)*

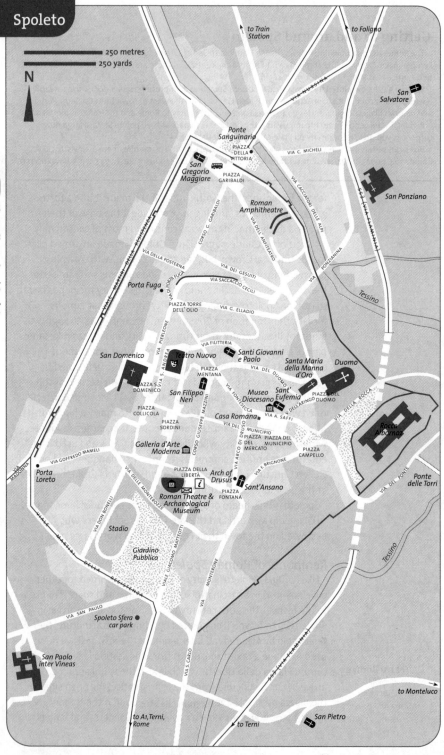

250 metres
250 yards

N

to Train
Station

to Foligno

San
Salvatore

Ponte
Sanguinario

PIAZZA
DELLA
VITTORIA

VIA C. MICHELI

San
Gregorio
Maggiore

PIAZZA
GARIBALDI

San Ponziano

Roman
Amphitheatre

CORSO G. GARIBALDI

VIA DELL'ANFITEATRO

VIA CACCIATORI DELLE ALPI

VIA PONZIANINA

VIA DELLA POSTERNA

VIA DEI GESUITI

VIA DI PORTA FUGA

Tessino

Porta Fuga

VIA SACCACCIO CECILI

PIAZZA TORRE
DELL' OLIO

VIA G. ELLADIO

VIA FILITTERIA

San Domenico

Teatro Nuovo

Santi Giovanni
e Paolo

Santa Maria
della Manna
d'Oro

Duomo

VIA S. ANDREA

VIA DEL DUOMO

PIAZZA S.
DOMENICO

PIAZZA
MENTANA

San Filippo
Neri

Sant'
Eufemia

PIAZZA DEL
DUOMO

VIA DELL'ARINGO

VIA DELLA ROCCA

VIA PIERLEONE

VIA FONTESECCA

Museo
Diocesano

PIAZZA
COLLICOLA

Casa Romana

VIA A. SAFFI

PIAZZA
SORDINI

CORSO GIUSEPPE MAZZINI

VIA DEL

Roccu
Albornoz

Galleria d'Arte
Moderna

VIA ARCO DI DRUSO

PIAZZA DEL
MUNICIPIO

PIAZZA
MUNICIPIO

PIAZZA
CAMPELLO

VIA GOFFREDO MAMELI

VIA DELLE MONTEROZZA

PIAZZA DELLA
LIBERTA

Arch of
Drusus

VIA F. BRIGNONE

Ponte
delle Torri

VIA MADONNA

Porta
Loreto

Sant'Ansano

VIA DEL PONTE

Roman Theatre &
Archaeological
Museum

PIAZZA
FONTANA

VIA DON BONELLI

Stadio

Giardino
Pubblica

VIALE GIACOMO MATTEOTTI

VIA MONTERONE

Tessino

to Monteluco

VIA SAN PAULO

VIA S. CARLO

Spoleto Sfera
car park

San Paolo
inter Vineas

to A1, Terni,
Rome

to Terni

San Pietro

during the music festivals; most of the theatre's impressive substructure of arches and tunnels has survived, as well as the pretty marble pavement in the *scena*. In the Middle Ages, the stage building was replaced with the formidable church, charming cloister and Benedictine **monastery of Sant'Agata**. The restored convent houses Spoleto's **Museo Archeologico** with inscriptions and architectural fragments, busts of Julius Caesar and Augustus and other distinguished Romans, and a stone found in a sacred grove dedicated to Jupiter, warning against profaning the place (or chopping wood). The convent refectory has a good cinquecento fresco of the Last Supper.

**Museo Archeologico**
*t 0743 225531; open daily 8.30–7.30; joint adm with Roman theatre (see p.177)*

East through Piazza Fontana and then left, you pass under the travertine **arch of Drusus and Germanicus**, erected in AD 23 by Tiberius' son (Drusus would have made a good emperor, but he died, and the Roman world got Caligula instead). The arch marked the entrance to the Forum, and on the adjacent modern building is the outline of the columns of a temple, as well as its actual foundations beneath. **Sant'Ansano** built over a Paleochristian church and a Roman temple, incorporates more ancient fragments, though its original medieval appearance was sacrificed for fashion in the late 18th century. The 11th-century **crypt of San Isacco** has stayed the same, decorated with rare frescoes in the Byzantine style: the *Beheading of John the Baptist*, *Christ in Glory*, the *Last Supper* and the *Life of St Isaac the Hermit*, a 5th-century Syrian monk who took refuge near Spoleto. The crypt's columns are Roman, the capitals Lombard.

**Sant'Ansano**
*t 0743 40305; open daily April–Oct 8–12.30 and 3–7, Nov–Mar 8–12.30 and 3–6*

Via Arco di Druso empties into the Roman forum, now **Piazza del Mercato**, where glistening tomatoes and aubergines compete for your attention with the 18th-century **Fonte di Piazza**, a provincial version of Rome's Trevi Fountain, which incorporates Carlo Maderno's monument to Urban VII of 1626.

The nearby 1st-century BC **Casa Romana** is believed, perhaps fancifully, to have been the house of Emperor Vespasian's mother, Vespasia Polla. The atrium and wellhead, bedrooms, bath and beautiful mosaic floors survive.

**Casa Romana**
*Via di Visiale, t 0743 234250; open daily 10–8; adm*

## Piazza Campello, the Rocca and the Ponte delle Torri

From Piazza del Municipio, Via Saffi climbs up to panoramic **Piazza Campello** with another good fountain, the 17th-century **Mascherone**, with a huge, grotesque face spitting out the water from the Roman and medieval aqueduct. The monument on the square is from 1910, built to honour all the Spoletines who fought to free their city from the Papal States. The symbol of the oppression looms just above: the **Rocca Albornoz** an impressive, six-towered citadel by Gattapone from Gubbio, commissioned in 1359 by that indefatigable papal enforcer Cardinal Albornoz, who

**Rocca Albornoz**
*t 0743 43707 or t 0743 551 0813; open Mon 10–6, Tues, Wed and Sun 9–6, Thurs–Sat 9–7.30; adm*

09

The Valle Umbra | Spoleto

made this his personal HQ. Most of the stone used is at least third-hand: first employed in the Roman amphitheatre, then cannibalized by the Goth Totila for his fortress, then dragged up here. When Spoleto was firmly in the papal pocket, the Rocca became a popular country resort for the popes, frequented in particular by Julius II, accompanied on occasion by Michelangelo, who loved the peace of these hills. Until fairly recently, the Rocca served as a prison (among inmates was Mohammed Ali Agca, would-be assassin of Pope John Paul II); work is under way to install a laboratory for the restoration of books and art. Ruins of a 7th-century **church of Sant'Elia** have been found on the hill. There are beautiful views of Spoleto and the valley below.

**Museo Nazionale del Ducato di Spoleto**

*Rocca Albornoz,*
*t 0743 223055; open*
*Tues, Wed and Sun*
*9–1.30; Thurs, Fri and*
*Sat 9–7.30; adm*

The contents of the former **Pinacoteca** have moved to the new **Museo Nazionale del Ducato di Spoleto**, housed in the Rocca Albornoz. Among the highlights are works by Spoleto-born Lo Spagna, including his finest, the Raphaelesque *Madonna, Child and Saints* (1512), painted for the Rocca Albornoz. Another of his commissions, an allegorical *Charity, Mercy and Justice*, was painted for Julius II even though they were hardly that Pope's strong points; in 1824 the work was adjusted to fit a bust of another pope, Leo XII, a Spoleto native. There are portraits of the Teutonic dukes of long ago and coins from the days of the Lombard duchy, as well as a beautiful crucifix reliquary and painting of Christ in a lavish filigree frame by the Maestro di Sant'Alò, who worked in Spoleto at the end of the 1200s. There's a bejewelled Byzantine-style icon from the 13th century and frescoes on the lives of SS. Peter and Paul. Anyone who has read the conspiracy book *Holy Blood, Holy Grail* may want to take a close look at the Magdalene by Guercino.

The pedestrian-only **Via del Ponte** from Piazza Campello leads down to one of the greatest engineering works of the 1300s, the spectacular 230m **Ponte delle Torri**, a bridge and aqueduct of 10 towering arches built by Gattapone for Cardinal Albornoz, to guarantee the water supply to the Rocca. It dizzily spans the 79m-deep ravine of the Tessino river far, far below, and was one of the unmissable sights for Grand Tourists, who thought it was Roman; Turner painted a fine picture of it. The bridge does stand on a Roman foundation; you can cross it to the towers that gave it its name, and to Monteluco's San Pietro (*see* p.184). From here, Via del Ponte circles around under the Rocca back to Piazza Campello.

**Sant'Eufemia**

*t 0743 231022;*
*open 16 Mar–31 Oct*
*Mon–Fri 10–1 and 3–6,*
*Sat, Sun and hols 10–6;*
*Aug daily 10–6;*
*1 Nov–15 Mar Tues–Fri*
*10.30–1 and 3–5.30, Sat,*
*Sun and hols 11–5; adm*

## Sant'Eufemia and the Museo Diocesano

Behind the Palazzo Comunale on Via Saffi, an archway leads into the small courtyard of the archbishop's palace, facing one of the finest Umbrian Romanesque churches, **Sant'Eufemia**, completed about 1140. It has a plain façade, but its interior in luminescent white stone is remarkable. Fragments of Roman buildings are built into the walls and columns in surprising ways, and it has an anachronistic *matroneum*, the Byzantine-style second-floor gallery where women were segregated during Mass – although this was a common practice in Rome and Ravenna, it's the only *matroneum* in Umbria. The altar, brought from Spoleto's first cathedral, is good Cosmatesque work, with symbols of the four Evangelists surrounding the Paschal lamb.

**Museo Diocesano**
*details as for Sant'Eufemia*

Part of Sant'Eufemia's convent, built over an important and still partly visible 1st-century Roman structure, became the Palazzo Arcivescovile, home of the **Museo Diocesano** This has works garnered from the diocese, with an array of early painted crucifixes and trecento Madonnas, including a lovely one by the First Master of Santa Chiara di Montefalco. Highlights among later works are an *Adoration of the Child* by Domenico Beccafumi of Siena, the *Madonna delle Neve* by Neri di Bicci and a *Madonna and Child with SS. Montano and Bartolomeo* by Filippino Lippi. One room has an excellent collection of medieval Umbrian sculpture, and there's a fascinating assortment of popular 16th–19th-century *ex votos*.

## Via dell'Arringo

Via dell'Arringo, a grand, shallow stairway behind Sant'Eufemia, opens into the Piazza del Duomo. In early medieval times Spoletani gathered here to make communal decisions by acclamation after hearing speeches. It must have been this theatrical ensemble that sold Menotti on Spoleto, with its naturally tiered seating set against the cathedral façade and the Umbrian hills as a backdrop.

**Teatro Caio Melisso**
*t 0743 222209, www. teatrostabile.umbria.it; open for performances*

Among the buildings, there's the **Teatro Caio Melisso** an exquisite little late-19th-century theatre named after the Spoleto-born dramatist and librarian of the Emperor Augustus; the pink-and-white striped **Casa dell'Opera del Duomo** (1419); and an octagonal church, **Santa Maria della Manna d'Oro**, built after 1527 as a votive after the Sack of Rome, with four paintings by Sebastiano Conca. Note the Roman sarcophagus used as a fountain, the memorial to US conductor Thomas Schippers, who loved the view and festival so much he asked to be buried here. Nearby is the 16th-century **Palazzo Racani**, designed by Giulio Romano, with faded *sgraffito* decoration in dire need of restoration.

## The Duomo

**Duomo**
*t 0743 44307; open daily Mar–Oct 7.30–12.30 and 3–7; Nov–Feb 7.30–12.30 and 3–5*

The magnificent cathedral was rebuilt after Emperor Frederick Barbarossa, the most powerful of papal enemies, razed its predecessor to the ground in 1155. Consecrated by the most powerful of medieval popes, Innocent III, in 1198, it has several unusual features. A graceful Renaissance portico (1491) incorporates two pulpits; four rose windows and four circular emblems of the Evangelists adorn its façade, surrounding a gold-ground Byzantine-style mosaic of *Christ Enthroned with Mary and John the Baptist* (1207), signed by Solsternus. The lower middle *rosone* is an exceptional example of the Cosmatesque work imported from Rome – stone or enamel chips in sinuous patterns. The campanile is built from Roman odds and ends.

The Latin cross **interior** was redone in the 1630s, a misguided gift to the city by the Barberini family of Rome: Maffeo Barberini had been cardinal of Spoleto before he was elected Urban VIII in 1623, and his nephew, another cardinal of Spoleto, funded the works and commemorated his uncle with the bronze bust by Bernini inside the central door. Several treasures survived the interior redesigners, including the fine Cosmati pavement in the central nave. Pinturicchio, not on one of his better days, painted the frescoes of the Madonna and saints in the first chapel on the right, his usual amusing detail including St Jerome's lion frisking about the landscape. His pupil Jacopo Siculo painted the frescoes in the next chapel. In the right transept, a Baroque chapel by Giambattista Mola holds the 12th-century *Santissima Icona*, a highly venerated icon from Constantinople donated as a peace offering to Spoleto by Frederick Barbarossa. The chapel has two paintings by the Cavalier d'Arpino, who painted the dome of St Peter's.

In the apse are the exquisite, rich frescoes of the life of the Virgin (1467–69), a masterpiece by Florentine Fra Filippo Lippi, beautifully restored. Not only did Lippi paint larger-than-life figures, he fitted them expertly into the space, through a canny use of perspective and architectural features, including columns and friezes from Spoleto itself. The splendid *Coronation of the Virgin*, in the upper part of the apse, is the best-preserved of the cycle, crowded with the angel musicians and female figures Lippi loved to paint, here in the guise of Sibyls and women from the Old Testament. Lippi portrayed himself (in a white habit with a black hat), his son Filippino (the young angel) and his assistants among the mourners in the central scene of the Virgin's death. The fun-loving monk (he ran off with a nun but was permitted to leave his order and marry her) died in Spoleto while working on the project, and the *Nativity* was finished by his chief helpers, Fra Diamanti and the Umbrian Pier Matteo d'Amelia. When Lippi's great patron Lorenzo de' Medici asked that the artist's body be returned to Florence, the Spoletini refused, claiming they had no notable dead while Florence had a great many. Lorenzo had to be content with commissioning a handsome Florentine tomb for him, now in the right transept.

In the left aisle, the original sacristy was converted into a chapel of reliquaries in the 1560s, with lavish intarsia cupboards made mostly by local craftsmen, although the two with architectural perspectives are by the great Fra Giovanni da Verona; the most important relic is a very rare letter in the hand of St Francis to Fra Leone. Hanging by the first altar on the left is a large and colourful *Crucifix*, dated 1187 and signed by Alberto Sotio, the first Umbrian artist whose name has come down to us.

## Lower Spoleto

**Galleria Civica d'Arte Moderna**
*Via Collicola,*
*t 0743 46434;*
*open Wed–Mon 10.30–1*
*and 3.30–7; adm*

Much of the city's contemporary art has gone to the Palazzo Collicola, the **Galleria Civica d'Arte Moderna** with works by Italy's 20th-century masters (Pomodoro, Burri, Guttoso, Accardi) and Spoleto's Leoncillo Leonardi (1915–68), who evolved a distinctive, colourful style in highly textured glazed terracotta. The custodian keeps the key for **Santi Giovanni e Paolo**, consecrated in 1178. It has excellent frescoes; on the left wall is a scene, attributed to Alberto Sotio, of the martyrdom of St Thomas Becket, canonized five years before (1170).

Via Tobagi leads you to Spoleto's fanciest Baroque church, **San Filippo Neri**, with an ornate façade and lofty dome, by local architect, Loreto Scelli, who studied in Rome. It has a fine Baroque bust of St Philip Neri by Bolognese sculptor Alessandro Algardi and paintings by Sebastiano Conca and Gaetano Lapis da Cagli.

**Teatro Nuovo**
*t 0743 40265*

Via Filitteria leads into Via Sant'Andrea, site of the **Teatro Nuovo** headquarters of the Two Worlds festival and the older Festival of Experimental Opera.

**San Domenico**
*t 0743 223240;*
*open daily 8.30–12.30*
*and 3.30–6*

Down the steps from here, the colourful pink and white striped preaching church of **San Domenico** was built in the 13th century; the interior has been restored to its original medieval appearance and has a colourful crucifix hanging in the centre of the nave. The walls are decorated with interesting if fragmented 13th–15th-century frescoes: the first chapel has an especially good *Triumph of St Thomas Aquinas* from the early 1400s, representing the triumph of Aquinas' scholastic philosphy; in a little chapel in the right transept is a *Life of Mary Magdalene* and there's a *Madonna and Child* behind the high altar, both from the early 15th century. The crucifix over the altar is 14th-century. Near here is a fine fresco of the Pietà, and a painting of St Peter Martyr, the overly efficient Dominican inquisitor who was axed in the head for his trouble.

From San Domenico, walk down Via Leone to the tall-towered 13th-century **Porta Fuga** (Put-to-flight Gate – as experienced by Hannibal in 217 BC) and along Via Saccocchio Cecili to take in a stretch of Spoleto's **walls**, with their *millefeuille* layers of history. The Umbrii built the 6th-century BC cyclopean base using huge blocks, later heightened by the Romans and all the other occupants of Spoleto up to the 15th century. The street ends in Piazza Cairoli; from here, Via dell'Anfiteatro leads past the ruined 2nd-century AD **Roman amphitheatre**, turned into a fortress by Totila and still part of a barracks.

**San Gregorio Maggiore**
t 0743 44140;
open 8–12 and 4–6

Down on Piazza Garibaldi is the 12th-century **San Gregorio Maggiore**; through the gate are the ruins of the Roman **Ponte Sanguinario** (Bloody Bridge), supposedly named after the Christians martyred in the amphitheatre, though more probably a corruption of the Latin name of a nearby gate, the *Sandapilarius*. It was built in the 1st century BC to carry the new Via Flaminia over the river and rediscovered in 1817.

## Outside Spoleto

### San Ponziano and San Salvatore

**San Ponziano**
t 0743 40655; to visit, ring bell of custodian's house near church

From the bridge and Piazza Vittoria, it's a short drive or an unpleasant 15-minute walk on the road under the *superstrada* to the cemetery, passing the 12th-century **San Ponziano**. Ponziano is Spoleto's patron, martyred here in 1169. The façade of his church, once faced with marble, is divided horizontally by a cornice and has a pretty Cosmatesque door and a round window surrounded by symbols of the Evangelists. The interior was redone by Giuseppe Valadier in 1788 but has the original crypt, with an upside-down Roman column, two turning posts (*metae*) from a Roman circus, three ancient sarcophagi and some fresco fragments. In the corridor, embedded like fossils in the wall, are huge Corinthian columns.

**San Salvatore**
t 0743 49606; open daily Nov–Feb 7–5; Mar, Apr, Sept and Oct 7–6; May–Aug 7–7

Even more Roman material went into building the charming 4th-century **San Salvatore**, just down from San Ponziano by the cemetery. Spoleto's oldest church has its façade and apse despite rebuildings and loss of its marble facing; the three doors have fine marble architraves and three curious old windows. The fluted Corinthian columns inside originally supported a Roman temple; the fresco of the jewelled cross in the apse is 8th or 9th century.

## Monteluco

✪ Monteluco

Just east of town, beautiful, forested Monteluco is Spoleto's holy mountain. The name is derived from *lucus* (sacred wood), and in Roman times it was forbidden to chop down the trees. In the 5th century, Isaac the Hermit from Antioch founded the first cenobitic community here; the Benedictines and the Franciscans followed.

**San Pietro**
t 0743 44882; closed for restoration but due to reopen in late 2009

You can get to Monteluco by car, by bus from Piazza della Libertà, or on foot over the Ponte delle Torri (*see* p.180). Near the base of the mountains stands the great Romanesque church of **San Pietro**, with a magnificent 12th-century façade, the last hurrah of the Lombard dukes of Spoleto. The Lombards delighted in portraying real and imaginary animals: here is a fox playing dead to capture some too-curious chickens, battles with lions, oxen, peacocks, eagles, a wolf in monk's clothing, animals devouring one another and the occasional armoured knight; devils contest souls, and St Michael slays his dragon. On the top level are two bulls, statues of St Peter and St Andrew and reliefs of Christ washing St Peter's feet and Christ calling St Peter and St Andrew. An elaborate frieze of vines and plants links allegorical scenes; on the left, the pious could compare the post-mortem destinies of the righteous and the sinful. The interior was Baroqued in 1699.

A steep, hairpinning road leads up through ilex forests to the lonely 12th-century church of **San Giuliano**, with a façade incorporating 6th-century elements of its predecessor. In the 7th century, anchorites and hermits, refugees from the wars in the Holy Land, settled here and set up monasteries; St Francis, who tried to emulate them, came to meditate here and in 1218 founded the tiny **monastery of San Francesco** near the summit of the mountain, a serene spot overlooking the countryside. Monteluco now has more summer villas and hotels than hermitages but it's still a cool and tranquil place to spend an afternoon.

## San Paolo Intervineas

Founded in Paleochristian times and mentioned in the 6th century by St Gregory the Great, this was rebuilt in the 10th century and again in 1234, when it was consecrated by Gregory IX as a church for a convent of Clarisse. It has a pretty façade with a rose window and frescoed lunette over the door; the interior contains a good series of frescoes from the period, including an account of the Creation, and an old altar.

**San Giuliano**
*visits by appt with monastery of San Francesco,* **t** *0743 40711*

**San Francesco**
**t** *0743 40711 or* **t** *0743 47797; open daily 9–12 and 3–6*

**San Paolo Intervineas**
*1km southwest of Spoleto (take Via San Paolo off Via Martiri della Resistenza); closed for restoration since earthquake; ask at tourist office (see below) for latest information*

**ⓘ Spoleto >>**
*Piazza della Libertà 7, t 0743 238920, www.regioneumbria.eu; closed Sun pm in winter*

## Tourist Information in Spoleto

**Post office:** Viale G. Matteotti 2, **t** 0743 201521, *www.postei.it.*
The main **market** takes place on Via Cacciatori delle Alpi on Fridays. There's also a sporadic farmers' market on Piazza del Mercato, and an antiques/fleamarket the 2nd Sun of the month.

## Festival in Spoleto

**Festival dei Due Mondi** (Festival of Two Worlds), Piazza del Duomo 8 and Piazza della Libertà (info and tickets), **t** 45028 220320, **t** 0743 45028 or freephone **t** 800 565600,

*www.spoletofestival.it*, 3wks end June–mid-July. Italy's leading arts festival, with music, theatre and dance.

## Where to Stay in and around Spoleto

**Spoleto ✉ 06049**
If Spoleto is full for the Two Worlds Festival, try the smaller outlying towns of Trevi, Campello and Spello, or ask the tourist office for a list of rooms to let and *agriturismo*, though it's still vital to book ahead. Con-Spoleto, Piazza della Libertà 7, **t** 0743 220773, *www.conspoleto.com*, can help find rooms.

### Luxury (€€€€€)

****Albornoz Palace**, Viale Matteotti 4, t 0743 221221, *www.albornozpalace. com*. A refined, stylish option just outside the historic centre, with babysitting, a restaurant (half and full board possible). and parking.

****Gattapone**, Via del Ponte 6, t 0743 223447, *www.hotelgattapone.it*. The most spectacular option: a stone house clinging to the slope near the Rocca and Ponte delle Torri, with good views. Rooms (breakfast included) are spacious and finely furnished, and there's free Internet access, babysitting and a beautiful garden.

****San Luca**, Via Interna delle Mura 21, t 0743 223399, *www.hotelsanluca.com*. A charming little hotel situated within Spolet's historic centre, boasting a sophisticated 19th-century ambience. Some of the rooms have baths with hydromassage.

**Palazzo Dragoni**, Via del Duomo 13, t 0743 222220, *www.palazzodragoni.it*. A beautiful *residenza d'epoca* in a central 16th-century building, retaining much of its original atmosphere, with rooms furnished in an elegant Umbrian style.

### Very Expensive (€€€€)

****Dei Duchi**, Viale Matteotti 4, t 0743 44541, *www.hoteldeiduchi.com*. An attractive contemporary hotel and restaurant, popular among visiting artists and performers. Half and full board available.

***Clitunno**, Piazza Sordini 6, t 0743 223340, *www.hotelclitunno. com*. A good option close to the centre of town, with a restaurant offering Umbrian cuisine (half and full board available).

### Expensive (€€€)

***Charleston**, Piazza Collicola 10, t 0743 220052,*www.hotelcharleston.it*. A pretty 17th-century *palazzo* in the *centro storico*, with comfortable rooms and apartments (let by the week), a sauna, an *enoteca* and two bars.

***Clarici**, Piazza della Vittoria 32, t 0743 223311, *www.hotelclarici.com*. A more modern choice in the lower part of town, decorated with taste, with babysitting and parking.

### Moderate (€€)

****Il Panciolle**, Via Duomo 4, t 0743 45677. Simple rooms and a good restaurant where meat is grilled over an open fire. *Closed Wed.*

**Il Casale Divino**, Loc. Colle del Marchese 101, Castel Ritaldi, t 0743 252029, *www.ilcasaledivino.it* (€70). A few kilometres from Spoleto on the *strada del vino* (wine route) near Castel Ritaldi, this is the perfect place for wine lovers. A beautiful country house with comfortable en-suite bedrooms, each named after a famous wine. Owners Raffaelle and Giacometta Rendano go out of their way to make guests feel welcome and will point you in the direction of the best *cantine* for wine tasting.

### Inexpensive (€)

****Due Porte**, Piazza della Vittoria 5, t 0743 223666. Basic rooms, a beautiful garden and parking.

## Outside Spoleto

**Il Barbarossa**, Via Licina 12, just outside town walls, t 0743 235083, *www. countryhouse-ilbarbarossa.it* (€€€). Guestrooms with all comforts set the middle of an olive grove, plus meals by prior arrangement.

***La Macchia**, Loc Licina 11, just north of centre off Via Flaminia, t 0743 49059, *www.albergolamacchia.it* (€€). A quiet, good-value option with rustic local furniture and a pretty garden. The restaurant specializes in *cucina spoletana*, using lots of mushrooms, truffles and asparagus; half board is available. The owners also let a flat in the nearby Castel San Felice.

***Michelangelo**, Loc.Monteluco, t 0743 40289, *www.michelangelohotel.net* (€€). Large, simple rooms near the top of the town, very friendly staff, and a good restaurant-pizzeria (full board available). *Closed 7 Nov–7 Dec.*

***Paradiso**, Loc Monteluco 19, t 0743 223082, *www.albergoparadiso.net* (€€). Comfortable rooms, a restaurant (half/full board available), a garden, great views, and peace and quiet.

****Ferretti**, Loc Monteluco 20, t 0743 49849, *www.albergoferretti.com* (€€).

A charming *pensione*, with some of its guest rooms boasting balconies overlooking the pretty piazza. There's a restaurant offering typical local cuisine, and full board is offered.

(★) **Il Tempio del Gusto>>**

**Il Casale Divino**, Loc. Colle del Marchese 101, Castel Ritaldi, **t** 0743 252029, *www.ilcasaledivino.it* (€€). A few kilometres from Spoleto on the *strada del vino* (wine route) near Castel Ritaldi, this is the perfect place for wine lovers. A beautiful country house with comfortable en-suite bedrooms, each named after a famous wine. Owners Raffaelle and Giacometta Rendano go out of their way to make guests feel welcome and will point you in the direction of the best *cantine* for wine tasting.

**Pecoraro**, Fraz. Strettura 76, Strettura, about 12km down SS3 towards Terni, **t** 0743 229697, *www.ilpecoraro.it* (€€). A pretty, welcoming *agriturismo*, albeit on the main road, with cosy rooms (breakfast included in rates), a small outdoor pool, a billiards table, horseriding, trekking, canoeing and a good restaurant offering a wide range of regional dishes and strong home-made grappas (full board available). *Closed 15–30 Nov, 1–15 Feb.*

(★) **Osteria del Matto >>**

## Eating Out in and around Spoleto

### Spoleto ✉ 06049

Expensive (€€€)
**Apollinare**, Via S. Agata 14, near Roman theatre, **t** 0743 223256. A romantic 13th-century Franciscan convent, though it can have its off days. Try gnocchi with fried leek and pigeon sauce or smoked eel with lentils. Booking is recommended. *Closed Tues.*

**Pentagramma**, Via Martani 4, near Piazza della Libertà, **t** 0743 223141. A welcoming former stable owned by Arturo Toscanini's daughter, serving perfectly prepared local dishes such as *strangozzi di Spoleto* (with olive oil, garlic, tomato and basil). Book ahead. *Closed Mon and part of Jan and Aug.*

**Tartufo**, Piazza Garibaldi 24, **t** 0743 40236. The black diamonds of the Valnerina in various combinations:

try *risotto al tartufo* or guinea fowl with truffles and potatoes (there are non-truffle dishes too). Booking is required. *Closed Sun eve, Mon, 2wks in Feb and 3wks in July.*

**Il Tempio del Gusto** Via Arco di Druso 11, **t** 0743 47121, *www.iltempiodelgusto. com*. Husband and wife Eros and Manuela Patrizi run this small restaurant with flair and passion, producing dishes that are original and unfailingly delicious. For starters, try the *cannolo croccante*, a crunchy tube made of sesame seeds and filled with soft white cheese, and the excellent pasta with seafood. Main dishes include a good choice of well-cooked fish and meat dishes. There are tables inside, or outside on the pretty courtyard. *Closed Thurs.*

Moderate (€€)
**Del Festival**, Via Brignone 8, **t** 0743 220993. A pretty place for *millefoglie* with *caciottina* cheese and the like, plus pizza. *Closed Thurs and 1–15 Feb.*

**Osteria del Matto** Vicolo del Mercato 3, **t** 0743 335506. The owner Filippo used to work as a butler in a stately home in Scotland, and will show you a picture of him in his kilt to prove it. He is a real character, and ably helped by Mamma, who does the cooking, serves a seemingly endless stream of small but mouthwatering dishes, based on local ingredients. There's no choice, but so much food that you're bound to find something you like. *Closed Tues.*

**Sabatini**, Corso Mazzini 54, **t** 0743 221831. Traditional Umbrian fare. *Closed Mon, 2wks Jan and 2wks Aug.*

**Sportellino**, Via Cerquiglia 4, **t** 0743 45230. A simple, homely place for *frittatina* with truffles, *ossobuco* with peas, and more. *Closed Thurs and 10 days in July or Aug.*

### Outside Spoleto
**Il Capanno**, Loc. Torrecola 6, 10km south on Via Flaminia, **t** 0743 54119 (€€€). Umbrian dishes such as *pappardelle* with pigeon ragout. *Closed Mon.*

**La Ginestra**, Loc. Pompagnano, **t** 0743 47010 (€€). Just outside the pretty village of Pompagnano, 1km from Spoleto, this is a pizzeria with a

**Palazzo del Papa >>**

difference, serving many of the classics but also a number of new variations, all cooked in a wood oven. You can even have a pizza with nutella to finish off with!

**Palazzo del Papa**, Strettura, on SS3, t 0743 54140 (€€). A *trattoria* with some of the best home cooking around, plus pizzas in the evening. *Closed Wed*.

# The Tiber Valley

South of Perugia, Old Father Tiber flows below the proud medieval eagle's eyrie of Todi then swells to form the Lago di Corbara and takes a sharp left under lofty hills to form the border with Lazio. This corner of Umbria closest to Rome has a character all its own, much of it concentrated in Orvieto, where mementos of Etruscans rub elbows with those of medieval popes and the papal nobility, in the shadow of one of Italy's great cathedrals. Charming Amelia, wrapped in walls built by the ancient Umbrii, is often overlooked. Between the three big hill towns are vineyards and steep wooded ridges, a score of smaller villages and lovely churches, and a handful of oddities, from a fossil forest of sequoias at Dunarobba to a tiny theatre at Montecastello di Vinio and the bizarre gardens of La Scarzuola at Montegiove.

# 10

## Don't miss

⭐ **A medieval civic ensemble**
Piazza del Popolo, Todi **p.192**

⭐ **Renaissance perfection**
Tempio della Consolazione **p.195**

⭐ **A jewelbox theatre**
Montecastello **p.196**

⭐ **The 'golden lily of cathedrals'**
Orvieto **p.203**

⭐ **A dream garden**
La Scarzuola, Montegiove **p.215**

See map overleaf

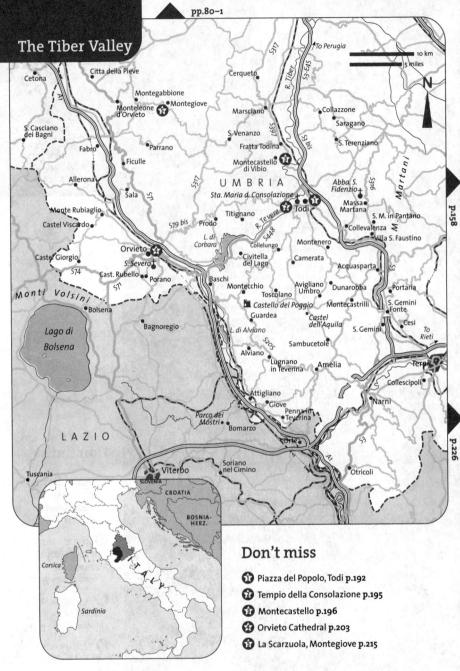

## Don't miss

## Todi

Todi (population 17,200) may be small but it has everything a
self-respecting central Italian hill town needs. There's the hill in a
gorgeous setting, a cathedral and medieval public buildings, one

## Getting to and from Todi

Todi is linked by **bus** to Terni (33km/45mins; ATC, **t** 0744 492711, *www.atcerni.it*), Perugia (41km/1hr; APM, **t** 800 512141, *www.apmperugia.it*) and Rome (130km/2hrs 30mins), and by the FCU's little **trains** (**t** 075 575401, *www.fcu.it*) to Perugia and Terni. Trains (FS, **t** 892021, *wwwtrenitalia.com*) and coaches (to Perugia, Terni, Rome and Orvieto) come and go from Ponte Rio, **t** 075 894 2092, linked to the centre by city bus.

There's only 1 bus a day between Todi and Orvieto (SULGA, **t** 800 099661, *www.sulga.it*), but the route takes in the lovely scenery over the Tiber valley. There are SSIT buses to Spoleto (**t** 074 321 2208 and **t** 0743 212229 for timetables, *www.spoletina.com*).

great Renaissance monument, a long and tortuous history, a saint (uncanonized, this time), and a proud *comune* escutcheon, a fierce eagle over the inevitable device 'SPQT'. In the past few years it has consistently been voted the world's most livable-in town by the University of Kentucky, an accolade that has brought American tycoons rushing to buy its villas and castles as holiday retreats, inviting comparisons with the Hamptons. But Todi was always a sophisticated little place, famous for its carpentry and woodworking. In April it hosts one of Italy's major antiques fairs, the Rassegna Antiquaria d'Italia, and in August and September the Mostra Nazionale dell'Artigianato, a national crafts fair. Since 1986, the Tudertini have added the latest fashion accessory: a festival, which brings the town opera, ballet and stage companies from late August to early September.

### History

It was the eagle that showed the ancient Umbrii where to build the city they were to call the 'Border' or *Tuter*, above modern Todi, on what is now the Rocca. The border was an uncomfortable one with the Etruscans, who settled lower down around the Piazza del Popolo; one day, the Etruscans became kings of the whole hill when they surprised, slaughtered and enslaved their Umbrian neighbours. As *Colonia Julia Fida Tuder*, dedicated to the war god Mars for its role in the wars against Hannibal, the town prospered through Roman times, and its nearly impregnable site kept the barbarians out; there's no evidence that Todi was ever part of the Lombard duchy of Spoleto, and it's possible that it may have maintained its independence all along.

By the 1200s, Todi had accumulated a little empire, including Terni and Amelia, and its soldiers were kept in trim by constant dust-ups with their peers in Spoleto, Narni and Orvieto. In 1227 their *podestà* was the notorious Mosca dei Lamberti, exiled from Florence after the killing of Buondelmonte dei Buondelmonti (*see* p.38); Dante would consign him to the Eighth Circle of Hell. But, above all, Todi took special pride in its good deeds. In 1249 the *comune* founded the Ospedale della Carità, where the poor were treated free – even Florence wasn't to have the like until 1316 – and it produced one of the greatest Italian poets of the Middle Ages in Fra Jacopone (*see* pp.193–5). By the end of the century, the government and the political effectiveness of the free *comune* were failing. The Atti family established themselves as *signori* during the early 1300s but were pushed out by the Malatesta of Rimini and Francesco Sforza of Milan among others, until eventually, in the 1460s, the pope gobbled up the town definitively for the Papal States.

🌟 Piazza del Popolo

## Piazza del Popolo

Todi's streets converge on this magnificent 13th–15th-century piazza, centre of civic life since the Etruscans and Romans. In the 15th century, as Todi's existence as an independent city-state came to an end, the square was preserved in aspic, leaving a medieval pageant in grey stone. The sternest building, the **Palazzo dei Priori** (1293–1337), has square battlements with a chunky tower; the **Palazzo del Popolo** (1213), with swallow-tail crenellations, and its adjacent **Palazzo del Capitano** (1290) are all grace by comparison. Linked by a grand Gothic stairway, these make up one of the most remarkable medieval town halls in Italy. These outer stairs emphasized how easy it was for the citizenry to have access to local government, who invariably held their meetings on the first floor. They now provide access to Todi's attic, the **Museo Pinacoteca di Todi** on the fourth floor of the Palazzo del Popolo. This harbours fond civic memories: retired eagles, archaeological pieces, 16th-century scenes of charity by local painter Pietro Paolo Sensini, among portraits of saints and worthies linked to the city, a model of the Tempio della Consolazione from *c.* 1570, a fine *Coronation of the Virgin* by Lo Spagna, and works by a 16th-century so-so painter, Ferraù da Faenza, who spent a lot of time here. Todi is especially proud of a saddle it made for the ailing pregnant Anita Garibaldi.

Museo Pinacoteca di Todi
*t 075 894 4148,
todi@sistemamuseo.it;
open Tues–Sun Apr–Oct
10–1 and 3–6, Nov–Mar
10.30–1 and 2.30–5;
adm (beware: stairs can
be slippery when wet)*

To the right of Palazzo del Capitano stands a cypress that was planted in 1849 in honour of Garibaldi's visit – which was a fleeting one, because the Republic of Rome had just fallen to the French allies of the pope and they were pursuing the hero, his wife and a handful of loyal Garibaldini.

Duomo
*t 075 894 3041;
open 28 Mar–Oct
daily 8.30–12.30 and
3–6.30; Nov–27 Mar
Tues–Sat 8.30–4.30, Sun
and hols 8.30–12.30
and 3–5.30; adm to
lapidary museum*

On the far side of the Piazza del Popolo, the **Duomo** is at the top of another distinguished flight of steps. Begun in the 12th century and finished 200 years later, it has a handsome flat screen façade, fine rose window and delicately decorated portal. Inside are good capitals, a Gothic arcade by a fourth aisle and a 14th-century altarpiece. Parishioners who turned to gossip during Mass were confronted by a not-too-terrifying vision of the Last Judgement by Ferraù da Faenza, a reworking of Michelangelo's in the Sistine Chapel. The large crypt is now a **lapidary museum** with bells, a copy of Todi's patron deity *Mars*, now housed in the Vatican, and fragments of statue groups by the school of Giovanni Pisano.

Left of the Duomo stands the 16th-century **bishop's palace** and the **Palazzo Rolli**, attributed to the younger Antonio da Sangallo; it was home to Paolo Rolli (d. 1765), who translated Milton into Italian.

## Down to Porta Perugina

Right of the Duomo, the road twists round, allowing a view of its beautiful apse. Some of Todi's **Etruscan–Roman walls** survive nearby, off Via Mure Antiche. Via Santa Prassede leads down to the pink and white **church of Santa Prassede**, from the 14th century but with a Baroque interior. The early medieval town ended here; beyond, Via Borgo Nuovo descends steeply past the **monastery of San Francesco**, also from the 14th century, with an allegorical fresco on salvation from the same period by the altar. Further down, a round tower marks the 13th-century **Porta Perugina**, offering views over the countryside. The only hitch is walking back up the hill.

## San Fortunato and the Rocca

**San Fortunato**
t 329 848 9080; open Tues–Sat April–Oct 9–1 and 3–7, Nov–Mar 9.30–12.30 and 3–5

From Piazza del Popolo, Via Mazzini leads past the **Teatro Comunale** (1872) to Todi's other great monument, **San Fortunato** (1292). In a prominent position at the top of a broad stair, this was one of many churches built during the late-13th-century Franciscan spending spree, when the Order received permission from the popes to administer as well as 'use' the substantial property it received as donations from the pious. In Todi they built on a grand scale, but the façade remains unfinished. According to scurrilous legend, when the Orvietani heard that the Tuderini had commissioned Lorenzo Maitani to decorate it, they had the sculptor murdered to prevent Todi from having a church as good as their cathedral. The late Gothic central portal was completed only in the 1400s and has little figures hidden among the acanthus and decorative bands: there's St Francis receiving the stigmata and the damned in hell with a little salamander, who doesn't seem to mind because salamanders were believed to be fireproof. The statues on either side of the door are of the *Annunciation*; the beautiful angel has been attributed to Jacopo della Quercia. The airy, luminous and remarkably wide Gothic interior, divided into three naves of equal height, is one of the best in central Italy. Large fragments of frescoes decorate many of the chapels, including a *Madonna and Child* (1432) by Masolino da Panicale, his only work in Umbria. The fine wooden choir is by Antonio Maffei of Gubbio (1590). But for the Tuderini the focal point is the **tomb of poet and mystic Jacopone da Todi** in the crypt, the subject of much local if unofficial devotion.

## God's Fool

Todi in its golden age was the home of Jacopo dei Benedetti (1228–1306), the greatest of the *laudesi*, or medieval Franciscan poets. For the first half of his life, however, Jacopone was anything but saintly: a worldly, money-grubbing notary, his one good point was his love for his wife, whom he married in 1267. But the next year she died in a freak accident, when a platform set up for a dance collapsed. Mad with grief, Jacopone brought her body home and found that, under all the finery he had made her wear, she had dressed in a hair shirt.

The shock of her death and discovery of her secret piety made him repent – slowly. The wrestling match with his soul lasted for 10 years, which he amply documented in a new-found talent for poetry. Rather than Latin, he wrote in Todi's dialect, employing the popular ballad form of the *laude*, the hymns chanted by the people in the streets, modelled on St Francis' great *Canticle of All Things Created*. Jacopone's previous career taught him the virtues of brevity and getting straight to the point – his staccato verse stands in marked contrast to the younger Dante's courtly measured Italian. Jacopone was the first to make the *laude* an art form, the perfect vehicle for communicating to the uneducated his message, of love for Christ, warnings of death, of the conflicts in his own soul, of the foibles of the worldly great and proud – he was a satirist almost by nature. His language is vivid and unconventional: in coming to terms with his unworthiness, for instance, he begs for sickness and even death, with his grave in the belly of a wolf, so his relics would be excrement.

His well-bred family in Todi disowned him. As a wandering penitent, a *bizocone*, he became 'Big Jim' the town eccentric, liable to do anything. He followed the medieval countercultural example of Francis himself in acting out his inner life, becoming 'God's fool': when his brother asked him not to show up at his wedding reception and ruin it with his usual follies, Jacopone crashed the party in the middle of the dance, naked and covered all over with honey and brightly coloured feathers.

In 1278, Jacopone joined the Franciscans at San Fortunato, although at first they were reluctant to accept him, convinced he was mad. Jacopone had reservations about Todi's friars as well; although the first Franciscan convent, founded in 1220, had been a very humble place outside the walls, in 1254 they had traded houses with the rich Vallombrosians of San Fortunato in the town centre, and were constantly in the courts arguing over the considerable lands and possessions they had amassed in Todi.

Franciscans by then had become learned scholars and priests, but Jacopone followed Francis's path and remained a friar, one who constantly upset his fellow brothers. To combat his gluttonous urges, for instance, he hung up a piece of meat in his cell, and let it rot until the whole convent stank; his peers threw him in the latrine for revenge, which he claimed to enjoy. This was the period of his most famous and unique poem, *Donna del Paradiso*, a dramatic dialogue on the grief of Mary at the Crucifixion; it quickly spread throughout Italy and developed into Passion plays, the first theatrical representations in Italy since Roman times (although Jacopone is often credited with the *Stabat Mater*, which has a similar theme and appeared at the same time, its Latin elegance shows that it is by another hand).

As a Franciscan, Jacopone soon found his niche with the Spirituals, the most unworldly branch of the order, which sought to keep to the letter of Francis's ideals of poverty. This involved Jacopone in the big events of the day, when the pro-Spiritual 'angel pope', Celestine V, was in 1294 compelled to resign by the irascible lawyer Cardinal Benedetto Gaetani, whose subsequent election as Boniface VIII was regarded by many as illegitimate. Boniface abrogated all of Celestine's acts, imprisoned the old man until he died (he was canonized in 1313) and forced the Spirituals back into the Franciscan fold. He then got down to the serious business of enriching his family, embezzling Church funds and spending the equivalent of two years' worth of the Curia's income, a tremendous sum, to buy up land around Rome.

Threatened by his acquisitiveness, the great Roman family of the Colonna became his sworn enemy, and Jacopone, who knew the pope well (he had lived in Todi for a long time), joined in the fray, signing a Colonna statement that declared that Boniface was not the true pope. Holed up in Palestrina with the Colonna, Jacopone let the pope have it in his vitriolic *Lauda LVIII*, listing his vainglorious and greedy acts, accusing him of being a desperado and heretic. When the pope's forces proved to be too strong for the Colonna in 1298, Jacopone was seized, excommunicated and tossed in prison, where he would remain in solitary confinement until Boniface died in 1303, mad and paranoid after the famous 'Slap of Anagni' administered by Sciarra Colonna.

When he was freed from prison by the next pope, Jacopone retired to a small friary in Collazzone, where he spent his last three years; Todi wanted no part of the old rebel. Now at peace, beyond good and evil, he wrote his greatest mystical poetry on divine love and joy, including the famous *Amor de Caritate*. His home town's attitude to him began to change when he became a hero for the new back-to-basics Observantist movement, founded in Umbria by Paolo de' Trinci in the 1360s; later the famous preacher Bernardino of Siena would be a great exponent of Jacopone's *laude*.

With his revolt against Boniface, Jacopone may have blown all hopes of ever being canonized, but Todi regards him as a saint, and in 1906, on the 600th anniversary of his death, erected the bronze statue in the niche at the bottom of San Fortunato's steps.

Next to San Fortunato stands the **Palazzo Ludovico Atti**, built for the town's *signori* and attributed to Galeazzo Alessi. From the garden right of the church, a lane leads up to the top of the town and the massive round tower of the Rocca, what remains of Todi's 14th-century citadel; the public gardens and belvedere offer an unforgettable view of the Tiber valley and Tempio della Consolazione. Here, too, is a Roman cistern converted into a chapel, known as the Carcere di San Cassiano for an account that it also at one point served as St Cassian's prison cell.

## Piazza Mercato Vecchio and Santa Maria in Camuccia

The most impressive reminder of Roman *Tuder* is in **Piazza Mercato Vecchio**: take the stepped Via San Fortunato down to Via Roma, walk through the handsome medieval **Porta Marzia** (made out of Roman pieces) then turn left. A temple of *Tuder*'s patron Mars stood near here, and in the old market square is a series of imposing arches with a Doric frieze called the **Nicchioni** (niches) from an Augustan-era basilica. Below the piazza is the little Romanesque **church of San Carlo** and the **Fontana Scarnabecco**, which was built in 1241 by a *podestà* from Bologna.

Santa Maria in Camuccia
*t 349 8392338; open daily summer 8–1 and 3–8, winter 8–1 and 3–5*

Return to the Porta Marzia, continue down Via Roma and turn right for **Santa Maria in Camuccia** a 13th-century church with Roman columns by the door; inside is the 12th-century wooden statue of the Virgin and Child known as the *Sedes Sapientiae* (Seat of Wisdom). From here, you can walk down to the Tempio della Consolazione (if you don't mind the slog back up the hill); you can also reach it by car on the ring road around Todi.

⚄ Tempio di Santa Maria della Consolazione
*open Wed–Mon April–Oct 9–12.30 and 2.30–6.30, Nov–Mar 9.30–12.30 and 2.30–5*

## Tempio di Santa Maria della Consolazione

This is the most ambitious attempt in Umbria to create a perfect Renaissance temple, and it is a beautiful ornament for Todi, an ivory-coloured essay in geometric forms, isolated amid wooded slopes and farmlands. Dedicated to an apparition of the Virgin, it was begun by the unknown Cola da Caprarola in 1508 but shows the influence of the great Roman architect Bramante, who may indeed have helped with the design. Scholars attempting to unravel the building's origins found only more puzzles, as a picture of the temple was discovered among the architectural sketches of Leonardo da Vinci from 1489.

Begun in 1508, the church was not completed until 99 years later. By that time, every celebrity architect of the late Renaissance had stuck his oar in, including many who worked on St Peter's: Antonio da Sangallo the Younger, Baldassare Peruzzi, Vignola and Sanmicheli among others. In 1589 Perugian architect Valentino Martelli designed the drum and dome. But unlike St Peter's in Rome, the Tempio's purity of form, geometrically harmonious restraint, patterns of semicircles and triangles and careful proportions of the fine dome and four apses (three polygonal and one semicircular) emerged as if the work of a single architect. Four Tudertini eagles guard the corners of the terrace and the classical interior, in the form of a Greek cross, is white, spacious and serene, with Baroque statues of the 12 Apostles and an elaborate altar with a 15th-century fresco of the Madonna della Consolazione.

### Convento di Montesanto

**Convento di Montesanto**
*Viale Montesanto; call t 075 894 8886 for opening hours*

Another sacred site outside Todi's walls is the 13th–14th-century fortified Convento di Montesanto 1km below the Porta Orvietana. A famous Etruscan bronze statue of Mars (probably made in Orvieto) was found here in what may have been an Etruscan temple. The great lime tree by the entrance is one of the oldest in Italy, planted in 1428 by San Bernardino of Siena. The church contains a massive 16th-century fresco of the Nativity, and another by Lo Spagna, and has lovely views over the Tempio della Consolazione.

🐸 Montecastello

**Teatro della Concordia**
*t 075 878 0737 or t 328 918 8892, prenotazioni@ teatropiccolo.it; open Mar and Oct Sat, Sun and hols 10–12.30 and 3–6; Apr–Sept Sat, Sun and hols 10–12.30 and 4.30–7.30; Nov–Feb Sat 3–6, Sun and hols 10–12.30 and 3–6*

# Around Todi

## North of Todi: Montecastello and the Smallest Theatre in the World

Todi's lovely surrounds are dotted with minor attractions. If you have to choose one, make it **Montecastello di Vibio**, 10km northwest, a walled medieval hill town high over the Tiber valley, home to an American art school. When Montecastello became its own master under Napoleon, the village's nine leading families decided to commemorate the Revolution by pooling their money to build the delightful (now restored) **Teatro della Concordia**, a mini-version of La Scala, with its boxes, decorations and 99 seats.

## Beyond Montecastello

Just north of Montecastello, the little hill town of **Fratta Todina** was a bone of contention between Perugia and Todi before it became a favourite country retreat of the rich families of Todi; it has a handsome Franciscan convent, La Spineta.

There's a 12th-century castle 7km further north in the industrial sprawl of **Marsciano**, built by its *signori* the Bulgarelli, who gave their fief to Perugia rather than let it fall into the talons of Todi. North again is part of a fresco, *St Sebastian and the Plague Saints*, by a young Perugino (1478), in the parish church of **Cerqueto**.

On the other side of the Tiber from Marsciano, charming **Collazzone** is a near-intact walled medieval hill town that was once a Perugian outpost. Like Todi, it enjoys a lovely setting among olive groves and forests, so perhaps Jacopone, who spent his last years here in the monastery of San Lorenzo, wasn't too homesick. The monastery was restored by Todi's bishop Angelo Cesi and now serves as Collazzone's town hall.

South, similarly charming **San Terenziano** has a handsome Palazzo Cesi and a pink Romanesque church outside the centre; don't miss the crypt with its funny old capitals.

## East of Todi: Massa Martana and Around

These days, pilgrims tend to ignore the Tempio della Consolazione and Montesanto, preferring the hideous **Santuario dell'Amore Misericordioso**, situated 6km east of Todi in **Collevalenza**. Founded in 1955 by Mother Speranza Alhama Valera (d. 1983), it was so popular it had to be enlarged 10 years later.

East a further 10km is **Massa Martana**, behind a 10th-century gate and 13th-century walls; it was founded as *Vicus ad Martis*, a waystation along the western branch of the Via Flaminia. Massa was the epicentre of the first earthquake – in May 1997 – of the many that would shake Umbria for the next two years, restoration of its *centro storico* is continuing. Like Orvieto, the town is built on a *rupe*, or spongey bluff made of tufa, which adds to the restoration difficulties; it requires major infrastructure work and buttressing as well as the more obvious repairs to walls and roofs. Just outside the centre, a late Renaissance church, the octagonal **Santa Maria della Pace** is a minor jewel, with an interior reminiscent of the Tempio della Consolazione.

To the west of Massa, in a beautiful setting, the pink and white 11th-century **Abbazia Santi Fidenzio e Terenzio** was constructed over the tomb to Umbria's first saints, who came from Syria to spread the Good Word and were martyred under Diocletian. The campanile stands on a 12-sided pedestal of tufa blocks, which was

**Abbazia Santi Fidenzio e Terenzio**
*call tourist office,
t 075 889371, for
opening hours*

10 **The Tiber Valley** | Around Todi

cannibalized from a Roman structure; there's an unusual crypt and Lombard reliefs, and a marble pulpit dating from the 1200s.

**Santa Maria in Pantano**
*key held at house next door*

South of Massa, **Santa Maria in Pantano** was built in the 7th or 8th century out of a Roman structure along the Via Flaminia. The oldest section is the apse; the adjacent campanile was converted from a medieval defensive tower. Inside there are Roman bits and a Roman altar, columns erected in the 12th century and frescoes from the 14th century and earlier; it also has a beautiful wooden Christ on the cross, halfway down the nave.

**Abbazia di San Faustino**
*key held next door*

**Catacomba di Villa San Faustino**
*open Tues, Thurs, Sat and Sun 9–1; book with tourist office on t 075 889371*

Further south, the little walled town of **Villa San Faustino** is synonymous in Umbria with its bottled mineral water. Just outside the walls, the **Abbazia di San Faustino** was also built using Roman stone, this time in the 12th century. It's an old, mysterious place, set among other buildings cobbled together over the centuries. One was a Paleochristian funerary chapel built over **catacombs** dating back to the 4th century AD and decorated with Christian symbols, the fish and lamb.

## Where to Stay in and around Todi

ⓘ **Todi ›**
*Comprensorio del Tuderte, Piazza Umberto I 6, t 075 894 3395 or t 075 894 5416*

★ **Poggio d'Asproli ›**

### Todi ✉ 06059

Ask at the tourist office for a full list of *agriturismi* around Todi.

**★★★★Bramante**, Via Orvietana 48, t 075 894 8381, *www.hotelbramante.it* (€€€€€). A 13th-century convent just outside town, in a lovely setting, with half/full board in its restaurant. The decor and service need an overhaul.

**Relais Todini**, on road to Collevalenza di Todi, t 075 887521, *www.relaistodini.com* (€€€€€). A 14th-century *palazzo* with a pool, tennis court, gym, restaurant and lovely views. The park houses camels, kangaroos, zebras and penguins, and there are horses or carriages to ride, and boating lakes. Choose from rooms, suites, studios and apartments.

**★★★★Fonte Cesia**, Via L. Leoni 3, t 075 894 3737, *www.fontecesia.it* (€€€€). Stylish rooms in an 18th-century building. Full board available.

**Poggio d'Asproli**, Loc. Asproli 7, 15mins from Todi, t 075 885 3385, *poggiodasproli@email.it* (€€€€). A quirky 16th-century convent filled with the artist-owner's works, with a pool and meals by request. Music and theatre evenings take place in summer.

**★★★Villa Luisa**, Via A. Cortesi 147, t 075 894 8571, *www.villaluisa.it* (€€€). A pleasant place with a beautiful pool surrounded by trees, elegant rooms, room service and a restaurant (half and full board available).

**San Lorenzo Tre**, Via S. Lorenzo 3, t 075 894 4555, *lorenzotre@tin.it* (€€€). A *residenza d'época* in a *palazzo*, with most rooms en suite.

**L'Arco**, Loc. Fossaccio 19, Cordigliano, t 075 894 7534, *www.umbria-villa.it* (€€). A luxurious villa for up to 9, with a lovely pool. *Closed Oct–April*.

**Castello di Porchiano**, Porchiano, t 075 885 3127, *www.agriturismotodi.it* (€€). An *agriturismo* with en-suite rooms with a medieval atmosphere, studios and 2-bed apartments. *Closed Feb*.

**Poponi**, Via delle Piagge 26, t 075 894 8233, *www.agriturismopoponi.it* (€€). Simple rooms, most with shared facilities. *Closed mid-Jan–mid-Feb*.

### Montecastello di Vibio ✉ 06057

**★★★Il Castello**, Piazza G. Marconi 5, t 075 878 0660, *www.hotelilcastello.it* (€€€). A charming 15th-century building with a pool, solarium and restaurant with half/full board. *Closed Jan; restaurant Tues Dec–Mar*.

### Collazzone ✉ 06050

**Relais il Canalicchio**, Canalicchio di Collazzone, **t** 075 870 7325, *www.relaisilcanalicchio.com* (€€€€€). A medieval hilltop idyll decorated *à la* English country home, with a pool, a sauna, a gym, mountain bikes, tennis, billiards, a library and a cigar room. The great restaurant uses produce from the owners' farm.

## Eating Out in Todi

Local specialities include pigeon, lamb and *porchetta*, and fat homemade spaghetti called *ombricelli*, served *alla boscaiola* (with tomatoes, piquant black olives and hot peppers). The dry white wine Grechetto di Todi dates back to the Roman Republic.

**La Torre**, Via Cortesi 57, **t** 075 894 2694 (€€€). Sophisticated fare such as risotto with pigeon and *linguini* with crab, followed by homemade ice cream. *Closed Tues and 1–15 Nov.*

**Ristorante Umbria**, Via San Bonaventura 13, **t** 075 894 2737, *umbria@todi.net* (€€€). In the heart of the *centro storico* with a beautiful terrace and an attractive interior with a huge fireplace for winter dining. Specialities include game and mushrooms collected from the surrounding woods.

**Antica Osteria de la Valle**, Via Ciuffelli 19, **t** 075 894 4848 (€€). An atmospheric bar with a daily menu of homemade fare, including a good *antipasto della casa* featuring cheese fondue flavoured with truffles, rustic pâté and *bruschette. Closed Mon.*

**Italia**, Via del Monte 27, **t** 075 894 2643 (€€). A typical family *trattoria* using local ingredients; try the speciality *capriccio* (a bit like lasagne). *Closed Fri.*

**Jacopone (Da Peppino)**, Piazza Jacopone 3, **t** 075 894 2366 (€€). Umbrian specialities served by friendly staff. *Closed Mon and 2wks July.*

**La Mulinella** Loc. Pontenaia, 3km from centre, **t** 075 894 4779 (€€). A reliable favourite with a fine view towards Todi from its garden. Try *bruschetta* with mushrooms and gnocchi in duck sauce. Booking is advisable. There are a few rooms too. *Closed Wed and 1–15 Nov.*

⭐ **La Mulinella »**

*(sidebar, vertical)* 10 — The Tiber Valley | Orvieto

# Orvieto

There's no mistaking Orvieto (pop. 20,700), a remarkable town that owes much of its success to an ancient volcano. First it created the city's *rupe*, its magnificent pedestal of golden tufa – a 1,066ft, sheer-cliffed mesa that wouldn't look out of place in the American southwest – and then it enriched the hillsides below with a special mixture of volcanic minerals that form part of the secret alchemy of the eponymous wine that has made the place famous well beyond Italy.

On top of this unique crag, the town, made out of the same tufa, looks much the same as it has for the last 500 years, crowned by its stupendous candy-striped cathedral. Because of this, and its proximity to the Rome–Florence *autostrada*, Orvieto gets more visitors than most hill towns in Umbria, and you may want to time your visit for a weekday to avoid the worst crowds.

## History

Attracted by Orvieto's incomparable natural defences, the Etruscans settled here by the 6th century BC and named their city *Velzna* (or *Volsinium* as the Romans pronounced it). It was one of

Funivia

↑ to Train station and P

Pozzo di San Patrizio

Rocca

Tempio del Belvedere
(Etruscan Temple) 🏛

PIAZZA CAHEN

VIALE CRISPI

VIA ROMA

CORSO CAVOUR

VIA POSTIERLA

VIA QUATTRO CANTONI

VIA ROMA

200 metres
200 yds

N

VIA ANGELO DA ORVIETO

San Domenico

VIA CESARE NEBBIA

Palazzo Apostolico

Palazzo Buzi

PIAZZA
VENTINOVE
MARZO

VIA CAVALLOTTI

CORSO CAVOUR

VIA DI MAURIZIO

Duomo

Palazzo
dei Papi

PIAZZA
DEL DUOMO

VIA DELLA PACE

Museo Claudio
Faina e Museo
Civico

VIA LUCA SIGNORELLI

VIA DEL DUOMO

VIA MATTANI

Palazzo
del Popolo

PIAZZA
DEL POPOLO

San Francesco

VIA IPPOLITO SCALZA

Torre
del Moro

VIA DEL POPOLO

San Lorenzo
de Arari

Sant'Andrea

PIAZZA
DELLA
REPUBBLICA

Palazzo Comunale

VIA ALBERICI

Crocifisso
del Tufo

VIA FILIPPESCHI

VIA LOGGIA DEI MERCANTI

VIA GARIBALDI

Porta
Romana

PIAZZA DEI
RANIERI

VIA MALABRANCA

Sant' Agostino

San Giovanni

CAMPO
DELLA
FIERA

P

VIA DELLA CAVA

Pozzo della Cava

Palazzo
Caravajal

San
Giovenale

VIA VOLSINIA

Porta
Maggiore

to
Viterbo ↙

# Getting to and around Orvieto

Orvieto, at least its lower version, Orvieto Scalo, is on the main **train** line between Rome (121km/2hrs) and Florence (152km/2hrs); from Perugia it's 86km and just over 1hr.

It is also linked by ATC **coach**, t 0763 301224, *www.atcternit.it*, with Amelia, Narni, Terni, Viterbo in Lazio, etc. The once-daily trip to Todi (48km/2hrs) down the SS79bis is magnificently scenic. All coaches stop by the *funivia* at the railway station.

There are **car parks** at Piazza Cahen and the ex-Campo della Fiera under the cliff; from here take a lift up to the church of San Giovanni, or bus C to Piazza della Repubblica. It may be easier to park by the station; from here bus 1 makes the steep trip up a couple of times a day, or take the scenic *funicolare* (every 10–15mins) from the station to Piazza Cahen next to the Rocca and Etruscan temple, then shuttle bus A directly to the cathedral, or bus B around the *centro storico* (save your tickets for a discount at the Museo Faina).

For **car hire**, try Avis, Viale I Maggio 46, Orvieto Scalo, t 0763 390030, *www.avisautonoleggio.it*, or Hertz, Via Sette Martiri 32f, Orvieto Scalo, t 0763 301303, *www.hertz.it*. For **bike and motorbike hire**, try: Gulliver, Strada del Piano 6a, Orvieto Scalo, t 0763 302969, or Ciclo e Trekking Natura e Avventura, Via dei Tigliza, Orvieto Scalo (near the station), t 0763 301649 (Mar–Oct), which also runs **bike tours** in the countryside.

the 12 cities of the Etruscan confederation, and the probable site of its main shrine, *Fanum Voltumnae*, where the usually independent-minded Etruscans gathered to discuss issues of mutual defence and to compete in sacred games; it was their Olympia, although the site has never been identified. Unlike Umbria's other great Etruscan city, Perugia, *Velzna* was a major art centre, noted in particular for its fine bronze work, and it prospered into the 4th century BC, although increasingly at odds with Rome, especially after the latter conquered nearby *Veii* in 396.

The Romans first invaded the territory of *Velzna* in 294 BC, and although the Gauls and Etruscans of Vulci came to their aid, the city was conquered and put to the sack in 280 BC. The historians record the Romans carting home 2,000 bronze statues as their swag, many of which had probably decorated the *Fanum Voltumnae*. The Roman victory led to severe social turmoil: Velzna's plebeians revolted against the aristocrats, and demanded the right to sit in the Senate and even to wed noblewomen. The Etruscan élite appealed to the Roman senate for aid, and the senators sent in troops to quell the uprising and incidentally destroy the city in the process. A new *Volsinium* was founded for the inhabitants on the shores of Lake Bolsena, and the old site remained uninhabited until the fall of Rome.

By the 5th century AD, the easily defensible butte was resettled as the 'Old City' (*Urbs Vetus*, hence Orvieto). The Goths took it, Belisarius captured it, Totila took it back, the Lombards settled and it became a *comune* early on in the Middle Ages, sometimes allied with Rome and sometimes with the new power up the road to the north – Florence. It was often visited by popes, especially popes whose polls were down with the fickle Romans or when Rome was occupied by foreign armies; it was here that Pope Gregory X received England's Edward I in 1271 after the Eighth Crusade. For most of the Middle Ages, however, Orvieto was embroiled in wars with its neighbours and internal wars between two leading families and their factions, the Guelph Monaldeschi and the Ghibelline Filippeschi, whose feud was recorded by Dante in his *Purgatorio* as being just as bitter as the struggle between Verona's Montecchi and Cappello families, whom Shakespeare turned into Montagues and Capulets.

The event that tipped their quarrel into the worst incident of bloodshed in Umbrian history was the announced visit in 1313 by Henry VII, Count of Luxembourg, King of Germany, and uncrowned Holy Roman Emperor, who was making his way to Rome with a German army. The Ghibellines began to swagger, thinking their moment had come and all the wrongs they had suffered at the hands of the Monaldeschi would soon be righted, while the Guelphs, in a panic, offered to give the city to the Ghibellines on the condition that the German army remained outside the town walls. The Ghibellines refused to accept the terms, precipitating two days of fighting in the streets, in which the Ghibellines came out on top. But then Guelph reinforcements arrived and the battle started anew, and when it seemed the Ghibellines would have to give up, reinforcements arrived from Spoleto, Terni, Todi and Amelia. Now outnumbered, the Bishop of Orvieto surrendered the city to the Ghibellines, who insisted that all the Guelphs leave town. As they filed out of the gate, the Perugian cavalry came to their rescue and the battle began again, and this time the Guelphs came out on top. In the fury, some 4,000 Ghibelline men, women and children were massacred, many hurled off the cliffs. Their houses were burnt, and for the next few years the Monaldeschi and their Guelph junta systematically destroyed all Ghibelline property it laid its hands on, and Guelph and papal rule was never threatened again. As for Henry VII, he never made it to Orvieto after all; while the Orvietani were killing each other, he died in Siena.

Over the last 20 years the big news in Orvieto has been the shoring up of its fantastical perch. Tufa is soft and the *rupe* absorbs water, then starts to break up. A few small landslides set off the alarm bells in the 1980s, and since then much of the bluff has been encased in scaffolding while the *rupe* was reinforced and a whole new waterworks and sewer system were dug for the town – another, if rather unglamorous, reminder of how expensive Italy is to keep up.

## The Duomo

 **Duomo**
*t 0763 341167; open
daily Mar and Oct
7.30–12.45 and 2–6.15,
April–Sept 7.30–12.45
and 2–7.15, Nov–Feb
7.30–12.45 and 2.30–5.15*

The 13th century may have been an age of faith but it certainly wasn't an age of fools. The popes were having trouble putting over the doctrine of transubstantiation, an archaic, genuinely pagan survival that many in the Church found difficulty accepting. But then the necessary miracle occurred, during a visit to Orvieto by Pope Urban IV in the 1260s. A Bohemian priest named Peter, on his way to Rome, was asked to celebrate Mass in Bolsena, just to the south. Father Peter had long been sceptical about the doctrine of the Host becoming the body of Christ, but during this Mass the Host itself answered his doubts by dripping blood on the altar linen. Peter took the linen to show to the Pope, who declared it a miracle and instituted the feast of Corpus Christi. St Thomas Aquinas, also visiting Orvieto at the time, was asked to compose a suitable office for the new holy day, while Urban IV promised Orvieto (rather unfairly to poor old Bolsena) a magnificent new cathedral to enshrine the bloodstained relic. The cornerstone was laid by Pope Nicholas IV in 1290 and the nave was built in the Romanesque style, probably to a design by Arnolfo di Cambio, builder of Florence cathedral. In 1300 the plan was changed into Gothic by local architect Giovanni di Uguccione, who replaced the stone vaults with an open truss roof. When the walls began to sway in 1305, architect and sculptor Lorenzo Maitani of Siena was summoned to remedy the situation. He built four lateral flying buttresses and made the apse square to stabilize the building, then designed the façade. The grateful Orvietani made him a citizen and let him choose his assistants. Subsequent architects included his son, followed by such luminaries as Nicolò and Meo Nuti, Andrea and Nino Pisano, Andrea Orcagna and Michele Sammicheli. Ippolito Scalza of Orvieto oversaw the works for 50 years.

The result is one of Italy's greatest cathedrals, visible for kilometres around, with a stunning, sumptuous 52m façade resembling a giant triptych. This is Maitani's masterpiece, the 'golden lily of cathedrals' or 'the greatest polychrome monument in the world,' as Burckhart called it, designed as an architectural and decorative whole, the simple geometric forms and gables emphasized to make them strong enough to take the lavish detail. Colour it certainly has, especially when the late-afternoon sun inflames the dazzling Technicolor **mosaics** that fill every flat surface, though artistically there's not much to say about them – all were replaced after the façade was struck by lightning in 1795, except the restored *Nativity of Mary* (1364) over the south door.

N

20m
20 yds

The magnificent **rose window** (1360) by the great Florentine artist
Orcagna is surrounded by 16th-century statues of the Apostles.

Close up, the richness and beauty of the sculptural detail is
simply breathtaking. It is said that 152 sculptors worked on the
cathedral, but it was Maitani himself who contributed the best
work – the remarkably designed and executed (with his son Vitale,
and Nicolò and Meo Nuti) **bas reliefs** (1320–30) on the lower
pilasters that recount the story of the Creation to the Last
Judgement. This Bible in stone captures the essence of the stories
with vivid drama and detail – the Last Judgement, in particular.
Maitani also cast the four bronze symbols of the Evangelists, the
ox, eagle, man and winged lion, all ready to step right off the
cornice of the façade, and the bronze angels in the lunette over the
central portal. The bronze doors, portraying the Works of Mercy
(1965), are by Emilio Greco. The 16th-century sibyls on the corners
of the façade were sculpted by Fabiano Toti and Antonio Federighi.

In contrast with the soaring vertical lines of the façade, the
cathedral's sides and little rounded chapels are banded with
horizontal zebra stripes of yellow tufa and grey basalt. On the right
(south side) is the oldest door, the Porta di Postierla. On the left,
the Porta del Corporale had three statues by Andrea Pisano in its

lunette; along with Pisano's *Madonna* from the Duomo, these are being stored by the Museo dell'Opera del Duomo (*see* p.208).

One of the best times to come to Orvieto is after Easter, when you can witness the Pentecost **Festa della Palombella**, a tradition founded by the Monaldeschi in 1404: a steel wire is suspended from the roof of the church of San Francesco (*see* p.210) to a wooden tabernacle on the porch of the cathedral, and on the stroke of noon a white dove tied with red ribbons on an iron wreath-like contraption gets the ride of its life hurtling down to the tabernacle, greeted by a round of firecrackers to symbolize the flames of the Holy Spirit that lit up over the heads of the Apostles. The dove is later presented to the last couple to have been wed in the cathedral, who are charged to keep it as a pet until the end of its natural days. Another high day after Easter, **Corpus Christi**, occasions a procession of the *Corporale* in its glittering reliquary through town, accompanied by Orvietani in their trecento finery.

## The Interior

Filtered through stained-glass and alabaster windows, the muted light adds to the serene beauty of the striped Romanesque nave, divided into three by fine columns and capitals and rounded arches, topped in turn by a clerestory. The lack of clutter – much of the art is stowed away in the Museo dell'Opera del Duomo (*see* p.208) – reveals the lovely proportions and the subtle asymmetries that give the interior its unique dynamism. Note how neither the five semicircular chapels on each wall nor the windows are centred between the arches of the aisles, nor the upper clerestory windows. The floor rises gently up to the altar, and each striped column is slightly shorter as you approach, producing a magical effect as you walk down the nave.

Look for Gentile da Fabriano's delicate fresco of the Madonna and Child (1426) by the left door, near the baptismal font of 1407. Many of the side chapels have remains of votive frescoes. In the left transept is a *Pietà* (1579) by Ippolito Scalza, its figures carved from a single block of marble. Beyond is the **Cappella del Corporale**, built c. 1350 to house the famous relic and decorated by Sienese masters: the frescoes of the Miracle of Bolsena and Crucifixion by Ugolino di Prete Ilario (1360s) and, in a niche in the right wall, the exquisite *Madonna dei Raccomandati* (1339) by Lippo Memmi, brother-in-law of Simone Martini. The altar, with Gothic tabernacle by Nicola da Siena and Orcagna, shelters the venerated blood-stained linen. To the left, encased, is the silver gilt **Reliquario del Corporale** (1338), echoing the façade of the cathedral and decorated with

12 enamelled scenes from the Life of Christ by goldsmith Ugolino di Vieri of Siena. In the nave, the magnificent **organ**, built in 1584 is the second largest in Italy. The restored **choir frescoes** are by Ugolino di Prete Ilario and other Sienese painters, the intarsia **stalls** by another Sienese, Giovanni Ammannati, and the **stained glass** by Giovanni di Bonino from Assisi (1334). To the right is Ippolito Scalza's last work, an *Ecce Homo* (1608). In the little south transept, the **altar of the Magi** was sculpted by a young Sammicheli, before he became Venice's great military architect.

## Cappella di San Brizio

**Cappella di
San Brizio**
*t 0763 342477; open
Mar and Oct Mon–Sat
9–12.45 and 2–6.15, Sun
and hols 2.30–5.45;
April–Sept Mon–Sat
9–12.45 and 2–7.15, Sun
and hols 2.30–6.45;
Nov–Feb Mon–Sat
9–12.45 and 2.30–5.15,
Sun and hols 2–5.45;
buy tickets at tourist
office; only 26 people
admitted at a time*

This contains one of the finest and most powerful fresco cycles of the Renaissance, but its genesis was hit and miss. In 1408, the Monaldeschi financed the construction of the Cappella Nuova, which became known as Cappella di San Brizio after the pretty 14th-century altarpiece of the Madonna di San Brizio. In 1447 they hired Fra Angelico to fresco it; he began with the ceiling vaults, completing two scenes near the altar – the serene *Christ in Judgement* and the *Prophets* – while his pupil Benozzo Gozzoli contributed the hierarchies of angels. Then the pope summoned Fra Angelico to Rome and he died before returning to finish.

Years later, Perugino was commissioned to complete the work, but he left after a few days. Finally, in 1499, Luca Signorelli of Cortona, a student of Piero della Francesca and already sufficiently famous to have painted a fresco in the Sistine Chapel, was hired to complete the vaults. The patrons liked what they saw and commissioned him to fresco the walls. Signorelli made the end of the world his theme, and worked on the project until 1504. This chapel is, in many ways, the stylistic and psychological precursor of Michelangelo's *Last Judgement* in the Sistine Chapel; Signorelli's remarkable draughtsmanship and foreshortening, his dynamic male nudes inspired by Antonio Pollaiuolo and what he learned from Piero about simplifying nature and architecture into essential geometrical forms give the frescoes tremendous power.

The six scenes in the Cappella di San Brizio are iconographically taken from the *Divine Comedy* and St Augustine's *City of God*. The first, 'Preaching of the Antichrist', is a rare subject and evokes the confusion and turmoil in Florence after the Dominican preacher Savonarola was burned at the stake in 1498. If you look in the crowd attending the Antichrist (whose words are prompted by the Devil), you can see Dante's beaky profile and red hat as he stands with Petrarch and Christopher Columbus – symbolic of the beginning of the modern era – while in the background, around the Temple of Solomon, chaos and catastrophe are at work in the last throes of the Middle Ages. Far left of the Antichrist, the artist portrays himself and Fra Angelico dressed in black, watching the anarchy with a quiet detachment that seems almost chilling. Signorelli's mistress jilted him while he painted this, so he put her in the scene as the prostitute taking money. Overhead St Michael keeps the Antichrist from ascending to heaven.

Next to this is 'End of the World', where a prophet foretells doomsday: the sea floods, the earth shakes, the stars fall from the firmament and the darkened sky is shot with streaks of fire. In the next scene, Signorelli gives us 'Resurrection of the Dead' in unforgettable, literal detail as the corpses and skeletons pull themselves out of the curiously glutinous earth and form new coats of flesh, though the fellow on the right merrily conversing with six skeletons adds a humorous touch. This is one of the most powerful nude studies of the quattrocento, only surpassed by the next scene, 'The Damned Consigned to Hell', a crowded writhing Inferno; even the cruel devils, one per person, are more or less human, except for their metallic colours, horns and shaggy hips (Signorelli made sure to put his mistress here, too, caught in the embrace of a flying devil). 'The Blessed' in the next scene get to go to Paradise with the lovely angels (parts of this fresco, concealed by the 18th-century altar, can be seen by way of video), while the final fresco is 'Coronation of the Chosen'.

Below the frescoes Signorelli painted medallions of Cicero, Homer (though since the restoration, he's been identified as Statius), Dante, Virgil, Ovid, Lucan and pre-Socratic philosopher Empedocles (right of the entrance). He also painted the scenes from the *Divine Comedy* and myth in the *tondi*, and the *Deposition*, where one mourner is Pietro Parenzo, who served Orvieto as *podestà* in the 13th century and was killed by heretics.

## Piazza del Duomo

The cathedral shares the piazza with Ippolito Scalza's handsome **Palazzo Buzi** (1580), the deteriorating neoclassical church, **San Giacomo Maggiore**, and other *palazzi* housing Orvieto's five museums.

Opposite the cathedral, the 19th-century Palazzo Faina contains two of these, the **Musei Archeologici Claudio Faina e Civico**. The ground floor, the **Museo Civico**, has terracotta decorations from the Belvedere temple – male figures, a warrior, a horse and the goddess Artemis that show a strong Greek influence. The *Venus of Cannicella*, an Archaic Greek statue made of Naxos marble from the 6th century BC, was found in Orvieto's oldest tombs; a giant warrior's head from the same period came from the Crocifisso del Tufo. A 4th-century BC sarcophagus is decorated with gruesome

**Musei Archeologici Claudio Faina e Civico**
*t 0763 341511, www.museofaina.it; open April–Sept daily 9.30–6; Oct–Mar Tues–Sun 10–5; guided tours 11 and 3; adm*

scenes from the Trojan War, of Achilles sacrificing Trojan prisoners to Patroclos, and Neoptolemos killing Polyxena, Priam's daughter, on Achilles' tomb. The **Museo Claudio Faina**, one of Italy's top private archaeological collections, garnered in the last century by the Faina counts and donated to the city in 1954, fills the two upper floors and is rich in finds from Orvieto's necropolis: 3,000 ancient coins, Etruscan gold, an excellent collection of vases and bronzes, a beautiful selection of the black and red figure Attic vases imported by wealthy Etruscans, *bucchero* ware, and an Etruscan sarcophagus with traces of its bright paint. Ask about the special kid's booklet (in English and Italian) with information and a quiz, and about concerts held in the garden in summer.

The south side of the cathedral was the heartbeat of papal Orvieto. The austere, crenellated tufa **Palazzo Soliano** was begun by Boniface VIII in 1297, who didn't think the slightly older Palazzo Apostolico (*see* below) was up to snuff. It was finished in the 1500s and contains the **Museo dell'Opera del Duomo**, with works that filled the cathedral – statues by grand masters such as Arnolfo di Cambio and Andrea Pisano, grand statues by little-known hands, especially the colossal *Apostles*, and two early Baroque figures of the Annunciation by Bernini's teacher, Francesco Mocchi. Paintings include a *Crucifixion* by Spinello Aretino, a *Madonna* by 13th-century master, Coppo di Marcovaldo, a *Self-portrait* and a *Magdalene* by Signorelli (like the one painted by his master Piero, in Arezzo), a reliquary of San Savino's head by Ugolino di Vieri and, most lovely of all, two richly coloured *Madonnas* by Simone Martini. There are two beautiful sketches on parchment of the cathedral façade, one by Maitani, and an older one attributed to Arnolfo di Cambio. The ground floor houses the **Museo Emilio Greco**, with a large collection of works from 1947 to the 1980s, donated by the sculptor.

Adjacent, the restored 13th-century **Palazzo Apostolico** (or Palazzo Papale), begun by Urban IV and finished in 1304, holds the **Museo Archeologico**, with an excellent collection of Etruscan bronzes, vases (including some fine Greek ones), mirrors, bronze armour and a fresco of an Etruscan butcher's stand. Best of all are two painted 4th-century BC tombs from Settecamini, reconstructed here, representing scenes of the banquet all good Etruscans expected to find when they went into the underworld. Those in the first tomb, of the Leinie, show scenes of the kitchen, as servants (all carefully named) prepare the meat. On the opposite wall the banquet takes place, presided over by the gods of the underworld, Pluto in a wolfskin cap and spear decorated with a serpent, and Persephone, holding a sceptre topped by a bird. The dead guest of honour arrives in a chariot with a demon.

**Museo dell'Opera del Duomo**
*t 0763 343592; open April–Sept daily 9.30–7; Nov–Feb Wed–Mon 9.30–1 and 3–5; Mar and Oct Wed–Mon 9.30–1 and 3–6; guided tours by appt; adm (joint ticket with Cappella di San Brizio; see p.206)*

**Museo Emilio Greco**
*t 0763 344605; open Oct–Feb Fri–Sun 10.30–4.30; Mar–Apr Fri–Sun 10.30–1 and 3.30–5; May–Aug Tues–Sun 10.30–1 and 3.30–5; Aug Tues–Sun 11–5; Sept Tues–Sun 10.30–1 and 2.30–5; adm; combined ticket available with Pozzo della Cava, see p.210, and Pozzo di San Patrizio, see p.211*

**Museo Archeologico**
*t 0763 341039; open daily 8.30–7.30; adm*

**Città Sotterranea**
*t 0763 344891, www.
orvietounderground.it;
tours daily 11, 12.15, 4
and 5.15 (call t 0763 334
0688 for tours in English
or extra tours); adm*

From the tourist office at Piazza del Duomo 24, tours depart for **Orvieto Underground**, a shadow, alternative city that residents of the *rupe* excavated from within their obliging tufa, an underground labyrinth of galleries (or *grotte*) containing wine cellars, silos, wells, cisterns, ovens, aqueducts, little religious shrines, medieval rubbish pits, dovecotes and more.

## Piazza del Popolo and Around

In contrast to its heavenly cathedral (Pope John XXIII said that on Judgement Day the angels would bear it up to Paradise), the rest of Orvieto is a solid medieval town, dotted with *palazzi* built for Roman and local bigwigs by many of the architects who worked on the cathedral. **Corso Cavour** has been Orvieto's main street since Etruscan times, and where it meets Via del Duomo towers the 42m

**Torre del Moro**
*t 0763 344567; open
daily Mar, April, Sept
and Oct 10–7, May–Aug
10–8, Nov–Feb 10.30–1
and 2.30–5; adm*

**Torre del Moro**, built in the 12th century and affording a sublime view over the city. The big bell, decorated with 24 symbols of Orvieto's guilds, was cast in 1316; the cathedral builders timed their workday by it. Next to it, the **Palazzo dei Sette** (1300) was built for the seven magistrates elected by the guilds to govern the *comune*.

One block north, in Piazza del Popolo, the **Palazzo del Popolo**, a tufa palace begun in 1250, has mullioned windows and an open loggia in the Lombard style. Turned into a prison and warehouse by the popes, it is now a conference centre. The restoration uncovered the sacred area of an Etruscan temple, a medieval aqueduct and a cistern. Also in the piazza, Palazzo Simoncelli is the site of the

**Museo delle
Ceramiche
Medioevali
Orvietane**
*ask at tourist
office, see p.212,
for opening hours*

**Museo delle Ceramiche Medioevali Orvietane**; Orvieto was an important centre for ceramic production in the Middle Ages.

From here, Via della Pace leads back to a piazza with the **church of San Domenico**, built in 1233, just after St Dominic's canonization, making it the first ever Dominican church. St Thomas Aquinas taught at the former monastery here and is recalled with several mementos in the **Cappella Petrucci**, built by Sammicheli below the church. None of these claims to fame spared the church from amputation of its naves in 1934 to make room for a barracks.

## Four Churches and a Palazzo

From the Torre del Moro, Corso Cavour winds down through 16th-century *palazzi* and medieval buildings to **Piazza della Repubblica**, Orvieto's main square and site of the Etruscan and Roman forums. Here is 12th-century **Sant'Andrea** with its unusual 12-sided campanile, pierced by mullioned windows and topped by

**Resti Etruschi**
*sacristan of church has
key to excavations*

bellicose crenellations. The mosaic pavement of a 6th-century church was discovered beneath Sant'Andrea; an even lower level has an **Etruscan street and buildings**. Decorated with 14th-century frescoes, Sant'Andrea was the most important church in Orvieto before the construction of the cathedral and basks in the memory of the events that took place within its walls: here Innocent III proclaimed the Fourth Crusade, and here in 1281, Charles of Anjou and his glittering retinue attended the coronation of Martin IV.

Piazza della Repubblica's 13th-century **Palazzo Comunale**, hidden behind a late Renaissance façade, is the starting point for exploring Orvieto's most picturesque medieval streets, such as Via Loggia dei Mercanti, lined with *tufa* houses; at its end, beyond Piazza dei Ranieri, octagonal **San Giovanni** was first built in 916 and rebuilt in 1687; it has a 14th-century detached fresco of the Madonna from the original church and a handsome cloister used for exhibitions. At this point, Orvieto's pedestal is almost sheer; a narrow lane follows along the edge down and around to the oldest corner of the town and delightful **San Giovenale**, begun in 1004, with a fortified tower, 12th–15th-century frescoes and charming bits of ancient sculpture. The big adjacent Gothic church of **Sant'Agostino**, with its handsome door, has been restored as an exhibition space.

## To Porta Maggiore

Picturesque Via Malabranca leads back to the centre by way of the 16th-century **Palazzo Caravajal** by Ippolito Scalza, with its handsome portal and an inscription in Spanish informing passers-by that the house was built for the comfort of the owner's friends. Here, too, is the 15th-century **Palazzo Filippeschi** (or Pietrangeli), the most beautiful in Orvieto. Florentine rather than Roman in style, it has such a lovely courtyard and portico that it has been attributed to Bernardo Rossellino. From here, Via della Cava descends to the old gate, **Porta Maggiore**; at the restaurant at Via della Cava 26, you can peer into the depths of the Pozzo della Cava a deep public well excavated by the Etruscans and used from 1428 to 1546.

**Pozzo della Cava**
*t 0763 342373,*
*www.pozzodellacava.it;*
*open Tues–Sun*
*8am–8pm; other times*
*by appt; adm; joint*
*ticket available with*
*Pozzo di San Patrizio,*
*see opposite, and*
*Museo Emilio Greco,*
*see p.208*

## San Lorenzo and San Francesco

The 13th-century Romanesque church of **San Lorenzo de Arari**, reached by Via Ippolito Scalza from Corso Cavour (or on Via Maitani from the Piazza Duomo) was named for its venerable altar (*ara*), supported by a cylindrical Etruscan altar, the whole protected by a lovely 12th-century stone *ciborium*. The Byzantine-style frescoes in the apse add an ancient feel, especially the elongated figures and staring eyes of *Christ Enthroned with Saints*. Other frescoes, from the 1330s and restored with more goodwill than skill, depict the life of St Lawrence, who retains his sense of humour even while being toasted on the grill ('Turn me over, I'm done on this side,' he said). In the Middle Ages, when no body part was too kinky to stick in a reliquary, some churches claimed to have vials of his melted fat.

Nearby, in Piazza dei Febei, the 13th-century preaching **church of San Francesco** has been much changed over time. Its size came in handy for important events – it was here that Boniface VIII canonized St Louis of France in 1297. Inside you can see a wooden *Crucifixion* attributed to Maitani or a close follower and some 14th-century frescoes in the sacristy.

## The Citadel, a Temple and St Patrick's Well

Orvieto's northeastern end and funicular terminus, **Piazza Cahen**, is dominated by the ruins of the **Rocca**, a citadel built in 1364 by Cardinal Albornoz. The people of Orvieto, always willing to host a pope or two (33 spent extended periods in the city), showed their appreciation of this direct attempt at papal domination by destroying it in 1390; only the walls, a gate and a tower survive, now encompassing a garden of umbrella pines. Views from the ramparts stretch from the shallow Paglia river to the Tiber valley.

Next to the citadel is the massive podium of an Etruscan temple, the 5th-century BC **Tempio del Belvedere**, made of travertine: it had a double row of columns in front, a *pronaos*, and three *cellae* – a perfect example of the typical Etruscan–Italic temple described by Vitruvius. The podium was rediscovered by accident in 1828 and fragments of its terracotta decoration are in the Museo Civico.

Much of the temple's stone was cannibalized for the building of a nearby well, the ingenious **Pozzo di San Patrizio**, designed in the 1530s by Antonio da Sangallo the Younger, and the most celebrated of all Orvieto's subterranean wonders. Its name comes from St Patrick's well in Ireland, where according to legend, Patrick found Paradise after passing through the depths of Hell. The well was built on the orders of calamitous Medici pope Clement VII. After surviving the sack of Rome – and sneaking out of the city disguised as a greengrocer – Clement became paranoid about the security of the papal person. He commissioned this unique work of engineering to supply Orvieto in the event of a siege; to reach the spring, Sangallo had to dig the equivalent of seven storeys. To haul the water to the surface, he built two spiral stairs of 248 steps in a brick double helix – one for the water-carriers and their donkeys going down, another for going up, meeting at a narrow bridge at the base. The stairs are lit by 72 windows on the central shaft. Despite the labour that went into its construction, the well was never needed. But it didn't harm the Church as much as another decision hapless Clement made during his stay – his refusal to annul Henry VIII's marriage to Catherine of Aragon.

**Pozzo di San Patrizio**
*Valle Sangallo, t 0763 343768; open daily May–Aug 9–7.45, Mar–Apr and Sept–Oct 9–6.45, Nov–Feb 10–4.45; adm, joint ticket available with Museo Emilio Greco, see p.208, and Pozza della Cava, see opposite; bring a sweater as it is cold and damp at the bottom*

## Around Orvieto

The base of Orvieto's bluff is pocked with Etruscan tombs excavated off and on for centuries; back in the finders-keepers age of archaeology, many of the most beautiful finds went to the Louvre and the British Museum. Unlike Perugia's impressive Ipogeo dei Volumni, few of these have any decoration; the tombs resemble streets of low houses, sparsely furnished with a pair of benches where the urns of the departed were arranged. The most impressive is the 6th-century BC **Crocifisso del Tufo** on the SS71 north of Orvieto; along the pleasant walkways of the Percorso Archeologico. Excavations began in the 1800s and continue slowly. More than 100 rectangular chamber tombs have been found, one per nuclear family, sharing walls, each with a little entrance with the family and given names inscribed on the lintel. Originally they were closed with a stone door. Piles of clay and earth sealed the roofs, which would be topped with a *cippus* – the head of the warrior in the Museo Civico was one of these. By the unique wealth of inscriptions found here, it seems Velzna was unusually multicultural for an Etruscan town – the oldest burials were of Greek origin; other families have Latin, Umbrian and even Gothic names.

**Crocifisso del Tufo**
*t 0763 343611;
open daily April–Sept
8.30–7; Oct–Mar
8.30–5; adm*

Still on the SS71, about 2.5km south from the Porta Romana, the 12th–13th-century Benedictine **abbey of Santi Severo e Martirio** (renovated in the 19th century and now partly a hotel, La Badia; *see* below) retains much of its original work – a Cosmatesque pavement and some trecento frescoes, as well as another dodecagonal campanile similar to the peculiar one at Sant'Andrea. Further south in Loc. Porano is the painted Etruscan **tomb of the Hescanas** near Castel Rubello Just over the border in Lazio, medieval **Bagnoregio** is piled on a smaller version of Orvieto's tufa pedestal.

**Castel Rubello**
*open by request;
custodian lives nearby*

## Tourist Information in Orvieto

ⓘ **Orvieto >>**
*Piazza del Duomo 24,
t 0763 341772 and
t 0763 341911,
www.orvienet.it,
www.regioneumbria.eu,
www.comune.
orvieto.tr.it*

Ask at the tourist office about the **Carta Orvieto Unica**, which admits you to various sights, and gives you a free round-trip on the *funicolare* plus minibus A or B or 5hrs' parking in the Campo della Fiera and lifts to the centre. It's also sold in museums and in booths in car parks.

Tourist information is also available from **Consorzio Orvieto Promotion**, Piazza dell'Erba 1/A, t 0763 393453, *www.orvietoturismo.it*, a consortium of hotels, restaurants, and more.

**Post office**: Largo Ravelli, t 0763 398311.

## Where to Stay in Orvieto

**Orvieto** ✉ 05018
There are plenty of *agriturismi* in the Orvieto area; ask at the tourist office for their list.

**Luxury (€€€€€)**
****La Badia**, Loc. La Badia 8, 5km south on Bagnoregio road, t 0763 301959, *www.labadiahotel.it*. An old abbey with lovely views up to the *tufa*-crowned citadel. Rooms are elegant, and there's an outdoor pool, a tennis court, a restaurant (half and full board available) and parking.

### Very Expensive (€€€€)

****Villa Ciconia**, Via dei Tigli 69, north along SS71, t 0763 305582, www.hotelvillaciconia.com. A 16th-century villa in an oasis of green in the ugly sprawl of Orbetello Scalo. There's a beautiful pool, parking and a frescoed restaurant (half and full board available) serving fine food.

### Expensive (€€€)

****Aquila Bianca**, Via Garibaldi 13, t 0763 341246, www.hotelaquilabianca. it. An old-fashioned, central choice, with spacious rooms, Internet access, a restaurant and a garage. Rates are at the lower end of this price range.

****Maitani**, Via Maitani 5, t 0763 342011, www.hotelmaitani.com. Comfy rooms opposite the cathedral, with Internet access and parking.

****Palazzo Piccolomini**, Piazza dei Ranieri 36, t 0763 341743, www. hotelpiccolomini.it. A gorgeous medieval palace in the historic centre, with half/full board in its restaurant.

***Duomo**, Vicolo di Maurizio 7, t 0763 341887, www.orvietohotelduomo.com. Basic rooms (at the lower end of this category), plus a garage.

### Moderate (€€)

***Valentino**, Via Angelo da Orvieto 30/32, t 0763 342464, www. valentinohotel.com. Simple but comfortable rooms in a 16th-century house near the old church of San Domenico, with a garage.

***Virgilio**, Piazza Duomo 5, t 0763 341882, www.hotelvirgilio.com. A trecento building just across from the cathedral, with en-suite rooms.

### Inexpensive (€)

**Pergoletta**, Via Sette Martiri 5, t 0763 301418, alberto.mon@libero.it. Rooms with or without bath, a restaurant (half and full board available) and a garage.

**Picchio**, Via G. Salvatori 17, t 0763 301144, www.bellaumbria.net/hotel-picchio. Simple rooms with parquet flooring and good baths, plus an Internet point and private garage.

**Posta**, Via Luca Signorelli 18, t 0763 341909, www.orvietohotels.it. Rooms off Corso Cavour in the historic centre, most with shared facilities, plus a garage and a patch of garden.

⭐ I Sette Consoli >>

⭐ Palazzo Piccolomini >

# Eating Out in Orvieto

Besides wine (see p.214), specialities are cinghiale in agrodolce (sweet and sour boar) and gallina ubriaca ('drunken chicken'). Tourists have helped keep some mediocre venues in business – choose with care. If you book at a restaurant in the historic centre, you can park free in Via Roma: restaurants have vouchers for your dashboard.

**Le Grotte del Funaro**, Via Ripa Serancia 41, t 0763 343276, www. grottedelfunaro.it (€€€). An elegant restaurant in tufa caves, with solid Umbrian cuisine. Book ahead. Closed Mon exc July/Aug; 1wk Jan; 1wk July.

**I Sette Consoli**, Piazza Sant'Angelo 1A, t 0763 343911, mstopp@tin.it (€€€). The best local ingredients cooked with imagination: try lasagne with broccoli and sausage. Closed Sun eve in winter and Wed.

**Osteria dell'Angelo**, Piazza 29 Marzo 8a, t 0763 341805 (€€€). Local products prepared with flair: try gnocchi with tomatoes and tuna. Closed Sun eve, Mon and Tues lunch and 1–15 Aug.

**L'Asino d'Oro**, Vicolo del Popolo 9, t 0763 344406 (€€). Excellent, innovative fare such as saltcod in tomato sauce, and charming service. Closed mid-Jan–mid-Mar and mid-Oct–mid-Nov.

**Etrusca**, Via Lorenzo Maitani 10, t 0763 344016 (€€). Great traditional food; try umbrichelli with white or black truffles.

**Maurizio**, Via Duomo 78, t 0763 341114, www.cantinamartinelli.com (€€). Inspired Umbrian homemade pasta and other dishes with game, mushrooms and truffles. Closed Tues and 1st half Jan.

**La Volpe e L'Uva**, Via Ripa Corsica 1, t 0763 341612 (€€). A busy place with unusual secondi: try eels with peppers and onions. Closed Mon, Tues (winter only), and Jan.

**Zeppelin**, Via G. Garibaldi 28, t 0763 341447 (€€). Excellent lunches and dinners, plus residential cooking courses where you can learn to cook treats such as umbrichelli with wild boar sauce. There's a veggie menu.

## Wine tasting

**Consorzio per la Tutela dei Vini Doc Orvieto e Rosso Orvietano**, Corso Cavour 36, **t** 0763 343790, *www. consorziovinidiorvieto.it*. Information on visiting the area's estates, with a list and map.

**Antinori**, Castello della Sala, Loc. Sala, Ficulle, **t** 0763 86051. A place famous for its Cervara; visits by appointment.

**Barberani**, Loc. Cerreto (Lago di Corbara), Baschi, **t** 0763 341820. Weekend visits by appointment.

**Cantina Foresi**, Piazza Duomo 2, **t** 0763 341611. The best place to taste and buy.

**Cantina Monrubio**, Loc. Le Prese, Monterubraglio, **t** 0763 626064. No visits weekends, hols or harvest.

**Cooperativa Vitivinicola per la Zona di Orvieto**, Vini Cardeto, Via Constanzi 51, **t** 0763 300594. Visits Tues–Fri except hols and harvest, but call first.

**Enoteca Regionale**, Piazza S. Giovanni 1, **t** 0763 793342, in the old cellars of the ex-convent of San Giovanni. Wine tastings and wine tours Mon–Fri 11–1 and 3–5; Sat and Sun open to groups if booked in advance; adm.

**Palazzone**, Rocca Ripesena 68, **t** 0763 344166. Open year round Mon–Sat.

**Tenuta Le Velette**, Le Velette, near Orvieto Scalo, **t** 0763 29090. Visits by appointment (exc Sun).

# Hills, Lakes and Gardens around Orvieto

## North of Orvieto

The rather empty territory high in the hills to the north of Orvieto on either side of the *autostrada* isn't one of Umbria's better-known regions – which you may find part of its appeal.

**Castel Viscardo**, 13km from Orvieto, in an isolated setting to the northwest, takes its name from a really fancy, if crumbling, castle, an archaic sort of family palace built for the Monaldeschis of Orvieto in the 1400s – it's still privately owned and not open to visitors. It was later owned by the Spada family, one of whom was a cardinal and received a beautiful ivory crucifix from Louis XIV, which is now by the high altar of the parish church. The village is known for its brick production – the paving of the Campo in Siena was made here.

**Monte Rubiaglio**, the next village north, has a 13th-century castle now converted into apartments, as well as something you don't find every day in Umbria: a church from the early 1900s, with an Art Nouveau interior. **Allerona**, north by indirect roads, is another out-of-the-way spot, the westernmost *comune* in Umbria, and the site of some well-preserved stretches of a minor Roman aqueduct. Two old gates, named Sun and Moon, and a few walls remain of Allerona's castle, demolished by Charles VIII of France in his ill-omened Italian tour of 1495; in nearby Selva di Meana park, don't miss another Art Nouveau work, the Villa Cahen.

Other possible destinations are along the winding SS71 to Città della Pieve: walled medieval **Ficulle**, founded by the Lombards and long home to potters who make earthenware wine pitchers (*panate*), oil containers (*ziri*) and bean pots (*pignatte*), which you can purchase. All the houses in Ficulle have little terracotta numberplates by the doors. The Collegiata in town was designed by Ippolito Scalza, while the little church of **Santa Maria Vecchia**, outside the walls, has 15th-century frescoes and preserves an ancient *cippus* from a mithraeum. Other residents of Ficulle are the Marchesi Antinori, who make some of the finest Orvieto wines and live six kilometres south at the imposing, beautifully preserved

**Castello della Sala**, built by the Monaldeschi in the 1300s; it has a Gargantuesque cylindrical tower, linked to the square castle by a covered gallery.

**Parrano**, to the northeast, has a castle begun in the year 1000 and in the vicinity a number of *Tane del Diavolo* ('Devil's Lairs') – not that old Nick spends more time here than anywhere else, but the peculiar shape of these water-carved caves led the locals to suspect a supernatural origin. Back in the Upper Palaeolithic era, these lairs were home sweet home for the first Umbrians for thousands of years.

**Fabro**, west of the A1, also has a castle for a landmark, occupied by the Germans in 1944, which made both castle and town a target for bombers. Further north, **Monteleone d'Orvieto** is better preserved, a pleasant hill town founded by Orvieto in the 11th century. It once had a fortress which went through a score of owners before it bit the dust in a battle between the Papal States and the Grand Dukes of Tuscany, in 1643. The houses are packed densely on three parallel streets over the surrounding cliffs, and the Collegiata dei SS. Pietro e Paolo has paintings by Perugino's followers. Città della Pieve is just north (*see* p.113).

## The Dream Garden of La Scarzuola

East of Monteleone, there's yet another Art Nouveau church in **Montegabbione**, and near Montegiove, up a signposted unpaved road through a forest, lie the gardens of La Scarzuola. In 1956, the architect Tomaso Buzzi (1900–81) purchased a 13th-century Franciscan convent and its grounds to create a garden based on the beautiful woodcuts and descriptions in the celebrated *Hypnerotomachia Poliphili* (Polyphilus' Dream of the Strife of Love), a nearly incomprehensible philosophical romance on love, beauty and architecture written by a Dominican friar named Francesco Colonna and published in Venice in 1499.

Buzzi's fantasy garden is very much in the offbeat Italian tradition: Renaissance gardens often had follies and water games, and not far from here, just over the border in Lazio, is the ultimate crazy garden, the 16th-century Monster Park at Bomarzo, while in southern Tuscany there's Niki de Sainte-Phalle's Giardino dei

**Castello della Sala**
*t 0763 86051; open for visits Mon–Fri exc Aug; advance booking needed*

⭐ **La Scarzuola**
*2hr guided visits for groups of 8 or more by appt with Convento della Scarzuola e Città Buzziana, t 0763 837463; adm*

## Orvieto's Wine, in Legend and in a Glass

When Signorelli drew up his contract to fresco the Cappella di San Brizio, he made sure to add a certain clause: 'that he be given as much as he wanted of that wine of Orvieto'. And, fuelled on the stuff, Signorelli never painted better. First made by the Etruscans and Romans, and shipped down the Tiber at Palianum, near Baschi (where archaeologists have found large caches of amphorae), the wine legendarily saved the city from the barbarians, who partook so generously of the golden nectar that they found in the city's temples that all the locals had to do was gather up the drunks in the middle of the night and give them the old heave-ho.

Now refined over the centuries, Umbria's most famous wine is grown in 16 designated areas in the provinces of Terni and Viterbo, and consists of a careful mixture of grapes, with Tuscan Trebbiano and Verdello dominant. Light straw-coloured Orvieto DOC comes in four different varieties: dry (Orvieto secco), which now predominates because of the market, although you can still find the more authentic moderately dry (*abboccato*, often served with appetizers), medium-sweet (*amabile*) and sweet (*dolce*), made like a Sauternes from noble rot (*muffa nobile*). If made in the oldest growing zone, right near Orvieto, it's called Classico.

Possibly the best place to taste local wines in the city is at the **Enoteca Regionale**, situated in the old cellars of the ex-convent of San Giovanni. There are tours of the cellars and wine tastings accompanied by appropriate nibbles, while the first floor hosts art exhibitions. Wines can also be tasted and bought at cantine around town. A number of vineyards also welcome visitors. Many of the vineyards also sell their own olive oil. *See* p.214 for wine-tasting details.

Tarocchi, full of large fantastical statues. At La Scarzuola, Buzzi has created a series of ruins and stage sets meant to be viewed by following a special itinerary: there's even a transparent pyramid (predating the one at the Louvre) and a musical staircase. Although it's unfinished, Buzzi's nephew is continuing the project according to his uncle's plans. There is also a Franciscan church, with a fresco portrait of St Francis from the mid-13th century.

### East and South of Orvieto: Lakes Corbara and Alviano

Between Orvieto and Todi, a dam stops up the Tiber to form the **Lago di Corbara**, Umbria's second largest lake, with good fishing. Both Orvieto–Todi routes are scenic: the slower SS79bis passes **Prodo**, with its pink medieval castle, and the turn-off for **Titignano**, a 16th-century fortified villa connected to a hamlet; the more southerly SS448 passes along the lake shore and **Civitella del Lago**, known for its restaurant (*see* p.218). The convent by the lake was founded by St Francis in 1218 on land donated by the Baschi family and rebuilt in 1703. Nearby, at the confluence of the Paglia and the Tiber, stands their fief, **Baschi**, a hill town with a medieval centre enjoying spectacular views. Below lie the ruins of the ancient Roman port of Palianum, from where Orvieto's wine (*see* above) was shipped to Rome. Baschi's **church of San Nicolò**, designed by Ippolito Scalza (1584) has a lovely triptych by Sienese painter Giovanni di Paolo and a Murano chandelier.

From Baschi, the SS205 climbs high over the valley of the Tiber, taking in splendid scenery on the way to **Montecchio** and the

**Castello del Poggio**
*t 0744 903379;*
*open 2nd Sat and 3rd*
*Mon of month 9–12.30*

15th-century **Castello del Poggio**. On a wooded hill, with beautiful views over lakes Corbara and Alviano, the *castello* is reached by a hard-to-find road from the village of Guardea. This peaceful area was busy in the Greek–Gothic wars; the castle was founded by the Byzantines and occupied by the Normans when they took over the Greek lands of southern Italy; it was restored by Antonio Sangallo the Younger and is now being restored again, as a cultural centre and residence.

South, just off the SS205 at medieval **Alviano**, St Francis hushed the swallows drowning out his preaching. Alviano has a perfectly preserved **castle** (1495–1506) built by *condottiere* Bartolomeo d'Alviano. Its fine Renaissance courtyard affords access to the

**Museo di Alviano**
*t 07444 905028,*
*www.comunedialviano.*
*it; open Tues–Fri*
*4–7; adm*

**Museo di Alviano**. A scion of the Liviani family, Bartolomeo was employed by the Republic of Venice and gave such satisfaction he was made lord of the Venetian city of Pordenone. In 1651 his castle was purchased by grasping Olimpia Pamphili, sister-in-law of Pope Innocent X; in 1920 her family donated it to Alviano, which uses it as a town hall. On the round tower, note the Medusa head designed to ward off enemies. The **chapel** in the castle courtyard is frescoed with scenes of St Francis and the swallows; in the old storage cellars is the **Museo della Civiltà Contadina**, dedicated to farm tools from the good old days. Alviano's charming **parish church** (1505) has kept most of its original features, and has Umbria's only fresco (the *Madonna and Saints*) by the painter Pordenone. The commission came from Pentesilea Baglione, widow of the *condottiere*; she is the elderly woman on the right. The church also contains one of Niccolò Alunno's finest paintings, the *Madonna in Gloria* (1480s).

**Oasi di Alviano**
*entrance at Madonna*
*del Porto, on Mutano–*
*Scalo–Baschi road;*
*t 0744 903715,*
*www.oasidialviano.it;*
*open Sept–mid-May*
*Sun and hols 10–sunset;*
*other times guided*
*tours by appt; adm*

The Tiber has been dammed near here to create another small artificial lake, the **Lago di Alviano**; its banks are nothing to look at now, but come back in a century or so. The surrounding marshes are a nature reserve, the **Oasi di Alviano**, with hides from which you can watch herons, bitterns and ducks.

⭐ **La Casella >**

## Where to Stay and Eat around Orvieto

### Ficulle ✉ 05016

**La Casella**, near Parrano, t 0763 86684 or t 0763 86588, *www.lacasella.com* (€€€€). An *agriturismo* in a 1,000-acre forest. Rooms (breakfast included) are in 12 stone houses in an old hamlet, and there is riding (including tuition), a pool with hydromassage, tennis, volleyball and 5-a-side football facilities, mountain bikes, an antique billiards table, an Internet point and a good restaurant (half and full board available). In summer the moonlit rides followed by a candlelit dinner in the forest are popular.

### Titignano ✉ 05010

**Fattoria di Titignano**, Loc. Titignano, t 0763 308000, *www.titignano.com* (€€). A simple guesthouse on a working farm producing wine and oil. The rooms (breakfast included) and self-catering apartments are in the main house or in cottages in the grounds, and there's a pool. The restaurant (€; half and full board available) serves wonderful rustic food, including superlative roasts; non-residents must book ahead. Ask about tasting and Italian courses.

### Baschi ✉ 05023

***La Penisola**, Pian delle Monache 138, Lago di Corbara on SS448, **t** 0744 950521/2/3, *www.albergolapenisola.it* (€€€). A handsome complex of three old farmhouses in its own grounds on the shore of Lake Corbara, with comfy rooms in a traditional Umbrian style (breakfast included), all with a private garden or terrace. There's also a pool and a restaurant specializing in giant *bistecca alla fiorentina* (half and full board offered).

**Pomurlo Vecchio**, Loc. Pomurlo Vecchio (5km east of Baschi on Montecchio road), **t** 0744 950190, *www.pomurlovecchio-lecasette.it* (€€). An *agriturismo* on a 350-acre farm producing wine, oil, fruit, honey and jams, and offering horseriding. There are 2 apartments in the house – actually a tower – and 14 very simple doubles (breakfasts included) in outbuildings. The good restaurant uses produce from the estate; half and full board available.

**Vissani**, on SS448 Todi–Baschi towards Civitella del Lago, **t** 0744 950206, *www.casavissani.it* (€€€€). A restaurant gourmets rank among Italy's top five – an almost passionately religious inner sanctum of *cucina altissima* serving such marvels as risotto in red wine sauce with cinnamon, quail casserole with grape flan, and seabass with lettuce, mushrooms, spelt and blueberries. *Booking required. Closed Mon, Wed, Thurs lunch, Sun eve and Aug.*

### Montecchio ✉ 05020

**Semiramide**, Via Pian dell'Ara, Melezzole, **t** 0744 951008, *penta.gigi@libero.it* (€€). A fine place in lovely woods above Montecchio, offering the likes of tagliatelle in chicken sauce, roast chicken or lamb, and ravioli in tomato and basil sauce, at fair prices in a family atmosphere. *Closed Tues, except in summer, and 3wks Sept.*

## Amelia

Authorities as important as the Elder Pliny and Cato claimed *Ameria* was among the oldest cities in Italy – perhaps founded in the 12th century BC, three centuries prior to Rome. It didn't take advantage of its headstart, but it was an important Roman *municipium* by 90 BC, and it gave its name to the Via Armerina, linking Perugia and Todi to southern Etruria. When it became a *comune* in the Middle Ages, its sympathies lay with the Ghibellines, even after it was officially incorporated into the Papal States. In 1571 the town was excommunicated after refusing to pay a war tax the popes had levied to raise money to fight the Turks.

In a beautiful setting on the ridge dividing the valleys of the Tiber and Nera, modern Amelia (population 11,200) is far enough off the busy *autostrada* to Rome to retain its tranquillity, at least in its *centro storico*; the surroundings are gritty and prosperous. Once there, reward yourself with one of the town's famous candied figs, made with cocoa and almonds.

# Getting to and around Amelia

Amelia is on the ATC **bus** routes from Terni, Orvieto and Orte. Less frequent buses from Amelia go on to Lugnano in Teverina, Attigliano and Alviano.

**Cars** are forbidden in the centre on weekdays; there are car parks outside the Porta Romana with a minibus link into the centre.

## The Walls, San Francesco and the Archeological Museum

The great age that was attributed by the Romans to Amelia is most tangible today in its **Mura Poligoni**, the 5th-century BC Cyclopean walls that were constructed by the Umbrii without using mortar. A section remains substantially intact, 3.5m thick in places and standing some 7.5m high, near the Renaissance **Porta Romana**. These walls are about all that survived after the Goths devastated the town in 548, though parts of the Roman town can still be seen in bits and pieces of ancient masonry and columns in some houses; sections of Roman street paving have been revealed along Via della Repubblica.

**Museo Archeologico**

*Palazzo Boccarini, Piazza Augusta Vera 10, t 0744 978120, info@sistemamuseo.it; open April–June and Sept Tues–Sun 10.30–1 and 4–7; July and Aug Tues–Sun 10.30–1 and 4.30–7; Oct–Mar Fri–Sun 10–1 and 3.30–6; adm*

Near the Porta Romana, the **Museo Archeologico** has a restored bronze statue of Germanicus, father of Caligula, found near the town in 1963 and displayed for years in the Museo Nazionale Archeologico in Perugia, which eventually agreed to its return. Also on display are relics of the Umbrii in Amelia and the **Pinacoteca**'s collection of paintings.

Just off Via della Repubblica, Piazza Vera opens up with the town war memorial and the church of **San Francesco** (or SS. Filippo e Giacomo), built in 1287 and remodelled inside in the 18th century. The one chapel that was left alone houses six fine Renaissance tombs of the Geraldini family, one of which (Matteo and Elisabetta) is by Agostino di Duccio, exquisite if somewhat worse for wear. The best-known member of the family, Alessandro Geraldini (1455–1525), lobbied in the court of Ferdinand and Isabella for Columbus' voyage and was rewarded by being appointed Bishop of Santo Domingo, the first in the New World.

## To Piazza Marconi and the Duomo

Continuing up Via della Repubblica, take the narrow stepped alley that leads under the arch on the left to reach Amelia's most impressive palace, the **Palazzo Farrattini** (1520), designed by Antonio da Sangallo the Younger as a smaller version of the famous Palazzo Farnese in Rome; inside it has two Roman mosaics.

Via della Repubblica continues up steeply past some more Renaissance *palazzi* to the **Arco della Piazza**, which was made up in the Middle Ages of Roman fragments and a frieze. Through here is Amelia's charming old main square, rectangular **Piazza Marconi** with its original paving, more proud Renaissance palaces, and the **Loggia dei Banditori**, from which public proclamations were read. **Palazzo Petrignani** has frescoed Mannerist and Baroque rooms, some of them by Zuccari .

**Palazzo Petrignani**
*visits by appt
on t 0744 976219*

From here, Via Duomo ascends steeply towards the cathedral, passing pretty Via Pellegrino Carleni as it rises into the medieval part of town. At the summit, the **Duomo** was almost completely rebuilt in 1640 with a brick façade. The handsome dodecagonal **campanile** was built in 1050 as a Torre Civica, reusing Roman stones and a portion of another frieze. The cathedral features a worn Romanesque column where Amelia's patron saint Firmina is said to have been bound and tortured to death under Diocletian in 303. It also contains reliefs by Agostino di Duccio's followers in the tomb of another Bishop Geraldini (1476), in the first chapel on the left. Another Duccio, the great Sienese Duccio di Buoninsegna, painted the cathedral's finest painting, an *Assumption*, but you have to come in May or between 15 and 20 August to see it on display. In the right transept is a *Last Supper* by Francesco Perini of Amelia (1538), and in the Oratorio del Sacramento are two restored paintings by Niccolò Pomarancio. The octagonal chapel in the right aisle is said to be the work of Antonio da Sangallo. Here there are also two Turkish flags captured in the battle of Lepanto in 1571 – most peculiar for a town excommunicated for refusing to contribute its share to the Christian cause. There are lovely views from the nearby belvedere.

**Duomo**
*open daily 10–12
and 4–6.30*

## Sant'Agostino to Piazza Matteotti and the Roman Cisterns

From the Duomo, Via Geraldini descends to the **church of Sant'Agostino** which boasts a good, squarish Gothic façade that was rebuilt in 1477, a beautiful ogival doorway and a large rose window. The interior was enthusiastically Baroqued and frescoed by Francesco Appiani in 1747–62. The first altar to the right contains a *Vision of St John at Patmos* by Pomarancio. Of the older church, only the pavement remains, but work in the sacristy has revealed some very curious *sinopie* dating from the 11th century. A *sinopia* is the rough sketch made for a fresco in red earth pigment: these show saints, floral patterns and stars in the vault that were never completed.

**Sant'Agostino**
*open mornings*

From here, Via Poserola descends to a little 13th-century gate, passing the large **convent of San Magno**; the church has a rare old organ of 1680, restored and used for concerts.

Heading in the opposite direction, Via Garibaldi passes some medieval alleys and takes you into Piazza Matteotti, the home of

**Sala Consiliare**
*open by request*
*Mon–Fri 10–12*

**Cisterna Romana**
*open April–Sept Sat*
*4.30–7.30, Sun and hols*
*10.30–12.30 and 4.30–*
*7.30; Oct–Mar Sat 3–6,*
*Sun and hols 10.30–*
*12.30 and 3–6; or call*
*Associazone I Poligonali,*
*t 0744 978436 or*
*t 339 756 1479, to*
*arrange a visit; adm*

**Teatro Sociale**
*t 0744 976219/20;*
*performances*
*Nov–May; rest of year*
*guided tours by appt*

**Cantina dei**
**Colli Amerini**
*t 0744 989721; open*
*Mon–Sat 9–1 and 3.30–6*

Amelia's delightful **Palazzo Comunale**. Fragments of Roman *Ameria* decorate its courtyard and a *Madonna with Saints* presides in the **Sala Consiliare**, painted by Pier Matteo d'Amelia (d. 1508), who, through art history sleuthing, has been identified with the Master of the Gardner Annunciation. In 1996 a steep staircase was built to allow access to the remarkable vaulted **Roman cisterns** beneath, which are capable of holding more than 4,000 cubic metres. Constructed for emergencies in the 1st century BC, they comprise 10 chambers into which rainwater was channelled; another channel was employed to release the waters periodically in order to keep them fresh.

Amelia has an especially delightful theatre, the **Teatro Sociale**, near Piazza Matteotti. Built in 1783 on the model of La Fenice in Venice, its boxes and stalls are well preserved. Notice how some of the boxes are equipped with cupboards to store food; in the late 18th century only a magnificently sung aria had the power to make an audience shut up or stop eating.

The surrounding hills are famous for their figs and wine: for the latter, visit the **Cantina dei Colli Amerini** near Amelia at **Fornole**. On the first Sunday in October, the wine is miraculously made to pour from Amelia's fountains.

## Around Amelia

### Lugnano in Teverina

Lugnano in Teverina (population 1,650), which lies 11km northwest of Amelia, is a walled town set on a ridge that long served as a bone of contention between the *comuni* of Amelia, Orvieto and Todi; in 1503 it was sacked by Cesare Borgia. Nowadays it attracts a few Romans and foreigners for summer-holiday *villeggiatura*. The enormous **Palazzo Pennone** that was built in the 1500s by wealthy cardinals has been converted into the town

**Antiquarium**
*t 0744 902321 or*
*t 199 151123; Apr–Sept,*
*Sun and hols guided*
*tours at 4, 5 and 6;*
*Oct–Mar, Sun and hols*
*at 3, 4, 5 and 6*

hall, with a little **antiquarium** on the first floor, where you can see fragments of frescoes and mosaics from a 1st-century BC Roman villa unearthed at Poggio Gramignano. Excavations began in 1988 in collaboration with the University of Tucson, Arizona. Among finds was an infant cemetery that may be unique – dozens of babies died from malaria and were buried in a series of amphorae; their skeletons (still in the vessels) can be seen among the artefacts in the antiquarium.

Lugnano's main attraction is one of the finest, most exotic Romanesque churches that you'll ever see, the 12th-century **Collegiata di Santa Maria Assunta**. This has a striking roof and columned portico or *pronaos*, which was added in 1230 reusing older columns on a design derived from the ancient Roman basilica. The shallow arches above bear a few traces of their once-glorious Cosmati decoration, and there is a fine large window in the form of a double wheel. On the wall left of the portico, a curious three-headed figure represents the Trinity. The barrel-vaulted interior, not remodelled to everyone's taste, retains its fine proportions. Like so many churches of the period, the presbytery at the end of the central nave is raised over the crypt. The pavement is beautifully worked and there are fine carved capitals along the nave; the third one to the left shows a scene of a Byzantine-style Mass and a man with a snake coming out of his mouth, symbolic of evil, almost like an editorial comment on the Great Schism. There are finely carved *ambones* (twin pulpits) and *transennas* from the original choir, with bas-reliefs showing St Michael killing the dragon and two men exchanging the kiss of peace, and a rare *ciborium* restored in 1937. The apse has a fine tripytch of the Assumption by Nicolò Alunno, and Mannerist painter Livio Agresti from Forlì checks in with a surprising *Beheading of John the Baptist* of 1571, in the chapel to the right.

## South of Amelia: Penna in Teverina, Giove and a Dip into Lazio

To the southwest of Amelia, towards the Tiber and the big road and railway junction at Orte, you'll find **Penna in Teverina**, a charming old fortified town with houses built directly into the walls. It was disputed by Rome's eternal Punch and Judy factions, the Colonna and Orsini families, until the Colonna got tired of the show and sold it to the Orsini, who constructed a Palazzo Orsini in town with a fine 19th-century Italian garden attached (now privately owned). Other relics of the same era are the Mammalocchi, allegorical herms in travertine standing at the entrance to villas on the road to Amelia.

To the north of Penna are a pair of crumbling medieval villages, **Giove** and **Attligliano**. Giove was smashed in 1503 by the troops of Cesare Borgia, who dismantled the walls and castles; what was left was reconstructed in the next century as the imposing and elegant **Palazzo Ducale** overlooking the Tiber; it was built by the Mattei, a great Roman family, and is still in the hands of their heirs. Members of great Roman families can be on the lazy and decadent side; one of the original features of this palace is the proto-parking garage ramp spiralling up to the first floor, big enough for horse-drawn carriages.

Most of the truly remarkable sights in these parts are situated over the border in **Lazio**, especially the **Monster Park** in the woebegone village of **Bomarzo** – a mad garden full of colossal cinquecento sculptures that brings the neurosis of late Renaissance Italy to the surface.

Just south, the pretty Cimini hills shelter fine towns such as **Soriano nel Cimino** and **San Martino al Cimino**, and beautiful, unspoiled **Lake Vico**, an ancient volcanic crater. **Caprarola**, nearby, sits in the shadow of one of the greatest, strangest and most arrogant of all Renaissance palaces, the Farnese, built with papal booty by Perugia's arch enemy Paul III.

## North of Amelia

Much of the countryside lying north of Amelia towards Todi is *terra incognita*, with hamlets standing abandoned. Yet in Roman times this area was important enough for a road, the Via Falisca Armerina – traces of this and a Roman bridge can be seen by **Sambucetole**, and the modern hamlet lies in the shadow of the abandoned medieval town.

Further north the road passes the tower of the medieval **Castel dell'Aquila**, then forks: to the west, surrounded by forests, is the unusual circular walled village of **Toscolano**, once owned by Todi (note the eagle over the gate), now used as the summer base for the Centro Europeo Toscolano, dedicated to the renewal of popular Italian music, among other things. Just outside the centre, the **chapel of the Santissima Annunziata** contains restored frescoes attributed to Pier Matteo d'Amelia.

A scenic road continues north to **Collelungo**, which was the last outpost of the Monaldeschi on the frontier of Todi. Inside its restored church you can see a Lombard-era altar and some frescoes dating from the late 1200s.

The east fork of the road from Castel dell'Aquila leads to **Avigliano Umbro** with its castle-like water tower. To the north, little **Dunarobba** with its big 16th-century castle stood on the banks of the prehistoric Lago Tiberino that filled the Tiber valley to the brim. During the 1980s, diggers in a quarry nearby came upon 40 specimens of the 200,000-year-old ancestors of the sequoia that once stood on the lake shores. The mighty trunks of this **Foresta Fossile**, some standing 7.5m high, were so well preserved that they were still upright in thick clay. They are the most important palaeobotanical finds in the region; a research centre has been set up to study them.

The surrounding countryside is truly lovely, whether you decide to heard northwards to Todi or east towards **Montecastrilli**, a traditional fortified Umbrian hamlet that was an outpost of Todi for several centuries.

**Foresta Fossile**
*open for guided tours Fri–Sun and hols Apr–mid-Oct 10–1 and 4–7; mid-Oct–Dec 10.30–3.30; Jan–Mar 10.30–3.30; or by appt with Pro Loco in Avigliano Umbro,* *t 0744 940348; adm*

ⓘ **Amelia >**
*Via Roma 2,*
*t 0744 981453,*
*www.regioneumbria.eu,*
*info@iat.amelia.tr.it*
*(closed summer Sun*
*and Mon pm, winter Sat*
*and Mon pm);*
*and Pro Loco,*
*Piazza A. Vera 8,*
*t 0744 982559,*
*http://web.tiscali.it/*
*proloco.amelia*

# Where to Stay and Eat in and around Amelia

## Amelia ✉ 05022

**★★★Scoglio dell'Aquilone**, Via Orvieto 23, t 0744 982445, *scogliodellaquilone@ tiscali.it* (€€). A quiet place in the woods, with comfortable rooms with panoramic views and a restaurant (half and full board offered).

**Parco degli Ulivi**, Strada Statale Amerina 27, on road into Amelia, **t** 0744 982681 (€€). Umbrian cuisine plus pizzas in a little natural park. A highlight is the *spaghetti alla Spoletina*. On Tues, Thurs and Fri there's fresh fish if you order ahead. In summer you can enjoy use of a swimming pool. *Closed Wed.*

## Lugnano in Teverina ✉ 05020

**Podere Ceoli**, Vocabolo Ceoli 117, **t** 0744 347448, *podere_ceoli@yahoo.it* (€€). An atmospheric little *affittacamere* in the countryside, with 2 self-catering apartments, a beautiful pool and horses. Weekly stays are better value.

**Ostello Casa Laboratorio Vallenera**, Casale di Vallenera, **t** 0744 902674, *www.vallenera.it* (€). The youth hostel, offering full board if you wish.

**La Frateria dell'Abate Loniano**, Loc. San Francesco 6, just outside Lugnano, **t** 0744 902180 (€€). An atmospheric restaurant in the restored 13th-century refectory of a former convent, serving traditional seasonal fare based on organic produce. *Closed Wed.*

# The Valnerina

*The clear Nera, one of the main tributaries of the Tiber, flows across the southern edge of Umbria. Nera means 'black' in Italian, but the name derives from Naharkum, a tribe of the Umbrii, the valley's mysterious first-known inhabitants.*

*The Nera is the region's special river: 'There would be no Tiber if the Nera did not give it to drink' is an old Umbrian saying; the Umbrians have long memories and know deep in their hearts that the ancient Romans learned all their simple and honest virtues from their ancestors. Much of the Valnerina is still an Italian secret, though its black truffles and saints have global reputations, and its superb, often dramatic, natural beauty is now protected as a natural park.*

# 11

## Don't miss

⭐ **An ancient Roman jewel**
Carsulae **p.232**

⭐ **Europe's highest waterfall**
Cascata delle Marmore **p.238**

⭐ **Byzantine-style frescos**
San Pietro in Valle **p.241**

⭐ **Boar salami and basilicas**
Norcia **p.248**

⭐ **A dream landscape**
Piano Grande **p.252**

*See map overleaf*

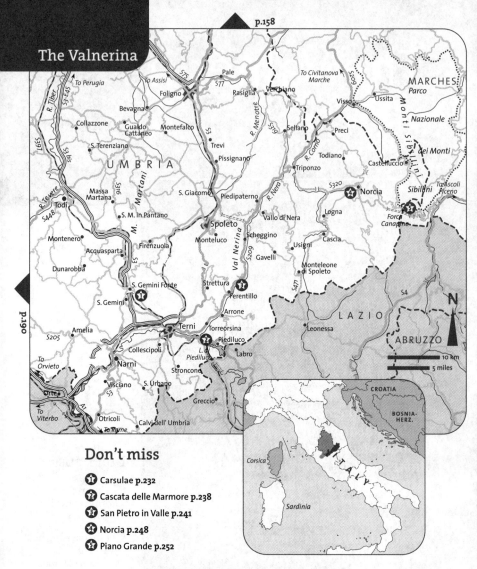

p.158

p.190

p.190

## Don't miss

⭐ Carsulae **p.232**

⭐ Cascata delle Marmore **p.238**

⭐ San Pietro in Valle **p.241**

⭐ Norcia **p.248**

⭐ Piano Grande **p.252**

# Narni, Terni and Around

## Narni

Once an important stop on the Via Flaminia, Narni (population 21,000) is a fine old hill town in a dramatic position, guarding the steep gorge as you enter the Valnerina. Originally the Umbrian *Nequinum*, it renamed itself *Nahar* or *Narnia* after the river when it changed its allegiance to Rome in 299 BC. Pliny wrote of its unassailable defences; the emperor Nerva was born here in AD 32; and the city can also claim a pope, John XIII (965–72), as well as a great *condottiere*, Gattamelata (1370–1443), who went on to fame

# Getting to and around Narni

Narni is easily reached by **train** from Rome (89km/1hr), Terni, Spoleto or Assisi on the main Rome–Ancona line; it is 15km from the main Florence–Rome rail and *autostrada* junction at Orte. Frequent buses link the station and the city on the hill.

ATC **buses, t** 0744 492711, *www.atcterni.it*, also departing from the train station, connect Amelia, Terni, Otricoli and surrounding hamlets.

and fortune in Venice. However, many people never bother to breach the modern industry and electrocarbon plant at Narni Scalo in the river valley to discover the fine town within – which, *pace* Foligno, is in reality the closest to the geographic centre of Italy.

## To Piazza Garibaldi

The sight in Narni that most engaged the Grand Tourist of the past two centuries, the romantically ruined **Ponte d'Augusto** (27 BC), is now just visible from the bridge at lower, industrial Narni Scalo, or from the train window as you approach from the south. This

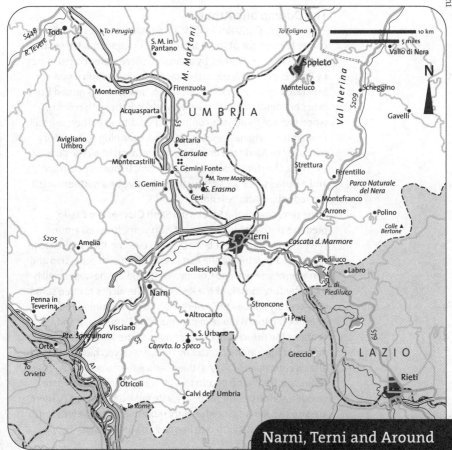

Narni, Terni and Around

11 The Valnerina | Narni

lofty massive arch in the river is all that survives of a bridge famous even in Roman times for its size – it stretched 130m and stood 27m high – built to carry the newer Via Flaminia towards Terni and Spoleto. It fell into ruins in the Middle Ages, and until 1855 it had two arches and a much more picturesque setting. If it looks familiar, you may have seen Corot's famous painting in the Louvre.

Many of Narni's old city gates are intact, especially the eastern **Porta Ternana**, with its twin round towers built by Sixtus IV where the Via Flaminia entered Narni proper. This bustling ancient road served the city well through history, except in 1527, when the brutal mercenary troops of Charles V, having sacked Rome, were marching home and stopped to sack and pillage Narni as well. The Flaminia (here called Via Roma) leads to Narni's main crossroads: the busy, colourful, irregularly shaped **Piazza Garibaldi**, overlooked by the side door of the cathedral and a neoclassical palace. The whole square was originally a Roman *piscina*, and steps from the restored 15th-century fountain descend into a 12th-century cistern.

### The Duomo and Around

From Piazza Garibaldi, main Via Garibaldi squeezes round the corner to the front of the Duomo and its elegant quattrocento portico, which is adorned by a classical frieze. Consecrated in 1145 by Pope Eugenius III, the cathedral originally had three naves, separated by a wide variety of capitals and columns reused from other buildings. A fourth nave was added in the 15th century, when most of its art was commissioned, although there are still remnants of original frescoes. There's a charming 15th-century fresco of the Madonna and Child by a local artist by the door. On the right, the third chapel boasts a Cosmati mosaic pavement and a Renaissance architectural perspective by a northern artist named Sebastiano Pellegrini.

The next chapel, the **Sacello dei Santi Giovenale e Cassio**, predates the cathedral by almost 800 years, founded around the tomb of Narni's first bishop, San Giovenale. Its marble screen was pieced together in the Renaissance from Paleochristian and Romanesque reliefs and Cosmati work, and on the upper wall is a 9th-century mosaic of the Redeemer. The niches contain some 15th-century statues of Giovenale and a German-made *Pietà*. The inner chapel is made in part from the Roman wall and contains the 6th-century sarcophagus of the saint; there's a picture of him on the pilaster by the Sienese Vecchietta. The high altar was completed in 1714; there are a pair of marble pulpits and choirstalls from 1490 and, in the left nave, a large polychrome wooden statue of Sant'Antonio Abate by Vecchietta (1474). There are also two Renaissance funerary monuments to the left; Pietro Cesi's has been attributed to Bernardo da Settignano.

**Pinacoteca**
*Palazzo del Vescovile;*
*open Tues–Sun 9–1*
*and 2–7; adm*

Opposite the Duomo, in little Piazza Cavour, is the **Pinacoteca**, with an *Annunciation* by Benozzo Gozzoli. Tucked behind Piazza Cavour is the **Roman arch**, reworked into a medieval gate.

Right of the cathedral, off Via Garibaldi, the Via del Campanile leads to the sturdy Roman base of the cathedral's **bell tower**; the upper section was added in the 1400s and adorned with colourful ceramic plates. The 14th-century **church of San Francesco** near the top of the next street to the left is on the site of an oratory founded in 1213 by St Francis. It burnt down in a fire in 1998, but its fine façade remains and the interior has been restored.

## Piazza dei Priori

Via Garibaldi, the main street since Roman times (note the pretty 19th-century restored Teatro Comunale), widens to form Piazza dei Priori, centre of Narni's civic life in the Middle Ages. Here sits the **Palazzo del Podestà** (14th–15th centuries), now seat of the *comune*, an old tower melded with three medieval towerhouses and decorated with four bas-reliefs depicting a joust, a lion and dragon, the beheading of Holofernes, and a hunt with falcons. The palace shows some cracks from Narni's very own earthquake in 2000, which left 250 homeless. In the **Sala Consigliare** hangs Narni's finest painting, a magnificent *Coronation of the Virgin* (1486) by Florentine Domenico Ghirlandaio, in a lovely frame with a *predella* showing *St Francis Receiving the Stigmata*, a *Pietà* and *St Jerome*.

**Sala Consigliare**
*open Fri–Sun*
*10–1 and 3–7*

The circular **fountain** dates from 1303. Opposite is the medieval **Casa Sacripanti**, with more reliefs, and the **loggia** and **clock tower** of the once-massive 14th-century Palazzo dei Priori, built by Matteo Gattapone, all that survived the sack of Charles V's *Landsknechten* in 1527; the pulpit was used for reading public proclamations.

**Santa Maria**
**in Pensole**
*visits by appt*
*with Associazione*
*Culturale Subterranea,*
*t 0744 722292;*
*April–Oct Sat 3–6, Sun*
*10–1 and 3–6; Nov–Mar*
*Sun 11–1 and 3–5; adm*

At the end of the piazza, **Santa Maria in Pensole** (1175) has a beautiful Romanesque façade fronted by a handsome portico made with columns borrowed from older buildings and three beautiful doors with elaborate marble decoration. Other reused columns line the three naves, many of which have charming capitals. The church was built over the vaults (*in pensole*) of an 8th-century Benedictine church and a Roman cistern once believed to be a temple of Bacchus. Opposite are two attractive palaces: the 17th-century **Palazzo Bocciarelli** and 16th-century **Palazzo Scotti**.

The iron fixtures in the walls, here and all around Narni, hold torches for the May medieval pageant of San Giovenale (*see* p.233), one of the most colourful festivals of the Umbrian calendar.

## San Domenico

**San Domenico**
*open daily 11–1 and 3–7*

Further down tower- and palace-lined Via Mazzini, the deconsecrated 12th-century pink and white **church and campanile of San Domenico**, now the public library, has a door adorned with worn medallions of the 12 apostles, and 13th- to 16th-century fresco fragments inside. On the east end is a wall memorial (1494) near a tabernacle by the workshop of Agostino di Duccio; on the left side are faint frescoes by the Zuccari family and the tusk of a prehistoric elephant found on the banks of the Nera in 1988.

The Dominicans' convent, demolished in the 1950s, was replaced by the **Giardino di San Bernardo**, with ruins of a lofty tower and an great view towards the Romanesque abbey of San Cassiano over the narrow gorge of the Nera. Near Narni the river turns robin's-egg blue from the copper and lime deposits in the soil. The Associazione Culturale Subterranea discovered an earlier church under the apse of San Domenico, dating from the 1100s with frescoes, another Roman cistern and a prison cell with 18th-century graffiti left by poor souls imprisoned by the Dominican-run Inquisition; the ensemble is called the **Sotterranei della Chiesa di San Domenico**.

**Sotterranei della Chiesa di San Domenico**
*t 0744 722292; open for guided tours April–Oct Sat 3–6, Sun 10–12.30 and 3–5.30; Nov–Mar Sun 11–1 and 3–4.15*

## Lower Narni, and the Rocca

At the end of Via Mazzini, in Piazza Marzio, is the 15th-century well, the **Pozzo della Comunità**; from here follow the 15th-century walls along Via della Mura, or cut down the steps of Vicolo degli Orti to the most picturesque bit, around the tall tower of the **Porta della Fiera**. Via Gattamelata continues back to the centre, passing the so-called **house of Gattamelata** (No.113). The 'Honeyed Cat' (Erasmo da Narni) was born here in 1370 to a baker, and became such a successful, reliable and honest *condottiere* for Venice that he received the highest honour that the usually stingy Republic bestowed on anyone: a paid funeral and an equestrian statue by Donatello, the first since Roman times and one of Padua's gems.

Via Gattamelata continues to **Sant'Agostino**, its severe façade decorated with a faded fresco in a niche, attributed to Antoniazzo Romano. The interior has good quattrocento frescoes, a *Crucifixion* by the school of Antoniazzo Romano and a *Madonna* by Pier Antonio d'Amelia, a fine Renaissance wooden crucifix and a lofty carved ceiling holding a 16th-century painting on the Triumph of St Augustine by Carlo Federico Benincasa of Narni.

From Piazza Garibaldi, Via del Monte winds up through a picturesque medieval neighbourhood to the restored four-square **Rocca Albornoz** that dominates all views of Narni from the plain of Terni, built in the 1370s by the indefatigable Cardinal Albornoz.

About 3km east of town you can see inside the narrow tunnel of the **Ponte Cardona**, part of a 1st-century Roman aqueduct.

**Rocca Albornoz**
*t 0744 717117; open daily 11–1 and 3–6*

**Ponte Cordona**
*visits by appt with tourist office (see p.233)*

## South of Narni

South of Narni, the ancient Via Flaminia (SS3) continues towards the Rome of the Caesars, now just a back road in an obscure corner of Umbria. At about the 83km mark, it passes through a small plain with rugged cliffs near the road, an ancient holy site, **Grotte d'Orlando** (Roland's Cave). Badly worn Roman reliefs can be made out on the rocks and there are remains of an altar, 'Roland's Seat'.

On a steep slope below the hamlet of **Visciano**, southwest of Narni off the Otricoli road, is a lovely 11th-century church dedicated to Santa Pudenzia, surrounded by trees, with an exceptionally tall slender campanile. The portico has two Roman columns with fine capitals and some other Roman bits embedded in the walls. The polygonal apse is similar to those in Ravenna. Where the road branches off for Calvi, you'll see scanty remains of another Roman bridge, the **Ponte Sanguinario**.

The first Umbrian town a Roman would find along the Via Flaminia was **Otricoli** (16km from Narni), a town of the Umbrii destroyed by the Romans in the Social War in the 1st century BC. It was rebuilt down on the then-navigable Tiber as the city and port of *Ocriculum*. When this became swampy in the Middle Ages, the inhabitants moved back up to their hill, and what was once a thriving city became by the 18th century a wretchedly poor village. The rest of Otricoli is concentrated in a walled hill town with medieval streets of cannibalized Roman stone. The constantly rebuilt and reworked parish church of Santa Maria seems to have something from every century somewhere, from Roman columns within to a 19th-century campanile.

**Resti della Città Romana di Ocriculum**
*always open*

The ruins of Ocriculum are located 1.6km below town, overlooking the Tiber. Excavations began under Pope Pius VI in 1776, enriching the Vatican Museum with an enormous head of Jupiter and other pieces, but little has happened since, and many ruins, including the big baths, a theatre, amphitheatre, funerary monuments and a section of the original Via Flaminia, are overgrown and crumbling from exposure.

Fine oak forests and scenery surround **Calvi dell'Umbria** (south of Narni, 11km east of Otricoli), the southernmost *comune* of Umbria, prosperous until the plague crippled it in 1527. It was the home of Bernardo da Calvi, a follower of St Francis martyred in the first Franciscan mission to Morocco; the church of San Francesco is built on land Bernardo donated to Francis. Calvi's pride, however, is the 16th-century *presepio* of unusually large terracotta figures in the church of Sant'Antonio.

**Convento del Sacro Speco**
*guided tours daily 8–11.30 and 3–4.45; churchyard and cloisters open daily 8–11.30, 3–5 and 6–7.30*

To the southeast, 13km from Narni beyond Altrocanto and Sant'Urbano, the Convento del Sacro Speco was founded in 1213 by St Francis, who often sojourned in a nearby cave; the legend goes that once when he fell ill here, an angel comforted him with some sweet violin music. It was reconstructed during the 1300s and is one of the most evocative Franciscan monuments in all Italy. In recent years, it has been reoccupied by friars living according to the saint's First Rule.

## San Gemini, Carsulae, Acquasparta and Cesi

North of Narni, the SS3bis to Todi passes two towns known for their waters since the Etruscans. The first, **San Gemini**, keeps its spa a few kilometres to the north; the old centre remains the essential Umbrian hill town, despite being wrecked on two occasions, by the Saracens in 882, and the Imperial mercenary army of the Constable of Bourbon in 1527, practising for the Sack of Rome. There's a handy car park near the 1291 church of **San Francesco**, with a carved portal and doors from the 14th century and 15th–17th-century frescoes.

**San Francesco**
*open daily 9–7.30*

In the medieval centre (take narrow Via Casventino), in Piazza Palazzo Vecchio, the restored 12th-century **Palazzo Pubblico** has an external stairway and encompasses an older defensive tower converted into a campanile in the 1700s; here, too, is the 13th-century **Oratorio San Carlo**, with a striking, fresco-covered *ciborium*. Further along, the curiously shaped church of **San Giovanni Battista** started out in the 12th century as an octagon; it has a Romanesque door on its left side, with scant remnants of its Cosmati decoration and an inscription of 1199. Near San Gemini's 18th-century **gateway** stands its **cathedral**, with a tarted-up 19th-century interior.

**San Nicolò**
*open summer Fri–Sun 3–6; winter Fri–Sun 10–1 and 3–5; ask keeper for key*

Outside the gate, in a pretty garden, the church of **San Nicolò** was built as a dependency of the once-mighty abbey of Farfa near Rieti and is now privately owned; the frieze and lions on its portal are copies of the originals, now in the Metropolitan Museum in New York. The columns within have fine sculpted capitals, several from Carsulae (*see* below), and among its 13th-century frescoes, most of which are detached, is the only known work of Rogerino da Todi.

The spa, **San Gemini Fonte**, is in a pretty park full of old oaks, where you can try the carbonated diuretic waters (May–October). Near here, under the steep green hills, are the remains of Imperial era **Carsulae**, a Roman city abandoned and never rebuilt after a quake in the 800s. In its day, *Carsulae* was famous for its waters and wines. From the handsome gate built by Trajan (a favourite spot for wedding photos), you can follow a stretch of the original Via Flaminia, dotted with funerary monuments, among them two large, well-preserved tombs and a head of Claudius. There are the remains of a residential district, a theatre and an amphitheatre; in the pink marble forum are the bases of twin temples that may have been dedicated to the heavenly twins, the Dioscuri, and the basilica used as a council house or Curia. One temple was rebuilt in the 11th century to become a little chapel of **Santi Cosma e Damiano**.

⭐ **Carsulae**
*t 0744 334133; open daily April–Sept 8.30–7.30, Oct–Mar 8.30–5.30; adm*

North of San Gemini, the village of **Portaria** is known for its restaurants and for possessing one of the oldest postboxes in Italy (1674, under the clocktower). Further north, **Acquasparta** (Latin *Ad Aquas Partas*) is another quiet spot in which to sort out your digestive problems, recommended by no less than St Francis;

Amerino and Furapane waters are bottled here. In the centre is the Palazzo Cesi, from 1565, owned by the University of Perugia, with has Renaissance frescoes and a beautiful courtyard filled with ancient inscriptions. Here Roman prince Federico Cesi established a country branch of the scholarly Accademia dei Lincei he founded in Rome in 1609; his friend Galileo came out to visit for a month in 1624. Though the Accademia died with the prince, the idea caught on across Italy and most towns of any consequence managed to create a little academy. Normally peaceful and very typical of the region, the town alarms its neighbours every summer by hosting, of all things, a German lieder-singing competition.

**Palazzo Cesi**
*visits by appt*
*on* t 075 5851

From Acquasparta, you can follow a mountain road, the SS418, across to Spoleto – just don't think you've somehow got lost in Tuscany when you see signs for Arezzo. There are pleasant picnic spots along the way, overlooking deep-set **Lake Arezzo**, and nearby a Romanesque church with an unusual portico at **Firenzuola**.

On the last craggy slope of the Monti Martani, 6km east of San Gemini Fonte, **Cesi** thrived between the 12th and 16th centuries, though it lies under a much older town. The entrance, through the Porta Ternana, leads into the medieval centre and the church of **Santa Maria Assunta** (1515–25), with a trecento wooden sculpture of the Virgin and Child, and underneath, a room that belonged to a former church on the site, frescoed with a *Crucifixion* of 1425 by Giovanni di Giovannello of Narni. Outside the second gate, the **Porta Tudertina**, is the handsome church of **Sant'Andrea**, built of Roman stones from Carsulae, as well as another impressive 16th-century Palazzo Cesi. A road twists up Monte Eolo to the site of the ancient town, with remains of the 6th-century BC walls and splendid views. **Sant'Erasmo**, a 12th-century church with a pretty window, stands near the remains of the medieval fortress. An unpaved road continues to the top of **Monte Torre Maggiore** (1,121m).

## Festival in Narni

**Festival of San Giovenale**, last wk April and 1st wk May. Medieval pageantry at its brightest, with a torchlit costumed procession the night before the Corsa dell'Anello, in which knights from the town's three neighbourhoods compete to pierce a ring suspended over the street with their lances.

## Where to Stay and Eat

ⓘ Narni ›
*Piazza dei Priori 3,*
t 0744 715362,
www.narni.it

**Narni** ✉ 05035
**Podere Costa Romana**, SS. Flaminia, Strada per Itieli, t 0744 722495, *www.poderecostaromana.com* (€€€).

A beautifully restored stone farmhouse on a wooded hillside just outside Narni, with rustic apartments sleeping 2–5, with all comforts and panoramic views. There's a big garden and a pool overlooking the hills. Choose from B&B (mininum 2-night stay) and self-catering (min. 1wk).

**\*\*\*Dei Priori**, Vicolo del Comune 4, t 0744 726843, *www.loggiadeipriori.it* (€€). A medieval palace in the centre, with very comfortable rooms and suites (breakfast included) and a restaurant that has long been popular for dishes such as pasta with onions, tomatoes and peppers (half and full board available). *Closed Mon.*

**Il Cavallino**, Via Flaminia Romana 220, road to Terni, **t** 0744 761020 (€€). A good, old-fashioned little inn with simple rooms and a restaurant offering local cuisine. *Closed Tues, part of July, and Dec.*

**Monte del Grano 1696**, Strada Guadamello 328, Loc. San Vito, 15km south of Narni on SS3bis, **t** 0744 749143 (€€). A typical Umbrian trattoria specializing in meat dishes and with an excellent cheese selection. *Closed Mon, lunch Tues–Fri, and Jan.*

**San Gemini** ✉ 05029

**\*\*\*Locanda di Carsulae**, Via Tibernia 2, Loc. Fonte, on SS3bis, **t** 0744 630163, *www.gruppobacus.com* (€€). Simple rooms with private baths and a restaurant and *enoteca* (half and full board available).

**\*\*Duomo**, Piazza Duomo 4, **t** 0744 630015 or 630005, *www.gruppobacus.com* (€€). Basic en-suite rooms in the town centre (breakfast included), plus a restaurant specializing in meat and truffle dishes (half/full board offered).

# Terni

Sprawling, mouldering, modern – you may not want to spend long in southern Umbria's capital, but at least muster some respect for Terni's accomplishments. In 1867, as the city closest to the geographical centre of Italy, it was intended to be the nation's capital (this was before Rome was wrested from the occupying French), but the idea flew like a penguin. If Italy's politicians couldn't appreciate Terni's location, far from the country's vulnerable coasts and frontiers, the military did. Its location on the river Nera, and the vicinity of the Cascata delle Marmore, Europe's highest waterfall, sealed its destiny: in the 1870s the beautiful thundering waters were diverted for cheap hydroelectric power, and Italy's first steel mill went up to build ships for its navy to pester Africa, pushing Umbria to lurch belatedly into the Industrial Revolution (even though Italy has no iron ore to speak of; the mill has never made a profit, but it's still there on the east end of town).

**Centro di Documentazione sul Patrimonio Industriale**
*t 0744 428753; open July and Aug Mon 9–12 and 4–7, Tues–Fri 4–7; rest of year Mon, Tues and Thurs 9–12 and 4–7, Wed and Fri 4–7, Sat and Sun 9–12; adm*

The **Industrial Heritage Documentation Centre** offers guided tours on themes such as 'The City Factories' and 'The Culture and Conditions of a Worker's Life'. Before the First World War, Terni employed a third of Umbria's workforce, and what was an insignificant medieval town before Unification became Umbria's second city after Perugia. In the 1920s Terni scientists created the first practical plastic. Terni also has the State arms factory (the rifle that killed John Kennedy was made here); these three industries together were enough of an attraction in the last war for Allied air forces to smash the place. They also keep Terni ardently Communist, the heart of Red Umbria, and a fun place to be on 1 May for a parade of humorous floats made by towns in the province.

For the past few years, Terni has hosted an Easter holiday instalment of the Umbrian Jazz Festival, with an emphasis on gospel and spirituals. It has taken a new pride in its industrial past: the mills, employing over 2,000, though recent lay-offs have hit

## Getting to and around Terni

The SS209 from Terni to Visso is the main route of the upper Valnerina; you can reach Norcia and Cascia by turning off at Sant'Anatolia di Narco or Triponzo (the latter offers prettier routes). Both towns have frequent SSIT buses (*www.spoletina.com*) to Spoleto. From Terni, ATC **buses, t** 0744 492711, *www.atcterni.it*, leave from the park near the station to go to Narni, the Cascata delle Marmore (bus 21), Piediluco (bus 24), Arrone, Ferentillo, Spoleto, Orvieto, Viterbo and Scheggino; another bus picks up passengers along the SS209 daily to Rome.

Terni is the terminus of the FCU **train** line (*www.fcu.it/www.trenitalia.com*) through Todi, Perugia and Città di Castello to Sansepolcro, **t** 0744 59741, and a stop on the FS's Rome–Ancona line, though from Rome you often have to change at Orte; travelling from Assisi and the east usually requires a change at Foligno.

For **bike hire**, contact Blob Service, Via G. di Pergamo 66, **t** 0744 287686, *www.cuoreverde.com*.

hard, and specializing in stainless and other speciality steels, have been tarted up. Major intersections and *piazze* are decorated with imposing rusty chunks of raw industrial art. And as Italian film-makers grow estranged from the high costs and confabulations of Rome and Cinecittà they are falling into the seductive clasp of Terni: cheap, spacious and just over an hour's drive from the capital. Some of Italy's best special effects gizmos and wizardry are concentrated in the increasingly important **Centro Multimediale di Terni**, which lent its support to Roberto Benigni's *Pinocchio* and *Life is Beautiful*, much of which was shot in the suburb of Papigno.

### St Valentine's City

During the building of the steelworks, bulldozers uncovered an important Iron Age necropolis, and the mysterious Umbrii Naharkum were here around 7th century BC. Terni's name derives from their *Interamna Nahars* (from *inter amnes*, 'between two rivers', namely the confluence of the Nera and the torrential Serra). *Interamna* was conquered by the Romans in the 3rd century BC, and grew into a major station along the newer, easterly route of the Via Flaminia. It was traditionally considered the birthplace of the historian Tacitus, although scholars now quibble that Terni's was a more meagre Tacitus, Claudius Tacitus, one of the many Roman emperors for a day.

More certainly identified with the city is its first bishop, the martyred St Valentine, beheaded in 273. Several stories attempt to explain how he became the patron saint of lovers: one claims he miraculously united a 4th-century Romeo and Juliet, a Christian and a pagan (who converted after matrimony); another that his feast day coincided with the traditional mating day of Umbrian birds. He was buried in a cemetery 2km south of the centre, where the first chapel was built; in the 17th century this was rebuilt rather modestly as the **Basilica di San Valentino**. Valentine's mummified head was stolen in 1986 but found three years later, unharmed, wrapped in newspaper under a park bench at the Cascata delle Marmore. Until then, the city seemed unaware of its patron's fame abroad. Now, on 14 February, it hosts the traditional Mass, market and fireworks, a full range of international chocs and schlock, and a jewellery exhibition and prize for the best piece dedicated to St Valentine. An 'Act of Love' prize is solemnly awarded by the city to a person or organization who has performed one (in 1996 it was dedicated to the memory of Itzhak Rabin), and modern lovers have an all-night Latino dance party.

## In the Heart of the City of Love

Much of the rest of Terni has relatively little to show in spite of a history of more than 2,500 years. The post-war rebuilding, however, was left in the expert hands of architect Mario Ridolfi (d. 1984) who, after working on the reconstruction of Rome, moved here and laid out Terni's more pleasant residential districts, filling in the gaps left by the bombs. Of Roman Terni only part of the **amphitheatre** (32 AD) remains, in the south of the city near the pretty public gardens, where gladiators once tussled to the death before a crowd of 10,000, and pensioners now play *bocce*.

**Pinacoteca Comunale**
*Palazzo Gazzoli, Via del Teatro Romano 16, t 0744 459421, pinacoteca@ ternimusei.it; open Tues–Sun 10–1 and 4–7; adm*

The **Pinacoteca Comunale** has a lot of paintings by Anonymous (a strange 16th-century *Circumcision*; a portrait of St Charles Borromeo, a light of the Counter-Reformation here almost caricatured, with an enormous nose; and, in the same Counter-Reformation vein, a nightmarish scene of Franciscan martyrdoms in the Low Countries). The highlight is a *Marriage of St Catherine* from 1466 by Benozzo Gozzoli, inspired by Beato Angelico, and there is also a triptych, *The Madonna, Child and Saints*, by Pier Matteo d'Amelia, a gonfalon from Siena and a *Crucifixion* painted by L'Alunno, a triptych by the late 14th-century Maestro della Dormitio di Terni, and small works by Chagall, Picasso, Carrà, Severini, Mirò, Kandinsky and Léger. Best of all, there's a large collection of works by Terni's own **Orneore Metelli** (1872–1938), a shoemaker who spent his evenings painting, as Bernard Berenson said, the most naive of naive art. The two rooms of his paintings alone make a trip to this industrial city worthwhile, with their disarming, colourful scenes of Terni, its steel mill and its surroundings, of shoemakers, of Mussolini's motorcade, of Dante, and even of the Venus of Terni.

**Duomo**
*open daily 9–12 and 3.30–7*

Nearby, the **Duomo**, which was founded in the 6th century, rebuilt in the 12th and redone in the 17th, has a handsome portico and a pair of original portals, the front one topped with a 12th-century frieze. The interior has an elaborate high altar and a *Circumcision* by Livio Agresti. The 10th-century crypt, with its Roman columns and altar, was restored in 1904. In the cathedral square is a fountain and Terni's most elegant palace, the **Palazzo Bianchini-Riccardi**, both 16th century.

From here, Via Aminale leads around to Terni's old main street, **Via Roma**, where a number of *palazzi* survived the bombing; a towerhouse marks the crossroads. Turn left here into Piazza Europa; at the south end is the massive **Palazzo Spada** (1546) by Antonio da Sangallo the Younger, perhaps his least inspired effort (some scholars have absolved him from all responsibility), now used as the town hall. To its right is the charming round church of

**San Salvatore**
*open daily 9–12 and 4–6*

**San Salvatore** the oldest building in Terni, from the 5th century, which may have been a Roman temple to the Sun. In the 12th century, a nave and some frescoes were added.

From Piazza Europa, Via Cavour leads past the severe medieval **Palazzo Mezzancolli** back to Via Febbraio; off this is the Knights of St John's 12th-century church of **Sant'Alò**, with a pretty exterior, incorporating Roman and medieval fragments. Turn off onto Via Fratini, follow it north to Via Noblini and turn left for 13th-century

**San Francesco**
*open daily 8–12.30 and 3.30–7.30*

**San Francesco** Its landmark campanile with colourful ceramic edgings (1345) is by Angelo da Orvieto; in the Cappella Paradisi are the Dominican friar Bartolomeo di Tommaso's fascinating restored 15th-century frescoes based on Hell, Purgatory and Paradise as described in the *Divine Comedy*.

Piazza della Repubblica is the starting point for modern Terni's main thoroughfare, **Corso Tacito**, which passes through the piazza of the same name, where there's a fountain by Mario Ridolfi (1932) with mosaics of astrological signs. From Piazza della Repubblica the Corso Vecchio passes other signs of medieval Terni, around to

**San Pietro in Trivio**
*open daily 8–12 and 3.30–7.30*

**San Pietro in Trivio** a church that was built in the 14th century and rebuilt in the 1700s and again after the war, yet somehow retains some original frescoes. Nearby **Palazzo Carrara** is a 17th-century reconstruction of a medieval palace; its Iron Age artefacts found under the steel mills are now in the

**Museo Archeologico**
*Via Lungonera Savoia t 0744 221801; open Tues–Sun 10–1 and 4–7; adm*

**Museo Archeologico** Another church along Corso Vecchio, **San Lorenzo** has Terni's oddest interior, with one short and one tall nave, and a good 16th-century painting on the martyrdom of San Biagio. Opposite are a set of medieval towerhouses, the **Case dei Castelli**.

**San Lorenzo**
*open daily 9–12.30 and 4–7*

**Santa Maria del Monumento**
*open daily 8.30–9.30am*

**Santa Maria del Monumento** is west near the cemetery, 1.5km along the extension of Via Cavour (Viale di Porta Sant'Angelo); partly built from a Roman funerary monument, it was enlarged in 1474. Inside, frescoes depict the legend of the golden apples, and there is an early 16th-century *presepio*.

## Around Terni

Overlooking Terni to the southwest is medieval hilltop **Collescipoli**. Long a defensive outpost of the city, it is now being engulfed in urban sprawl. Among its churches, **Santa Maria Maggiore** has a handsome Renaissance door and one of the most beautiful Baroque interiors in Umbria, and an unusual painting on the death of St Joseph. There are some popular votive frescoes and a *Coronation of the Virgin* (1507) painted by Evangelista Aquili in the church of **San Nicola da Bari**. The **church of Santo Stefano** has an odd bell tower, a *Crucifixion* and an inscription from 1093.

The pretty, old walled village of **Stroncone** lies at the crossroads 8km south of Terni, leading to a series of alpine meadows and chestnut forests called **I Prati**. Here there are grand views over Terni's plain from the highest point, **Cimitelle** (840m).

## The Cascata delle Marmore and Lago di Piediluco

Terni, appropriately enough as the city of St Valentine, has its own Niagara Falls for honeymooners: the 126m green and misty **Cascata delle Marmore**. Falling in three stages, this is one of Europe's tallest, most beautiful waterfalls – when it's running. Surprisingly, the Cascata is an artificial creation, albeit an ancient one. In 271 BC Curius Dentatus, conqueror of the Sabines, dug a channel to drain the marshlands of Rieti, diverting the river Velino into the Nera. Although the falls are usually swallowed up by hydroelectric turbines, the thundering waters are let down at regular times, and illuminated after dark. The surrounding area is open for picnics except in December and January.

There are two places from which to view the falls – the Belvedere Inferiore below on the SS209 (with a large car park, a tourist pavilion and a dozen *porchetta* vans, just beyond the tunnel) and the Belvedere Superiore, in the village of Marmore. A path through the woods connects the two, although it's steep, muddy in the off season, and much nicer to walk down than up (the path at the bottom begins 100m downstream from the falls). There are some pleasant places to swim near the bottom, but you can't use them when the falls are on (the siren sounds 15 minutes before the falls are turned on to warn swimmers).

For guided canoeing and rafting down the Corno and Nera rivers, contact **Centro Canoa e Rafting Le Marmore**.

Up near Marmore, lovely **Lago di Piediluco** zigzags in and out of wooded hills, crowned by a 12th-century fortress. There are a couple of beaches but the water is cold and a bit dirty, and has dangerous undercurrents. There are other diversions; the lake has become the capital of sport rowing in Italy and the site of international competitions. On its shores, the medieval village and modest resort of **Piediluco**, named after a sacred Roman grove of trees (*lucus*), has a fine late-13th-century church, **San Francesco**, up a flight of steps. The bricked-up door has a striking frieze decorated with knots and lions; inside are 16th-century frescoes, among them a *Madonna and Two Saints* by Marcantonio di Antoniazzo. The stoup was a Roman capital and there's a Roman statue of a lady in a niche. Above the church is a ruined castle (1364) by Cardinal Albornoz.

**⓲ Cascata delle Marmore**
*t 0744 62982; top and bottom of falls easily reached by bus from Terni 6km west, www.marmore.it; falls let down on following schedule: Jan: Sat and Sun 12–1 and 3–4; Feb: Sat and Sun 11–1 and 3–5; Mar: Mon–Fri 12–1 and 4–5, Sat and Sun 11–1 and 4–9; April: Mon–Fri 12–1 and 4–5, Sat and Sun 10–1 and 4–9; May: Mon–Fri 12–1 and 4–5, Sat and Sun 10–1 and 3–10; June–Aug: Mon–Fri 11–1, 4–6 and 9–10pm, Sat and Sun 10–1 and 3–10; Sept: Mon–Fri 12–1, 4–5 and 8–9pm, Sat and Sun 10–1 and 3–10; Oct: Fri 3–5, Sat–Sun 11–1 and 3–7; Nov and Dec: Sat and Sun 12–1 and 3–4; adm*

**Centro Canoa e Rafting Le Marmore**
*t 330 753420, www.raftingmarmore.com*

High above the east shore of the lake is lovely **Labro**, former nest of noblemen on the run, now colonized by Belgians after a Belgian architect bought and restored the village. Below the lake, the Arrone road passes **Villalago**, which has an outdoor theatre for summer events and lovely grounds for picnicking.

## Shopping in Terni

**Post office**: Piazza Solferino, t 0744 546711, *www.poste.it*
**Market day**: Wed, off Piazza Briccialdi, near the stadium.

## Where to Stay in and around Terni

ⓘ **Terni >**
*Via C. Battisti,*
*t 0744 423047,*
*www.regioneumbria.eu*
*(closed Sun)*

**Terni** ✉ 05100

This is a good base for the Valnerina if you're relying on public transport.

**\*\*\*\*Valentino**, Via Plinio il Giovane 5, t 0744 402550, *www.hotelvalentinoterni. it* (€€€). A central option with comfy modern rooms (breakfast included), all air conditioned (important here in summer), and one of Terni's classiest restaurants, La Fontanella (*see* right). Half and full board are available. Internet access and babysitting.

**\*\*\*Garden**, Viale Bramante 6, t 0744 300041, *www.gardenhotelterni.it* (€€€). Terni's prettiest hotel, near the motorway exit, with plant-filled balconies, a pool, a sauna and rooms with all the usual mod cons (breakfast included). There's also babysitting, an Internet point and a restaurant (half and full board available).

**\*\*\*Hotel de Paris**, Viale Stazione 52, t 0744 58047, *www.hoteldeparis.it* (€€). A decent option right by the station. Breakfast is included in the rates and there's an excellent restaurant, which specializes in fish (€€€).

**\*\*\*Allegretti**, Strada dello Staino 7b, t 0744 426747, *hotelallegretti@ virgilio.it* (€). Comfy en-suite rooms with balconies amid greenery.

**\*\*\*Brenta II**, Via Montegrappa 51, t 0744 273957 (€). En-suite modern rooms in a shady neighbourhood near the Nera and Corso del Popolo. There's an Internet point.

**\*\*\*Vecchia Osteria**, Loc. Valle Spolentina, just below Villalago, t 0744 369111, *www.vecchiaosteria.it* (€).

A recommended alternative to staying in town, up at Lake Piediluco, with simple rooms in a traditional Umbrian style, with iron beds. The restaurant (€€) serves seasonal local fare. *Closed Mon, and lunch in winter.*

## Eating Out in and around Terni

Viparo, the local *aperitivo*, has all the charm of flat rum and cola.

**Terni** ✉ 05100

**La Fontanella**, Valentino hotel, Via Plinio il Giovane 3, t 0744 402550 (€€€). Tasty and imaginative dishes featuring fresh, natural ingredients.

**Villa Graziani**, Via Villavalle 11, Papigno, 4km from centre, t 0744 67138 (€€€). An 18th-century place once graced by Byron, offering seasonal cuisine (you have to pre-order fish dishes). *Closed Sun eve, Mon and 2nd half Aug.*

**La Piazzetta**, Via Cavour 9, t 0744 58188 (€€). Marinated fish *antipasti*, lamb *cacciatora* with potatoes and so on. *Closed Sun and 2wks Aug.*

**Lu Somaru**, Viale Cesare Battisti 106, t 0744 300208 (€€). A popular choice for Umbrian specialities. *Closed Fri.*

### Stroncone ✉ 05039

**Taverna di Portanova**, t 0744 60496 (€€). A family-run spot in an old cloister, with good *scottadito*, grilled meats, soup and pizzas. *Closed Wed, lunch exc Sun, 1wk Jan, 1st half Aug.*

### Piediluco ✉ 05038

**Ristorante Eco**, Corso IV Novembre 12, Piediluco, t 0744 368124 (€€€). A beautiful terrace overlooking the lake makes this a good choice. Specialities include imaginative dishes using lake fish, though seafood is also available.

**L'Amaca all'Eco**, Localita Montagna dell'Eco, t 0744 368555 or t 335 5700552 (€€). This lovely restaurant, on the far side of the lake, is best reached by water, using the free boat service available to ferry guests to and from the village of Piediluco. Pizzas and a limited but good range of pasta dishes and *secondi* are available. *Closed Oct–May.*

⭐ **Peppe Scappa** >

**Peppe Scappa**, Vocabolo Algerini 7, over lake on Arrone road, **t** 0744 368416 (€€). Some of the tastiest and

best-priced Umbrian cuisine in the area, and great valley views. *Closed Mon.*

**Tavoletta**, Vocabolo Forca 4, off the SS79, **t** 0744 368196 (€€). A lakeside venue with a seasonal menu based largely on its fish: try trout with peppers. *Closed Mon, and some wks June–Oct.*

# The Upper Valnerina

The further you head up the Valnerina, the more wild and beautiful the scenery becomes, and the tastier the truffles. The Parco Naturale del Nera begins at the Cascata delle Marmore. This part of Umbria had just about finished repairs, after tremors in 1979, when the 1997 earthquake caused fresh damage. Some villages are still undergoing repairs.

## Arrone and Ferentillo

After the Cascata delle Marmore, the SS209 passes beneath the pretty townlets of **Torreorsina** and **Casteldilago** before arriving at the more substantial and picturesque market village of **Arrone**, spilling over its isolated rock. In the centre, the church of **Santa Maria** has remarkably good frescoes, including a *Life of the Virgin*, by Vincenzo Tamagni and Giovanni di Spoleto, inspired by Lippo Lippi's work in Spoleto's Duomo. The *Madonna della Misericordia* (1544) by Jacopo Siculo is to the right of the main altar, and there's a *Supper at Emmaus* by Caravaggio's school. In the apse left of the altar is a Renaissance terracotta, *The Madonna Suckling the Child, Between Two Saints*.

In the old days, Arrone and its neighbours indulged in fierce warfare. The *signori* of Arrone, who built the landmark tower on top of the town (with a tree growing out of it), were bitter enemies of the lords of Polino. A pretty 10km drive along a winding road, passing under the great white arch of a Mussolini-built aqueduct, the Ponte Canale, at **Rosciano**, brings you to **Polino**, Umbria's tiniest *comune*. It, too, has its feudal tower, as well as a monumental Baroque fountain and a road up to the **Colle Bertone** (1,223m), a modest winter sports resort and summer picnic area.

**Santo Stefano**
*t 0743 54395;*
*open daily Mar and*
*Oct 9.30–12.30 and*
*2.30–6.30, April–Sept*
*9–12.30 and 2.30–7.30,*
*Nov–Feb 10–12.30*
*and 2.30–5; adm*

The biggest rivals of the lords of Arrone were the powerful abbots of **Ferentillo**, the next town up the Valnerina, guarded by twin 14th-century citadels on rocks that dominate the narrow valley like matching bookends; their sheer walls are popular with rock-climbers. In Precetto, the oldest quarter, the **crypt of Santo Stefano** contains **mummies**, accidentally preserved by a microfungus in the soil, complete with brown papery skin and organs, hair, whiskers, teeth and even eyeballs in some cases, and displayed in shiny glass cases. Among them are Chinese newlyweds who came here more than 100 years ago on a pilgrimage to Rome and got cholera; two French prisoners hanged in the Napoleonic wars; a woman who died of bubonic plague; a lawyer stabbed 27 times and one of his murderers; and an eagle, placed here as an experiment and perfectly mummified in less than a year.

## San Pietro in Valle

**3 San Pietro in Valle**
*church open daily summer 9.30–6, winter 10–12, but call ahead, t 0744 780316; custodian's house clearly marked on road up to abbey*

The former Benedictine abbey of Ferentillo, San Pietro in Valle, is 4km up the valley on the lovely slopes of Monte Solenne. You won't find a more charming abbey to visit, or stay in – it's been converted into a *residenza d'epoca*. Founded *c.* 710 by the duke of Spoleto, Faraoldo II, it is on the site of a Syrian hermitage from the 6th century, and has an ornate 12th-century campanile embedded with 8th-century fragments, in a style more common to Rome than Umbria.

The church is full of rare treasures. The nave is covered with restored **frescoes** from 1190, a rare and important early example of

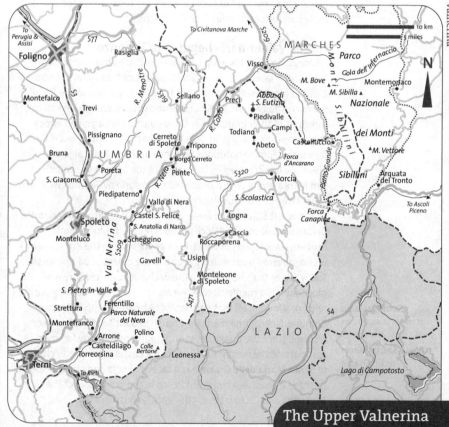

The Upper Valnerina

the Italian response to the Byzantine style – here already moving away from the stylized hierarchy to a more natural 'Latin style' where figures are individuals rather than types; the only comparable frescoes of the period are in the Roman church of San Giovanni a Porta Latina. The left wall has Old Testament scenes (note 'Adam Naming the Animals' and 'Noah'), and there are New Testament scenes on the right. The high **altar** (*c.* 740) is a rare example of Lombard work, sculpted front and back, with a self-portrait of the sculptor, signed Ursus Magester. The apse contains good 13th-century frescoes, with a pretty *Madonna* by the school of Giotto. At the back is a cylindrical altar said to be Etruscan. Among the stone fragments on the wall is a real rarity – a bas-relief of a monk with oriental features, believed to be one of the two Syrian monks who set up a hermitage here. The side door is usually open so you can peek into the charming two-storey **cloister**, built in the 12th century, where the hotel rooms are; the two 11th-century figures guarding the door of the church are Peter and Paul.

The views extend across the valley to the abandoned citadel of **Umbriano**, legendary first village of Umbria. If you walk up there, be sure to make a lot of noise to scare off any unexpected vipers. It makes an unforgettable place for a picnic.

## Up the Valnerina: Scheggino to Triponzo

**Scheggino**, next town up the valley, occupies both banks of the Nera and is laced with tiny canals full of trout and a rare species of crayfish (*gamberettini*) imported from Turkey; it is also the fief of Italy's truffle tycoons, Paolo and Bruno Urbani, who thanks to the foresight of their grandfather Carlo control about 70 percent of the Valnerina's black gold. Scheggino has 12th-century walls that famously repelled notorious brigand Girolamo Brancaleoni in 1522. There are late frescoes by Lo Spagna in the apse of the **church of San Nicolò**, along with a *Madonna del Rosario* by Pierino Cesari and other late-16th-century works.

On the left bank of the Nera, 3km from Scheggino, **Sant'Anatolia di Narco** is another bailiwick of the black truffle. In the 19th century, a necropolis of Naharkum going back to the 8th century BC was discovered here, making it one of the oldest of all Umbrii sites. Today fewer than 600 people live within its 14th-century walls. Its glory days as a medieval *comune* are recalled in an archway with a relief of a knight, all that survives of the 13th-century Palazzo del Comune. Nearby, the medieval church of **Sant'Anatolia** has been restored since the quake, revealing fragments of early frescoes. Just outside the west gate, the Porta di Castello, the pretty church of **Santa Maria delle Grazie** has a façade of 1572 and popular votive frescoes, as well as a beautiful fresco in the presbytery of the Madonna and Child by the 15th-century Master of Eggi.

**Sant'Anatolia**
*if locked, ask at house next door for key*

**Santa Maria delle Grazie**
*keyholder for Sant' Anatolia will show you to priest's house for key*

Just up from Sant'Anatolia, medieval **Castel San Felice** is a pretty little hamlet on its hill, restored after 1979. The delightful 12th-century **abbey church of San Felice in Narco** is on an unpaved road at the foot of the village; there is a great picnic spot just beyond it, by the little bridge over the Nera. The façade has an intricate rose window surrounded by Evangelist symbols, sculpted columns and capitals, Cosmatesque decoration and reliefs on the life of St Felice, who moved here with his father Mauro from Palestine in the 5th century. Locals were having serious problems with a dragon; with the help of an angel, Felice dispatched it and performed other miracles. When he died, Mauro built an oratory over his grave. The interior is equally beautiful, with a pair of *transennae* with Cosmatesque remains and some early 15th-century frescoes. The crypt contains the ancient sarcophagus of St Mauro and St Felice.

**San Felice in Narco**
*t 0743 613427; key held at Via Orichelle 34*

High over the left bank of the Nera, walled medieval **Vallo di Nera** has fortified walls, twisting steep cobbled streets, covered alleys, little piazzas and stone houses, all immaculately restored, and two churches with frescoes. One is the 13th-century **Santa Maria** with a Gothic portal and frescoes by Cola di Pietro from Camerino and Francesco di Antonio, painted in 1383; other frescoes are votive and feature some delightful pigs. Even better are the beautifully coloured frescoes in pink and white **San Giovanni Battista** at the top of the village; these, on the life of the Virgin (1536), are by Pinturicchio's assistant, Jacopo Siculo.

**Santa Maria**
*key from house through gate left of church, by fountain*

**San Giovanni Battista**
*key kept next door, or ask any local*

This upper part of the Valnerina has been less remote since the opening of a road and tunnel from Spoleto to Piedipaterno, replacing the old narrow winding road. The next village, **Borgo Cerreto**, lies at an important crossroads and has a late-13th-century Franciscan church, **San Lorenzo**. Above it, on a high hill, tiny **Ponte** overlooks the confluence of the Tissino and the Nera. In the 9th century, this village was a major Lombard stronghold ruling both Cascia and Norcia. The views are lovely, and the **Pieve di Santa Maria Assunta** (1201) has a beautifully carved rose window with symbols of the Evangelists and a *telemon* on its tall façade, and a fine apse decorated with hanging arches and funny little heads. The handsome restored interior contains ancient fragments, a fine pavement and some damaged frescoes by the Umbrian school. From here, it is a steep but pretty walk up to the ruined castle.

**Pieve di Santa Maria Assunta**
*custodian's house in Via Nortosce*

Across the valley and just off the main road, **Cerreto di Spoleto** sits high on its spur, offering splendid views towards Ponte. This was the birthplace of the humanist and Latin poet Giovanni Pontano (1426–1503), better known as Pontanus. While he was attending university in Perugia, his family's home in Cerreto was burned down, so he went to live with relatives in Naples, advising the court and running the literary academy that was later to take his name, the Accademia Pontana. Cerreto has a number of fine *palazzi*, as well as a pretty main piazza with a 15th-century **Palazzo Comunale** and fountain; just beyond is the tall 15th-century **Torre Civica**. The churches here were all damaged in 1997, though most of the restoration is now complete. **San Giacomo** on the edge of the hill has beautiful 15th-century frescoes.

**Triponzo**, last Umbrian village in the Valnerina, was the epicentre of the 1979 quake but is now inhabited again. The road continues on to Pontechiusita, and from there, you can pick up the road to Preci and Norcia (*see* pp.248–52).

## Towards Monteleone di Spoleto and Cascia from Sant'Anatolia

A spectacular mountain road rises east of Sant'Anatolia di Narco to the hamlet of **Caso**, with interesting churches: **Santa Maria delle Grazie** with some frescoes by the school of Lo Spagna; and, outside the village, Romanesque **Santa Cristina**, with frescoes dating from the 14th–16th centuries.

**Santa Maria delle Grazie/ Santa Cristina**
*ask in village for keys to both churches*

Further along, the road rises and rises to **Gavelli** (1,152m), a tiny village on the cliff, home to the 15th-century church of **San Michele Arcangelo**, beautifully frescoed by Lo Spagna and his school. The remote hamlet of **Usigni**, signposted off the main road, has a remarkable 17th-century Roman–Baroque church, **San Salvatore**, attributed to Bernini. It was commissioned by Fausto Poli, who was born here and became a cardinal in the court of Urban VIII; he is best remembered for promoting the beatification of St Rita.

**San Michele Arcangelo**
*key kept next to door*

Further south, high above the Corno valley, remote little **Monteleone di Spoleto** has a pretty setting that has been inhabited for centuries: a large 6th-century BC cemetery on the road from Usigni, discovered in 1902, yielded a wooden chariot of Etruscan manufacture, decorated with magnificent bronze reliefs of the life of Achilles (now in the Metropolitan Museum in New York and a source of bitter contention with the locals). Monteleone was ruled by Spoleto until 1559 but suffered earthquakes in 1703 and 1979. In the upper part of town, a couple of fine quattrocento *palazzi* and a porticoed **Palazzo dei Priori** are testimony to its former importance. Here, too, is the massive 13th-century church and **convent of San Francesco**, with a beautiful Gothic door. The restored interior has a fine high altar, an 18th-century painted ceiling decorated with symbols of the Madonna and fascinating remains of 15th-century frescoes, especially a magnificent *Christ in Majesty*. The arcaded cloister has more frescoes, as does the lower church, with a good one of St Anthony Abbot and animals.

For stupendous views over much of southern Umbria, take the remote SS471 south through the mountains to Leonessa in Lazio and follow the signs west to Labro, Lake Piediluco and the Cascata della Marmore near Terni.

## Activities in the Upper Valnerina

**Fiume Corno**, t 348 351 1798, *www. raftingumbria.it*. Rafting, kayaking, hydrospeed, hiking and mountainbike tours in the Valnerina and an impressive aerial walkway, with rope bridges strung through the treetops.

**Valnerina Verticale Sport**, Piazza Vittorio Emanuele 9, Ferentillo, t 0744 780003. Rock-climbing at various levels around Ferentillo, Montefranco and Arrone.

## Where to Stay and Eat in the Upper Valnerina

### Arrone ✉ 05031

**\*\*/\*\*\*Rossi**, Loc. Isola 7, on SS209, t 0744 388372, *www.rossihotelristorante. it* (€). Modern ensuite rooms (breakfast included), a nice pool and a good restaurant (€€), offering tasty river shrimps and more, served in a pretty garden in summer. Book ahead for the deservedly popular Thursday seafood feasts. *Closed Fri.*

**Locanda Paradiso**, Via del Colle Buonacquisto 9, t 0744 368526 (€). A few simple rooms with baths, and a restaurant for reliable pizza and other basic fare (€23).

### Ferentillo ✉ 05034

**Abbazia San Pietro in Valle**, Case Sparse 4, Loc. Macenano, t 0744 780129, *www.sanpietroinvalle.com* (€€€). Well-furnished, comfortable rooms, some with frescoes, in the old monks' quarters of a former abbey (breakfast included). There's also a solarium, sauna, Internet point and restaurant serving typical local fare (€€€). *Closed Nov–Mar.*

**Il Borgo**, Via S. Anselmo 1, Ferentillo t 0744 780186, *www.ilborgo-countryhouse.it* (€€). A pleasant alternative to a hotel, this small family-run establishment has a few attractive en-suite rooms and an apartment for families.

**\*\*\*Monterivoso**, Via Case Sparse 5, Loc. Monterivoso on mummy road (*see* p.240), t 0744 780772, *www. monterivoso.it* (€€). A converted mill

with simple rooms with great views, a lovely garden and a good restaurant (€€). Half/full board available.

**Il Capanno**, Localita' Torrecola-Acquaiura 6, t 0743 54119 (€€€). You can reach this restaurant via the winding back roads from Ferentillo (follow the road for Ancaiano) or by taking a right turn off the main Terni–Spoleto road (restaurant is signposted). Either way, it's worth the trek, as the setting, with a big well-kept garden and a huge fireplace inside, is sublime and the food is memorable. *Popular with locals so book ahead and ask for directions.*

**Piermarini**, Via Ancaiano 23, t 0744 780714 (€€€). Wonderful local dishes; try rabbit with lentils and sage, and duck breast in balsamic vinegar with radicchio. *Closed Sun eve and Mon.*

**Ai Tre Archi**, on SS. Valnerina 29km, t 0744 780004 (€€). Good workaday pasta dishes, such as *gnocchi al sugo di pecora*, and pizza, plus four simple rooms. *Closed Mon.*

**Pizzeria Collestatte**, Collestatt, t 0744 62625. Up mountain from Montefranco towards Spoleto (signposted at pass) (€€). Delicious pizzas smothered in rocket, and views over the lower Valnerina. *Booking essential. Closed Mon in winter.*

### Montefranco ✉ 05030

**Roccaranne** Via del Palazzo 10, Montefranco, t 0744 388338 (€€). A very pretty hotel in the beautifully restored *centro storico* of Montefranco, a few kms up the hill from Ferentillo, this makes a good base for visiting the area. There is also a restaurant, with lovely views (€€).

### Scheggino ✉ 06040

**\*\* Del Ponte** Via Borgo 15, t 0743 61253, *www.bellaumbria.net/hotel-delponte* (€€). A charming hotel on the Nera, with mainly en-suite rooms and delicious meals (€€) based on river shrimps, trout and truffles. *Closed Mon.*

### Sant'Anatolia di Narco ✉ 06040

**\*\*Tre Valli**, Strada Valnerina, t 0743 613385 (€). A place offering simple rooms and typical Umbrian cuisine (€€). Half/full board available.

⭐ Roccaranne >>

ⓘ Ferentillo >
*Comune,*
*Via della Vittoria,*
*t 0744 780521, www.*
*comune.ferentillo.tr.it*
*and Pro-Loco,*
*t 0744 780990*
*(closed mornings)*

⭐ Del Ponte >>

# Cascia

The narrow SS471 running north from Monteleone takes you to the top of Cascia (population 4,000), a hill town that sees more pilgrims than truffles; more, in fact, than any Umbrian town except Assisi. Santa Rita, the 'Saint of Impossibilities', was born near here in 1381 but had to wait until 1900 to be canonized, then hold on until the inauspicious period of 1937–47 for her sanctuary. Poor Rita! After a wretched marriage to a roughneck, who was killed by his enemies, she persuaded her two sons not to take vengeance; when they died soon afterwards of disease, she became a nun, only to develop such a foul-smelling sore on her forehead that none of the sisters would come near her. Then she received the Stigmata and spent the rest of her life in pain.

Cascia itself has similarly known more than its fair share of bad luck. Originally Roman *Cursula*, it was wiped out by an earthquake and refounded on a different site. That didn't stop other earthquakes periodically destroying it, in 1599, 1703 and 1979. The Lombards and Saracens sacked it in the three digit years. Afterwards, Cascia was a freewheeling *comune* like the others, sometimes under Spoleto's sway, sometimes under that of the Emperor or the Trinci family in Foligno. When it came under the Church with the rest of Umbria in 1516, it rebelled but was quickly put in its place.

**Basilica di Santa Rita da Cascia**
*www.santaritada cascia.org; open daily Mar 7–6.30, April 6.30am–7.30pm, May–Sept 6.30am–8pm, Oct 6.30am–7pm, Nov–Feb 7–6; Monastero t 0743 76221; open for guided tours daily April 8–4, May–Sept 8–6, Oct 8.30–4.30, Nov–Mar 10–4*

## The Basilica of Santa Rita

This proto-Disney castle with a pseudo-Byzantine interior and ghastly frescoes has been described as the most vulgar basilica in all Christendom. Rita's dried-up body is on display in a glass coffin, surrounded by votive offerings from the Terni and Rome football clubs; every year tens of thousands of unhappily married women and victims of bad luck come here to pray for relief. The art inserted into the basilica, the high altar by Giacomo Manzù, doesn't really stand a chance.

The **Monastero di Santa Rita**, left of the basilica, marks the spot where she spent here 40 years as a nun, the 15th-century cloister, her cell and miraculous rose bush.

**Museo Comunale di Palazzo Santi**
*Via G. Palombi, t 0743 751010; 18 Mar–April Sat, Sun and hols 10.30–1 and 3–6; May, June and 1–18 Sept Fri–Sun and hols 10.30–1 and 3–6; Aug and 24 Dec–6 Jan daily 10.30–1 and 3–6; 19 Sept–6 Nov Sat and Sun 10.30–1 and 3–6; adm, inc Sant'Antonio Abate*

## The Rest of Town

Other spots around Cascia receive less devotion but offer a good deal more substance in the art department. The **Museo Comunale di Palazzo Santi**, which is located within a 17th-century palace, has an archaeological collection and a number of works of art that were taken from the town's churches, including some beautiful early medieval wooden sculpture. You can also see a lovely carved doorway and rose window on the Gothic **church of San Francesco** in nearby Piazza Garibaldi; it's worth venturing inside for the

## Getting to Cascia

The Società Spoletina, t 0743 212211, *www.spoletina.com*, runs **buses** from Norcia, Spoleto, Terni, Foligno and Perugia to Cascia.

---

frescoes dating from the 15th and 16th centuries, a fancy Baroque pulpit, the Gothic choirstalls and the last painting by Niccolò Pomarancio, an *Ascension* (1596).

There are some more good frescoes, together with a pretty 14th-century statue of the Virgin and Child, in the nearby **Collegiata di Santa Maria**, a large church that was founded in 856 but reconstructed several times; one of the Romanesque lions that held up a porch is now a fountain, while the other peers out from a niche over the door.

**Sant'Antonio Abate**
*open same hrs as Palazzo Santi (see opposite)*

Below Piazza Garibaldi, the austere church of **Sant'Antonio Abate** forms part of the Museo Comunale. Despite frequent earthquake repairs over the course of centuries, it preserves in the apse a delightful 14th-century fresco cycle on the life of St Anthony Abbot, which has been attributed to the Maestro della Dormitio di Terni. The nun's choir contains another fine fresco cycle, on the passion of Christ (1461), by Nicola da Siena. Most beautiful of all is the painted 15th-century wooden statue, *The Archangel Raphael with Tobias*, by Antonio Rizzo's workshop.

### Around Cascia

Above Cascia (you need to follow signs for Monteleone) you can see the ruins of its 15th-century **citadel**, which was destroyed by the papal army after the town's revolt. Below this, the pink and white 14th-century **Convento di Sant'Agostino** has more good 15th-century frescoes.

The last site on the Rita trail is the saint's birthplace, at **Roccaporena**, 6km to the west of Cascia in the Corna valley. The setting, under a mighty rock that has been renamed the Scoglio della Preghiera (Cliff of Prayer) is exactly the kind of slightly otherworldly place in which you might expect a saint to be born. Rita's house was transformed into a church in 1630 by Cardinal Fausto Poli, chief promoter of her beatification; a little chapel crowns the big rock like a cap.

## Where to Stay and Eat in Cascia

**ⓘ Cascia >**
*Piazza Garibaldi,*
*t 0743 71147,*
*www.regioneumbria.eu*
*(closed Sun afternoon)*

Cascia ✉ 06043
***Cursula**, Via Cavour 3, t 0743 76206, *www.hotelcursula.com* (€€€). Pleasant and comfortable rooms with typical Umbrian furniture,

breakfast included, and Umbrian fare in the restaurant (€€). Half and full board offered.

**\*\*Mini Hotel La Tavernetta**, Via Palombi, t 0743 71387, *www.minihotellatavernetta.com* (€€). A family-run choice offering clean, comfortable en-suite rooms (with breakfast included in rates) and a restaurant (€€) where you can enjoy good *pappardelle* with wild boar, tagliatelle with mushrooms, grilled *pecorino* cheese, sausages with lentils, and mixed grills. Of the three tasting menus on offer, one is wholly

vegetarian. Half and full board are available. *Closed Tues.*

**Centrale**, Piazza Garibaldi 36, t 0743 76736 (€). En-suite rooms in a handy location. Breakfast is included in the room rate.

# Norcia and the Monti Sibillini

Here in its southeast corner, in the shadow of the Monti Sibillini, Umbria achieves its highest heights and widest open spaces. Norcia, in ancient times the northernmost of all Sabine towns, stands battered yet proud on its high plain, famous for its saint and its butchers. Because of the frequent earthquakes, an 18th-century law limited buildings to two storeys and the result is a town unlike any other in Umbria.

## Norcia

 ✪ **Norcia**

Old Norcia (population 4,900) or, as the gate reads, VETUSTA NURSIA, can seem bright and cheerful or morose and gloomy, barricaded like a Foreign Legion outpost in its 14th-century walls on the edge of the lofty **Piano di Santa Scolastica**, with mountains on all sides. Virgil called it *Frigida Nursia*, so one can imagine when he visited. But the last Roman emperor was still warm in his grave when this old, cold town offered the world St Benedict (480–543), father of Western monasticism.

During the Middle Ages, Norcia was a *comune* to be reckoned with. Nor was it long before the Nursini lost their early reputation for sanctity; they were known at various times for witchcraft (there was a sorcerers' college here in the Middle Ages, when *nursino* or *norcino* became synonymous with 'wizard'), as well as for its pork butchers and surgery. Practitioners of both of the latter were renowned for their expert knife work – after all, in the days when doing autopsies on cadavers was illegal, the famous surgeons of Preci (*see* p.252) practised on pigs. To this day, Norcia is synonymous with *prosciutto* (which is taken from both domestic pork and wild boar) and for having the best *norcinerie* in Umbria, as well as some fine cheeses.

As a sideline, the Nursini were also experts in the art of keeping male voices unnaturally pure and sweet – the parents of a boy with operatic potential would bring him to Norcia, where he would be drugged with opium and put in a very hot bath until he was quite insensible, when the dirty deed was done (the ducts leading to the testicles were severed so the organs would eventually shrivel and disappear). Too bad for the lad whose voice never made the grade,

# Getting to Norcia

Società Spoletina (t 0743 212211, *www.spoletina.com*) runs **buses** to Norcia from Spoleto, Cascia, Perugia, Terni, Foligno, Rome and Ascoli Piceno in the Marches.

---

but those who did became the darlings of society and quite wealthy besides. Some were such charming prima donnas that Casanova wasn't the only one to keep falling in love with them. One of the last 'graduates' of Norcia, Domenico Mustafa (d. 1912), was director of the Sistine Chapel choir and stayed long enough to cut the only recording by a *castrato*.

### Piazza San Benedetto

Norcia's history has been plagued by earthquakes: the one of 1328 destroyed the medieval city, and others in 1703, 1730, 1859 and 1979 all took their toll. However, the city escaped any damage in the 1997 earthquake.

The city's chief monuments are situated on the rounded Piazza San Benedetto, which is presided over by a stern statue of St Benedict dating from 1880. Directly behind stands the 13th-century Gothic **Basilica di San Benedetto**, with a charming portal, framed by statues of Benedict and Scholastica and painted angels, with a Madonna on top and a rose window. On the side of the church, a portico shelters 16th-century grain measures and ends at a sturdy campanile. The interior, remodelled in the 18th century, with unexceptional paintings and restored for the 2000 Jubilee, seems unduly modest for the shrine to the Patron Saint of Europe. In the crypt you can study the ruins of a late Roman house, which tradition says belonged to Europroprio Anicio and Abbondanza Reguardati, parents of twins Benedict and Scholastica, the first Western monk and nun.

The handsome **Palazzo Comunale**, also in the piazza, boasts a 13th-century campanile and portico of 1492, and a **Cappella dei Priori** containing a 15th-century silver reliquary of St Benedict. Next door and in the nearby streets are the boar and truffle gastronomic shops – Norcia's real attraction for Italians.

**Castellina**
*t 0743 817030; open Tues–Sun Oct–Mar 10–1 and 3–5, Apr–May 10–1 and 4–6, June–Sept 10–1 and 4–7.30*

The other side of the piazza is occupied by the square **Castellina**, built over the ruins of an ancient temple. Designed in 1554 for Pope Julius III by his favourite architect Vignola, its upper floor houses the **Museo Civico Diocesano**, with pretty and precious things, including a late-12th-century painted *Crucifixion* with the two Marys on either side of Christ, a not uncommon Romanesque conceit; there were originally two others but they fell off. Another remarkable *Cross*, signed Petrus, was made half a century later. There's a life-sized *Deposition* group in wood from Ruccataniburo, from the late 1200s, high reliefs of the Madonna and Child, and

**Museo Civico Diocesano**
*t 0743 817030; open June daily 10–1 and 4–7.30; rest of year Tues–Sun 10–1 and 4–6; adm*

**11** The Valnerina | Norcia

paintings of the same by Antonio da Faenza (whose architectural training shows in his use of perspective) and others in the Salone, under its handsome panelled ceiling, along with a *Risen Christ* by Nicola da Siena. Another room has stone sculptures by Giovanni Dalmata (1469) from an altarpiece formerly in San Giovanni, and further on are two terracotta statues of the Annunciation by Luca della Robbia. The loggia is dedicated to detached frescoes.

Next to the Castellina is Norcia's **Duomo**, built by Lombard masons in 1560 and remodelled in the 1700s; the massive campanile was rebuilt in 1859. The 17th-century chapel of the Madonna della Misericordia shelters a venerated 16th-century fresco, *Madonna between SS. Scholastica and Benedict*.

### Elsewhere in Norcia

From the Castellina, Via Battisti leads to the 14th-century Gothic church of **San Francesco**, with a rose window and handsome portal; insider are 16th-century frescoes and a fine painting by Jacopo Siculo, *Coronation of the Virgin*. Opposite is the building, now a restaurant, that held the public pawn shop, the Monte di Pietà, founded in 1466. Norcia's straight main street, Corso Sertorio, runs just east; the town's rebuilt **Teatro Civico** is in Piazza Vittorio Veneto, at the north end of the Corso by the handsome 19th-century **Porta Romana**. Just outside, the **Cripto Portico Romano Museo Archeologico** displays finds from the area.

From Corso Sertorio, Via Gioberti leads to 15th-century **San Giovanni**, with its bell tower built into the walls. This is one of the most important churches in Norcia, with a good interior and art, but it has long been closed. From nearby Piazza Carlo Alberto with its fountain, turn down Via Umberto to see the most curious building in Norcia, the square limestone **Tempietto**, built on the street corner by local stonemason Vanni Tuzi in 1354. No one is sure what it was used for, but it has pretty reliefs. Via Umberto continues past here to Via Anicia, where a left turn takes you to the 13th-century Gothic church of **Sant'Agostino** with an ogival portal and a frescoed lunette from 1368 and good 15th- and 16th-century frescoes inside. The **Oratorio di Sant'Agostinuccio**, further up Via Anicia, belongs to a local confraternity and has a charming interior covered in fine woodwork of the early 1600s.

The **cemetery church of Santa Scolastica**, 3km south, was built not long after the lifetime of the holy twins, according to tradition on the site of their mother's house. Largely rebuilt in the 17th century, it has a late-14th-century fresco cycle on the life of St Benedict.

## North of Norcia: the Valcastoriana

North of Norcia, the rugged Valcastoriana is one of the most remote Umbrian valleys, making it a favourite residence for

**Teatro Civico**
*t 0743 816022*

**Cripto Portico Romano Museo Archeologico**
*open June daily 10–1 and 4–7.30; rest of year Tues–Sun 10–1 and 4–6*

**Sant'Agostino**
*open in summer*

hermits in the early Middle Ages; in addition to its natural beauty, it has a fine collection of small churches, villages and an important abbey, all of which have suffered in recent quakes. The east of the valley is now part of Monti Sibillini National Park.

The road from Norcia (follow signs for Visso) rises through pines to a 1,008m pass, the **Forca d'Ancarano**. Descending into the Valcastoriana it passes the delightful, beautifully restored and maintained church of **Santa Maria Bianca**, rebuilt and added to over the centuries. Early Romanesque capitals support a 15th-century loggia, and there's a funny old campanile. Inside is an ancient font, and the high altar shelters the eponymous *Madonna* (1511), a marble in high relief attributed to the Florentine Francesco di Simone Ferrucci; votive frescoes adorn the walls.

**Santa Maria Bianca**
*signposted right; pick up key at nearby house*

The valley road continues towards Campi; before it, on the right, is a sign for **Campi Castello**, a tiny hamlet with a pretty public wall fountain. Its handsome church, **Sant'Andrea**, has a prominent portico that acts as a belvedere over the valley. Two sweet lions guard the Gothic door; a hotchpotch of votive paintings and colourful gilded wooden altars lines the attractive 16th-century interior. **Campi Basso**, back on the main road, is equally proud of its church of **San Salvatore**, with a lovely old asymmetrical façade with a pair of rose windows; inside are fine frescoes by Giovanni and Antonio Sparapane (1464) and an old immersion baptismal font.

**Sant'Andrea**
*key at Via Entedia 15*

North beyond Piedivalle is the sign for the **Abbazia di Sant'Eutizio** up in its own sub-valley. In the early Middle Ages, Sant'Eutizio owed much of its success to its remoteness: according to St Gregory the Great, it was founded by hermits Eutizio and Spes in the late 400s, who were visited by the young St Benedict. It became an abbey under Benedictine rule, and between the 800s and 1200s prospered under the dukes of Spoleto who, along with emperors and popes, gave it large grants of land, so that by the first millennium it owned more than 100 villages and churches. It had a famous library (with Umbria's oldest examples of vernacular Italian from the 11th century) and an infirmary renowned for the skill of its doctors, a skill handed to Preci when the Benedictines were barred from practising surgery. The abbey enjoys a beautiful setting, hugging the steep wooded mountain, with its campanile high on a rock over the cloister. The Romanesque **church** with its rose window and handsome portal was rebuilt in 1190 by a Master Petrus, who gave it a majestic interior, with a single nave culminating in a lofty presbytery over the crypt. A fine funerary monument to St Eutizio stands behind the altar, attributed to Rocco da Vicenza (1514), and the intarsia choirstalls are 16th century. The abbey was restored after the 1997 quake as a hostel for pilgrims of the 2000 Jubilee; from the courtyard, you can visit the grottoes where the first hermits lived.

**Abbazia di Sant'Eutizio**
*t 0743 99659 or t 0743 231635; open April–Aug Mon and Wed–Sat 10–12.30 and 3.30–7, Sun 10–6; Sept–Mar Sun and hols by appt; if closed, try custodian at 1st door on left inside abbey, or ask at bar*

**Preci**, up the road, was badly damaged in the quakes of 1979 and 1998, but much of it has been restored. A small fortified village rebuilt after an attack by Norcia in 1528, it has proud palaces built by its famous surgeons, who learned the art from the Benedictines and passed it down through generations into the 18th century. They had very sharp knives and tools and specialized in eye operations: when Queen Elizabeth I of England needed a cataract operation in 1588, Cesari Scacchi of Preci was summoned. The **museum** displays some surgical instruments from Preci's school, and a jumble of wooden sculpture, paintings (some from earthquake-damaged churches in the area), archaeological bits and pieces and ancient crafts.

From **Preci**, you can circle back to the Valnerina by way of Triponzo, or return to Norcia via the more remote but wonderfully scenic Valle Oblita, where only a handful of people live year-round, at **Abeto** and **Todiano**, both home to handsome *palazzi* and churches holding important Baroque canvases attesting to their former importance, when the inhabitants made their fortunes as itinerant pork butchers in Tuscany.

## The Piano Grande and Castelluccio

Since 1993 all of the territory to the east of Norcia has been encompassed in the majestic **Monti Sibillini National Park**, which Umbria shares with the Marches. A protected area covering some 70,000 hectares, it is off the tourist track, remote and wildly beautiful. You can see some of the most spectacular scenery along the narrow road from the church of Santa Scolastica south of Norcia (*see* p.250), which winds a magnificent 21km up to **Forca Canapine** (1,540m), high enough to support a modest ski station in winter, with a refuge and hotel.

On the same Forca Canapine road, 18km from Norcia, a road descends into one of the most poetic landscapes you'll fine in all these pages, affording the best possible ending to a journey in Umbria. This is the sublime **Piano Grande** a karstic basin, former glacial lake and now an extraordinary meadow measuring 16 square kilometres, surrounded by bare rolling hills and mountains that look as if they are covered with velvet during late spring, when the entire meadow explodes into swathes of wildflowers that go on and on for kilometres, reaching their peak in June. It is a rarefied dream landscape (one used by Franco Zeffirelli in his Franciscan film *Brother Sun, Sister Moon*), large enough to distort distances; the flocks that produce Norcia's famous cheese graze here, and its fields produce the tiny lentils of Castelluccio, which come in three colours and are among the tastiest and rarest in Italy.

⊕ Piano Grande

### The Sibyl of the Mountains

One of the most popular medieval Italian romances was Guerino il Meschino ('Guerino the Wretch'), written in 1391 by Andrea da Barberino. Guerino, a bold and clever young orphan in search of his parents, meets the Devil in a mountain pass above Norcia. The Devil, playing the role of a pimp, advises Guerino to go up into the mountains and seek out Sibilla, a lovely fairy whose cave is a bower of bliss. The price of her charms, of course, is his soul. But Guerino doesn't hesitate, and finds that Sibilla is everything the Devil promises. He also finds out her true identity: she is the Cumean Sibyl from Campania, the most famous of the dozen prophetic wise women who were honoured by the Church for their predictions of Christ's birth and Passion, thus earning a place on Michelangelo's Sistine Chapel ceiling, on Siena Cathedral's inlaid floor, and elsewhere before the Counter-Reformation put on the brakes. In the Aeneid, the Cumean Sibyl was visited by Aeneas on his way to founding Rome and offered him a brief tour of hell; she was later visited by the last king of Rome, Tarquin, who came to her to purchase the nine Sibylline books of prophesy. When he tried to dicker down the price, the Sibyl threw three of the precious books into the fire; when he still tried to bargain, she threw in three more, until, in a panic, he paid the original price for the last three. In Guerino il Meschino we learn something else about her: that she had expected God to have chosen her to be the virgin mother of His son and was miffed when He chose Mary, then a nobody. When the new Christianity she had predicted took hold, the Sibyl left her cave in Campania and took refuge in a cave.

Guerino in the nick of time discovers that Sibilla and her ladies turn into monsters on Saturdays, and after spending a year in their pleasant company he goes to Rome to seek the Pope's absolution. The humanist Aeneas Sylvius (the future Pope Pius II) identified Sibilla as the goddess Venus, and the popular tale inspired several variants, all casting their spell of magical eroticism and forbidden knowledge over the Monti Sibillini. The most famous story these days, thanks to Wagner, is Tannhäuser. Soon so many amorous pilgrims and necromancers were making their way to Norcia, the lake, and the cave (near Montemonaco), that by the 1490s, Rome threatened to excommunicate anyone who went to visit the Sibyl. So many people continued to defy the pope with their profane pilgrimages that the long corridors that descended into the magical realm of the Sibyl were filled in during the 17th century, and dynamited in the 19th to keep all the wickedness within from ever escaping. But in Montemonaco they still know where it is, if you're interested.

A long straight road crosses the Piano Grande, then rises to the lentil village of **Castelluccio**, which at 1,452m is the highest and loneliest settlement in all Umbria. Castelluccio had around 700 inhabitants in 1951 and now has just 40 or so; not so long ago, it was often cut off by the winter snows, a problem that has now been alleviated by ploughs. It is also the one old village in Umbria with no pretence to charm, but it does attract hikers, hang-gliders and cross-country skiers.

## The Rooftop of Umbria: the Monti Sibillini

Castelluccio lies near an important crossroads under the dark, legendary **Monti Sibillini**, the most dramatic mountains in the Apennines. To the east of Castelluccio a secondary road skirts the slopes of **Monte Vettore** (2,476m), the tallest in the Sibillini, covered with snow for much of the year. Its summit (the usual approach is from the east, from the hamlet of Foce near Montemonaco in the Marches) is one of the very few places on the Italian peninsula where both the Adriatic and Tyrrhenian seas are visible, at least on a clear day.

ⓘ **Norcia** ›
*Piazza Garibaldi,*
**t** *0743 71147,*
*www.norcia.net*

⭐ **Dal Francese** ››

## Tourist Information in and around Norcia

**Monte Sibillini National Park** has an information office at Casa del Parco, Norcia, Via Solferino 22, **t** 0743 817090, *www.sibillini.net* (closed afternoons).

## Market Day in Norcia

There's a market every Thursday, and a truffle fair each February.

## Events and Activities in and around Norcia

**Feast of St Benedict,** 20–21 Mar. A crossbow tournament between six *quaite* or districts of town.

For **outdoor activities,** contact:
**Associazione Piangrande,** Castelluccio, **t** 0743 817279. Mountain bike excursions and horse-trekking.

**Cooperativa Monte Patino,** Via Foscolo 2, Norcia, **t** 0743 817487. Hiking trips, mountainbiking and horse-trekking.

**Prodelta,** Via delle Fate 3, Castelluccio, **t** 0743 821156. A paragliding and hang-gliding school.

**Rafting Centre Monti Sibillini,** c/o Ristorante dei Cacciatori, Biselli di Norcia, **t** 0742 23146.

## Where to Stay and Eat in and around Norcia

### Norcia ✉ 06046

**\*\*\*Grotta Azzurra,** Via Alfieri 12, **t** 0743 816513, *www.bianconi.com* (€€€). An attractive inn dating back to 1850, with comfortable rooms, a disco and a good restaurant serving a monthly changing menu of traditional local fare such as lamb with red peppers (€€€). Breakfast is included in rates; half and full board are available. *Closed Tues.*

**\*\*\*Nuovo Hotel Posta,** Via C. Battisti 10, **t** 0743 817 434, *www.bianconi.com* (€€). A fine establishment, with a beautiful garden and a restaurant (€€€) serving robust Castelluccio lentils, boar salami, *tortellini alla norcina* (with ricotta) and lamb with

truffles – topped off, if you dare, by a tumbler of Norcia's nasty *grappa*, which is flavoured with black truffles. Half and full board available.

**Dal Francese** Via Riguardati 16, **t** 0743 816290 (€€€). A place offering bumper meals of mainly truffle-based dishes. Among the highlights are the pasta medley of *tris al tartufo,* the *gnocchi al tartufo* and the *tortellini con crema di tordi* (thrushes) *e tartufi.* *Closed Fri exc in summer, 2wks Jan and 2wks July.*

**Il Beccafino,** Piazza San Benedetto 12, **t** 0743 816086 (€€€). Located right in the heart of Norcia, this small and welcoming restaurant produces variations on the usual truffle and *norcineria* theme and has a well-stocked wine cellar. Popular with locals as well as tourists.

**Restaurant Granaro del Monte,** Via Alfieri 12, **t** 0743 816 513 (€€€). Good meats grilled right before your eyes over a large open fire, *tagliolini* with black truffles, *pappardelle* with wild boar, and spelt soup. *Closed Tues.*

### Castelluccio di Norcia ✉ 06046

To stay in *rifugi* – modest **mountain huts** offering modest meals at modest prices – contact Parco Nazionale dei Monti Sibillini, Largo G. B. Gaola Antinori 1, Visso (Mc), **t** 0737 972711, *www.sibillini.net.*

**\*\*Sibilla, t** 0743 821113, *hotelsibilla@ hotmail.com* (€€). Simple, en-suite rooms (breakfast included) and a restaurant (€€; with half/full board). *Closed Tues.*

**Il Guerrin Meschino,** Via Monte Veletta 22, **t** 0743 821125, *www. guerinmeschino.it* (€€). Basic bedrooms and apartments on a working lentil farm.

**Taverna Castelluccio,** Via dietro la Torre 8, **t** 0743 821158, *tavernacastelluccio@libero.it* (€€). The place to come for the best food in town, including Norcia-style *antipasti* and the village's famous lentils in soup or with sausages, plus pizzas. It also has a few reasonably priced rooms (€€). *Closed Wed exc summer.*

# Glossary

**acroterion**: decorative protrusion on the rooftop of an Etruscan, Greek or Roman temple. At the corners of the roof they are called *antefixes*.

**ambones**: twin pulpits (singular: *ambo*), often elaborately decorated.

**ambulatory**: aisle round the apse of a church.

**atrium**: entrance court of a Roman house or early church.

*badia*: abbey or abbey church (also *abbazia*).

*baldacchino*: baldachin, a columned stone canopy above the altar of a church.

**basilica**: a rectangular building, usually divided into three aisles by rows of columns. In Rome this was the common form for law courts and other public buildings, and Roman Christians adapted it for their early churches.

*borgo*: from the Saxon *burh* of Santo Spirito in Rome: a suburb or village.

**bucchero ware**: black, delicately thin Etruscan ceramics, usually incised or painted.

**Calvary chapels**: a series of outdoor chapels, usually on a hillside, that commemorate the stages of the Passion of Christ.

**campanile**: a bell tower.

*campanilismo*: local patriotism; the Italians' own word for their historic tendency to be more faithful to their home towns than to the abstract idea of 'Italy'.

*campo santo*: a cemetery.

**cardo**: the transverse street of a Roman *castrum*-shaped city.

*carroccio*: a wagon carrying the banners of a medieval city and an altar; it served as the rallying point in battles.

**cartoon**: the preliminary sketch for a fresco or tapestry.

**caryatid**: supporting pillar or column carved into a standing female form; male versions are called *telamones*.

*castrum*: a Roman military camp, always neatly rectangular, with straight streets

and gates at the cardinal points. Later the Romans founded or refounded cities in this form, hundreds of which survive today (Lucca, Aosta, Florence, Pavia, Como, Brescia, Ascoli Piceno, Ancona are clear examples).

**cavea**: the semicircle of seats inside a classical theatre.

*cenacolo*: fresco of the Last Supper, often on the wall of a monastery refectory.

**chiaroscuro**: the arrangement or treatment of light and dark areas in a painting.

**ciborium**: a tabernacle; the word is often used for large, free-standing tabernacles, or in the sense of a *baldacchino* (*see* above).

*comune*: commune or commonwealth, referring to the governments of the free cities of the Middle Ages. Today it denotes any local government, from the Comune di Roma down to the smallest village.

*condottiere*: leader of a band of mercenaries in late medieval and Renaissance times.

**confraternity**: a religious lay brotherhood, often serving as a neighbourhood mutual-aid and burial society, or following some specific charitable work (Michelangelo, for example, belonged to one that cared for condemned prisoners in Rome).

*contrapposto*: the dramatic, but rather unnatural twist in a statue, especially in a Mannerist or Baroque work, derived from Hellenistic and Roman art.

*convento*: a convent or monastery.

**Cosmati work** (or *Cosmatesque*): referring to a distinctive style of inlaid marble or enamel chips used in architectural decoration (pavements, pulpits, paschal candlesticks, etc.) in medieval Italy. The Cosmati family of Rome were its greatest practitioners.

*crete*: found in the pasturelands of southern Tuscany, chalky cliffs caused by erosion. Similar phenomena are the *biancane*, small chalk outcrops, and *balze*, deep eroded ravines around Volterra.

**cupola**: a dome.

**decumanus**: street of a Roman *castrum*-shaped city parallel to the longer axis, the central, main avenue called the Decumanus Major.

**Dodecapolis**: the federation of the 12 largest, strongest Etruscan city states (*see* p.21).

*duomo*: cathedral.

*ex voto*: an offering (a terracotta figurine, painting, medallion, silver bauble or whatever) made in thanksgiving to a god or Christian saint; the practice has always been present in Italy.

**forum**: the central square of a Roman town, with its most important temples and public buildings. The word means 'outside', as the original Roman forum was outside the first city walls.

**fresco**: wall painting, the most important Italian medium of art since Etruscan times. It isn't easy; first the artist draws the *sinopia* (*see* below) on the wall. This is covered with plaster, but only a little at a time, as the paint must be on the plaster before it dries. Leonardo da Vinci's endless attempts to find clever shortcuts ensured that little of his work would survive.

**Ghibellines**: one of the two great medieval parties (*see* Guelphs), the supporters of the Holy Roman Emperors.

**gonfalon**: the banner of a medieval free city; the *gonfaloniere*, or flag-bearer, was often the most important public official.

**graffito**: originally, incised decoration on buildings, walls, etc.; now means casually scribbled messages in public places.

**Greek cross**: in the floor plans of churches, a cross with equal arms. The more familiar plan, with one arm extended to form a nave, is called a Latin Cross.

**grisaille**: painting or fresco in monochrome.

**grotesques**: carved or painted faces used in Etruscan and later Roman decoration; Raphael and others rediscovered them in the 'grotto' of Nero's Golden House in Rome.

**Guelphs** (*see* Ghibellines): the other great political faction of medieval Italy, supporters of the Pope.

**intarsia**: decorative inlaid wood or marble.

**loggia**: an open-sided gallery or arcade.

**lozenge**: the diamond shape – this, along with stripes, is one of the trademarks of Pisan architecture.

**lunette**: semicircular space on a wall, above a door or under vaulting, either filled by a window or a mural painting.

**matroneum**: elevated women's gallery round the nave of an early church (adopted from the Byzantines in the 6th and 7th centuries).

**narthex**: the enclosed porch of a church.

**naumachia**: mock naval battles, like those staged in the Colosseum.

**opus reticulatum**: Roman masonry consisting of diamond-shaped blocks.

*palazzo*: not just a palace, but any large, important building (though the word comes from the Imperial *palatium* on Rome's Palatine Hill).

**Palio**: a banner, and the horse race in which city neighbourhoods contend for it in their annual festivals. The most famous is at Siena.

**Pantocrator**: Christ 'ruler of all', a common subject for apse paintings and mosaics in areas influenced by Byzantine art.

**pietra dura**: rich inlay decoration that uses semi-precious stones, perfected in post-Renaissance Florence.

*pieve*: a parish church.

**pluteo**: screen, usually of marble, between two columns, often highly decorated.

*podestà*: in medieval cities, an official sent by the Holy Roman Emperors to take charge; their power, or lack of it, depended on the strength of the *comune*.

**polyptych**: a painting (usually a panel painting) that is divided into four or more sections, or panels.

**predella**: smaller paintings on panels below the main subject of a painted altarpiece.

*presepio*: a Christmas crib.

*putti*: flocks of plaster cherubs with rosy cheeks and bottoms that infested much of Italy in the Baroque era.

**quattrocento**: the 1400s – the Italian way of referring to centuries (duecento, trecento, quattrocento, cinquecento, etc.).

*sbandieratore* (or *alfiere*): flag-thrower in medieval costume at an Italian festival.

**sinopia**: the layout of a fresco (*see* above), etched by the artist on the wall before the plaster is applied. Often these are works of art in their own right.

**stele**: a vertical funeral stone.

**stigmata**: a miraculous simulation of the bleeding wounds of Christ, appearing in holy men such as St Francis during the 12th century, and in Padre Pio of Puglia in our own time.

**telamone**: *see* caryatid.

**thermae**: Roman baths.

*tondo*: round relief, painting or terracotta (plural: *tondi*).

**transenna**: a marble screen separating the altar area from the rest of an Early Christian church.

**travertine**: hard, light-coloured stone, sometimes flecked or pitted with black, sometimes perfect. The most widely used material in ancient and modern Rome.

**triptych**: a painting, especially an altarpiece, in three sections.

**trompe l'œil**: art using perspective effects to deceive the eye – for example, to create the illusion of depth on a flat surface, or make painted columns and arches seem real.

**tympanum**: the semicircular space, often bearing a painting or relief, above the portal of a church.

**voussoir**: one of the stones of an arch.

# Language

The fathers of modern Italian were Dante, Manzoni and television. Each did their part in creating a national language from an infinity of regional and local dialects; the Florentine Dante, the first 'immortal' to write in the vernacular, did much to put the Tuscan dialect in the foreground of Italian literature. In the 19th century Manzoni's revolutionary novel, *I Promessi Sposi* (*The Betrothed*), heightened national consciousness by using an everyday language all could understand. Television in the last few decades has been performing an even more spectacular linguistic unification; although the majority of Italians still speak a dialect at home, school and work, their TV idols insist on proper Italian.

Perhaps because they are so busy learning their own beautiful but grammatically complex language, Italians are not especially apt at learning others. English lessons, however, have been the rage for years, and at most hotels and restaurants there will be someone who speaks some English. In small towns and out-of-the-way places, finding an Anglophone may prove more difficult. The words and phrases below should help you out in most situations, but the ideal way to come to Italy is with some Italian under your belt; your visit will be richer and you're much more likely to make some Italian friends.

## Pronunciation

Italian words are pronounced phonetically. Every vowel and consonant (except 'h') is sounded. Consonants are the same as in English, except the 'c' which, when followed by an 'e' or 'i', is pronounced like the English 'ch' (*cinque* thus becomes 'cheenquay'). Italian 'g' is also soft before 'i' or 'e' as in gira, pronounced 'jee-ra'. 'H' is never sounded; 'z' is pronounced like 'ts'. The consonants 'sc' before the vowels 'i' or 'e' become like the English 'sh' as in 'sci', pronounced 'shee'; 'ch' is pronouced like a 'k' as in Chianti, 'kee-an-tee'; 'gn' as 'ny' in English (*bagno*, pronounced 'ban-yo'), while 'gli' is pronounced like the middle of the word 'million' (Castiglione, pronounced 'Ca-steely-oh-nay').

Vowel pronunciation is: 'a' as in English 'father'; 'e' when unstressed is pronounced like 'a' in 'fate' as in *mele*, when stressed can be the same or like the 'e' in 'pet' (*bello*); 'i' is like the 'i' in 'machine'; 'o', like 'e', has two sounds, 'o' as in 'hope' when unstressed (*tacchino*), and usually 'o' as in 'rock' when stressed (*morte*); 'u' is pronounced like the 'u' in 'June'.

The accent usually (but not always) falls on the penultimate syllable. Also note that, in the big cities, the informal way of addressing someone as you, *tu*, is widely used; the more formal *Lei* or *voi* is commonly used in provincial districts.

## Useful Words and Phrases

For a list of vocabulary relating to Italian food and drink, *see* pp.53–56.

### General
**yes/no/maybe** *sì/no/forse*
**I don't know** *Non lo so*
**I don't understand (Italian)**
   *Non capisco (l'italiano)*
**Does someone here speak English?**
   *C'è qualcuno qui che parla inglese?*
**Speak slowly** *Parla lentamente*

Could you assist me? *Potrebbe aiutarmi?*
Help! *Aiuto!*
Please/Thank you (very much)
  *Per favore/(Molte) grazie*
You're welcome *Prego*
It doesn't matter *Non importa*
All right *Va bene*
Excuse me *Mi scusi*
Be careful! *Attenzione!*
Nothing *Niente*
It is urgent! *È urgente!*
How are you? *Come sta?*
Well, and you? *Bene, e Lei?*
What is your name? *Come si chiama?*
Hello *Salve* or *ciao* (both informal)
Good morning *Buongiorno* (formal hello)
Good afternoon, evening *Buonasera*
  (also formal hello)
Good night *Buonanotte*
Goodbye *Arrivederla* (formal),
  *arrivederci/ciao* (informal)
What do you call this in Italian?
  *Come si chiama questo in italiano?*
What?/Who?/Where? *Che?/Chi?/Dove?*
Where is/are... *Dov'è/Dove sono...*
When?/Why? *Quando?/Perché?*
How? *Come?*
How much? *Quanto?*
I am lost *Mi sono smarrito(a);*
  *mi sono perso(a)*
I am hungry/thirsty/sleepy; I am tired
  *Ho fame/sete/sonno; sono stanco(a)*
I am sorry *Mi dispiace*
I am ill *Mi sento male*
Leave me alone *Lasciami in pace*
good/bad *buono bravo/male cattivo*
hot/cold *caldo/freddo*
slow/fast *lento/rapido*
up/down *su/giù*
big/small *grande/piccolo*
here/there *qui/lì*

## Transport

airport *aeroporto*
bus stop *fermata*
bus/coach *autobus/pullman*
railway station *stazione ferroviaria*
train *treno*
platform *binario*
port *porto*

port station *stazione marittima*
ship *nave*
car *macchina*
taxi *tassì*
ticket *biglietto*
customs *dogana*
seat (reserved) *posto (prenotato)*

## Travel Directions

One (two) ticket(s) to Naples, please
  *Un biglietto (due biglietti) per Napoli,*
  *per favore*
one way *semplice/andata*
return (round trip) *andata e ritorno*
first/second class *Prima/seconda classe*
I want to go to... *Desidero andare a...*
How can I get to...? *Come posso andare a...?*
How do I get to the town centre?
  *Come posso raggiungere il centro città?*
Do you stop at...? *Ferma a...?*
Where is...? *Dov'è...?*
How far is it to...?
  *Quanto siamo lontani da...?*
What is the name of this station?
  *Come si chiama questa stazione?*
When does the next ... leave?
  *Quando parte il prossimo...?*
From where does it leave? *Da dove parte?*
How long does the trip take?
  *Quanto tempo dura il viaggio?*
How much is the fare? *Quant'è il biglietto?*
Have a good trip *Buon viaggio!*

## Driving

near/far *vicino/lontano*
left/right *sinistra/destra*
straight ahead *sempre diritto*
forwards/backwards *avanti/indietro*
north/south *nord/sud*
east *est, oriente*
west *ovest, occidente*
round the corner *dietro l'angolo*
crossroads *bivio*
street/road *strada/via*
square *piazza*
car hire *noleggio macchina*
motorbike/scooter *motocicletta/Vespa*
bicycle *bicicletta*
petrol/diesel *benzina/gasolio*
garage *garage*

13 Language

This doesn't work *Questo non funziona*
mechanic *meccanico*
map/town plan *carta/pianta*
Where is the road to...? *Dov'è la strada per...?*
breakdown *guasto, panne*
driving licence *patente di guida*
driver *guidatore*
speed *velocità*
danger *pericolo*
parking *parcheggio*
no parking *sosta vietata*
narrow *stretto*
bridge *ponte*
toll *pedaggio*
slow down *rallentare*

## Numbers

one *uno/una*
two/three/four *due/tre/quattro*
five/six/seven *cinque/sei/sette*
eight/nine/ten *otto/nove/dieci*
eleven/twelve *undici/dodici*
thirteen/fourteen *tredici/quattordici*
fifteen/sixteen *quindici/sedici*
seventeen/eighteen *diciassette/diciotto*
nineteen *diciannove*
twenty *venti*
twenty-one *ventuno*
thirty *trenta*
forty *quaranta*
fifty *cinquanta*
sixty *sessanta*
seventy *settanta*
eighty *ottanta*
ninety *novanta*
hundred *cento*
one hundred and one *centouno*
two hundred *duecento*
one thousand *mille*
two thousand *duemila*
million *milione*

## Days

Monday *lunedì*
Tuesday *martedì*
Wednesday *mercoledì*
Thursday *giovedì*
Friday *venerdì*
Saturday *sabato*
Sunday *domenica*

## Time

What time is it? *Che ora è?*
day/week *giorno/settimana*
month *mese*
morning/afternoon *mattina/pomeriggio*
evening *sera*
yesterday *ieri*
today *oggi*
tomorrow *domani*
soon *fra poco*
later *dopo/più tardi*
It is too early *È troppo presto*
It is too late *È troppo tardi*

## Shopping, Services and Sightseeing

I would like... *Vorrei...*
How much is it? *Quanto costa questo?*
open/closed *aperto/chiuso*
cheap/expensive *a buon prezzo/caro*
bank *banca*
beach *spiaggia*
bed *letto*
church *chiesa*
entrance/exit *entrata/uscita*
hospital *ospedale*
money *soldi*
newspaper (foreign) *giornale (straniero)*
pharmacy *farmacia*
police station *commissariato*
policeman *poliziotto*
post office *ufficio postale*
sea *mare*
shop *negozio*
tobacco shop *tabaccaio*
WC *toilette, bagno*
men *signori, uomini*
women *signore, donne*

## Useful Hotel Vocabulary

I'd like a single/twin/double room please
   *Vorrei una camera singola/doppia/matrimoniale, per favore*
with/without bath *con/senza bagno*
for two nights *per due notti*
We are leaving tomorrow morning
   *Partiamo domani mattina*
May I see the room/another room, please?
   *Posso vedere la camera/un'altra camera?*

**Is there a room with a balcony?**
*C'è una camera con balcone?*
**There isn't (aren't) any hot water/soap/
light/toilet paper/towels**
*Manca (Mancano) acqua calda/sapone/
luce/carta igienica/asciugamani*
**May I pay by credit card?**
*Posso pagare con carta di credito?*

**Fine, I'll take it** *Bene, la prendo*
**Is breakfast included?**
*E' compresa la prima colazione?*
**What time do you serve breakfast?**
*A che ora è la colazione?*

# Further Reading

**Blasi, Marlena de**, *The Lady in the Palazzo: At Home in Umbria* (Algonquin, 2006). Tales of Umbrian life by the quixotic American food writer who fixes up a *palazzo* in Orvieto.

**Della Croce, Maria Laura**, *Treasures of Umbria* (White Star, 2006). Lavishly illustrated coffee table book covering the region's art, architecture and landscapes.

**Francke, Linda Bird**, *On the Road with Francis of Assisi: A Timeless Journey Through Umbria, Tuscany and Beyond* (Random House, 2005). Following in the footsteps of St Francis' life in the form of a spiritual and often amusing travelogue.

**Gelmetti, Susanna**, *Italian Country Cooking: Recipes from Umbria and Apulia* (Ten Speed Press, 1996). Written by a chef who runs a cooking school, and a lavishly illustrated book.

**Goethe, J. W.**, *Italian Journey* (Penguin, 1982). An excellent example of a genius turned to mush by Italy; good insights, but big, big mistakes. Interesting section on Umbria.

**Hutton, Edward**, *The Cities of Umbria* (London, Methuen, 1905). You'll have to go to a big library for this classic of 'Umbria, the true Italia Mystica' from the glorious age of travel writing.

**Lasdun, James** and **Pia Davis**, *Walking and Eating in Tuscany and Umbria* (Penguin, 2004). A detailed guide to exactly that, with beautiful itineraries.

**McIntyre, Anthony**, *Medieval Tuscany and Umbria* (Viking, 1992). Recent account of Umbria's golden age of the *comuni* to the rise of the signoria.

**Peck, George T.**, *The Fool of God: Jacopone da Todi* (University of Alabama, 1980). Fine account of his life and times in medieval Todi, along with a sympathetic analysis of his poetry.

**Procacci, Giuliano**, *History of the Italian People* (Penguin, 1973). An in-depth view from the year 1000 to the present – also an introduction to the wit and subtlety of the best Italian scholarship.

**Richards, Charles**, *The New Italians* (Penguin, 1995). An observant and amusing study of life in Italy during and since the political upheaval and the financial scandals in the early 1990s.

**Ross, Ian Campbell**, *Umbria: A Cultural History* (Viking, 1996). Well researched and sympathetic account that explains how Umbria arrived at its current state of affairs.

**St Aubin de Terán, Lisa**, *A Valley in Italy: Confessions of a House Addict* (Penguin, 1995). Life in rural Umbria, and one of the more eccentric but entertaining expat sagas of recent years.

*The Little Flowers of St Francis (I Fioretti): The Acts of Saint Francis and His Companions*, trans. E. M. Blaiklock and A. C. Keys (Hodder & Stoughton, 1985). The poems and original source of the Franciscan legend.

**Vasari, Giorgio**, *Lives of the Painters, Sculptors and Architects* (Everyman, 1996). Readable, anecdotal accounts of the Renaissance greats by the father of modern art history.

**White, John**, *Art and Architecture in Italy 1250–1400* (Yale University Press, 1993). Puts Umbria's golden age into context with the rest of Italy.

# Index

Main page references are in **bold**. Page references to maps are in *italics*.

## 4th edition published 2009

**Cadogan Guides** is an imprint of
New Holland Publishers (UK) Ltd
London • Cape Town • Sydney • Auckland

| | | | |
|---|---|---|---|
| New Holland Publishers (UK) Ltd | 80 McKenzie Street | Unit 1, 66 Gibbes Street | 218 Lake Road |
| Garfield House | Cape Town 8001 | Chatswood, NSW 2067 | Northcote |
| 86–88 Edgware Road | South Africa | Australia | Auckland |
| London W2 2EA | | | New Zealand |

*cadogan@nhpub.co.uk*
**t** 44 (0)20 7724 7773

Distributed in the United States by Interlink

Copyright © Dana Facaros and Michael Pauls 1989, 1990, 1992, 1994, 1996, 1998, 2001, 2003, 2006, 2009
© 2009 New Holland Publishers (UK) Ltd

Cover photographs: front cover © Doug Pearson/JAI/Corbis; back cover © World Pictures/Photoshot
Photo essay photographs: p.1 © Doug Pearson/JAI/Corbis; p.3 (t) © Travel Pix Ltd/PCL, (b) Terry Harris/PCL;
p.4 © Adrian Pope/PCL; p.5 © Terry Harris/PCL; p.6 © Terry Harris/PCL; p.8 © John Heseltine/CORBIS;
p.9 (t) © Adam Eastland/PCL, (b) © David Barnes/PCL; p.10 © Massimo Listri/CORBIS; p.11 © Chuck Pefley/Alamy;
p.12 © Elio Ciol/CORBIS; p.13 (t) © Sheila Terry/Robert Harding World Imagery/Corbis, (b) © PjrFoto/Phil
Robinson/Alamy; p.14 (t) © David Tomlinson/PCL, (b) © Terry Harris/PCL; p.15 © Travel Pix Ltd/PCL;
p.16 (t) © Justin Guariglia/Corbis, (m) © Angelo Hornak/CORBIS, (b) © Grant Rooney/PCL
Maps © Cadogan Guides, drawn by Maidenhead Cartographic Services Ltd
Cover design: Jason Hopper
Photo essay design: Sarah Gardner
Editor: Alison Copland
Proofreading: Susannah Wight
Indexing: Isobel McLean

Printed and bound in Italy by Legoprint
A catalogue record for this book is available from the British Library

ISBN: 978-1-86011-411-3

# Umbria touring atlas

**TUSCANY**

**MARCHES**

**UMBRIA**

**LAZIO**

Arezzo
Sansepolcro
Va Tiberina
Citta di Castello
Pietralunga
Morra
Montone
Umbertide
Abba. di Vallingegno
Gubbio
Scheggia
M. Cucco
Fossato di Vico
Gualdo Tadino
Jesi
R. Esino
Cortona
Castel Rigone
Passignano s. Trasimeno
Isola Maggiore
Lago Trasimeno
Magione
Sorciano
I. Polvese
Perugia
Assisi
Nocera Umbra
Castiglione del Lago
Sta. Maria d. Angeli
Torgiano
Bettona
Spello
Parco
Chiusi
Fontignano
Deruta
Foligno
Visso
Citta della Pieve
Montegiove
Marsciano
Bevagna
Montefalco
Trevi
Tempio di Clitunno
Nazionale dei Monti
Monti Sibillini
M. Vettore
Fabro
Ficulle
Triponzo
Castelluccio
Allerona
Todi
Massa Martana
Spoleto
Norcia
Sibillini
Castel Viscardo
Prodo
Castel Giorgio
Orvieto
Civitella del Lago
Acquasparta
Monteluco
S. Anatolia di Narco
Scheggino
Cascia
Lago di Bolsena
Baschi
Dunarobba
Carsulae
S. Pietro in Valle
Monteleone di Spoleto
S. Gemini
Ferentillo
Lugnano in Teverina
Amelia
Arrone
Torreorsina
Cascata d. Marmore
Lago di Campotosto
Penna in Teverina
Terni
Piediluco
Orte
Narni
L. di Piediluco
Viterbo
Rieti
Lago di Vico
Monti Sabini
Lago di Salto
Monti Sabatini
Lago di Turano
N
Lago di Bracciano
Via Flaminia
R. Tevere

10 km
5 miles

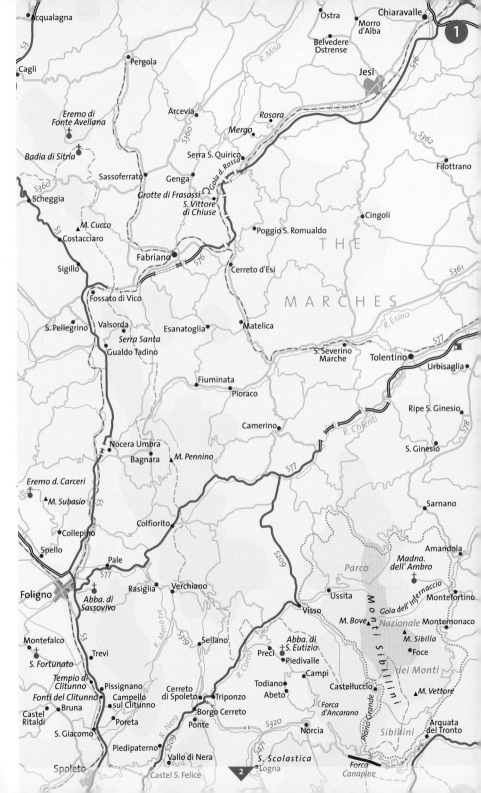

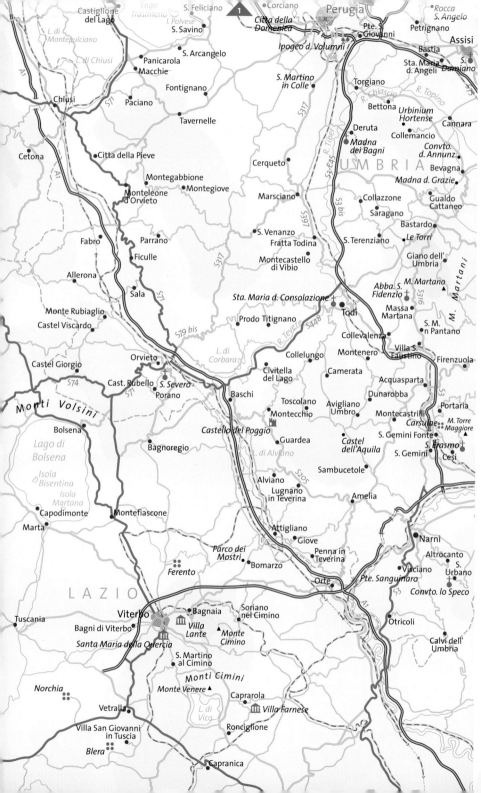

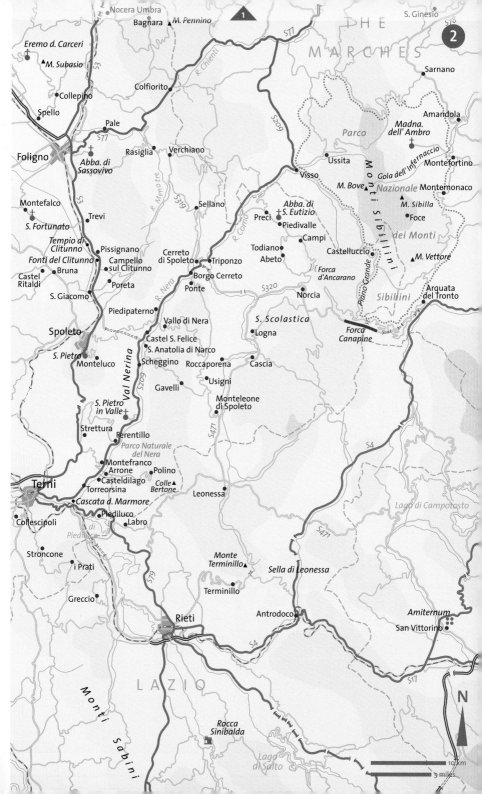

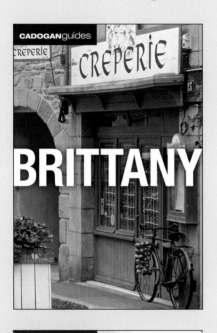
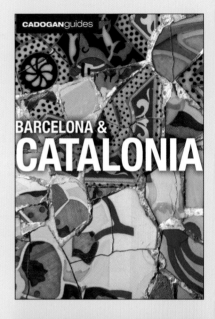

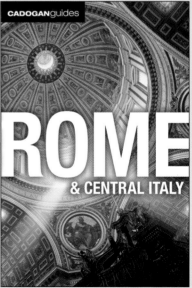

# there can only be one guide

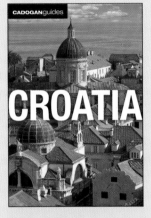

*'A balance of infectious enthusiasm and solid practicality.'*

Michael Palin

# CADOGANguides

# Working and Living

'Impressively comprehensive

*Wanderlust* Magazine

*Working and Living* Australia • *Working and Living* Canada • *Working and Living* France • *Working and Living* Italy • *Working and Living* New Zealand • *Working and Living* Spain • *Working and Living* USA